Anatomy of Liberty in
Don Quijote de la Mancha

Anatomy of Liberty in
Don Quijote de la Mancha

Religion, Feminism, Slavery, Politics, and Economics in the First Modern Novel

Eric Clifford Graf

LEXINGTON BOOKS
Lanham • Boulder • New York • London

Published by Lexington Books
Lexington Books is an imprint of The Rowman & Littlefield Publishing Group, Inc.
4501 Forbes Boulevard, Suite 200, Lanham, Maryland 20706
www.rowman.com

6 Tinworth Street, London SE11 5AL, United Kingdom

British Library Cataloguing in Publication Information Available

Library of Congress Cataloging-in-Publication Data Available

ISBN: 978-1-7936-0118-6 (cloth: alk. paper)
ISBN: 978-1-7936-0119-3 (electronic)

∞^{TM} The paper used in this publication meets the minimum requirements of
American National Standard for Information Sciences—Permanence of Paper
for Printed Library Materials, ANSI/NISO Z39.48-1992.

For Helena

"For in politics, as in religion, it is equally absurd to aim at making proselytes by fire and sword. Heresies in either can rarely be cured by persecution."

—Alexander Hamilton, *Federalist 1*

Contents

List of Illustrations

Introduction

Liberty and Classical Liberalism in Don Quijote

"*Don Quixote* is not 'about' the character of that name: the character is just a device for holding together different kinds of narrative technique."

—Terry Eagleton, *Literary Theory* (3)

The most famous passage about liberty in *Don Quijote de la Mancha* (part one, 1605; part two, 1615) by Miguel de Cervantes Saavedra (1547–1616) arrives like a capstone near the novel's conclusion. Having extricated himself from the Duke and Duchess's palace, and finally back on the road to Zaragoza, the hidalgo explains to his squire why he values freedom:

> La libertad, Sancho, es uno de los más preciosos dones que a los hombres dieron los cielos; con ella no pueden igualarse los tesoros que encierra la tierra ni el mar encubre; por la libertad así como por la honra se puede y debe aventurar la vida, y, por el contrario, el cautiverio es el mayor mal que puede venir a los hombres. (2.58.1094)[1]

> Liberty, Sancho, is one of the most precious gifts that the heavens gave to men; she is worth more than all the hidden treasures on land and beneath the sea; for liberty, as well as for honor, one can and should risk one's life, and, by contrast, captivity is the worst thing that can happen to men.

Don Quijote's speech suggests some fundamental and weighty ideas about liberty. One might even imagine arranging these into an overarching theory of liberty as it emerged in the early modern period. Liberty has divine or natural origins, it trumps material values, it echoes the nobility's right to resist tyranny, and its opposite is captivity.

1

Nevertheless, and as usually happens in *Don Quijote*, the hidalgo's penchant for grandiloquence muddles his point about liberty. He goes on to say that the reason he feels free is because he's no longer required to reciprocate the generosity of the Duke and Duchess: «las obligaciones de las recompensas de los beneficios y mercedes recebidas son ataduras que no dejan campear al ánimo libre» "the obligations to remunerate received benefits and largesse are bonds that restrain the independence of the spirit" (2.58.1094). A soaring reflection on liberty has now turned awkward, trite, and paradoxical. Awkward, because Don Quijote manifests hypocrisy, for he has often rebuffed Sancho Panza's own requests for remuneration and independence by promising him precisely benefits and largesse. Trite, because these are petty and resentful thoughts in the context of liberty just described as an inestimable gift from the heavens. Paradoxical, because suffering oppression on account of another's generosity will remain counterintuitive to most readers (cf. Mauss).

Compounding our difficulties, Cervantes's art is a game of perspectives, much like Diego Velázquez's *Las meninas*.[2] *DQ* 2.58, for example, offers different takes on the early modern transition from feudalism to bourgeois capitalism. In terms of the fading medieval caste system, the Duke (high noble) is to Don Quijote (low noble) what Don Quijote (low noble) is to Sancho (peasant laborer). In this context, the self-interest of Don Quijote's contradictory reflections is a major source of Cervantine irony. When evading service to the high nobility, the hidalgo rejects the hierarchical bonds of feudalism; but when refusing to pay his neighbor, he insists on them, preferring the medieval fantasy according to which he is a knight-errant and the peasant laborer is his squire. Predictably and comically, Sancho soon undercuts his master's position by pointing out that the Duke has paid them. Even granting what Don Quijote has just said about liberty, still, «no es bien que se quede sin agradecimiento de nuestra parte docientos escudos de oro que en una bolsilla me dio el mayordomo del duque» "it's not good that two hundred gold *escudos* in a small purse which the Duke's majordomo gave me should remain without acknowledgement on our part" (2.58.1095).

DQ 2.58, then, starts out epic enough. When Don Quijote calls liberty priceless, he echoes the first Latin phrase of the novel, which the first prologuist's friend had attributed to the Roman satirist Horace: «Non bene pro toto libertas venditur auro» "Liberty is not sold for all the gold in the world" (1.pro.14). But the squire intrudes on such idealism by noting that large sums of money have been exchanged and that obligations linger. Moreover, from Sancho's point of view, liberty actually can be priced. And bringing things even further back down to earth, there's a hint of governmental corruption in all of this. Recently returned from ruling over the Duke's Isle of Barataria, Sancho has tediously insisted that he was not bribed and that he ruled like an angel. But now the Duke's gift of 200 *escudos* makes Sancho seem just as capable of self-serving hypocrisy as Don Quijote (cf. Madison, *Federalist 51*).

A major thesis of this book is that Cervantes's great novel offers a realist bourgeois solution to the confusing labyrinth of tyranny, bondage, and corruption. Literary theorists and critics of all stripes have argued that in the early modern novel, realist and functional bourgeois options displace the fading idealist fantasies of feudalism (see Lukács, Auerbach, and Quint). I will emphasize, however, that bourgeois realism is also deeply related to the assertion of positive themes like freedom, harmony, and progress. For example, when he notes that paying for goods and services makes sense because it avoids violence, Sancho hints at the idea that economic activity has a civilizing effect on its participants: «que no siempre hemos de hallar castillos donde nos regalen, que tal vez toparemos con algunas ventas donde nos apaleen» "for we'll not always find castles where they welcome us; we might come across some inns where they'll beat us" (2.58.1095). This anticipation of Montesquieu's famous dictum *doux commerce,* or "sweet commerce," is just one of many ways in which *Don Quijote* counters chivalric idealism by stressing bourgeois common sense. Moreover, the effect is consistent throughout, surfacing early in the mad knight's difficulties with financial notions like bookkeeping and payment for goods and services in *DQ* 1.1, 1.3, and 1.4 and extending through to the novel's bourgeois finale, which consists of a salary negotiation between hidalgo and squire in *DQ* 2.71 followed by the settlement of Alonso Quijano's domestic accounts in *DQ* 2.74.

A particular difficulty in the study of Cervantes is how to manage the author's constant irony. Faced with so many slippery contradictions, how can we possibly locate meaning or intention? Moreover, we risk imposing rational discourse on what might be little more than a clever assemblage of topical allusions (cf. Curtius). The notion that Cervantes penned a broad, universal satire offers one way around these problems. In *DQ* 2.58, for example, we might observe that Cervantes simply highlights our fallible human nature. We are all potential hypocrites to the degree that we are ready to sacrifice transcendent principles like liberty in favor of our own egocentric and more worldly concerns. Though accurate, the generality of such pronouncements reveals the consequences of the irony and intentionality problems. The same problems cause many readers to seek refuge in the novel's slapstick humor or else in its endearingly sentimental hero. Either way, Cervantes's excessive disorientations lead us to sidestep the possibility of ever discovering his specific intentions and meanings. If we do so, of course, we are not alone; some very important literary critics, like Erich Auerbach, Leo Spitzer, and Peter Russell, have argued that *Don Quijote* is little more than lighthearted entertainment.

In this book, however, I'll argue that both professional and lay readers have missed key aspects of Cervantes's novel. Yes, *Don Quijote* is a beautiful, comical, ironical, and universal novel, but, of course, it's also intricate, specific, and historical enough such that analyzing its components can help us to resolve many of its other interpretive dilemmas. My literary criticism in this book accepts the following three premises:

1. We should try to deduce authorial intention, because even when unsuccessful, the process can be informative.
2. Evaluating different types and degrees of liberty is precisely the point in many of the novel's episodes.
3. Given the novel's influences on subsequent generations of readers, later interpretations of it by important thinkers can help us to better triangulate its original meaning.

A word is in order regarding the occasionally technical language of this book's last two chapters on politics and economics in *Don Quijote*. The political scientists and economists with whom I have worked in recent years have shown me how their fields can add layers of wonder to an already astonishingly baroque text. In deference to their patience with me, I have attempted to find some middle ground between their idioms and my own. Of course, all of the terminological and conceptual errors that may have resulted from this process are my own.

At the same time, however, if the goal is to understand the political and economic significance of Cervantes's masterpiece, then we should be prepared to move beyond popular, but simplistic, views of Don Quijote as mere entertainment, i.e., as either a clown or a hero. He's often a moral dilemma, even a counterexample who represents a true menace to society and someone in need of restraint and reform. He ought to pay for goods and services, for example, and he should also stop physically assaulting people who disagree with him. Likewise, Sancho Panza is not always the loveable, roly-poly sidekick that he is in the popular imagination. At different points in the narrative he endorses theft, slavery, corruption, price controls, misogyny, and ethnic cleansing. He, too, must transform away from his tendency to embrace tyrannical behaviors and learn instead to acknowledge social limits.

Despite their frequent protests to the contrary, most literary critics seek to clarify the meanings and intentions of texts and authors. In this book, I'll try to do this for Cervantes's novel *Don Quijote* in four basic ways:

a. I'll provide tangible historical context (e.g., Spain declared bankruptcies in 1557, 1575, and 1597, a moratorium on her debts in 1607, and further bankruptcies in 1627, 1647, 1656, and 1662).

b. I'll interpret specific details (e.g., when Dulcinea requests a loan from Don Quijote in the Cave of Montesinos in *DQ* 2.23, Cervantes is mocking Spain's fiscal predicament).

c. I'll connect, contrast, and analyze specific episodes (e.g., Don Quijote's intense chivalric fantasy is confronted by the details of earthbound bourgeois realism: money, contracts, debt, accounting ledgers, inflation, loans, salaries, market pricing, etc.).

d. I'll indicate other important texts that either influenced or echoed ideas that are also found throughout *Don Quijote* (e.g., later bourgeois novels in the English-speaking world).

This last idea leads in multiple directions. That Cervantes appreciated precursors like Plato, Giovanni Boccaccio, Niccolò Machiavelli, and Juan de Mariana suggests *Don Quijote* has something to do with symbolic caves, merchant-class humor, advice to princes, and monetary policy. That Cervantes was later appreciated by María de Zayas, Thomas Hobbes, Thomas Jefferson, and Mark Twain suggests *Don Quijote* has something to do with feminism, materialism, constitutionalism, and criticism of the institution of slavery.

These methods of literary criticism—historicizing, comparing, and interpreting at a global level while also linking, contrasting, and analyzing internally—also serve a broader goal of the book, which is to examine the ways in which Cervantes uses metaphors, dialogues, and stories to get readers to think about liberty. This involves disentangling what is admittedly a complicated and evasive text. For example, the source of that first Latin phrase about liberty found in the first prologue of *Don Quijote* is not the Roman satirist Horace, as the narrator's friend erroneously claims but, rather, the Greek fabulist Aesop, a slave who rose to become a counselor to princes. And that is the point. Cervantes is from the outset signaling that we should think about his textual contrasts between freedom and slavery.

While writing this book, I have attempted to be precise and categorical about the specific types of liberty that most interested Cervantes while writing *Don Quijote*. Essentially, I agree with Luis Rosales, who thirty-five years ago contended that «la libertad es, justamente, el eje mismo del pensamiento cervantino» "liberty is, precisely, the very axis of Cervantes's thinking," and proposed that we try to appreciate «el radicalísimo sentido de la libertad que tiene nuestro autor» "the extremely radical sense of liberty maintained by our author" (33). Attempting an updated version of Rosales's insight, I have therefore arranged the book according to what I think many would agree are five of Western Civilization's most important societal virtues early in the twenty-first century: (i) religious tolerance, (ii) respect for women, (iii) abolition of slavery, (iv) resistance to tyranny, and (v) economic freedom. I have tried to avoid tautological descriptions by supplying both the historical contexts and the theoretical consequences of my interpretations. On the one hand, I'll argue that Cervantes did not write in an intellectual vacuum, that he had reasons for writing critically about religion, sex, slavery, politics, and economics. On the other hand, I'll show how Cervantes anticipated, and often influenced, the ways in which subsequent generations of classical liberals approached these same categories of liberty.[3]

I have chosen to use the term "anatomy" for this book in deference to another critical literary genre which, like novels and princely advice manuals, was extremely popular during the late Renaissance. The *Encyclopedia Britannica* defines this exceedingly Aristotelian genre as "the separating or dividing of a topic into parts for detailed examination or analysis." Examples from Cervantes's day include John Lyly's *Euphues: The Anatomy of Wit* (1578) and Robert Burton's *Anatomy of Melancholy* (1621). Of course, there was also the early scientific study of the human body, such as that found in Mondino de' Luizzi's *Anathomia* (c.1316), which was very popular in the early sixteenth century. A spectacular combination of both allegorical and scientific anatomy was Andrés Vesalius's *De humani corporis fabrica* (1543).

From our own era, Northrop Frye's *Anatomy of Criticism* (1957) is particularly useful for the study of Cervantes. Frye defines anatomy as a genre resembling Menippean satire due to its tendency to apply a massive amount of information toward achieving an in-depth understanding of a given subject. At one point he even describes *Don Quijote* as a combination of "novel, romance, and anatomy" (313). Anatomy of what, Frye does not say. Here, I consider that *Don Quijote* can be read as an anatomy of liberty. From the Latin *anatomia*, and from the Ancient Greek ἀνατομία, from ἀνατομή, meaning "dissection," when we imagine this mode of analysis, we might think of Aristotle on the shore systematically tearing apart sea urchins and starfish.

Cervantes's work is often classified as a universal satire due to its tendency to deride a wide range of attitudes and behaviors. Nevertheless, insofar as modern liberty is a universal concept that is also divisible into a handful of specific categories, then the generic distinction allowed by a critical anatomy is not wholly unwarranted. I have chosen five categories which I would argue are the major objectives for Cervantes's novel conceived as an anatomy of modern liberty. Additionally, my intention has been that of facilitating navigation among the different parts of my book by readers who may have different interests. As with any dissection, however, my procedure has had to adapt itself to the contours of the object under analysis as well as the predispositions of the hand holding the blade. I fear that my blurred sense of thematic categories and my inconsistent subdivisions in places have made my anatomy of liberty in *Don Quijote* into something of a Frankenstein. I can only beg the reader's patience as I tend to follow critical continuities and theoretical sinews wherever they may go.

From its comparison to gold in the quote from Aesop in the first prologue to Don Quijote's final explication of its transcendental value to Sancho in *DQ* 2.58, liberty is a consistent enough theme in *Don Quijote* so as to merit systematic analysis. At the very least, Cervantes's most famous protagonist serves as a narrative device that sutures together specific calls for justice and liberty with respect to a variety of conflicts and a range of historical contexts. At a broader level, however, and most especially from the vantage of the Spanish Baroque, Cervantes's complex allusions to the Bible, Aesop, Horace, Ovid, Apuleius, Plato, and Aristotle form that mass of information that anatomies bring to bear on their topics. To put it another way, the first modern novel leverages its criticism using biblical and classical fables, allegories, dialogues, and satires to rail against phenomena like sadism, imperialism, colonialism, misogyny, and slavery. Especially in part two, the knight's constant desire to liberate victims and to crush tyrants focuses our attention on a theme that Cervantes inherits from sources as diverse as Virgil and the Bible: «el castigo de los soberbios y el premio de los humildes» "the punishment of the proud and the rewarding of the humble" (2.1.633); «se han de perdonar los sujetos y supeditar y acocear los soberbios» "the meek must be pardoned and the proud must be subdued and crushed" (2.18.781); «el principal asumpto de mi profesión es perdonar a los humildes y castigar a los soberbios» "the primary purpose of my profession is to spare the humble and punish the proud" (2.52.1054; cf. *Aeneid* 6.853 and Luke 1.52).

Some readers might be surprised to find that generations of classical liberal thinkers were intense fans of *Don Quijote*. Nevertheless, as far as truth claims go, this is a fairly mild one. *Don Quijote* remains one of the most read books in history. It has been the supreme example of creative fiction for four centuries and counting. A recent survey of the novel's impact on seventeenth-century England alone needed more than 700 pages (Randall and Boswell).

Thomas Hobbes openly deploys *Don Quijote* for his psychological theory in *Human Nature* (1650) and more covertly in his critique of metaphysical belief in *Leviathan* (1651). In his *First Treatise on Government* (1689), John Locke cites the tyrannical potential of Sancho's rule over Barataria. In number 78 of his *Persian Letters* (1721), Montesquieu perceives Cervantes's distaste for racism as well as his emphasis on the ennobling effects of work in lieu of conquest. David Hume compares the dragons and giants of knight-errantry to the fantasies of religious philosophers in his essay "Of the Academical or Skeptical Philosophy" (1748); and in "Of the Standard of Taste" (1757), he praises Sancho's abilities as a sommelier in *DQ* 2.13. Voltaire's episodic satire of imperialism and colonialism in *Candide* (1759) follows the basic contours of *Don Quijote*. Early in *Reflections on the Revolution in France* (1790), Edmund Burke refers to the episode of the galley slaves in *DQ* 1.20 as a lesson on the importance of the rule of law. The liberal political economist and feminist John Stuart Mill studied *Don Quijote* as a child. Among early US presidents, George Washington, John Adams, Thomas Jefferson, James Madison, and John Quincy Adams were all avid readers of Cervantes's great novel. In his short, epistolary sketch entitled "Barataria" (1848), Frédéric Bastiat unravels the anti-utopian essence of Sancho's contradictory governance of Barataria (see Hart).

Another thesis of this book is that it is no accident that so many of the classical liberal devotees of *Don Quijote* also articulated well-grounded economic ideas and maintained serious misgivings about political power. If not direct influences, then similar interests explain these parallels; either way, such comparisons can be helpful, especially for understanding the novel's political and economic dynamics.

A list of Hispanic classical liberals who were influenced by *Don Quijote* would also be long, although, as scholar and editor Francisco Rico has pointed out, it would crest later and be less populated than the Anglo list (*Anales cervantinos*, 113). In spite of his personal struggle to overcome the literary influence of Cervantes, Miguel de Unamuno was a powerful advocate of *Don Quijote* as a special kind of required reading: «debería ser la Biblia nacional de la religión patriótica de España» "it ought to be the national Bible of the patriotic religion of Spain" (qtd. by Iwasaki). Unamuno thought that, like Homer's *Iliad* was for the Greeks, Cervantes's novel could be a reference point or sourcebook for just about every important topic in Spanish life, things like manners, art, religion, politics, novels, etc. Additionally, like the rest of the writers of the Generation of 1898, Unamuno hoped that *Don Quijote* would have a grounding, rationalizing effect on what was still a mystically- and metaphysically-inclined culture at the turn of the twentieth century.

Important Hispanic liberal thinking with Cervantine contours can be found in Ricardo Palma's "El alacrán de fray Gómez" (1896), José Ortega y Gasset's *Meditaciones del Quijote* (1914), and Jorge Luis Borges's "Pierre Menard, autor del *Quijote*" (1939). More recently, in his essay "Una novela para el siglo XXI," Mario Vargas Llosa has argued that Cervantes anticipated the eighteenth- and nineteenth-century notion of "negative liberty," that is, liberty as freedom from external threats, as opposed to "positive liberty," which is the possession of sufficient wealth and circumstance to fulfill one's potential (see Berlin). Vargas Llosa also does well to note that the spirit of bourgeois republicanism animates *Don Quijote*: «Lo que anida en el corazón de esta idea de la libertad es una desconfianza profunda de la autoridad, de los desafueros que puede cometer el poder, todo poder» "What dwells in the heart of this idea of liberty is a profound suspicion of authority, of the outrages that power, all power, is capable of committing" (xix). I agree with both Unamuno and Vargas Llosa. I would only add that *Don Quijote* would make a good national Bible for systematic study in whatever remains of the Republic of Texas (fig. 1).

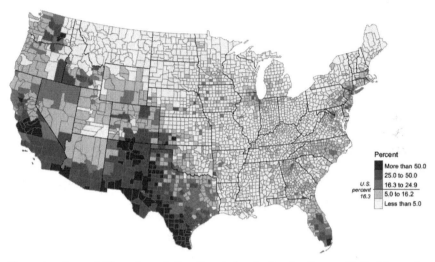

Figure 1. **Percent Hispanic or Latino Population in the Contiguous United States by County, 2010** *Source*: U.S. Census Bureau

Less surprising than the classical liberals influenced by Cervantes are the novelists who have modeled their work after the inventor of the modern form. A list would be daunting. In this book I will limit myself to observing helpful parallels between Cervantes and a handful of later novelists and essayists, especially María de Zayas, Madame de La Fayette, Daniel Defoe, Voltaire, Edgar Allan Poe, Cecilia Böhl de Faber, Mark Twain, and George Orwell.

Additionally, I argue that Cervantes's astonishing literary legacy indicates how creative fiction can be a cultural advantage for conservatives, classical liberals, and libertarians. Ayn Rand, for example, used novelistic discourse as a very successful vehicle for disseminating a lot of thinking about Aristotle, reason, and economics. Her novels, such as *The Fountainhead* (1943) and *Atlas Shrugged* (1957), echo the kind of impact that *Don Quijote* had on generations of classical liberals in the eighteenth and nineteenth centuries. In other words, bourgeois topics like Aristotle, reason, and economics have been essential and dominant aspects of novels since around 1600. Also, to the degree that the most radical forms of modern fiction continue to emphasize freedom, the influence of Cervantes will remain salient. The Spanish master appeared recently in a particularly metaliterary moment in Poul Anderson's "Iron," a novella that forms part of *The Man-Kzin Wars*, a "multiverse" science-fiction series created by radical libertarian author Larry Niven:

> The database in *Rover* contained books as well as musical and video per-formances. Both the Saxtorphs spent a considerable amount of their leisure reading, she more than he. Their tastes differed enough that they had separate terminals in their cabin. He wanted his literature, like his food, plain and hearty; Dorcas ranged wider. Ever since hyperwave made transmission easy, she had been putting hundreds of writings by extrasolar dwellers into the discs, with the quixotic idea of eventually getting to know most of them. (49)

There is historical context for this particularly bourgeois type of literary legacy. Cervantes's attention to Aristotle, reason, and economics parallels themes that also interested the early modern group of late-scholastic Iberi-ans collectively known as the School of Salamanca.[4] The work of many of these thinkers pioneered the non-interventionist economic ideas and the deep mistrust of political power that would later come to characterize classical liberalism. Men like Francisco de Vitoria (1492–1546), Domingo de Soto (1494–1560), Bartolomé de las Casas (1484–1566), Juan de Medina (1490–1547), Martín de Azpilcueta (1491–1586), Diego de Covarrubias (1512–77), Luis Saravia de la Calle (1500s), Tomás de Mercado (1525–75), Luis de Molina (1535–1600), Juan de Mariana (1536–1624), Jerónimo Castillo de Bobadilla (c.1547–c.1605), Juan de Salas (1553–1612), Francisco Suárez (1548–1617), Juan de Lugo (1583–1660), and Felipe de la Cruz Vasconcillos (1600s?) were keen to define, analyze, and debate concepts like individual human rights, slavery, democracy, and the power of kings, as well as interest rates, currency exchanges, the prices of goods and services, the causes and effects of inflation, and the nature and significance of the relation between supply and demand.

The novel form's manifestations of the political, theological, ethical, and economic theories of the School of Salamanca indicate the range of intellec-tual bridges that exist between the late scholasticism of early modern Spain and the classical liberalism of Northern Europe and North America. Friedrich A. Hayek noted this continuity in his Nobel Prize speech of 1974, especially in terms of the inadvisability and arrogance of rulers interfering in economic matters: "the chief point was already seen by those remarkable anticipators of modern economics, the Spanish schoolmen of the sixteenth century, who emphasized that what they called *pretium mathematicum*, the mathematical price, depended on so many particular circumstances that it could never be known to man but was known only to God" ("The Pretense of Knowledge").

This book's view of *Don Quijote* as a proto-liberal text already has its detractors, mainly from the far left. According to Marxist literary critics ranging from Georg Lukács to Terry Eagleton, modern creative literature as well as modern literary analysis are essentially little more than bourgeois ideology (excepting, of course, the cases of Marxist writers like Bertolt Brecht, Henrik Ibsen, and Jean-Paul Sartre). Within the narrower field of Spanish literature, this view has been voiced by critics like José Antonio Maravall (*Utopía y contrautopía en El Quijote*), Juan Carlos Rodríguez, Malcolm Read (*Language, Text, Subject*), and Carroll Johnson (*Cervantes and the Material World*), who have described either Golden Age cultural production or else its modern interpretation as the discursive manifestations of bourgeois individualism.

I have benefitted from the work of all of these critics and I concur with them on many of their points. However, as far as I can figure, I differ with them in four ways:

1. I'm more in agreement with thinkers like Friedrich Hayek, Irving Kristol, Deirdre McCloskey, Niall Ferguson, Victor Davis Hanson, and many others who have variously argued that bourgeois individualism can be an advantageous development.
2. I'm interested in a much longer trajectory of the novel as a merchant-class institution, one which extends from Apuleius in antiquity to Cervantes in the late Renaissance.
3. I'm interested in the specific degrees to which the political and economic thinking of the School of Salamanca influenced the novel's development in late-Renaissance Spain.
4. I argue that Cervantes was conscious that the materialistic world of bourgeois capitalism was overtaking that of feudalism and that he wrote *Don Quijote* precisely as a way of ushering in the new and escorting out the old.

Due to its primarily expositional nature, the main theses of this book are not as radical as are the particulars of their articulation. Generally, I'm reviewing evidence for an already given list of five societal virtues, with each chapter relating *Don Quijote* to one of them. Thus, the novel anticipated, and perhaps even provided the occasional impetus to, five important trends in modern Western Civilization: (i) religious tolerance, (ii) respect for women, (iii) abolition of slavery, (iv) resistance to tyranny, and (v) economic freedom.

Chapter one argues that Cervantes maintains an anti-orthodox and anti-Inquisitorial attitude throughout *Don Quijote*, such that it can sometimes even be useful to consider him proto-Protestant. At the very least, he is radically Erasmian in his opposition to religious coercion. He also opposes the Crown's policy of expelling the Moriscos, a specific group of Christians with

Moorish ancestry who still inhabited much of Andalucía, Murcia, Valencia, and Aragón at the beginning of the seventeenth century, i.e., more than a century after the expulsion of Spain's last Muslims by the Catholic Monarchs Isabella and Ferdinand at the beginning of the sixteenth century.

Chapter two reviews a range of characters and episodes in *Don Quijote* that should be of interest to modern-day advocates and defenders of women's rights. Although Cervantes is rightly credited with having invented all kinds of narrative fiction—Enlightenment detective fiction, modernist metanarratives, science fiction, etc.—it's important to emphasize that he also played a role in the invention of the feminist novel.

Chapter three assesses the theme of slavery in *Don Quijote*. Cervantes's experience of captivity during a five-year period in Algiers (1575–80) inclined him against the institution. But his novel also targets the new, transatlantic form of black African slavery, according to which skin color had become the newest signifier of slave status. Even given this advanced form of social criticism, Cervantes's most theoretically interesting take on slavery might well be his utilitarian vision of its economic obsolescence.

Chapter four considers the politics of *Don Quijote*. I argue that aggressive gestures directed against kings in both of the novel's prologues indicate how Cervantes imagined the political significance of his art. This regicidal tendency echoes the ideas of compatriots like Mariana as well as those of a group of radical Calvinists known as the Monarchomachs.

Chapter five investigates Cervantes's understanding of a range of economic topics, especially those that interested the late scholastics of the School of Salamanca. These include Gresham's law, the time value of money, inflationary monetary policy, supply and demand, the just price debate, monopolies, wealth creation, labor relations, and competing theories about the nature of value.

In the epilogue, I interpret the symbolic significance of three specific animals and show how these are useful for understanding Cervantes's art as an elaborate casuistic game of moral perspectivism. *Don Quijote* is essentially a series of intellectual exercises that guide readers toward the experience of humility. Pigs, asses, and felines are symbols used, respectively, to criticize the evils of orthodox fanaticism, chattel slavery, and monetary debasement. A common theme is that such symbols are also directed against the ignorant imperiousness of the self, in these cases the imperiousness of the religious, governing, and racist selves of early modern Europe, selves which are also common to most of human history.

Before beginning, I offer specialists and novices alike three short, technical paragraphs that describe how I have come to view Cervantes's masterpiece after years of study.

Don Quijote puts numerous literary genres into play. These include epic, tragicomedy, romance, lyric, exemplary tale, and many more, but the novel is most essentially a picaresque. Cervantes signals this by repeatedly alluding to Apuleius's *The Golden Ass* (c.175) and the anonymous *La vida de Lazarillo de Tormes* (c.1554), which were the picaresque genre's respective ancient and early modern models. A picaresque is an episodic and satirical type of narrative fiction; hence, the first modern novel consists of a wide range of moral, social, and political mockeries. Cervantes signals the importance of satire again in the second prologue, when he sarcastically thanks his rival Avellaneda for having attached the label to him: «le agradezco a este señor autor el decir que mis novelas son más satíricas que ejemplares» "I thank the gentleman author for saying that my novels are more satirical than exemplary" (2.pro.618). In this context, Cervantes signals satire again in *DQ* 2.16–17, when the mad knight heaps enormous praise on the poetry of Horace and Ovid and then attacks what appears to be the king's money cart. This sequence reveals part two as a more overtly political novel that takes particular aim at the Crown's monetary policy. The increased presence of politics also explains part two's tug of war between Plato and Aristotle. Like Garcilaso de la Vega and San Juan de la Cruz, Cervantes may be Platonic when thinking about individuals, but like Las Casas and Mariana, he's roundly Aristotelian when thinking about things like societies, laws, and constitutions (cf. Skinner, "Political Philosophy").

In terms of early modern religious politics, Cervantes is in many ways very Jesuit (see Unamuno, *Vida de don Quijote y Sancho*), while also maintaining a seriously Erasmian reformist attitude (see Castro's *El pensamiento de Cervantes*). There was a time around the middle of the sixteenth century when these were not necessarily such antithetical positions.[5] But why stop at Erasmus? If Stephen Greenblatt can claim that William Shakespeare (1564–1616) was a closet Catholic Augustinian, then surely Cervantes can express an occasional sympathy for Protestant Huguenots. Of course, to make Calvinist and Monarchomach gestures in early seventeenth-century Madrid was to run the risk of being accused of heresy and treason. Then again, why stop at Protestantism? Anticipating the more modern insights of thinkers as diverse as Alexander Hamilton, Carl Schmitt, Sigmund Freud, Eric Hoffer, Christopher Dawson, and Frederic Jameson, the first modern novelist highlights the dictum that religion is always a form of politics, and *vice versa*. To be even more specific, the particularly relativistic type of religious politics that Cervantes articulates throughout *Don Quijote* helps explain why the novel so impressed classical liberals like Hobbes, Hume, and Jefferson, who, for their part, gravitated toward ideas, institutions, and constitutions that would separate religion from political life.

Finally, the stylistic "perspectivism" famously associated with *Don Quijote* can be understood as both an early modern humanist's and a late scholastic's version of Hayek's dark lesson against economic planning ("The Use of Knowledge"). Given the lack of any absolute knowledge about dynamic problems like the variety of human wants and needs or the proper deployment of natural resources, Hayek underscores that economic planning drifts toward madness and tyranny, and that this tragedy occurs even in relatively advanced societies. Similarly, *Don Quijote* provides lessons about our ultimate lack of access to any ideal perspective and therein the need to embrace humility. Just prior to becoming Governor of Barataria, when Sancho claims to have gazed down upon the whole earth while flying atop the wooden horse Clavileño, the Duchess objects. Notably, she doesn't so much object to the possibility of flying wooden horses as she does to Sancho's totalitarian overreach in his description of his knowledge: «por un ladito no se vee el todo de lo que se mira» "one does not view the entirety of what one contemplates from just one side" (2.41.965).

NOTES

1. All translations are my own unless otherwise indicated. For the quotes in Spanish from *Don Quijote*, I use an earlier version (Barcelona: Crítica, 1998) of Francisco Rico's now standard edition. For those who read online, this is the same text used by the Centro Virtual Cervantes.

2. For more on Cervantes's "perspectivism," see Castro (*El pensamiento de Cervantes*), Spitzer, Foucault, Read ("Language Adrift"), Cascardi ("Perspectivism and the Conflict of Values"), and Rico.

3. Rosales's book, as well as a more recent study by Pedro Cerezo Galán, are to be commended for focusing on liberty as a key concept for understanding Cervantes's novel. What distinguishes my own approach is that I devote less attention to the well-established view of the fictional protagonist as a psychological, philosophical, or theological emblem of freedom and more attention to the author's anticipation of the categorical foundations of a more modern vision of freedom. Readers will also note my attempt to walk the academic line between my postmodern colleagues, who are rightly concerned with the new trinity of race, class, and gender oppressions, and my libertarian colleagues, who are rightly concerned with defending the utility of reason in the fields of politics and economics. While I think these groups have more in common than either usually admits, I also hold that the topics attended to by the prior ought to be attenuated by the more sobering conclusions of the latter.

4. Excellent introductions to the School of Salamanca are provided by the respective books by Alves and Moreira, Barrientos García, and Chafuen.

5. Historian Jorge Cañizares-Esguerra emphasizes that Calvinists and Jesuits represented uncannily similar subject positions in the seventeenth century, especially in the Americas where "the boundaries between Catholic and Calvinist colonialism were wafer-thin" (182).

Chapter One

Don Quijote and Religion

"He cannot be frightened by danger nor disheartened by obstacle nor baffled by contradictions because he denies their existence."

—Eric Hoffer, *The True Believer* (80)

Today's readers might find it hard to imagine that five hundred years ago Catholics and Protestants became enemies and then stayed that way for about three hundred more (fig. 2). Christopher Hitchens used to say that what brings an end to religious violence is not reason but exhaustion. Multiple geopolitical factors combined to unleash the Protestant Reformation, but the major spark was provided by Martin Luther's *Ninety-five Theses* (1517), a diatribe against papal corruption rumored to have been nailed to the door of All Saints' Church in Wittenberg.[1] As a consequence, early modern Europe soon became a battleground between rival forms of Christianity. The French Wars of Religion (1562–98), the Dutch War of Independence (1568–1648), and the English Civil War (1642–51) were all deeply religious struggles, and bloody enough to bring about exhaustion. People across Europe began to consider that what historian James Henderson Burns labeled the "confessional state" might not be such a good idea and that states should probably avoid demanding that their citizens profess specific faiths.

Niall Ferguson recently argued that, in the long run, the rise of Protestant sects saved Christianity from the agonizing statist extinction that plagues Catholicism on the European continent (*Civilization*). Protestants did this by bringing competition to faith, by making it local, personal, and voluntary rather than national, formal, and obligatory. But my point here is not to dispute the nature, existence, or even the utility of God; I'm merely observing

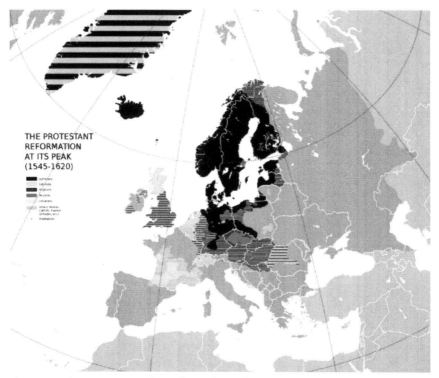

Figure 2.   The Protestant Reformation at its Peak *Source*: Wikipedia

that, during the sixteenth, seventeenth, and eighteenth centuries, thinkers across Europe had pretty good reasons for wanting to secularize public life.

One result of the Protestant Reformation was freedom of religion as a basic virtue of modern civilization. Such was the genius of thinkers like Hobbes, Hume, Jefferson, and Madison. Hobbes's mockery of spirits in *Leviathan* (1651); Hume's attack on metaphysical thinking in "Of Miracles" (1748); Jefferson's radical libertarian attitude while writing the *Virginia Statute for Religious Freedom* (1777); and Madison's culminating rejection of congressional laws "respecting an establishment of religion, or prohibiting the free exercise thereof" in the *First Amendment* (1789). These are logical aversive reactions to centuries of religious violence. Jefferson, Madison, Hume, and Hobbes were also excellent readers of *Don Quijote de la Mancha*. At the very least, this literary preference indicates the degree to which Cervantes's creative narrative satire against religious authority, coercion, and obeisance resonated with classical liberals.

For Americans, Jefferson's legacy of religious freedom has had additional benefits. Not only does religious toleration mean people can avoid killing each other over spiritual matters; not only does it make religion nimbler and more adaptable to modern life; ultimately, freedom of religious conscience implies nothing less than freedom of thought. Moreover, as Matt Ridley has pointed out, when thoughts can interact freely, when there exists a free market for the exchange of ideas, or, more figuratively, "when ideas have sex," then wealth and prosperity soon follow ("When Ideas Have Sex"). In the same vein, Christopher Phillips has argued that the keys to human flourishing lie in interaction, dialogue, and exchange, and often the weirder the better. Nevertheless, if ideas are to interact and to be productive, first they must be allowed to occur and to exist.

Religious freedom is a crucial early modern step in the direction of freedom of thought. Through a poetic kind of logic, religious freedom lays the groundwork for tolerating an infinite range of subsequent ideas. Many of these are admittedly dangerous, others rather banal and mostly useless, but still others have stimulated production capacity, scientific inquiry, and living standards throughout history. What is more, freedom of thought then calls forth additional freedoms. Ideas won't matter if they aren't allowed to circulate. Ergo, freedom of religion requires the freedoms of speech, press, and assembly. As messy as it has been at times, the idea that belief in God should be left up to the individual represents a great leap forward in the evolution of human society.

Biologists and psychologists can demonstrate that the notion that we have willful control over how our brains react to the world is largely an illusion. As animals, we're mostly designed for short-term goals, semi-conscious thinking at best, and with very basic mandates: find food, water, and shelter; procreate and care for offspring; avoid tigers and sharks, etc. But the primacy of the individual is still useful when thinking about the larger and longer-term legal, political, and cultural problems confronted by modern nations. The freedom to think what we want is the freedom to imagine and do what we want, which is effectively the freedom to live as we want.

In Cervantes's masterpiece, the boy caught fleeing while Governor Sancho Panza makes the rounds on Barataria figuratively articulates the limits of the state's ability to control the inner lives of its citizens: «¿será vuestra merced bastante con todo su poder para hacerme dormir, si yo no quiero?» "is all your grace's power enough to make me sleep if I don't want to?" (2.49.1029). Recoiling from the natural limits of his own tyranny, Sancho sets the boy free. Echoing Don Quijote's political advice in *DQ* 2.42, the case in *DQ* 2.49 exemplifies clemency. But it's also a clever enactment of the legal principle *in dubio pro reo*, meaning "when in doubt, rule for the accused" or, in more modern parlance, "innocent unless proven guilty." The principle of *in dubio pro reo* is soon demonstrated again at the beginning of *DQ* 2.51 in the paradox of the man who wishes to be hanged as penalty for crossing a bridge.

Sancho cannot and should not oblige him. In this light, then, the boy's right in *DQ* 2.49 to his inner will to sleep if he so wants is analogous to his right to his own body, and thus describes an essential limit that should be placed on the state's power over its subjects. As Sancho later observes, the bad thing about sleep «es que se parece a la muerte» "is that it resembles death" (2.68.1180).

Subsequent to these back-to-back cases of *in dubio pro reo* in *DQ* 2.49 and 2.51, the rather serious consequences of which include the state putting a person in jail and the state putting a person to death, Cervantes links these political and legal issues to issues of cultural and religious conflict. He does this by evoking the principle of *in dubio pro reo* prior to his treatment of one of the most heavily debated domestic issues of late sixteenth-century Spain. Soon after many of the Moriscos inhabiting the Mediterranean coastline south of Granada staged the Alpujarras Rebellion in the years 1568–71, King Philip II had the order for their expulsion, a kind of early modern plan for ethnic cleansing, placed before him, but he managed to avoid signing it. Philip III, however, embraced the policy and the Expulsion of the Moriscos was carried out in the years 1609–14. Note that this event occurred between the publications of the two parts of Cervantes's great novel in 1605 and 1615. Reflecting the shift in national policy toward the Moriscos, after his ruling over Barataria, ex-Governor Sancho is confronted by two characters who have suffered the antithesis of *in dubio pro reo*. His former neighbor Ricote and his daughter Ana Félix (Ricota), who surface like castaways in *DQ* 2.54 and 2.63–65, embody the consequences of the absolutist policy of expulsion. The state has deemed an entire people guilty of religious heresy, taken their property, and banished them from the country.[2]

The Moriscos were Christian descendants of those Moors whom the Catholic Monarchs had forced to convert in their edicts of February 14 and 17, 1502. Like more than a few priests in cities like Granada and like some important nobles with large agricultural holdings in southeast Spain, Cervantes saw the demographic and ethnic conflict between Old Christians and Moriscos as a matter of orthodox zealots condemning and expropriating a lot of innocent and productive people (fig. 3). As Francisco Márquez Villanueva has shown, Cervantes objected to Philip III's turn to religious conformity as a Machiavellian "reason of state" that justified the expulsion. The critical treatment of this issue in *Don Quijote* is yet another example of how, on theoretical, political, and moral grounds, the author of the first modern novel opposed religious coercion.

Cervantes adopted an essentially Protestant and humanist attitude in defense of the Moriscos. Thus, he often weaves in his concern for the Moriscos into his most Protestant moments. Of course, he would have found further support for this perspective among some of the late scholastics. The opposi-

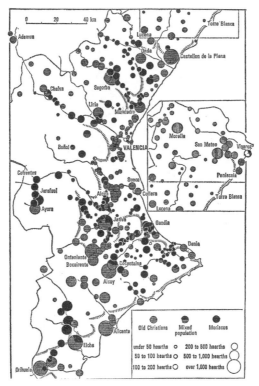

Figure 3. Old-Christian and Morisco Populations of Valencia from 1565 to 1609 *Source*: **Fernand Braudel**

tion to spiritual coercion asserted by Erasmians, Lutherans, and Calvinists was also asserted by major figures associated with the School of Salamanca, men like Francisco de Vitoria, Bartolomé de las Casas, Juan de Mariana, Luis de Molina, Fray Luis de León, and San Juan de la Cruz. Moreover, late-Renaissance intellectuals signaled anxiety about early modern confessional states by remaining ambivalent about their own religious orientations. On the one hand, religion was politics, and since religion and politics often brought violence, it was wise to hedge in case the other side won. On the other hand, the theological and moral distinctions driving events like the Reformation and the Expulsion of the Moriscos could be vague and absurd. Stephen Greenblatt has argued along similar lines that Shakespeare was a closet Catholic. Here, I'll argue that, at key moments in *Don Quijote*, Cervantes displays Protestant sympathies. I'll then conclude at the other end of the geographical and religious spectrum by attempting to distill Cervantes's attitudes toward the Moriscos and Islam.

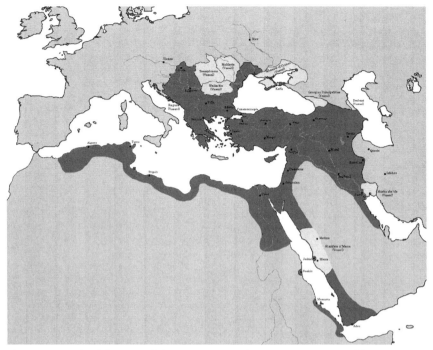

Figure 4. Territorial Extent of the Ottoman Empire in 1590 *Source*: Wikipedia

The Protestant Reformation interested Cervantes, inevitably. The political, religious, and military revolt against Rome peaked during his lifetime and his texts allude to it constantly. *La española inglesa* (c.1606) moves between Protestant England and Catholic Spain and *Los trabajos de Persiles y Sigismunda* (1617) follows a centripetal trajectory away from the pagan frontier in the Arctic North back toward Catholic Rome. Similarly, major characters in both parts of *Don Quijote* have encounters with the limits of the Protestant world. In *DQ* 1.39, having arrived at the inn with the Algerian princess Zoraida, Captain Viedma reports that he was present in Brussels in 1568 when the Duke of Alba executed the Catholic reformist martyrs Egmont and Horn. Later, in *DQ* 1.41, we learn of Viedma and Zoraida's recent encounter with Calvinist pirates headed for the Reformed Republic of La Rochelle. In *DQ* 2.54, Sancho's friend and neighbor, the Morisco Ricote, claims that he found «libertad de conciencia» "freedom of religious conscience" while in exile in Austria. Each of these examples from *Don Quijote* displays symbolic and geographical overlap between the Protestant and Morisco questions.

During the Reformation, sectarian sentiment and identity were fluid, often involving weird ideological distinctions and oblique cross-border allegiances. There were, for example, important Spanish Protestants at the court of Charles V (r.1516–56) as well as that of his son, the future Philip II. There were outbreaks of Lutheranism around 1550 in Seville and Valladolid. Protestantism in cities so politically and commercially vital to the Habsburgs was perhaps bound to elicit a military response. In fact, Cervantes's younger brother Rodrigo died in the Catholic campaign against Protestantism at the Battle of Nieuwpoort in Belgium in 1600. One might suppose this would have biased Cervantes against Protestants. Nevertheless, like the anonymous young soldier in *DQ* 2.24, Rodrigo enlisted out of necessity; and the novelist also seems to have disapproved of the attempt to subjugate the Low Countries, especially when that meant installing the Inquisition there and beheading men like Egmont and Horn. Cervantes's criticisms of Spain's war against Protestantism are also consistent with his other antimonarchical gestures.

There is perhaps still some lingering debate among Cervantes scholars regarding the exact degree to which the author was influenced by Erasmus, but the idea has the support of a consensus of critics. A religious reformer and humanist scholar, Erasmus of Rotterdam (1466–1536) was highly critical of ceremonial displays of faith and overreaching dogmas like papal infallibility. Advocating instead for a more bourgeois and private kind of "interior Christianity," Erasmus saw religion as a means to control the self, not coerce others. Although Catholic, Erasmus was about as Protestant as one could be without actually converting. Again, the situation was fluid. Erasmus refused to abandon the Church in the company of Protestant leaders like Luther or Calvin, but not surprisingly many of his followers eventually did.

Erasmus is important for understanding sixteenth-century Spain. He influenced an entire generation of intellectuals with substantial power at court, such as Antonio de Guevara (c.1481–1545), Juan Luis Vives (1492–1540), and the brothers Alfonso de Valdés (1490–1532), Latin secretary to Charles V, and Juan de Valdés (1509–41), who later converted to Protestantism. Erasmus also paved the way for the so-called Leuven School, a group of second-generation reformist Spanish scholars and theologians who gathered outside Brussels in search of refuge from the rising tide of religious tensions in Paris. These men appear to have believed that Philip II (r.1559–98) would continue Charles V's policy of religious toleration; some even thought that he would let them reform the Spanish Church. Important figures in this group include Felipe de la Torre (1500s), Fadrique Furió Ceriol (1527–92), and Sebastián Fox Morcillo (1526/28–59?).

When thinking about early modern religious politics as an aspect of the historical context that we need to keep in mind for a proper understanding of Cervantes's *Don Quijote*, it helps to consider the nature and degree of the sentiments expressed by the Spaniards at Leuven in the 1550s, that is, during the decade previous to Philip II's ascent to the throne in Spain. Members of the group openly dismissed the salvific power of confession; they approved of reading and publishing the Bible in translation; and they insisted that religious belief was a question of personal choice. They declared that the Inquisition was a murderous and tyrannical institution and they questioned the authority of Catholic Rome while declaring allegiance to Luther's Wittenberg. This was extreme thinking in the midst of the atmosphere of paranoia, conspiracy, and espionage taking hold at courts across Europe. Finally, the case of the Leuven School also reveals that, as religious parties jockeyed for political power, some very radical reformers had significant contacts within the entourage of the future Philip II (see Tellechea).

The year 1559, however, ended the dreams of early modern Spanish Protestants. As he would often do, Philip II changed political factions and attempted to establish a new ideological barrier, ordering all students living abroad to return to Spain and subjecting many of them to debriefings by the Inquisition. The group at Leuven dissolved and many of their compatriots were burned in the *autos de fe* at Seville and Valladolid, which were meant to symbolically coincide with Philip II's coronation. Also in 1559, the Grand Inquisitor Fernando de Valdés published his *Index of Prohibited Books* and brought his infamous charge of heresy against Bartolomé Carranza, the Archbishop of Toledo. Valdés's persecution of the reputable, reform-minded cleric would grind on for nearly eighteen years; Carranza died in 1576, just two weeks after being declared innocent. Events like these marked Philip II as the King of the Counter-Reformation, and the Inquisition now made clear that, in addition to Jews and Muslims, it would target Protestants and their sympathizers for surveillance, conversion, and persecution.

A solid group of esteemed literary critics, including Américo Castro (*El pensamiento de Cervantes*), Marcel Bataillon, Alban Forcione, Javier Herrero, Carroll Johnson (*Don Quixote: The Quest*), and Antonio Vilanova, have demonstrated that Cervantes was very much influenced by Erasmus. The novelist, however, set to writing after more than fifty years of Reformation and Counter-Reformation, and so we might expect to find allusions in his texts to even more radical expressions of religious politics. While it is true that Cervantes is buried in a Trinitarian convent, Hobbes and Hume were also correct to read the first modern novelist as embracing many of the essential aspects of the Protestant perspective. In particular, Cervantes treats formal religion quite harshly in *Don Quijote*, especially public displays of orthodoxy. This is why everything from rosaries to the infamous *auto de fe* take it on the chin in the first modern novel. That popular wisdom is correct which regards Don Quijote's quip «Con la iglesia hemos dado, Sancho» "We've come up against the Church, Sancho" (2.9.696) as indicating a basic conflict between Cervantes and the Church.

Here are six (6) aspects of *Don Quijote* that suggest it was authored by a reformer intent on articulating a case against the use of religious coercion by the confessional state, and therein a case very much in support of the modern notion of religious freedom.

(1) BLASPHEMIES, ROSARIES, AND GHOSTS

Cervantes's disrespect for religious formality and metaphysical belief is persistent. Everywhere in *Don Quijote*, for example, are to be found irreverent euphemisms for the Eucharist. These are often difficult to translate derivations of the phrase "Body of Christ," such as «¡cuerpo de tal!» "gosh darn body" (2.1.628, 2.62.1143), «¡cuerpo de mi padre!» "body of my father" (2.2.644, 2.14.738), «¡cuerpo del mundo!» "body of tarnation" (2.4.660), and «cuerpo del sol» "sun of a body" (2.9.695). Other euphemistic swearing, like «voto a tal» "dagnabit" (1.24.269), abounds as well. And there are more sophisticated examples. Sánson Carrasco's invocation of God in *DQ* 2.7 is an hilarious scribal pun with sexual connotations: «Plega a Dios todopoderoso, donde más largamente se contiene» "May it please Almighty God, where he is most observed at length" (2.7.682).

In a more elaborate blasphemy, the first innkeeper uses an accounting ledger as a sacred text while knighting the crazy hidalgo in *DQ* 1.3. Likewise, the reaction by the Toledan merchants at the end of *DQ* 1.4, when Don Quijote insists they acknowledge the beauty of Dulcinea, echoes the empirical objections lodged by Jews and Muslims against the Christian doctrine of the virgin birth: «mostrádnosla, que, si ella fuere de tanta hermosura como significáis, de buena gana y sin apremio alguno confesaremos la verdad» "show her to us, for if she be as beauteous as you suggest, then we will gladly and freely confess the truth" (1.4.68). Also radically irreverent is Vivaldo's point that knights-errant act like heretics: «se encomiendan a sus damas, con tanta gana y devoción como si ellas fueran su Dios, cosa que me parece que huele algo a gentilidad» "they commend themselves to their ladies with such zeal and devotion, as if these women were their God, something that smacks not a little to me of paganism" (1.13.139).

One might reasonably object that this type of religious disrespect is to some degree a continuation of the relatively harmless medieval legacy of carnivalesque and anticlerical humor found in writers like Juan Ruiz, Fernando de Rojas, or François Rabelais (see Bakhtin, *Rabelais and His World.*). Regardless of their medieval and Catholic origins, however, Cervantes's religious vulgarities in *Don Quijote* are part of a dramatically down-to-earth discourse aimed at subverting orthodoxy. In other words, it's just as difficult to separate these desecrations from the theological problems unleashed by the Reformation. The most radical Protestants, for example, went beyond their medieval precursors when they argued that the bread and wine of the Eucharist in no way experienced any mystical transubstantiations by way of priestly incantations in Latin.

Consider Cervantes's mockeries of public displays of religious faith. For starters, *Don Quijote* has a number of irreverent rosaries. In *DQ* 1.26, somewhere in the Sierra Morena, the penitent hidalgo improvises a string of prayer beads by tying knots into a strip of shirttail. This was the equivalent of making a rosary out of the era's toilet paper. How do we know this was especially offensive? Well, it's one of the few passages stricken by censors before the second edition of 1605.

Don Quijote's filthy rosary connects meaningfully to another one in the very next chapter. When Sancho, the barber, and the priest depart the inn in search of Don Quijote, Maritornes makes a specific vow: «prometió de rezar un rosario, aunque pecadora, por que Dios les diese bien suceso en tan arduo y tan cristiano negocio como era el que habían emprendido» "she promised to pray a rosary, even though she was sinful, so that God might grant them success in so arduous and so Christian an enterprise as was the one they had undertaken" (1.27.300). Don Quijote's unhygienic rosary in *DQ* 1.26 anticipates Maritornes's transethnic rosary in *DQ* 1.27, turning both into symbols of miscegenation. We know Maritornes is transethnic because she's a prostitute who attempts to service a Morisco mule driver, about whom the narrator even let it drop that Cide Mahamate Benengeli «era algo pariente suyo» "was one of his relatives" (1.16.171). In turn, these transgressive rosaries also recall the galley slaves whom Don Quijote and Sancho meet plodding through the Sierra Morena «como cuentas en una gran cadena de hierro» "like beads on a great iron chain" (1.22.235). This triad of rosaries suggests that Old Christians, the Church, and the Habsburgs all have interests in mandating religious orthodoxy, by which they stand to gain land, wealth, power, and conscripts for the ongoing galley war against the Turks. The rosaries are ways of satirizing the religious hypocrisy embodied by these institutions. Specifically, Spanish obsessions with religious and racial purity underwrote policies like the Expulsion of the Moriscos and forced military conscription as punishment for petty criminals and prisoners of war.

Cervantes's unruly use of rosaries continues in part two. The mad knight brandishes ridiculously large prayer beads when he confronts Altisidora in *DQ* 2.46. Teresa compares the coral necklace sent to her and her daughter by the Duchess to another absurd rosary in *DQ* 2.50. In part two, however, added to the criticisms of religious orthodoxy and racism we find the vindication of bourgeois values like trade and the work ethic. The Duchess seeks acorns in exchange for coral, and later, in *DQ* 2.70, both Don Quijote and Sancho Panza recommend that Altisidora dedicate herself to textiles. One way to read all of this is that Cervantes accentuates material commerce as an antidote to the fire and brimstone that often accompany religious orthodoxy. Perhaps most impressive of all, echoing and inverting the bourgeois gesture of the first innkeeper's sacred ledger in *DQ* 1.3, Don Quijote uses the novel's final rosary as a means of keeping proper count of the lashes for which he has agreed to pay Sancho in order to bring about the disenchantment of Dulcinea (2.71.1201).

Finally, when considering specific episodes that demonstrate the extent of Cervantes's religious radicalism, a major candidate would be the dead body adventure of *DQ* 1.19. The episode exhibits a dense series of anti-orthodox gestures mocking excommunication, the Pope, and belief in spirits. It's also a good example of how much *Don Quijote* impressed Hobbes, who borrowed a number of Cervantes's metaphors for his own demystifications of religious ceremony, Church authority, and metaphysical belief (see Graf, "*Don Quijote* and Materialism"). In *DQ* 1.19, Cervantes anticipates Hobbes's view in the final pages of *Leviathan* of the Roman Catholic Church as nothing but "the Ghost of the deceased Romane Empire" (47.480). The novelist turns what at first appears to be a nocturnal parade of phantoms into a procession of arrogant priests, one of whom Don Quijote ironically mistakes for a devil and then attacks. After the priest feebly excommunicates Don Quijote, the knight proudly recalls an episode in which the Cid defied the Pope. It's easy to see how both early modern materialistic atheists like Hobbes and Hume as well as fairly traditional nineteenth-century Protestants like Alexander Duffield could have all interpreted *Don Quijote* as relentless satirical protest against Catholic orthodoxy. Similar anti-metaphysical and anticlerical sentiments also characterized the thought of Erasmus (see "Exorcism").

(2) PRIESTS, BOOKS, AND HERETICS

In his essay "Of the Academical or Skeptical Philosophy," David Hume points to faith in chivalric novels as analogous to religious fanaticism. This works well as an explanation for Don Quijote's early aggressiveness. When he attacks the Toledan merchants in *DQ* 1.4, for example, he morphs into an inquisitorial menace, an anti-hero asserting the diabolical authority of the confessional state: «vosotros pagaréis la grande blasfemia que habéis dicho» "you will all pay for the great blasphemy you have uttered" (1.4.69).

Chivalric novels, however, have a deeper metaphorical meaning in *Don Quijote* shown by the fact that the genre is anathema to the purist and persecutorial literary tastes of the curate, the canon, and the ecclesiastic. Chivalric novels allow Cervantes's mockery of the Inquisition to be quite specific: chi-valric novels are people. When the curate and the barber are distracted from their scrutiny of Don Quijote's library, the narrator humanizes the books, not-ing that many innocent volumes went to the flames «sin ser vistos ni oídos» "without being charged or questioned" (1.7.88). This is very precise criticism of the Inquisition as too arbitrary and subjective. According to this logic, later, when the curate wants to burn more chivalric novels at the inn, Palomeque asks a painful question: «¿mis libros son herejes o flemáticos?» "are my books heretics or unrepentants?" (1.32.371). A debate over books—ironically a genre of books that everybody loves—now echoes the debate over burning and ex-pelling the enemies of the confessional state. We should keep in mind too that, like mule drivers, innkeepers were often Moriscos. On more than one level, then, Palomeque's objection makes hatred of chivalric novels and insistence on literary purity analogous to popular notions of ethnic or religious purity. It would seem that Cervantes considered both ideas ridiculous. So, it's a little more complicated than Hume's view of Don Quijote as the religious fanatic.

We again see the duplicity and hypocrisy of religious authority in *DQ* 1.47–48 when the canon of Toledo calls for the expulsion of chivalric novels, only then to reveal that he too is composing one. Siding with Palomeque, Don Quijote rebuffs the canon. Toledo, we should remember, had a particularly aggressive Inquisitional tribunal. In addition to being arbitrary and subjective, the Inquisition's *autos de fe* are now hypocritical. All this theological false-ness accords with the reformist perspective of the Leuven School: the real heresy is the violent persecution of heresy. For its part, the essence of the novel's satire of racial hypocrisy stems from the absurd idea that one Span-iard could possibly presume to judge the blood purity of another when nine centuries had passed since the Umayyad-Berber invasion of 711.

Early in part two, Don Quijote's niece Antonia recalls the gist of the burning of the books episode in *DQ* 1.6–7, saying that her uncle's chivalric novels are heretical and that if they are not put to death, then they should at least be made to dress like the victims of the Inquisition: «todo eso que dice de los caballeros andantes es fábula y mentira, y sus historias, ya que no las quemasen, merecían que a cada una se le echase un sambenito o alguna señal en que fuese conocida por infame» "all that you say about knights-errant is fake and false, and their histories, if they cannot be burned, deserve every last one of them to be clothed in a *sambenito* or with some sign that would make known their infamy" (2.6.673). This image of the book as a penitent heretic wearing a *sambenito* sets the stage for Cervantes's criticism in part two of the essential mechanisms of the confessional state, especially expulsion, cen-sorship, and the *auto de fe*. For this reason, when the aggressive ecclesiastic launches another tirade against chivalric books at dinner in the palace of the

Duke and Duchess in *DQ* 2.31, it's an ominous sign because the scene takes place in Aragón, a kingdom that was severely affected by the Expulsion of the Moriscos. The book-as-heretic theme reaches a crescendo in the novel's final chapters. In *DQ* 2.69, when the Duke and Duchess's minions dress Sancho for a mock Inquisitorial trial, he wears buckram, a material also used to cover books. In *DQ* 2.70, Altisidora witnesses books being burned by devils like sinners in hell. Finally, in *DQ* 2.73, when Sancho dresses his donkey like a book-as-heretic, draping it with his own buckram *sambenito* from *DQ* 2.69, the narrator marvels at the metamorphosis: «fue la más nueva transformación y adorno con que se vio jamás jumento en el mundo» "it was the most novel transformation and adornment with which a donkey was ever seen in the world" (2.73.1211).

This metaphor of books representing people who are tortured, burned, or exiled for heresy, then, is a crucial aspect of Cervantes's art of the novel. Many critics have noted that *Don Quijote* is a book about books. But we can be even more specific: *Don Quijote* is a book that deploys books in an extended allegory about the torturing, burning, and exiling of people. This is also the reason why three major representatives of the priestly caste are portrayed so negatively in *Don Quijote*. In *DQ* 1.6–7, the curate burns books like people; he wants to do so again in *DQ* 1.32. In *DQ* 1.47, the canon endorses the curate's efforts at literary purification, saying books of chivalry are «dignos de ser desterrados de la república cristiana, como a gente inútil» "worthy of being expelled from Christian republics, like unproductive people" (1.47.549). In *DQ* 2.31–32, when the ecclesiastic butts into the affairs of the nobility of Aragón, echoing the curate and the canon, he aims another round of bile in the direction of chivalric fiction. In a symbolic sense, the ecclesiastic's extreme, confrontational tone lays the groundwork for the Expulsion of the Moriscos theme which climaxes later upon the arrival of Ricote and Ana Félix in *DQ* 2.54 and 2.63–65.

Understanding the "books are people" metaphor helps us grasp one of the novel's major ironies. After his violent attempt to impose Catholic orthodoxy on the Toledan merchants in *DQ* 1.4, the mad knight is slowly transformed back into a tragic hero who increasingly defends various victims of orthodoxy. Throughout the remainder of the novel, this takes place in terms of Don Quijote's relation to books. First, he's traumatized by the erasure of his library in *DQ* 1.7. Later, in *DQ* 1.49, he rebukes the canon for his literary bias and essentially adopts the same attitude as Palomeque in defense of the exotic romantic messiness of his heretical novels. Extending the theme in part two, Don Quijote calls his niece's hatred of the books of chivalry «blasfemia» "blasphemy" (2.6.673), and he later roundly rejects the ecclesiastic's orthodox literary preferences.

The climax of the subversive satire involved in the "books are people" theme occurs when Altisidora claims that she has seen the apocryphal continuation of *Don Quijote* in hell being tortured by devils. Don Quijote calmly responds that he is not that other book: «Yo no me he alterado en oír que ando como cuerpo fantástico por las tinieblas del abismo, ni por la claridad de la tierra porque no soy aquel de quien esa historia trata» "I am not disturbed to hear that I move like a fantastical tome through the darkness of the abyss or even through the light of the world, because I am not the one about whom that history speaks" (2.70.1195). We might paraphrase as follows: by being passionate about his books, Don Quijote unwittingly comes to the defense of the *conversos*, Moriscos, and Protestants all targeted by the Spanish confessional state. And if Cervantes's hero ends up defending heretics against the fiery fates decreed by priests, then these fanatical burners of books and people are the true devils.

The dense, anti-orthodox dead body adventure of *DQ* 1.19 again offers a good example of Cervantes's irreverence toward ecclesiastics who banish and burn books and people. In one of only two episodes in which Don Quijote assumes a different moniker, the «Caballero de la Triste Figura» "Knight of the Sorrowful Face" breaks the leg of a priest. In response, the cleric excommunicates Don Quijote, at which point the hero recalls with approval that the Pope once excommunicated the Cid. This reads like secular nationalist nostalgia for the Cid (c.1043–99), a hybrid figure, a non-racist pragmatist, as opposed to the relatively more fanatical fury of Pope Urban II (c.1035–99), the founder of the modern Roman Curia and the instigator of the first crusade. It bears noting, too, that Erasmus savages another notoriously bellicose pope in his satire *Julius Excluded from Heaven* (1514). So, inspired by Erasmus, mildly nationalistic, and in anticipation of Hobbes in *Leviathan*, Cervantes tilts consistently against Rome in *Don Quijote*. At one point, Sancho even compares the pleasure of getting drunk with his Morisco neighbors to Nero's joy at watching Rome burn (2.54.1070–71).

(3) THE INQUISITION

Turning to that nefarious institution at the heart of the Spanish confessional state, the Inquisition, it is again helpful to keep in mind the radical views of the Leuven School. J. Ignacio Tellechea's description of the sentiments of these reformers around the middle of the sixteenth century, which cites the testimony of Fray Baltasar Pérez, shows how the Erasmian legacy underwent its own radicalization. The Spanish reformers at Leuven were an angry group:

... constantemente se criticaba de los Prelados de la Iglesia y de sus rentas, de los frailes y del Santo Oficio. De éste último afirmaban que era "carnicería", que hacía caso de testimonios falsos y prolongaba los procesos por no dar paso atrás; que condenaban libros por ignorancia; que los inquisidores eran "verdugos" y los frailes "sayones"; que la Inquisición no era sino "una tiranía, que se querían hacer adorar", etc. (Tellechea 29)

... there was constant criticism of the prelates of the Church and their incomes, of the friars and the Holy Office. Regarding this last, they affirmed that it was "butchery," that it allowed false testimonies and prolonged trails, so as not to have to withdraw their charges; that they condemned books out of ignorance; that the inquisitors were "executioners" and the friars "killers"; that the Inquisition was nothing but "tyranny, and that they wanted people to worship them," etc.

Similarly, *Don Quijote* attacks the Inquisition and the *auto de fe*. In *DQ* 1.6–7 and 1.32, banned and burned books are analogous to people. Allusions to the clothing of the victims of the Inquisition in *DQ* 1.52 (*capirotes*), *DQ* 2.6 (*sambenitos*), and *DQ* 2.45 (*caperuzas*) climax in scenes where Sancho and his ass are dressed as heretics on trial in *DQ* 2.69 and 2.73. Other ironies include Don Quijote's shock that the Inquisition has not investigated the diabolical Ginés de Pasamonte: «estoy maravillado cómo no le han acusado al Santo Oficio» "I marvel that nobody has denounced him to the Holy Office" (2.25.843); Sancho's formulation of the fallible nature of damnation: «Ahora yo tengo para mí que aun en el mesmo infierno debe de haber buena gente» "Now I am convinced that even in the depths of hell there are good people" (2.34.918); and the ride atop Clavileño, which Don Quijote compares to the flight made by a famous heretic processed as a wizard by the Inquisition: «acuérdate del verdadero cuento del licenciado Torralba, a quien llevaron los diablos en volandas por el aire caballero en una caña» "remember the true story of the licentiate Torralba, when those devils carried him through the air mounted on a reed" (2.41.962). In these ways, Cervantes criticizes the Inquisition as an immoral, brutal, random, superstitious, and hypocritical institution that suffers from considerable ideological inconsistency.

Many of the most provocative wordplays in *Don Quijote* also target the Holy Office. The dead body adventure typifies Cervantes's assault on orthodoxy and persecution by way of Don Quijote's attack on a priest and his praise for the Cid's anger at the Pope. However, modern readers might miss other anticlerical touches in the same scene. At the beginning of the episode, knight and squire metaphorically accuse each other of heresy, deploying technical terms used by the Inquisition. Don Quijote says that Sancho deserved his blanketing in the previous chapter—«de participantes no estás seguro» "you are not cleared of being an accomplice"—; then Sancho warns his master that certain ghosts might abuse him too «si le ven pertinaz» "if they deem you unrepentant" (1.19.199). Similarly, a few chapters later, when Don Quijote enters the Sierra Morena, in order to perform penance in imitation of the chivalric hero Amadís of Gual, phrases like «las generales» "general deposition questions," «pena de relasos» "penalty for reoffenders," and «cosa juzgada» "sentence with no appeal" (1.25.280–81) infuse the situation with the juridical language of the Inquisition. By implication, then, Don Quijote is not just a madman; he's often an apostate.

In his criticism of the Inquisition, Cervantes makes much use of the verb *reducir*, which means "to surrender" if used passively or "to convince" in the active, but with a very heavy confessional-state ring to it, meaning something along the lines of "to convert" or "to turn" sinners away from heresy. Cervantes defines the essence of the term at the conclusion of "The Captive's Tale," when the apostate renegade reports to the Holy Office: «se fue a la ciudad de Granada a reducirse por medio de la Santa Inquisición al gremio santísimo de la Iglesia» "he went to the city of Granada in order to surrender himself to the bosom of the Church by way of the Holy Inquisition" (1.41.492). In case we missed the discomfort of this official interrogation of the religious identity of Viedma's most important ally, we are soon confronted by the image of Don Quijote himself dangling in torture: «bien así como los que están en el tormento de la garrucha, puestos a *toca, no toca*» "much like those who are subjected to the torture of the *strappado*, left in a state of *touch, can't touch*" (1.43.511). Then, in *DQ* 1.46, Fernando parodies the Inquisition when he asks Don Quijote to forgive Sancho: «reducille al gremio de su gracia, *sic erat in principio*» "restore him to the bosom of your grace, *as it was in the beginning*" (1.46.535). These words are a kind of formula from the *Gloria Patri* prayer read during the Inquisition's ceremonies of religious reconciliation.

In *DQ* 2.7, the squire reports to Don Quijote that he has convinced his wife to let him go on another adventure. But his word choice is wrong: «Señor, ya yo tengo relucida a mi mujer a que me deje ir con vuestra merced adonde quisiere llevarme» "Sir, I've conwinced my wife to let me go with your grace wherever you might wish to take me," and so Don Quijote corrects him: «Reducida has de decir, Sancho» "*Convinced* you mean to say, Sancho" (2.7.679). The irony here is double. Don Quijote's *reducida* means "convinced" and implies religious coercion; and Sancho's *relucida*, a very fluid malapropism, means "shined" but also "severely whipped," which would certainly be a more Inquisitorial kind of convincing. Likewise, after Don Quijote and Sancho depart on their second sally together, in *DQ* 2.15, the narrator alludes again to the Inquisition, informing us that Sansón Carrasco, the hidalgo's neighbor and a bachelor student at the University of

Salamanca, has conspired with the priest and the barber «sobre qué medio se podría tomar para reducir a don Quijote a que se estuviese en su casa quieto y sosegado» "regarding what devices to use to convince Don Quijote to stay quietly and peacefully at home" (2.15.747). By implication, Don Quijote is again a heretic.

Similarly, the fencing duel in *DQ* 2.19 between the bachelor Corchuelo and the anonymous licentiate, both students at the University of Salamanca, offers an allegory for the precision of the era's scientific and moral debates among late-scholastic intellectuals. Allusions to geometry abound, for example, and the scene concludes upon the achievement of the social accord sought by philosophy and theology. Science here defeats force and the sarcastic allusion to the Inquisition appears when Corchuelo is left «reducido de su pertinacia» "turned away from his obstinacy" (2.19.789). Unlike the essence of the Holy Office, Corchuelo shows respect for his rival and recognizes his own error, displaying harmony which reads like a mixture of Salamanca and Erasmus— on the one hand, a lesson about the Golden Rule of natural law, "treat others as you want to be treated," and on the other hand, a lesson about Christianity, "love your enemies" (see Matthew 5.44).

Among Cervantes's most explicit mockeries of the Inquisition in *Don Quijote* are a series of ludic versions of the infamous *auto de fe*. These are of two types. First, the theme of books as heretics condemned by the Inquisition appears in episodes like the burning of the hidalgo's library in *DQ* 1.6–7, Palomeque's and Don Quijote's defenses of chivalric novels in *DQ* 1.32 and 1.49, and Altisidora's vision of the novel *Don Quijote* undergoing torture in hell in *DQ* 2.70.

Second are Sancho's grotesque trials throughout part two. At the Duke and Duchess's palace, the squire is assailed by «ministros de limpieza» "ministers of cleanliness" (2.32.903). During the hunting trip on their estate, Dulcinea appears and asks Sancho to accept 3,300 lashes, calling him «bestión indómito» "indomitable beast" and lamenting that he does not want to turn away from heresy: «si por mí no quieres ablandarte ni reducirte a algún razonable término, hazlo por ese pobre caballero» "if, on my behalf you do not wish to soften nor submit yourself in some reasonable period of time, then do it for this poor knight " (2.35.925). Returning from Barcelona, Sancho is brought before Altisidora's tomb and forced by «ministros infernales» "infernal ministers" to suffer «extraordinarios martirios» "extraordinary martyrdom" (2.69.1189). One of these infernal minions dresses Sancho as an unrepentant victim of the Inquisition condemned to die in an *auto de fe*: «le echó una ropa de bocací negro encima, toda pintada con llamas de fuego, y quitándole la caperuza le puso en la cabeza una coroza, al modo de las que sacan los penitenciados por el Santo Oficio» "he placed on him a garment of black buckram painted over with fiery flames, and he removed his cap and placed on his head a cone-shaped hat like those given to penitents by the Holy Office" (2.69.1185). All of this culminates in the final image of Sancho's own ass dressed in the same heretical garb (2.73.1211). A reasonably informed reader of *Don Quijote* cannot help but perceive Cervantes's unrelenting attacks on the Inquisition.

(4) ERASMUS, FELIPE DE MENESES,
AND BARTOLOMÉ DE CARRANZA

The argument that Cervantes was Erasmian is particularly convincing because it takes several forms. First, it's worth keeping in mind the violently censored engravings of Erasmus brought forward by Bataillon (fig. 5). The words «Sancho Panza y su amigo don Quijote» "Sancho Panza and his friend Don Quijote" scribbled in the margin of one of them indicate that orthodox censors read the first modern novel as a threat to their ecclesiastic power creatively articulated in the Erasmian mode.

Second, in terms of his biography, one of Cervantes's early teachers at the Estudio de la Villa de Madrid, Juan López de Hoyos (1511–83), was an enthusiastic Erasmian, as were many of the intellectuals at the University of Alcalá with whom Cervantes affiliated throughout his life. Then there's the fact that Seville and Valladolid, two cities where Cervantes lived for significant periods, had experienced Erasmian-inspired outbreaks of Protestantism in the 1550s. As a boy, the future novelist might have witnessed one of the *autos de fe* held in Seville or Valladolid in 1559 at the beginning of the reign of Philip II. As an adult he might have encountered lingering urban memories of those events. Cervantes was himself excommunicated, so he knew first-hand about confrontations with religious authorities. He was also a requisitions officer for the ill-fated Armada Invencible of 1588, and he later lost his own brother Rodrigo to the war against Protestant insurgency in the Low Countries in 1600. Such events may have been particularly frustrating for an Erasmian, adding further momentum to his satirical instincts.

Like Cervantes, Erasmus was highly critical of religious formalities, spectacles, and superstitions, as well as institutions like the Papacy and the Inquisition. Instead, he advanced the simple, reformist elegance of Matthew 5.44, which is also notably the first case of biblical Latin we find in *Don Quijote*: «diligite inimicos vestros» "love your enemies" (1.pro.15). Similarly, compassion, respect, and tolerance for others are major aspects of Erasmian humanism. As Alban Forcione showed, Cervantes's texts often echo the *sententiae* or "adages" for which the Dutch theologian was so famous. When

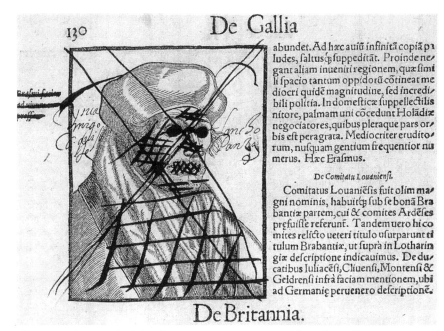

Figure 5. Erasmus in Sebastian Münster's *Cosmographia Uniuersalis*, 1550 **Source**: Biblioteca Nacional de Madrid, R/33638

Sancho refuses to duel Tomé Cecial, he articulates the Erasmian pacifist wisdom of minding one's own business: «lo más acertado sería dejar dormir su cólera a cada uno, que no sabe nadie el alma de nadie» "it would be best to let our angers sleep, for no man knows another man's soul" (2.14.739). As Javier Herrero observed, this liberal mode of "interior Christianity," which arrived in Spain from the Low Countries in the early sixteenth century, was roundly bourgeois in nature (see "Sierra Morena as Labyrinth").

Cervantes strikes another Erasmian chord soon thereafter in *DQ* 2.15–18. The temperate, yet also wealthy household of Diego de Miranda, also known as the "Knight of the Green Coat," represents grounded, earthly success. As such, Miranda is a counterexample to the mad hidalgo. Don Quijote takes pride in his nobility, but he's also dependent on a state pension and staggers toward poverty as he sells off his lands in order to buy chivalric novels. By contrast, Miranda properly manages his estate. His lifestyle is rural, like the hidalgo caste in question, but he also embodies bourgeois values popular in places like Antwerp, Brussels, Rotterdam, and Seville: frugality, work, attention to detail, discretion, and generosity. Most Erasmian of all, he's unpretentious in his religious practices: «no escudriño las vidas ajenas ni soy lince de los hechos de los otros, oigo misa cada día, reparto mis bienes con los pobres, sin hacer alarde de las buenas obras, por no dar entrada en mi corazón a la hipocresía y vanagloria» "I don't meddle in other people's lives, and I'm not a lynx when it comes to other people's business; I hear mass daily; I give of my wealth to the poor without making a show of my good deeds, so as not to allow hypocrisy and vanity into my heart" (2.16.754).

Other, more formal aspects of the Erasmian mode appear in *Don Quijote*. Two of the Dutchman's texts have global implications for the novel. *Encomium moriae* (1511), or *The Praise of Folly*, exhibits easygoing, often self-directed humor as an essential aspect of humanism; *Enchiridion militis Christiani* (1533), or *Handbook of a Christian Knight*, urges Christians to act in accordance with their religion's ideals rather than merely perform its requisite rituals. The hilarious misadventures of an overzealous medieval knight suggest Cervantes's familiarity with both works. Similarly, Cervantes exploits the outer-inner contrast that drives Erasmus's reformist message in *Sileni Alcibiadis*, or *The Sileni of Alcibiades* (1515). Thus, in metaphorical terms, Don Quijote turns his early defeat by the Yanguesan horse drivers into a moral victory by comparing himself to a major Erasmian emblem for Christianity's emphasis on humility and inner perfection: «me acuerdo haber leído que aquel buen viejo Sileno, ayo y pedagogo del alegre dios de la risa, cuando entró en la ciudad de las cien puertas iba muy a su placer caballero sobre un muy hermoso asno» "I remember reading that Silenus, that good old teacher and sage to the merry god of laughter, upon entering the city of the hundred gates, went most happily mounted upon a most beautiful jackass" (1.15.166).

Like *DQ* 1.19 in 1605, *DQ* 2.62 features Cervantes's anticlericalism in 1615. The extended and multipart episode in Barcelona involves a number of reformist themes and offers yet another indication of the range of the novelist's criticisms of the Inquisition. As elsewhere, he criticizes the Holy Office for its part in Spain's turn to censorship, expulsion, and racism, but now he further chastises the institution for repressing technology and diversion. In this sense, Cervantes investigates an entire range of negative externalities that are often brought about by imposing religious conformity, signaling the extent to which other bad things happen when the confessional state takes charge.

Cervantes signals the overarching importance of *DQ* 2.62 by making it the novel's most self-reflexive chapter. First, Don Quijote's host Don Antonio Moreno shows the hidalgo his prized «cabeza encantada» "enchanted head," a mechanized bronze bust with which he will later entertain guests by making witty prophecies. Moreno then parades him through Barcelona with a sign attached to his back which reads: «Este es don Quijote de la Mancha» "This is Don Quijote of La Mancha" (2.62.1136). Next, we have a dance in which women spin Don Quijote around until he collapses from dizziness. He even refers to the ritual of exorcism when he shouts out in Latin: «¡Fugite, partes adversae!» "Enemies begone!" (2.62.1138). And then we revisit the enchanted head.

We might read this sequence in *DQ* 2.62 as a kind of multipronged effort at *tabula rasa*, which constantly suggests that the character Don Quijote is a narrative device. This clearing of the deck has the effect of dropping symbolic pretense and hailing the reader, asking us to cogitate on the novel's meaning: "Look here, this is what my novel is really about." And as a final clue that the sequence targets the dangers and excesses of the Inquisition, it's the Holy Office that expressly orders the dismantling of Moreno's mechanical head:

> Y dice más Cide Hamete: que hasta diez o doce días duró esta maravillosa máquina, pero que divulgándose por la ciudad que don Antonio tenía en su casa una cabeza encantada, que a cuantos le preguntaban respondía, temiendo no llegase a los oídos de las despiertas centinelas de nuestra fe, habiendo declarado el caso a los señores inquisidores, le mandaron que lo deshiciese y no pasase más adelante. (2.62.1142)

> And Cide Hamete says more: that this marvelous machine lasted ten or twelve days, but word spread through the city that Don Antonio had an enchanted head in his house which responded to all questions, and so, fearing that the news would reach the ears of those vigilant guardians of our faith and having informed our lords the Inquisitors regarding the matter, they ordered him to dismantle it and to cease and desist.

The added detail that it's Cide Hamete Benengeli who provides all of this additional information about how Church authorities reacted to Moreno's machine ties the Inquisition problem back to the Morisco question. Moreover, Moreno's surname means "dark" and even "African." Like *moro* "Moor," it derives from the Latin *maurus* and the Greek μαῦρος. The link to the Morisco question is reconfirmed in *DQ* 2.65, when Moreno pledges to represent Ricote at court. In this way, Cervantes maintains that the Inquisition's tyrannical repression of intellectual and technological innovation is part and parcel of its persecution of the Morisco population.

But *DQ* 2.62 advances its message beyond the Morisco question. In the same chapter devoted to Barcelona, Don Quijote finally encounters that other important machine that drew the Inquisition's intense scrutiny and censure: the printing press. Don Quijote is drawn to a sign which reads «Aquí se imprimen libros» "Books Printed Here" (2.62.1142). As with Moreno's label on Don Quijote's back, the printer's shop incorporates a self-reflexive continuation of the "books are people" motif. There is irony, too, when Don Quijote, seated in the midst of this printer's shop, confesses that he has imagined that the apocryphal sequel by Alonso Fernández de Avellaneda has suffered some hellish torture: «pensé que ya estaba quemado y hecho polvos por impertinente» "I imagined that it had already been burned and turned to dust for being impertinent" (2.62.1146). This same self-reflexive irony resurfaces a few chapters later in *DQ* 2.70 when Don Quijote dismisses the possibility that he could have been the *Don Quijote* that Altisidora reports to have seen being tortured in hell.

This complex of reflexive gestures in *DQ* 2.62 produces an amplified and particularly bookish case of *mise en abîme*. In other words, Cervantes repeatedly violates our expectations of traditional, formal narrative frames of reference: a character, who is the titular subject of several books, including the one we are reading, enters the shop of a maker and seller of books, where he then discusses both a book about himself and the book industry more generally. Reflexive effects continue when Don Quijote refers to the Italian author Ariosto and the poet and painter Juan de Jáuregui. Informed readers recognize seriously personal gestures here. Ariosto ranks among Cervantes's favorite modern authors and Jáuregui once painted Cervantes's portrait.

It's a feature of great books that they teach us how to read them. In *DQ* 2.62, form telegraphs function. A vertiginously self-reflexive visit to a printer's shop amounts to more than a clever, existentialist effort by the author to make us aware that we're reading his novel; it's a pronouncement of intention. Through an obvious parallel, Cervantes uses the Inquisition's repression of Moreno's technological toy to signal disgust at the Holy Office's attempts to control the printing press. But he's more specific than that. Fittingly, *DQ* 2.62 has a Rube Goldberg quality to it. The enchanted mechanical head initiates a series of interlocking symbols and events that carry us along toward the chapter's most radical gesture, Don Quijote's praise for Felipe de Meneses's *Luz del alma cristiana* (Valladolid, 1554): «Estos tales libros, aunque hay muchos deste género, son los que se deben imprimir, porque son muchos los pecadores que se usan y son menester infinitas luces para tantos desalumbrados» "These are the kinds of books, even though there are many of its genre, that should be printed, because sin is now very much in fashion and an infinite number of lights are needed for so many unilluminated people" (2.62.1145). We know Cervantes thinks Meneses's book is important because Don Quijote alludes to it again on his deathbed in the novel's last chapter (2.74.1217).

The boldness of these gestures will escape modern readers. As a war hero injured at the Battle of Lepanto, Cervantes could get away with a lot. Nevertheless, referring to Meneses's book, the qualifying phrase «aunque hay muchos deste género» "even though there are many of this genre" seems designed to inoculate the passage against the consequences of a serious theological transgression. For starters, *Luz del alma cristiana* was influenced by Erasmus, and it was even more influenced by one of Spain's most eminent victims of the Inquisition, namely, the Archbishop of Toledo, Bartolomé Carranza (*DQ*

2.62.1145n72). Carranza's fate was a well-known example of the overzeal-ousness of the Holy Office. So, Cervantes has now signaled his concern for members of the Leuven School and their Erasmian brethren at Alcalá and To-ledo—men like Juan López de Hoyos, Sebastián Fox Morcillo, Fadrique Furió Ceriol, Felipe de la Torre, Felipe de Meneses, and Bartolomé de Carranza. These men represented a formidable generation of reform-minded Catholic humanists. They were critical of censorship, for example, and they approved of translating the Bible into the vernacular. They also criticized coercion in spiritual matters, often voicing deep hostility toward the Inquisition.

Of course, Cervantes echoes criticism of the Inquisition by Spanish late scholastics, too. Fray Luis de León, one of the School of Salamanca's most eminent victims of the Inquisition, reportedly scrawled «¡ni envidiado, ni envidioso!» "neither envied, nor envious" on his cell wall prior to his release in 1576. Cervantes's version of the phrase in part two of *Don Quijote* is fairly explicit, if comically mangled and redirected when the knight envies his squire's supposedly bucolic lifestyle utterly devoid of envy: «sin tener invidia ni ser invidiado» "without envy, nor being envied" (2.20.790). Beyond the irony of Don Quijote's envy meaning that Sancho is indeed envied, the affili-ation between Sancho and the persecuted *converso* Fray Luis has the effect of mocking the squire's insistence on his Old Christian status. Nevertheless, *DQ* 2.62 does go quite a long way toward linking Cervantes to some of the most radical Spanish Erasmians, men seemingly on the brink of power in the years prior to the *autos de fe* of 1559.[3]

(5) LUTHERAN DUCHESSES, CALVINIST PIRATES, AND PROTESTANT NEIGHBORS

Important critics have proven beyond reasonable doubt that Erasmus is fun-damental to a proper understanding of *Don Quijote*. I contend, however, that Cervantes insinuates even more extreme positions at crucial moments in the novel. This is especially evident in a series of references to the early modern period's major doctrinal debate over whether one gains access to heaven via faith or works. Protestants deployed the mantra that faith alone, *sola fide*, de-termined one's salvation; whereas orthodox Catholics argued that one could achieve justification through charitable acts or donations to the Church.

Cervantes begins to underscore this theme cautiously. At the climax of the adventure of the boiling lake in *DQ* 1.50, the mad hidalgo intervenes to explain that when he becomes a rich emperor, he will be generous and grate-ful. As he does this, however, he moves comically between the Protestant and Catholic positions on salvation through faith and works. First, he makes a Protestant point that Catholicism paradoxically discriminates against the poor, who can't afford the virtue of generosity; but then he makes a Catholic point against the idea of *sola fide* by arguing that the Christian faith loses meaning without virtuous works: «el pobre está inhabilitado de poder mostrar la virtud de liberalidad con ninguno, aunque en sumo grado la posea, y el agradecimiento que solo consiste en el deseo es cosa muerta, como es muerta la fe sin obras» "a poor man is disadvantaged when it comes to displaying the virtue of generosity, even if he be infinitely generous; and when gratitude consists solely of verbal expression or emotion, it is like a dead thing, just as faith is dead without works" (1.50.572). Is Don Quijote saying faith should suffice or is he insisting on generosity? It's easy to imagine a Counter-Reformation censor scratching his head about what to do with this passage.

Nevertheless, Cervantes gains confidence and takes more theological risks in part two. A less ambiguous case of the debate over faith and works appears in Diego de Miranda's qualified charity: «reparto mis bienes con los pobres, sin hacer alarde de las buenas obras» "I give of my wealth to the poor, without making a show of my good deeds" (2.16.754). Bolder still, when the Duchess warns Sancho Panza against whipping himself too lightly during his penance to free Dulcinea, she cites a Protestant notion: «advierta Sancho que las obras de caridad que se hacen tibia y flojamente no tienen mérito ni valen nada» "be advised, Sancho, that works of charity performed in a reserved or weak manner have no merit and are worth nothing" (2.36.930). The Duchess's phrase implies the Lutheran idea of *sola fide*, that is, she undermines the view that good works, no matter how trivial or transient, lead to grace. Moreover, since her intervention is part of an orchestrated trick played on Sancho, on some level she might just mock theology at large. Still, we do know that the phrase caused anxiety for orthodox readers because censors removed it in 1616 and it was expurgated from all Spanish editions after 1632 until Antonio Bergnes's Barcelona edition of 1839–40. As they did in the cases of Don Quijote's scatological rosary in *DQ* 1.26 and the secret marriage between Dorotea and Fernando in *DQ* 1.28, the censors sensed transgression in the Duchess's words and took action against them.

But there are even subtler and more aggressive allusions in *Don Quijote* to the theological and political tensions unleashed by Protestantism. In *DQ* 1.41, for example, readers of "The Captive's Tale" are confronted by pirates on their way to La Rochelle, a maritime port on the west coast of France with a large Huguenot population. In the early modern period, La Rochelle often functioned like a radically autonomous "state within a state." In 1568, the city declared itself an independent "Reformed Republic" modeled after Geneva. Just prior to the appearance of the Huguenot pirates in *DQ* 1.41, Captain Viedma's friend the renegade explains to Agi Morato that his daughter Zoraida has chosen to become a Christian: «ella va aquí de su voluntad, tan contenta, a lo que yo imagino, de verse en este estado como el que sale de las tinieblas a la luz» "she goes here of her own free will, as content, it seems to me, to see herself in this state as one who leaves darkness for light" (1.41.483–84). This last phrase refers to a biblical passage that became a Protestant motto, especially among Calvinists, during the sixteenth century: *Post tenebras spero lucem* or "I hope for light after darkness" (Job 17.12). An effect of *DQ* 1.41, then, is the construction of a bridge, an analogy between Zoraida and the Huguenots, who seek religious liberty in Spain and La Rochelle, respectively. To put it another way: on a relative gradient of religious freedom, Islam is to Catholicism as Catholicism is to Protestantism. This also makes Don Quijote's confusion about *sola fide* in *DQ* 1.50 seem like an anxious and disoriented reaction to Captain Viedma and Zoraida's recent brush with Calvinism at sea.

Most ingeniously, however, Cervantes has coopted the citation of Job 17.12 that appears on printer Juan de la Cuesta's shield found on the frontispieces of both editions of *Don Quijote*. Indeed, he fashions his novel into a kind of Calvinist shield, which he then wields in defense of the Moriscos. The fusion of Zoraida, Job, and the Huguenots at the end of part one is subtle; by contrast, Cervantes gathers together explicit Morisco and Protestant themes at the end of part two. Sancho's neighbor Ricote articulates the novel's most radical gesture in favor of freedom of religion. Criticism of the confessional state and a pro-Morisco attitude unite in Ricote's remark to Sancho that in Protestant Austria he has found «libertad de conciencia» "freedom of conscience" (2.54.1073). Some critics argue the phrase is ambiguous and that, rather than an affirmation of religious liberty, it could indicate an orthodox perspective, meaning something negative like "theological licentiousness." But given everything else Erasmian, Lutheran, and Calvinist in *Don Quijote*, Cervantes seems to intend the more modern, progressive sense of religious freedom. Similarly, Don Antonio Moreno resolves to defend Ricote and Ana Félix at court at the end of *DQ* 2.65, and then, at the beginning of *DQ* 2.68, the mad knight quotes the Calvinist motto in Latin while hoping for the disenchantment of Dulcinea: «que yo *post tenebras spero lucem*» "for I, *after darkness, hope for light*" (2.68.1179). Given the provocative ethnic status of characters like Zoraida and Ana Félix, and given Cervantes's nods to Huguenots and Lutherans in both parts of the novel, Don Quijote's final turn to Job 17.12 likely articulates another Protestant perspective on the Morisco question.

The chivalric quest to save Antonomasia in *DQ* 2.38–41 represents Cervantes's most complex case of a subversive approach to the Morisco question by way of an allegorical application of Reformation theology. The hilarious detail here is that the evil giant threatening Antonomasia's Kingdom of Kandy on the island nation of Sri Lanka is also a Christian: «Malambruno, aunque es encantador, es cristiano» "even though he is a sorcerer, Malambruno's still a Christian" (2.41.958). Informed readers sense similar confusion when Sancho dismounts Clavileño and frolics with «las siete cabrillas» "the seven she-goats" (2.41.965), which refer to the Pleaides, which, in turn, refer to Zoraida, whose name means this same group of stars in Arabic. In other words, the supposedly pure-blooded, Old-Christian squire is rolling around with the symbolic equivalent of the Algerian princess. Furthermore, Antonomasia's mother's name, «doña Maguncia» (1.38.942), refers to Mainz, the city in Germany which was the birthplace of Gutenberg's printing revolution at the very heart of the Holy Roman Empire. In multiple ways, then, Antonomasia's story anticipates: (1) the Christian persecution of the Morisco Ricote who finds religious freedom in Austria; (2) the love affair between Ricote's daughter Ana Félix and the Old-Christian Don Gregorio; (3) Don Quijote's triumphant visit to the reformist printer's shop in Barcelona. Her story also alludes rather overtly to the Christian Portuguese invasion of Sri Lanka in 1592, locating the Iberian colonizers in the evil giant Malambruno. The sum of these parts produces a Protestant allegory against the Expulsion of the Moriscos, as if it were a kind of illegitimate attack, an allegory which also happens to defend the radical technology of the printing press and the radical idea of religious liberty as two interrelated modes of social reform.

Now, several of the instances of Protestantism in *Don Quijote* exhibit a certain directionality away from Islam. Zoraida and Ana Félix, for example, embrace Catholic lovers and flee North Africa in search of asylum in Spain. Likewise, the renegades are apostates in both stories who heroically return to the bosom of the Catholic Church. So, what about Cervantes's attitudes toward Arabs and Islam?

(6) MORISCOS AND ISLAM

In sixteenth-century Europe, the Protestant Reformation threatened to infiltrate Spain from the northern frontier. At the other end of the geopolitical and religious spectrum was Islam, principally in the form of the menacing Ottoman Empire to the east. Notice the historical overlap of these conflicts, especially the temporal proximity between Spanish experiences of victory and defeat on two separate fronts. The Battle of Lepanto in 1571 ended Turkish ambitions to leverage Greece and North Africa for control of the Mediterranean Sea, and the Battle of the Armada in 1588 ended Catholic ambitions to repress massive Protestant uprisings in the Low Countries and England.

We should keep in mind, however, that liminal figures were common, that is, a lot of people existed somewhere in between the polar extremes of the era's religious identities. Moderate reformist Catholics like Erasmus, Castiglione, Vitoria, Montaigne, and Cervantes expressed hope for reasoned dialogue over warfare, forming what historian Paul Johnson called a humanist "third option," a middle way, albeit an ephemeral one which evaporated in the fanatical atmosphere of the religious conflicts of sixteenth- and seventeenth-century Europe. There were also many people in between the Islamic and Catholic Empires of Habsburg Spain and Ottoman Turkey. We see them in the crucial roles in *Don Quijote* played by the renegades, men who opt to flee Islam and return to Catholicism during the escapes and rescues of Captain Viedma, Zoraida, Ana Félix, and Don Gregorio. For their part, the Barbary Coast pirates, who operated out of ports like Tripoli, Tunis, and Algiers, were no friends of the Turks, and many were themselves apostates, former Christians from places like Greece, Italy, France, and Spain.

Within Spain proper, the Moriscos were a significant demographic presence in Andalucía, Murcia, Valencia, and Aragón. In the more rural areas of these provinces, the Moriscos were, depending on your perspective, either crypto Muslims or quasi Christians (see fig. 1). Tensions ran high between the Alpujarras War of 1568–71 and the Expulsion of the Moriscos in 1609–14. There was real fear in Spain that the Morisco population was a kind of fifth column which might rise up and assist a Turkish invasion. Philip II had the edict for the expulsion on his desk but did not sign it; Philip III, however, embraced the policy. *Don Quijote* echoes this growing anxiety: Muslim war cries are heard in the woods in *DQ* 2.34; Clavileño might be a Trojan horse with enemy soldiers in its belly in *DQ* 2.41; and Sancho's last challenge as governor is the sudden invasion of Barataria by mysterious forces in *DQ* 2.53.

Cervantes's fiction takes shape along multiple frontiers in the struggle between Protestants and Catholics for control of the North Atlantic and the struggle between Christianity and Islam for control of the Mediterranean. An effect of this crossover is that, throughout *Don Quijote*, Cervantes harmonizes Erasmian criticism of the Inquisition with opposition to the Expulsion of the Moriscos. We see this when Cervantes's mockeries of religious identity and religious persecution incorporate the racial and ethnic signifiers of the Mediterranean. A basic aspect of the first modern novel is its ironical representation of hypocritical obsessions with racial purity. This is the novel's "exemplary" sense, for it elicits thinking about the Morisco question and suggests a solution according to repeated narrative trajectories of miscegenation, i.e., stories that relate transgressions of cultural and racial orthodoxy and therein advocate assimilation over expulsion. Let's look at some examples of what we might call "limit encounters" with Moors and Moriscos in *Don Quijote*.[4]

Early on, the hidalgo exhibits confusion about religious and ethnic identities, both his own and those of others. In the first chapter, he praises the brave actions of Reinaldos de Montalbán: «cuando en allende robó aquel ídolo de Mahoma que era todo de oro» "when he went overseas and stole that idol of Mohammed that was made of pure gold" (1.1.40). Iconoclasm is an essential aspect of Islam; so, the very notion of an "idol of Mohammed" is absurd and signals Christian ignorance about the rival religion. At the end of his first sally, however, when the hidalgo retreats from his defeat by the merchants of Toledo, «se acordó del moro Abindarráez» "he remembered the Moor Abindarráez," which then makes Dulcinea analogous to Abindarráez's Moorish lover: «esta hermosa Jarifa que he dicho es ahora la linda Dulcinea del Toboso» "and this beautiful Jarifa that I just mentioned is now the lovely Dulcinea del Toboso" (1.5.73). In *DQ* 1.9, Cervantes forces readers to confront miscegenation as the very essence of the text when the second narrator pays and even provides housing to a Morisco in order to translate the remainder of the novel, which he purchased in Toledo's very Muslim Alcaná marketplace. Maritornes assumes significance with respect to the Morisco question when we learn from the second narrator that her lover was supposedly related to the original narrator «Cide Mahamate Benengeli», who «deste arriero hace particular mención porque le conocía muy bien, y aun quieren decir que era algo pariente suyo» "makes particular mention of this mule-driver because he knew him very well, and they even say that he was some kind of blood-relation to him" (1.16.171). A couple of chapters later, when the hidalgo narrates the battle of the sheep episode in *DQ* 1.18, it's effectively impossible to tell anymore whether he prefers Muslim or Christian knights.

Another major inflection point in the miscegenation theme occurs when Don Quijote decides to do penance in the Sierra Morena. In the middle of part one, we get a full-blown presentation of the ethnic and racial contradictions of his object of affection. He goes back and forth between an honest recognition of Dulcinea's identity as Aldonza Lorenzo and an irrational struggle to maintain an orthodox fiction. First, in keeping with his earlier parallel between Dulcinea and Jarifa in *DQ* 1.5, he claims not to care one bit about her bloodline: «en lo del linaje, importa poco, que no han de ir a hacer la información dél para darle algún hábito» "as concerns her lineage, it matters little, for nobody is going to investigate it in order to admit her to a religious order" (1.25.285). But, soon enough, he refers to Ariosto's *Orlando furioso* and considers what it was that caused Roland's insanity: «las nuevas que le dio el pastor de que Angélica había dormido más de dos siestas con Medoro, un morillo de cabellos enrizados» "the news given to him by the shepherd that Angelica had slept more than two naps with Medoro, a young Moor with curly hair" (1.26.290). This thought revives his repressed obsession with purity and he pushes away the idea that Dulcinea could be anything like Angelica: «Porque mi Dulcinea del Toboso osaré yo jurar que no ha visto en todos los días de su vida moro alguno» "Because I dare swear that my Dulcinea of Toboso has not in all the days of her life seen a single Moor" (1.26.291). Note how the mixed status of Dulcinea becomes an explicit problem upon entering the Sierra Morena, a toponym which we might translate as the racially intermediate "Brown Mountains." Maritornes's subsequent rosary in *DQ* 1.27 accentuates ethnic impurity in religious terms.

From this point forward, hybrid racial symbols incessantly echo the miscegenation in *DQ* 1.25–26. Thus, the barber's prophecy that Don Quijote, «el furibundo león manchado» "the furious spotted lion," and Dulcinea, «la blanca paloma tobosina» "the white Tobosan dove" (1.46.537), will marry and have offspring. Márquez Villanueva pointed out that Eugenio, who brags he is «limpio de sangre» "pure in bloodline" and whose name derives from the Greek word for "well-born," telegraphs his anxiety about Leandra in *DQ* 1.50 by humanizing and chastising the «cabra manchada» "spotted she-goat" who has escaped from his flock. We see a projection of the same contrast when Don Quijote attacks a black-clad statue of the Virgin Mary. If scholar Luis Andrés Murillo is right that "The Captive's Tale" is the moral endpoint of the original novel, and that Viedma is the palliative counterexample to the mad knight, then the hybrid figure of Zoraida-María in *DQ* 1.37 points to Aldonza Lorenzo's Morisca lineage, Don Quijote as the spotted lion, and Eugenio's anxiety about the spotted she-goat. Symbols and characters like these articulate and coordinate the miscegenation message. Even the last line of part one, «*Forse altro canterà con miglior plectro*» "Perhaps another will sing with better plectrum" (1.52.597), is a quotation from Ariosto's *Orlando furioso* (30.16.8), which invites us once again to contemplate the central importance of the interracial love triangle formed by Roland, Angelica, and Medoro in *DQ* 1.26. Indeed, Don Quijote's identity crisis in the «Sierra Morena» "Brown Mountains" indicates that Cervantes has an Ariosto-like racial irony in mind regarding his hero's place moniker «La Mancha», which also means "The Stain."

In part two, Dulcinea is again the subject of a lot of religious, ethnic, and racial confusion. Critics have long noted that the town of El Toboso had a disproportionate Morisco population in the late-Renaissance due to forced relocations after the Alpujarras War (see Castro, *Cervantes y los casticismos*; Selig). Cervantes indicates this situation at every turn. Cide Hamete makes one of his most radical interventions when Don Quijote and Sancho Panza finally set out for El Toboso, praising Allah four times at the beginning of *DQ* 2.8. Then in *DQ* 2.10, we meet Dulcinea in the company of a parade of different species of beasts of burden, which range from asses to camels to zebras.

The effect is a series of multicolored, multiracial metamorphoses of symbolic mounts in the heart of La Mancha (see Graf, "The Economy of Asses").

More racial mixing of this type underwrites Don Quijote's hilarious tale of the fortune-teller who predicts the birth of «tres perricos, el uno verde, el otro encarnado y el otro de mezcla» "three puppies, the one green, the other one red, and another one mixed" (2.25.844). Similarly, after the Clavileño adventure, Sancho claims to have frolicked with multi-colored she-goats who represent the Pleiades and echo the significance of Zoraida (from *al-Thurayya* or "the many little ones"; De Armas 137): «las dos verdes, las dos encarnadas, las dos azules y una de mezcla» "two of them green, two red, two blue, and one mixed" (2.41.966).

The ridiculous extremes of multicolored horses, goats, and dogs in *Don Quijote* are complemented by odd binary contrasts. The Virgin Mary serves as an emblem of black and white in *DQ* 1.52. Doña Rodríguez emphasizes that her husband was from León, considered the most racially pure region in all of Iberia, and yet he rides a conspicuous mule, «negra como el mismo aza-bache» "as black as jet itself" (2.48.1019), and he also escorts Doña Casilda, whose name refers to the symbolic Saint Casilda of Toledo, a Moorish king's daughter who converted to Christianity and was baptized in Burgos. Altisi-dora similarly alludes to miscegenation at the end of part two. Hard on the heels of Ricote, his daughter Ana Félix, and her Old-Christian lover Don Gregorio, Altisidora comically describes her own legs as «lisas, blancas y nègras» "smooth, white, and black" and then alludes to the injustice of the Expulsion of the Moriscos and *autos de fe*: «que justos por pecadores / tal vez pagan en mi tierra» "for the just for sinners it seems / will pay the price in my country" (2.57.1091). Later, when Altisidora visits Don Quijote and Sancho after her resurrection, she arrives «arrimada a un báculo de negro y finísimo ébano» "leaning on a cane of fine black ebony" (2.70.1193).

There's a lot of professional debate over the significance of Moriscos and Islam in Cervantes's fiction. Postmodern academia teems with postco-lonialist, Leninist, and neo-Marxist points of view. Accordingly, Cervantes supposedly despised orthodox Spain so much that he embraced Islam (see Goytisolo, López-Beralt, and Childers). While I disagree about the overdeter-mined leap from Cervantes's disapproval of the Inquisition to his approval of Islam, the confusion is understandable. Cervantes appreciated many aspects of Arabic and Islamic culture. Decentralized power structures, a universal sense of justice, advanced commercial networks, and mature mathematical and philosophical traditions characterized much of the Islamic Mediterra-nean. Adding to this positive tone, Cervantes was clearly concerned about the Moriscos. Figures like Abindarráez, Jarifa, Cide Hamete, Maritornes, Medoro, Zoraida, Ricote, and Ana Félix reveal the novelist's approval of ethnic and racial mixing and the idea that many Moriscos were good Christians and loyal Spaniards. Márquez Villanueva, who got Cervantes's political views about right, argued that Sancho Panza is the character whose judgment and behavior are under analysis in part two. Thus, immediately upon his resignation, the former Governor of Barataria must face the consequences of the "reason of state" thinking used to justify the expulsion of people like his neighbor Ricote.

In the end, I think we can be pretty specific about the central role played by the Moriscos in Cervantes's fiction. They are the focus of his criticism of orthodox rituals and official actions like *autos de fe* and ethnic expulsions. This is especially true of Ricote, whose name alludes to the Valle de Ricote in Murcia, home to Spain's most loyal Morisco population and among the very last to be expelled. Ricote twice describes the agonizing experience of expulsion in long passages in *DQ* 2.54 and 2.65, and he even justifies it according to what reads like a case of Stockholm syndrome. Ricote's role indicates the seriousness that Cervantes attached to the Morisco question, and Ricote clearly understands the principal actors and the logic that drove Philip III to finally sign the edict of expulsion:

> . . . no hay que esperar en favores ni en dádivas, porque con el gran don Bernardino de Velasco, conde de Salazar, a quien dio Su Majestad cargo de nuestra expulsión, no valen ruegos, no promesas, no dádivas, no lástimas; porque aunque es verdad que él mezcla la misericordia con la justicia, como él vee que todo el cuerpo de nuestra nación está contaminado y podrido, usa con él antes del cauterio que abrasa que del ungüento que molifica. (2.65.1165–66)

> . . . one should not expect favors or gifts, because with the great Don Bernardino de Velasco, Count of Salazar, whom His Majesty has charged with carrying out our expulsion, in vain are all prayers, promises, bribes, and lamentations; because, although it is true that he tempers justice with mercy, he also sees that the entire body of our nation is contaminated and rotten, and so he prefers cauterizing the wound to applying an ointment.

This notably medicinal-political (i.e., Platonic) discourse goes very much against the grain of the rest of Cervantes's sympathetic portraits of Moriscos in *Don Quijote*. The contrast suggests that Ricote's praise for Velasco is both melancholic and sarcastic. In *DQ* 1.32, when Palomeque confronts the priest who previously burned Don Quijote's library, Cervantes implies that both the innkeeper and his chivalric novels are Moriscos threatened by the Inquisition. Don Quijote, too, defends them. Similarly, at the end of part one, the second narrator claims that serendipity brought him a series of poems about Don Quijote in a strange box: «una caja de plomo, que, según él dijo, se había hallado en los cimientos derribados de una antigua ermita que se renovaba;

en la cual caja se habían hallado unos pergaminos escritos con letras góticas, pero en versos castellanos» "a lead box, which, as he told it, had been found among the destroyed foundations of an ancient hermitage which was being renovated; and in said box were found some parchments written in Gothic letters, but in Castilian verses" (1.52.591). This passage refers to the famous «Libros plúmbeos del Sacromonte» "Lead Books of Sacromonte," a series of forged archeological discoveries in Granada between 1588 and 1599, which were designed to defend the Moriscos against their pending expulsion (see Case). In *DQ* 2.69, dressed in a black tunic with decorative flames, Sancho himself becomes a figurative victim of the Inquisition. It's bitter poetic justice, especially given Sancho's intense pride in his Old-Christian lineage and his unwillingness to help his Morisco neighbor Ricote.

Also crucial for clarifying Cervantes's pro-Morisco program is Sancho's truly Solomon-like demonstration of the principle of *in dubio reo* in *DQ* 2.51, where instead of dividing a man's guilty half from his innocent half, the Governor of Barataria sets him free (cf. 1 Kings 3.16–28). Three chapters later, Ricote makes an Erasmian-inflected confession of religious ambivalence to Sancho: «yo sé cierto que la Ricota mi hija y Francisca Ricota mi mujer son católicas cristianas, y aunque yo no lo soy tanto, todavía tengo más de cristiano que de moro, y ruego siempre a Dios me abra los ojos del entendimiento» "I know for certain that my daughter, Ricota, and my wife, Francisca Ricota, are Catholic Christians, and even though I'm less of one, I'm still more Christian than Moor, and I always pray for God to open the eyes of my understanding" (2.54.1073–74). Ricote's discovery of «libertad de conciencia» "freedom of conscience" (2.54.1073) in Austria suggests that the solution to the Morisco question is for readers to judge not another's faith and instead take a hard look at their own.

The novel's climactic criticism of the Inquisition is the final image of Sancho's donkey in *DQ* 2.73. He appears dressed in the same black tunic with flames previously given to Sancho for his mock trial in *DQ* 2.69. This, in turn, connects to Basilio, who dresses similarly in *DQ* 2.21, transforming his romance with Quiteria into yet another of Cervantes's miscegenation tales that unite Christians and Moriscos. And all of this assimilative protest is reinforced at the level of subtle symbols, such as the *tobosescas tinajas*, urns produced by the Moriscos of El Toboso which Don Quijote spies in Diego de Miranda's basement in *DQ* 2.18, and the *albogues*, a strange Morisco woodwind instrument which attracts Sancho's attention in *DQ* 2.67.

There are good reasons why Cervantes's defense of Moriscos in *Don Quijote* is not a case of anachronistic interpretation by which we artificially impose our modern multicultural values on a text written over 400 years ago. For starters, Cervantes did not write in a vacuum. Nobles like the Duchess of

Cardona, the Count of Salinas, the Duke of Arcos, and the Duke of Gandía (see Monterde and Sánchez-Blanco), intellectuals like Diego Hurtado de Mendoza (see Darst), painters like El Greco, and mystic poets like San Juan de la Cruz (see Graf, "The Politics of Salvation"), as well as any number of creative priests in Granada (see Case) argued that people like Ricote should not be expelled from Spain.

More importantly, and more acutely than readers might imagine, Cervantes was conscious of Spain's debts to Islamic and Arabic culture. Labyrinthine storytelling, multiple narrative frames, and overarching didactic and episodic structure characterized the Islamic Golden Age, which, in turn, heavily influenced the early course of Spanish literature via works like Alfonso X's translation of *Calila e Dimna* (1251) and Don Juan Manuel's *Libro de los ejemplos del Conde Lucanor et de Patronio* (1335). The latter collection of exemplary tales was printed for the first time in Seville in 1575. Cervantes was impressed, later writing his own *Novelas ejemplares* in 1613. Like *Calila e Dimna, El conde Lucanor* makes extreme use of *mise en abîme*, the Russian-doll like narrative structure of frame tales containing their own inner series of tales within tales. Another major aspect of his aesthetic is that exotic oriental objects like *albogues* serve as symbols of religious, cultural, and racial mixing. Other texts in the Spanish tradition that model racial hybridity, cultural assimilation, and ethnic tolerance include the *Poema de mio Cid* (c.1200), Juan Ruiz's *Libro de buen amor* (1343), Jorge Montemayor's *La Diana* (1559), and San Juan de la Cruz's *Cántico espiritual* (c.1584). Simply put, Cervantes composed within a literary tradition that was quite conscious of its debts to Arabic culture.

Still, Cervantes draws two principal lines in the sand regarding Islam. First, he disapproves of Islam's treatment of women. This is not to say that he finds Spaniards incapable of similarly misogynistic behavior. Don Quijote's laughable effort to seduce Palomeque's daughter, Don Fernando's arrogant abduction of Luscinda, an anonymous peasant's attempted rape of Dorotea, Anselmo's repugnant test of Camila, and Eugenio's rage toward Leandra, these all indicate the universal nature of men's often despicable behavior towards women. That said, a defining feature of Cervantes's assessment of Islam in *Don Quijote* is that the Christian West has a moral and social advantage in terms of the relative respect it affords women. Zoraida near the end of part one and Ana Félix near the end of part two embody and voice this basic distinction.

Second, Cervantes writes against coercion in religious matters and so he draws another line in the sand at the confessional state. Islam in this respect is less desirable than Inquisitorial Spain. Supporting this view are his portrayals of the brutality of slavery in Algiers and the radical misogyny of Islam, as well as his pride at having fought against the Ottomans at the Battle of

Lepanto (1571). Captain Viedma lauds the heroes of Lepanto, especially Don Juan de Austria and Don Álvaro de Bazán, as great and noble leaders in the struggle against the Turk (1.39.455–56). Of course, Cervantes also saw Spain's heroes as human and fallible, criticizing, for example, Philip II, the Duke of Alba, and even Don Juan for their abuses in the Low Countries, North Africa, and Southeast Spain. Here is where I differ with postcolonialist critics who, paradoxically it would seem, either advance Cervantes's sympathy for Moriscos until it includes sympathy for Islam or else complain that he was irredeemably Islamophobic. Again, it's perfectly possible to be critical of the extremes of Catholic orthodoxy but still reject Islam.

Unfortunately, modern Islam is often to religious freedom what Stalinism is to democracy. Stalinists argue for popular votes until they manage to establish a dictatorship of the proletariat; Islamists urge religious tolerance until they find a way to suppress it. And yet, Cervantes seeks grounds for a respectful approach to Islam. In *DQ* 2.63, in the midst of what reads like both a social and a theological justification for war against the Ottomans, the viceroy of Barcelona urges the admiral general *not* to hang two Turkish soldiers who just killed two of his men. The viceroy's moral concern for the rights of prisoners of war trumps the admiral general's desire to avenge what he views as a war crime. Note how this reads like a case that would have interested the late-scholastic inventors of international law, men like Vitoria, Las Casas, Covarrubias, and Suárez. Different scholastics had nuanced opinions, of course, but they tended to emphasize natural law, especially when it came to encounters at sea or at frontiers between radically different nations or faiths. In such cases, the dogmatic persecution of heresy loses its theological grounds due to uncertainty regarding whether or not the enemy has been given the proper opportunity to accept the Christian faith. Vitoria and Las Casas applied this reasoning to the case of Spaniards encountering Amerindians in the New World; for Cervantes, international law would seem to apply even at the much older frontier with Islam.

What are the implications of Cervantes's opposition to the confessional state and his apparent drift toward religious relativism? One consequence is that, as Américo Castro argued in *El pensamiento de Cervantes* (1925), Cervantes's apparent *converso* lineage might be a major factor in his artistic production. We know that he gave false testimony on behalf of a *converso* friend who sought to join a religious confraternity. The cryptic rejection in 1590 by authorities of Cervantes's request for a post in America—«Busque por acá en que se le haga vuestra merced» "Find a way closer to home by which we can reward you" ("Representación")—also hints at the possibility of his *converso* ancestry. A *converso* perspective might explain Cervantes's reference to exiled Jewish mystic León Hebreo's *Dialogues of Love* (c.1502) in the first prologue of *Don Quijote*. The same could be said of the mad knight's defeat by the skeptical and blasphemous merchants of Toledo in *DQ* 1.4, and the *converso* theme surely adds weight to the second narrator's allusion to the presence of Hebrew in the same city: «y no fue muy dificultoso hallar intérprete; pues aunque le buscara de otra mejor y más antigua lengua le hallara» "and it was not difficult to find a translator; for even if I had sought one for another better and more ancient language, I could have found one" (1.9.107–08). For its part, the *converso* thesis reinforces the Erasmian thesis. *Conversos* logically welcomed the reformist message of personalized religion, as opposed to Catholic orthodoxy's constant requirements of public displays and works of faith.

The *converso* argument is convincing; in the end, however, I think *Don Quijote* signals Islam and Protestantism as greater concerns. Regarding Islam and the Moriscos, there is nowadays consensus that Cervantes disapproved of the policy of expulsion. He displays respect for aspects of Islamic and Arabic culture and seems to have envisioned the novel as a way to advocate for the selective readmission of loyal Moriscos like Ricote and Ana Félix. This is the general sense of Maritornes's carnal relations with a mule driver related to Cide Hamete in *DQ* 1.16, Zoraida's escape with Viedma from Algiers to Spain in *DQ* 1.37–41, the vocal praise for Allah when knight and squire set out for El Toboso in *DQ* 2.8, and Cide Hamete's multi-framed conversation with his cosmic pen upon Don Quijote's death in *DQ* 2.74. At first, the great Governor Sancho Panza refuses to assist his Morisco neighbor Ricote in *DQ* 2.54; so, it's poetic justice when he subsequently falls into a dark cave in *DQ* 2.55. When Sancho finally sees the light in *DQ* 2.55, Cervantes relates the Morisco question to a spectacular combination of Plato's Allegory of the Cave in the *Republic* and the Protestant motto "post tenebras spero lucem" from Job 17.12.

The Islamic aspects of *Don Quijote* also have implications for the intellectual history of Europe, especially for the trajectory of the kind of philosophical materialism that characterizes Aristotelian thinking. On multiple occasions in the novel, Cervantes initiates satirical criticism of Christianity from both Islamic and materialistic perspectives. These read like nods to Averroes (1126–98), the great Arab polymath of Córdoba whose commentaries on Aristotle greatly influenced the scholastics of places like Padua and Salamanca. Possible allusions to Averroes's materialism abound in *Don Quijote*. For example, when Quiteria decides to marry the outwardly heretical Basilio, the crowd shouts «¡Milagro, milagro!» "Miracle, miracle!" but the young man responds: «¡No milagro, milagro, sino industria, industria!» "No, not miracle, miracle but industry, industry!" (2.21.806). Take, too, the way that the original Moorish narrator rushes to explain the material reality behind the illusion of Don Antonio Moreno's enchanted head: «El cual quiso Cide Hamete Benengeli declarar luego, por no tener suspenso al mundo creyendo que algún hechicero y extraordinario misterio en la tal cabeza se encerraba» "Which Cide Hamete Benengeli wished to explain immediately, so as not to leave anyone still believing that some magical and extraordinary mystery was contained in the head" (2.62.1141). In much the same way, one of Cide Hamete's longest interventions echoes the capitalistic and materialistic reasoning of late scholasticism's attacks on Christianity's misguided fetish for poverty: «Yo, aunque moro, bien sé, por la comunicación que he tenido con cristianos, que la santidad consiste en la caridad, humildad, fee, obediencia y pobreza; pero, con todo eso, digo que ha de tener mucho de Dios el que se viniere a contentar con ser pobre» "Although I'm a Moor, I know well, from the communication I have had with Christians, that holiness consists of charity, humility, faith, obedience, and poverty; but, even so, I say that one has to have a lot of God in them to be content with a life of poverty" (2.44.984). Nevertheless, and tragically, we ought to recognize that Cervantes and the School of Salamanca are good examples of how Averroes had greater impact in Christian Europe than anywhere in the Islamic world.

At the other end of the religious spectrum, however, an appreciation of elements of Protestant discourse in *Don Quijote* helps us to see how modern materialism also evolved in conjunction with the doctrinal crisis caused by the Reformation. Consider Thomas Hobbes's remarkable criticism of the metaphysical logic of ecclesiastics:

> And in particular, of the Essence of a Man, which (they say) is his Soule, they affirm it, to be All of it in his little Finger, and All of it in every other Part (how small soever) of his Body; and yet no more Soule in the Whole Body, than in any one of those Parts. Can any man think that God is served with such absurdities? And yet all this is necessary to beleeve, to those that will beleeve the Existence of an Incorporeall Soule, Separated from the Body. And when they come to give account, how an Incorporeall Substance can be capable of Pain, and be tormented in the fire of Hell, or Purgatory, they have nothing at all to answer, but that it cannot be known how fire can burn Soules. Again, whereas Motion is change of Place, and Incorporeall Substances are not capable of Place, they are troubled to make it seem possible, how a Soule can goe hence, without the Body to Heaven, Hell, or Purgatory; and how the Ghosts of men (and I may adde of their clothes which they appear in) can walk by night in Churches, Church-yards, and other places of Sepulture. (*Leviathan* 46.466)

Along these same lines of thinking, Stephen Greenblatt has demonstrated how Shakespeare's *Hamlet* (c.1602) reflects psychological trauma caused by the Protestant rejection of the existence of Purgatory. One reason for the

prince of Denmark's brooding catatonia is that he simply cannot permit himself to accept the material reality of his father's ghost.

We have seen how early censorship of *Don Quijote* reflects the era's doctrinal debates about the effectiveness of rosaries, the validity of clandestine
marriages, and the primacy of faith or works. Still, it was impossible for a
censor to catch all such references. Don Quijote's allusion to *sola fide* in
DQ 1.51, for example, proved elusive. Another major example is the novel's
treatment of Purgatory (see Sullivan). Sancho insists that Don Quijote's penance in the Sierra Morena is Purgatory, not Hell: «volveré por los aires como
brujo y sacaré a vuestra merced deste purgatorio, que parece infierno y no
lo es» "I'll return flying through the air like a sorcerer and I'll rescue your
grace from this Purgatory, which seems to be Hell but is not" (1.25.282).
Returning the favor in part two, Don Quijote consoles his squire, who has
fallen into a cave: «si eres mi escudero Sancho Panza y te has muerto, como
no te hayan llevado los diablos, y por la misericordia de Dios estés en el
purgatorio, sufragios tiene nuestra santa madre la Iglesia Católica Romana
bastantes a sacarte de las penas en que estás» "if you are my squire Sancho
Panza and you have died, so long as the devils carried you off, and by the
mercy of God you are in Purgatory, our Holy Mother Roman Catholic Church
has plenty of prayers of intercession to deliver you from tortures you are suffering" (2.55.1081). These mockeries are Cervantes's hilarious approaches to
the same issue found in Hamlet's existentialist doubts about the ghost of his
father or Hobbes's mockery of oxymoronic notions like bodiless souls and
metaphysical places.

Averroes and Aristotle, then, prove remarkably compatible with the early
modern outlook of merchants, printers, and bankers in cities like Toledo,
Antwerp, Barcelona, and Mainz. This is to say that any latent Averroism in
Don Quijote also participates in a general bourgeois trajectory of materialistic
thinking in early modern Europe. Cervantes takes Erasmus's low regard for
ghosts and moves it towards Hobbes's aversion to metaphysical concepts and
Hume's ultimate demolition of miracles. The School of Salamanca, too, participated in the Renaissance's grounding of theological thinking by focusing
instead on rational, natural, and systematic explanations in fields as diverse
as history, law, and politics. As American philosopher Richard Rorty once
observed, "Lucretius and Hobbes tried to tell us that complexity is in fact
sufficient—that we, like everything else in the universe, are best understood
as accidentally produced assemblages of particles" (*Philosophy and Social
Hope* 263). Cervantes signals the seeds of this general trend in early modern
Spain. At a crucial and very otherworldly moment in the Cave of Montesinos,
Don Quijote is shocked to learn that enchanted spirits need cash loans, asking, «¿Es posible, señor Montesinos, que los encantados principales padecen

necesidad?» "Is it possible, Sir Montesinos, that distinguished enchanted spirits suffer from need?"; to which the magician ironically responds, «Créame
vuestra merced, señor don Quijote de la Mancha, que esta que llaman necesidad adondequiera se usa y por todo se estiende y a todos alcanza, y aun hasta
los encantados no perdona» "Believe me, your grace, Sir Don Quijote de la
Mancha, this thing called need is found everywhere and extends to all places,
and it reaches everyone, and it does not excuse even those who are enchanted"
(2.23.827). Insisting on the physical nature of the universe, Cervantes notably
incorporates the corollary that the study of economics is the science of material scarcity more than it is the science of metaphysical morality.

In terms of the religious politics of the first modern novel, we have come
full circle. The more interesting issue for scholarship on Cervantes is once
again the degree of the Erasmian influence. Could Cervantes have been a
crypto-Protestant or even a radical Calvinist? Perhaps a more useful question
is why would Cervantes allude to Protestantism at all? Just as the novelist
takes a flexible view of Islam, especially its defense of the gold standard and
its emphasis on racial diversity, so too does he embrace key aspects of Protestantism. The Erasmian interpretation of Cervantes emphasizes his moderate,
humorous, middle-of-the-road politics, what we might describe as an early
modern anti-fanatic and down-to-earth bourgeois perspective. Making room
for a Calvinist influence, however, we can better appreciate the occasionally deeper Protestant radicality that Cervantes's texts also project. All the
political, philosophical, and technological factors driving the Reformation
are here, most especially resisting the Inquisition, advocating freedom of
religion, and unleashing the printing press. As rebellious as ever, the city of
Barcelona in *DQ* 2.62 reverberates with the radical reformist spirit unleashed
by Gutenberg in Mainz.

On the one hand, the broadest implication here is that *Don Quijote* participates in the modern insight that religion is always political (cf. Schmitt,
Freud, Hoffer, Dawson, and Jameson, "Religion and Ideology"). On the other
hand, this is more than just philosophical speculation; it is one of the great
insights applied politically by American founders like Thomas Jefferson and
James Madison. The *Virginia Statute on Religious Freedom* (1777), authored
by Jefferson and introduced by Madison, was subsequently the model for the
First Amendment of the US Constitution, which guarantees the freedoms of
religion and the press. Both Jefferson and Madison were, of course, tremendous fans of *Don Quijote*, which simply confirms that their insight had its
own roots in the early modern period.

Cervantes's skepticism regarding the confessional state in combination
with his pro-Morisco outlook is neatly encapsulated in the exiled Ricote's
remark to Sancho that in Protestant Austria he now enjoys «libertad de con-

ciencia» "freedom of conscience" (2.54.1073). Many critics have argued that this phrase means "depravity" or "perversion of morals" rather than anything approaching religious freedom (2.54.1073n36). More general objections of this type have been raised by Malcolm Read, who warned that Cervantes is "not to be confused with the scientific empiricism and mechanical rationalism that correspond to the next stage of bourgeois development, which was to take place in England and France" (*Language, Text, Subject*, 6); and George Mariscal, who argued that Cervantes was no Enlightenment thinker and would've probably been unwelcome "in a Parisian salon presided over by Voltaire" (185).

These distinctions, however, are without differences. Voltaire's *Candide* (1759) discloses the cynicism and religious relativism of *Don Quijote*. If one can accept that Hobbes's mid-sixteenth-century declaration in *Leviathan* that "Miracles now cease . . ." (32.295) leads in the direction of Hume's essay "Of Miracles" (1748), then it's no great leap to see that *Don Quijote* has very direct descendants among a wide range of modern materialists.

Hume must rank among the eighteenth-century's most discerning readers of *Don Quijote*. In "Of the Standard of Taste" (1757), he got Cervantes's point that religion should be no more than something like literary taste or preference among wines or fashion, that is, a private, personal matter of no public consequence. Hume's reading of *Don Quijote* casts light on Cervantes's constant references to the lengths, colors, patterns, and styles of things like collars, tunics, cuffs, and all manner of dresses. Altisidora extends the matter of taste to a description of devils in hell: «todos en calzas y en jubón, con valonas guarnecidas con puntas de randas flamencas, y con unas vueltas de lo mismo que les servían de puños, con cuatro dedos de brazo de fuera, porque pareciesen las manos más largas» "all of them in tights and doublets, their collars trimmed with borders of Flemish lace, the same lace as their cuffs, which exposed four fingers' length of arm such that their hands would appear to be longer" (2.70.1194).

Cervantes's humorous catwalk of "religion as fashion" is a preview of the Enlightenment. Historian Peter Gay once described the Enlightenment as a kind of modern paganism which denoted an intellectual posture of skepticism regarding all religious belief. This is precisely the point of the Erasmian inset piece told by the barber in *DQ* 2.1. Not only does "The Madman of Seville" mock another corrupt aspect of the Inquisition, which expropriates the property of those it accuses of heresy, it also turns religious choice and persecution into a silly struggle between the devotees of Neptune and Jupiter. On the brink of freedom, the madman cannot resist responding to another madman's threat to bring drought to Andalucía: «No tenga vuestra merced pena, señor mío, ni haga caso de lo que este loco ha dicho, que si él es Júpiter y no quisiere llover, yo, que soy Neptuno, el padre y el dios de las aguas, lloveré todas las veces que se me antojare y fuere menester» "Your grace, sir, should not worry nor pay any attention to what this madman has said, for if he is Jupiter and does not wish to rain, I, who am Neptune, the god and father of all waters, will make it rain as often as I wish and deem necessary" (2.1.632). In such passages, it's hard not to read Cervantes's deep discontent with the ignorant brutality of religious orthodoxy of all stripes.

NOTES

1. An illustrative case of the level of corruption in the early modern Catholic Church is provided by Albert of Brandenburg (1490–1545), the Archbishop of Maguntia, who received the staggering sum of 20,000 ducats for his efforts promoting the sale of papal indulgences.

2. For a fascinating look at how the policy of expulsion was often successfully circumvented by both Moriscos and their supporters, see Rafael Benítez Sánchez-Blanco.

3. For Cervantes's early play *La Numancia* (c.1580) as simultaneous criticism of the Inquisition's *auto de fe* and the coronation of Philip II at Valladolid in 1559, see Graf ("La política teológica").

4. For a detailed survey of Cervantes's interest in Saracens in *Don Quijote*, see De Armas; see also, Graf ("When an Arab Laughs in Toledo").

Chapter Two

Don Quijote and Feminism

"The connexion between female beauty and male infatuation is one of the most regular sequences of cause and effect observable in everyday life."

—Edward Hallett Carr, *What Is History?* (129)

Don Quijote de la Mancha should be of great interest to feminists. With fair consistency, Cervantes's fiction defends women characters against the kinds of brutality often practiced and permitted by the Islamic, Protestant, and Catholic men of his day. It's important to keep in mind, however, that many saw Catholicism as a civilized bulwark against the barbaric exploitation and expropriation of women and their property made particularly possible by the explicit right to divorce in the other two faiths. Additionally, respect for women on a cosmic scale was an integral part of the ancient history of the novel form. *Don Quijote*, then, is a kind of intermediary text between the cult of Isis that informs Apuleius's *The Golden Ass* (c.175) and the feminist novels of the seventeenth century penned by aristocratic women like María de Zayas (1590–1661?), Madeleine de Scudéry (1607–1701), and Madame de La Fayette (1634–93). These writers, as well as powerful patronesses like Marguerite of Navarre (1492–1549), Eleanor of Toledo (1519–62), Catherine de' Medici (1519–89), Joanna of Austria (1535–73), and Marie de' Medici (1575–1642), dominated the elite salon culture of Renaissance Italy, Spain, Portugal, and France. This culture, in turn, heavily patronized the arts, in particular the novel form. One cannot overestimate the aesthetic and the political capacities of these women. Scholar Joan DeJean has gone so far as to link the dynamics of the early modern feminism of salon culture and its patronage of the novel form to the Fronde rebellion during the minority of Louis XIV (1648–53).

Precursors to early modern feminism include a lengthy medieval tradition of formal respect for women woven into exemplary texts like Christine de Pizan's *La Cité des dames* (1405) or Álvaro de Luna's *Libro de las claras e virtuosas mugeres* (1446). In the other historical direction, the legacy of early modern feminism includes major enlightenment, classical liberal, and modernist texts like Benito Jerónimo Feijoo y Montenegro's *Defensa de las mujeres* (1726), Mary Wollstonecraft's *A Vindication of the Rights of Women* (1792), John Stuart Mill's *The Subjugation of Women* (1869), and Simone de Beauvoir's *Le Deuxième Sexe* (1949).

One does not have to read very much of *Don Quijote* to realize that it contains many active, strong women characters: Marcela, Maritornes, the innkeeper Palomeque's wife, Aldonza Lorenzo, Torralba, Dorotea, Luscinda, Camila, Leonela, Zoraida, Doña Clara, Dulcinea, Quiteria, the Duchess, the Countess Trifaldi, Doña Rodríguez, Antonia Quijana, Don Quijote's house-keeper, Teresa Cascajo, Sanchica Panza, Antonomasia, Altisidora, Claudia Jerónima, Ana Félix, and many more who are mentioned or alluded to only in passing, such as Angélica, Leandra, Queen Doña Maguncia, or Doña Casilda. These women variously demand and assert their rights to choose their religion, remain unmarried, defend themselves against physical assault, marry their daughters as they wish, receive equal justice, and inherit, possess, and manage property.

The flipside of the feminist coin is that Don Quijote is often a pathetic example of male potency. At a general level, the novel constantly mocks *machismo* and criticizes the more tedious, oppressive, and violent aspects of male sexuality, especially men's tendency to obsess over the sexual purity of women. In part one, Cervantes seems to have reached the moral as well as the literary limitations of what initially seemed a rather one-dimensional hero. Instead, he pivots to offer readers a series of tangential stories in which the knight's role is diminished or absent and in which the active agency of women is a constant theme. Scholar Ruth Anthony El Saffar once pointed out that most of the male characters in *Don Quijote* are inept, and that it is always "the 'distressed damsel' who comes to the rescue, using vision, determination, courage, and ingenuity to untangle the web of confusion in which their lovers and husbands have become caught" (*Beyond Fiction* 218). Today, a consensus of critics has demonstrated that Cervantes was a feminist author (see El Saffar, Wilson, Rabin, Cruz, Hernández, Taddeo). The debate now turns to more technical questions. In what ways and to what degrees was Cervantes a feminist?

Mockery of the extremes of male sexuality is everywhere in *Don Quijote*. The very genesis of the idea of Dulcinea involves a ludicrous and dizzying *mise en abîme* series of narrators, at the end of which the hero imagines that he needs someone to whom to send his defeated enemies as signs of his devotion: «¿no será bien tener a quien enviarle presentado, y que entre y se hinque de rodillas ante mi dulce señora, y diga con voz humilde y rendida: ⟨Yo, señora, soy el gigante Caraculiambro, señor de la ínsula Malindrania, a quien venció en singular batalla el jamás como se debe alabado caballero don Quijote de la Mancha?⟩» "would it not be good to have someone to whom to send him to present himself, so that he might enter and drop to his knees before my sweet lady and say with a humble and defeated voice: 'I, my lady, am the giant Assfacimbro, lord of the Isle of Malindrania, defeated in single combat by the never sufficiently praised knight Don Quijote of La Mancha?'" (1.1.44). Just as funny, Don Quijote's loyalty to his imaginary Dulcinea proves rather ephemeral. As soon as he arrives at the second inn, for example, he tries to seduce the innkeeper Palomeque's daughter: «plugiera a los altos cielos que el amor no me tuviera tan rendido y tan sujeto a sus leyes, y los ojos de aquella hermosa ingrata que digo entre mis dientes: que los desta fermosa doncella fueran señores de mi libertad» "would that it were not the will of the heavens that love should hold me so defeated and subject to its laws, for then, instead of the eyes of that beauteous ingrate, whose name I pronounce through clinched teeth, those of the beauteous damsel of this castle would be the lords of my freedom" (1.16.170).

Over the course of the novel, several recognizable aspects of male desire emerge. An obsession with purity: Luscinda, Camila, and Leandra transfix characters like Cardenio, Anselmo, and Eugenio, who are enraged by sexual infidelity. Interest in exotic, oriental women: Jarifa, Zoraida, and Ana Félix attract supposedly Old-Christian men like Don Quijote, Captain Viedma, and Don Gregorio. Also, Cervantes tends to present each subsequent female character as the most beautiful on earth. Zoraida's removal of her veil, for example, results in her triangulation and elevation by way of Dorotea and Luscinda: «se lo quitó y descubrió un rostro tan hermoso, que Dorotea la tuvo por más hermosa que a Luscinda, y Luscinda por más hermosa que a Dorotea, y todos los circunstantes conocieron que si alguno se podría igualar al de las dos era el de la mora» "she lifted it and revealed a face so beautiful that Dorotea took her to be more beautiful than Luscinda and Luscinda took her to be more beautiful than Dorotea, and all those present recognized that if any beauty could equal that of the other two, it was that of the Mooress" (1.37.441).

Finally, and with hilariously absurd precision, Cervantes locates ideal female beauty at a very young age. Take the second Dulcinea in part two: «se descubría un hermosísimo rostro de doncella, y las muchas luces daban lugar para distinguir la belleza y los años, que al parecer no llegaban a veinte ni bajaban de diez y siete» "the lovely face of a young maiden was revealed, and the many lights allowed the discernment of her beauty and her age, which appeared to be no more than twenty and no less than seventeen" (2.35.921). Even more extreme is the case of Antonomasia: «llegó a edad de catorce años con tan gran perfección de hermosura, que no la pudo subir más de punto la naturaleza» "she reached the age of fourteen with a beauty of such perfection that nature could in no way improve upon it" (2.38.942).

These are comical, prosaic, and pathetic renditions of male fantasy. They are, however, also the conventions of a wide range of both urban and pastoral romance narratives from the Renaissance period, as well as the picaresque and byzantine novels of classical antiquity, especially Apuleius's *The Golden Ass* (c.175) and Heliodorus's *Aethiopica* (c.250 or c.363), both of which Cervantes took as models for his own craft.

Now, a cultural antidote to the violent extremes of unbridled male sexuality is the cultivation of chivalrous behavior in the modern sense. This option appears in the overt contrasts between characters like, on the one hand, the on-again, off-again aggressive madman Don Quijote or the sexually libertine Don Fernando, and characters like, on the other hand, the valiant and respectful Captain Viedma or the courteous and productive Don Diego de Miranda. In a similar way, Cervantes's novel makes much out of the fact that the term *caballero* has undergone a gradual metamorphosis away from its original and ancient meaning of "mounted warrior" as opposed to mere foot soldier. Below the patricians, the knights were the equestrian order of ancient Rome, from the Latin noun for old horse, *caballus*. After spending a long time meaning more or less "nobleman" in the middle ages and the early modern period, at some point the term finally evolved into its modern meaning of socialized "gentleman." Exactly when this occurred and whether or not the latter type of civilized gentleman exists in sufficient numbers at any given time or place in human history is, of course, always debatable.

We see Cervantes's intentions regarding this humanizing transformation from knight to gentleman in the heavy wordplay he inserts at the beginning of "The Captive's Tale." At the end of *DQ* 1.39, Viedma laments the deaths of many great Spanish and Italian *caballeros* during the Battle of La Goleta in North Africa in 1574. He also describes the Muslim siege against these *caballeros*, which proved successful due to a specific type of offensive fortification known precisely as a *caballero*. Notably, when one of Don Fernando's comrades interrupts Viedma to ask for more details, because he remains anonymous, their brief dialogue requires the narrator to rattle off the term *caballero* three times in rapid succession. All of the men present, it seems, are *caballeros*. But readers familiar with Don Fernando's nefarious role among the lovers in the Sierra Morena will recognize that he is the subject of a transformation from *caballero* meaning "highborn noble" to *caballero* meaning "gentleman." He must earn the title in every sense. The same problem can be seen in the contrast between the original titles of part one, *El ingenioso hidalgo don Quijote de la Mancha,* and part two, *El ingenioso caballero don Quijote de la Mancha.* Such details indicate that turning warriors and sexual vagrants into civilized gentlemen of character is an essential aspect of Cervantes's literary program.

In concert with its critiques of male desire, the first modern novel exhibits feminism in manifold ways. Let's start with three examples of relatively self-evident, natural-law feminism. First, women are no different from men when it comes to their moral status. Álvaro de Luna, the ill-fated advisor to Juan II (1405–54), but also a great apologist for women, once observed that «los que quieren culpar las mugeres mas que a los onbres, mucho yerran, pues que los yerros e viçios son comunes asi a los onbres commo a las mugeres, segund que las virtudes son comunes a ellos e a ellas» "those who would find fault with women more than men, are in serious error, for errors and vices are as common among men as women, just as virtues are common among both" (46). In *Don Quijote,* characters like Marcela, Luscinda, Zoraida, and Ana Félix model more or less virtuous behavior. But the shepherdess Torralba displays excess lasciviousness in *DQ* 1.20, Altisidora and Emerencia physically abuse Doña Rodríguez and Don Quijote in *DQ* 2.48, and Teresa, Sanchica, and the other women of their village are greedy, envious, and petty in *DQ* 2.50. This kind of feminist realism also admits to the existence of female desire in its cruder forms. Don Quijote tells the hilarious story of the rich widow who articulates a sexually utilitarian vision of a lowly friar in *DQ* 1.25. In cases like these, Cervantes effectively dismantles the simplistic polarizations by men of women into "virgin-whore" or "Mary-Eve" complexes. Thus, when Anselmo finally relinquishes his jealous domination of Camila, he makes manifest in his final letter that «no estaba ella obligada a hacer milagros» "she was not obliged to perform miracles" (1.35.422).

A second type of natural-law and realist feminism recognizes that since women get pregnant, their experience of sex is more consequential, both in terms of social stigma and material cost (see Miller, "Men's Reading, Women's Writing"). This major lesson appears in part one of *Don Quijote,* for example, when Don Fernando finally accepts the clandestine marriage that he previously promised to Luscinda (see Dudley; Herrero, "Sierra Morena as Labyrinth"; and Wilson, "Passing the Love of Women"). The same idea takes even more explicit form in part two, when the Countess Trifaldi explains the motive for the marriage between Doña Antonomasia and Don Clavijo: «Algunos días estuvo encubierta y solapada en la sagacidad de mi recato esta maraña, hasta que me pareció que iba descubriendo a más andar no sé qué hinchazón del vientre de Antonomasia, cuyo temor nos hizo entrar en bureo a los tres» "For some days this mess was kept hidden and concealed by my wise precautions, until it seemed to me that time would begin to reveal a certain swelling in the belly of Antonomasia, the fear of which made the three of us enter into deliberations" (2.38.945).

Thirdly, the physical differences between the sexes mean that women are at a natural disadvantage. American philosopher Richard Rorty once defined his brand of pragmatic feminism as critical attention to "the fact that the people with the slightly larger muscles have been bullying the people with the slightly smaller muscles for a very long time" ("Feminism" 233). This key issue of women's relative physical weakness drives the plots of many of the inset tales of *Don Quijote*, particularly in part one. Dorotea, for example, experiences the abuse unleashed by this natural law on three separate occasions. First, she feels threatened by Fernando—«en término le veo que, no usando el que debe, usará el de la fuerza» "he is of a mind, I think, that he will forget himself and turn to force"; second, her own servant attempts to rape her—«dejó aparte los ruegos, de quien primero pensó aprovecharse, y comenzó a usar de la fuerza» "he set aside his pleading, which he at first thought would suffice, and began to use force"; and third, an anonymous peasant attempts to rape her—«nació en él el mesmo mal pensamiento que en mi criado» "there was born in him the same evil thought as in my servant" (1.28.327–31). In this last case, Cervantes deploys the verb *nacer*, or "to be born," to ironically underscore the pregnancy issue as well. This also hints at the sociobiological reasons why we penalize rape as much as any crime short of murder. It's a particularly despotic act to deny a woman her choice regarding with whom to procreate.

In "The Tale of the Curious Impertinent," Leonela cautions Camila: «Mira, señora, que somos flacas mujeres, y él es hombre, y determinado» "Be careful, my lady, for we are women, and weak, and he is a man, and a determined one at that" (1.34.407). There is, however, a subtle difference here. There's feminist irony in the fact that these words form part of a theatrical scene that the two women are performing in order to deceive Camila's jealous husband Anselmo. On other occasions, too, Leonela and Camila manifest this storytelling type of ingenuity in order to free themselves from control by others. This suggests a natural alliance between novelists and women, and it goes a long way toward explaining why so many imaginative illusions and discursive manipulations performed by female narrators throughout both parts of *Don Quijote* echo Scheherazade's mercurial efforts to survive in *Arabian Nights*.

The sheer textual predominance of women in *Don Quijote* makes them an essential aspect of the creative, discursive art of the first modern novel, which consistently reorients the perspective of its readers away from an initial focus on the protagonist's madness onto multiple examples of female agency. This change in perspective is admirably represented by Antonio Muñoz Degrain's *Los molinos de viento* (fig. 6). Here, I'll review the grounds for feminist discourse in *Don Quijote* and then survey the novel's most emblematic and problematic women. I argue that Cervantes goes further than discarding the stigma of Eve. He advocates the need for a kind of global respect owed to women by men, respect which mandates special considerations, such as gentlemanly behavior and the marriage contract. Cervantes is perhaps more aligned with this particular ideological component of the Counter-Reformation than he is with any other.

Explanations for the many feminist features of *Don Quijote* include: (A) the author's personal experience; (B) the novels of classical antiquity; (C) the powerful aristocratic women of early modern Italy, Spain, and France; (D) consequent changes in reading practices throughout Western Europe; (E) the threats to their interests that many early modern Catholic women perceived in the neighboring sects of Protestantism and Islam.

(A) CERVANTES'S BIOGRAPHY

During his most prolific years, Cervantes's household was dominated by women. After returning from Algiers, he lived in the company of his elder sister Andrea, his illegitimate daughter Isabel, his niece Constanza, and his

Figure 6. Antonio Muñoz Degrain, *Los molinos de viento*, 1916–19 *Source*: Círculo de Bellas Artes

young wife Catalina (m.1584). In the Ezpeleta murder case, we glimpse the degree to which these women had a somewhat notorious aura about them. Andrea, Isabel, Constanza, and even Cervantes himself were all suspected of murder and briefly detained after a nobleman, Don Gaspar de Ezpeleta, died from his stab wounds on their doorstep in Valladolid in 1605. Cervantes also fathered his daughter Isabel via an earlier affair around 1582 with Ana Franca de Rojas, who was a nursemaid in the household of Marín Mújica, who, for his part, was later accused of aiding none other than Antonio Pérez, Philip II's estranged secretary and personal nemesis, during his escape from jail in 1590 (Pérez Lasheras 141). Don Quijote's drive toward the Ebro River in Aragón is certainly suggestive of the ensuing *Alteraciones de Aragón*, which Philip II ended by force in 1591. It's tempting to interpret the abuse of Don Quijote as a mockery of this particular use of force by the Crown necessitated by the rebellious actions of the employer of his former lover. The world was surely a smaller place in the sixteenth century, so Cervantes's connections to the Ezpeleta murder and the Antonio Pérez affair might just be coincidences. Still, it's probably no exaggeration to observe that Cervantes affiliated with some pretty strong and relatively scandalous women.

(B) EPIC AND NOVEL OF CLASSICAL ANTIQUITY

Cervantes was an excellent student of the history of narrative discourse and all the various genres that he recombined into the novel form. In the great epics of classical antiquity and the middle ages, such as Homer's *Odyssey*, Virgil's *Aeneid*, Dante's *Divine Comedy*, or the anonymous *Poema de mio Cid*, women like Penelope, Dido, Beatrice, and Ximena influence the trajectories of the male heroes (see Salinas). Cervantes's novel is no different. During the late Renaissance, more important than what we traditionally think of as epics were the picaresque and byzantine novels of classical antiquity. As an author of narrative fiction, Cervantes understood and overtly exploited the feminist implications of Andromeda and Diana in the respective origins and Venus and Isis in the respective conclusions of Heliodorus's *Aethiopica* and Apuleius's *The Golden Ass*. This classical facet of Cervantine feminism does not seem to be an exaggeration. As Margaret Doody has shown, ancient novels are practically gynocentric by definition, that is, they are designed and constructed around their goddesses. Zoraida and the Virgin Mary play similar roles with respect to the mad knight at the end of part one of *Don Quijote* as do Ana Félix and Altisidora at the end of part two.

(C) EARLY MODERN ARISTOCRATIC WOMEN

Another important factor in the rise of the modern novel was the patronage of powerful women at courts across Western Europe during the Renaissance. In turn, the early modern rise of the novel lends support to the idea that we can trace the origins of feminism back to the early modern period (see Cruz, De Jean, Miller, "Emphasis Added," and Wilson, "Homage to Apuleius"). The salon culture of Italy, Spain, and France produced radical feminist authors like Zayas, Scudéry, and La Fayette. How feminist were they? Scudéry's view is illustrative: "The equality of the sexes is no longer in dispute among worldly people" (qtd. by De Jean, 251–52n64). The early modern novel was an integral part of an artistic ethos that addressed women's concerns and featured complex women characters in situations familiar to women. The rise of the novel naturally reinforced values and institutions important to early modern aristocratic women, especially the marriage contract, religious convents, and salon culture. The early modern history of theoretical thinking about the novel form further supports these connections. The first treatise on the ancient origins of novels appeared in an essay entitled "Traité de l'origine des romans" by Pierre-Daniel Huet, which also served as the preface to La Fayette's byzantine romance *Zaïde: histoire espagnole* (1670). The same alliance between novels and women dominates the aesthetic program of the Château de Fontainebleau, in many ways an architectural remnant of early modern feminism. The statue in the garden of the goddess Diana by Tomasso Francini echoes Apuleius's *The Golden Ass* and several of the rooms display enormous paintings by Ambroise Dubois of different scenes selected from Heliodorus's *Aethiopica* (see Graf, "Heliodorus, Cervantes, La Fayette").

(D) EPIC TO NOVEL

The elite women of European salon culture hastened the death of epic and shifted early modern reading practices onto the novel, which then became a feminist mainstay. In *An Essay on Epick Poetry* (1727), Voltaire reflected on this literary sea change: "Notwithstanding, the veneration due, and paid to *Homer*, it is very strange, yet true, that among the most Learn'd, and the greatest Admirers of Antiquity, there is scarce one to be found, who ever read the *Iliad*, with that Eagerness and Rapture, which a Woman feels when she reads the Novel of Zaïda" (90).

This shift in reading practices also leaves its mark on sixteenth-century Spain. Saint Teresa of Ávila (1515–82) was a huge fan of chivalric novels. In *Don Quijote*, the innkeeper Palomeque's daughter is another fan, and the passages she likes most are suggestive of that eagerness and rapture later noted by Voltaire: «no gusto yo de los golpes de que mi padre gusta, sino de las lamentaciones que los caballeros hacen cuando están ausentes de sus señoras» "I do not delight in the blows that so please my father but, rather, in the lamentations made by the knights when they are absent from their ladies" (1.32.370). Other genres also held to collision courses with epic; Diego de San Pedro's sentimental romance *Cárcel de amor* (1492), Fernando de Rojas's urban dramatic dialogue *La Celestina* (c.1499), and Jorge de Montemayor's pastoral *La Diana* (1559) were all important near-term precursors to Cervantes's novels, and they all represented tonal, formal, and thematic shifts away from epic. Subsequent Spanish authors like María de Zayas sharpened this feminist narrative tradition, which later reached its zenith in the prose masterpieces of nineteenth-century authors like Charlotte Brontë, Jane Austen, Gertrudis Gómez de Avellaneda, Cecilia Böhl de Faber, Emilia Pardo Bazán, Gustave Flaubert, Emile Zola, and Benito Pérez Galdós.

(E) BETWEEN HENRY VIII AND THE KORAN

During the late Renaissance, a vigorous novelistic defense of the marriage contract and the rights of women served Catholicism on separate ideological fronts against Protestantism and Islam. From the perspective of a feminist in Europe, Thomas More's refusal to recognize the annulment of Henry VIII's marriage to Catherine of Aragón was inseparable from his opposition to the English tyrant's break with Catholicism. Like Zayas, Cervantes could be quite critical of domestic Spanish attitudes against women; nevertheless, the ends of each part of *Don Quijote* focus attention on two specifically trans-ethnic figures: Zoraida and Ana Félix, that is, Christian women of Moorish descent fleeing Islam. That both Zoraida and Ana Félix should also have curious, tangential brushes with representatives of Protestantism—the pirates of La Rochelle in *DQ* 1.41 and Ricote by way of his exile in Bavaria in *DQ* 2.53—suggests that they are meant to be symbolically opting for Catholicism between the two extremes of Muhammad and Luther.

Literary scholar Joan De Jean has shown, quite convincingly I think, how the seventeenth-century feminist novel opposed the Protestant tendency to use divorce and remarriage to expropriate the property of women, thereby consolidating alliances and strengthening the authority of certain princes. In terms of Cervantes's oeuvre, *La española inglesa* (1613) and *Los trabajos de Persiles y Sigismunda* (1617) contain the most explicit visions of the Protestant threat. *Don Quijote* is more focused on the Muslim frontier. Ana Félix's decision to marry a Christian and her father Ricote's eventual acceptance of her choice make them key exemplary figures in Cervantes's thinly veiled appeal for clemency toward some Moriscos. Similarly, Zoraida gazes at Viedma when the other women of the Sierra Morena beg her to unveil herself in public. He encourages her to do so, speaking Arabic: «Él en lengua arábiga le dijo que le pedían se quitase el embozo, y que lo hiciese» "In Arabic, he said that they were asking her to take off her veil, and that she should do so" (1.37.441). By contrast, Zoraida's father Agi Morato is the antithesis of positive, non-fanatical Moriscos like Ricote. If Morato learns that his daughter wants to flee to Christian Spain, in Zoraida's words, «me echará luego en un pozo y me cubrirá de piedras» "he will throw me straight into a well and cover me with stones" (1.40.467). I wager Cervantes found this a lamentable aspect of Islamic culture.

Here's a list of important female characters, types, and themes that readers should keep in mind when considering to what degree *Don Quijote* exhibits early modern feminism.

(1) MARCELA

Marcela is the first major liberated female figure in *Don Quijote*. Her name alludes to the Roman god of war. In 1981, this character played a central role in a somewhat heated exchange in the American academic journal *Cervantes*, between Cesáreo Bandera and Ruth Anthony El Saffar, the latter one of the pioneers of feminist criticism in the field of early modern Hispanism. Marcela establishes a serious, educated, and overarching feminist theme early in part one of the novel. As she mounts a spirited rejoinder to the jealous complaints voiced by Grisóstomo, Ambrosio, and the legion of suitors who now pursue her through the hills and valleys of La Mancha, her harangue is a conscious rejection of the stereotypes that men have always used in their libels against women. Among her more strident statements is her declaration of absolute physical independence, her natural right to decide what to do with her own body: «Yo nací libre, y para poder vivir libre escogí la soledad de los campos» "I was born free, and in order to live free I chose the solitude of the fields" (1.14.154).

At numerous points in her speech, her sophisticated rhetoric and reasoning echo those of a trained humanist lawyer. Here is one of the more famous passages:

> Hízome el cielo, según vosotros decís, hermosa, y de tal manera, que, sin ser poderosos a otra cosa, a que me améis os mueve mi hermosura, y por el amor que me mostráis decís y aun queréis que esté yo obligada a amaros. Yo conozco,

con el natural entendimiento que Dios me ha dado, que todo lo hermoso es amable; mas no alcanzo que, por razón de ser amado, esté obligado lo que es amado
por hermoso a amar a quien le ama. Y más, que podría acontecer que el amador
de lo hermoso fuese feo, y siendo lo feo digno de ser aborrecido, cae muy mal
el decir «Quiérote por hermosa: hasme de amar aunque sea feo». Pero, puesto
caso que corran igualmente las hermosuras, no por eso han de correr iguales
los deseos, que no todas hermosuras enamoran: que algunas alegran la vista y
no rinden la voluntad; que si todas las bellezas enamorasen y rindiesen, sería
un andar las voluntades confusas y descaminadas, sin saber en cuál habían de
parar, porque, siendo infinitos los sujetos hermosos, infinitos habían de ser los
deseos. Y, según yo he oído decir, el verdadero amor no se divide, y ha de ser
voluntario, y no forzoso. (1.14.153)

Heaven has made me, as you say, beautiful, and so much so that, rendering you
incapable of anything else, my beauty moves you to love me; and because of
the love you show me, you say, and even urge, that I am obliged to love you
in return. I know, by that natural understanding which God has given me, that
everything beautiful is loveable, but I cannot see how, by reason of being loved,
that which is loved for being beautiful is obliged to love that which loves it.
Furthermore, it may happen that the lover of that which is beautiful may be
ugly, and since ugliness is worthy of being avoided, it is most absurd to say, "I
love thee because thou art beautiful; ergo, thou must love me even though I be
ugly." But supposing the beauty to be equal on both sides, it does not follow that
their desires must therefore be alike, for not all beauties fall in love: some are
pleasing to the eye without surrendering their wills; because if all beauties fell
in love and surrendered, then there would be a chaos of confused and misguided
wills wandering about vaguely, unable to make any choice; for since there is
an infinity of beautiful subjects, there must also be an infinity of desires. And
true love, according to what I have heard, is indivisible, and must be voluntary
and not coerced.

Cervantes also deploys Marcela to further indulge his mockery of the emo-
tional and behavioral extremes of machismo, which often leads men to ignore
the basic meaning of female discourse. As soon as the beautiful shepherdess
finishes her speech and disappears into the woods, «dejando admirados tanto
de su discreción como de su hermosura a todos los que allí estaban» "leaving
all who were there filled with admiration, as much by her intelligence as by
her beauty," Don Quijote steps forward and forbids anyone to follow her:
«Ninguna persona, de cualquier estado y condición que sea, se atreva a seguir a la hermosa Marcela, so pena de caer en la furiosa indignación mía»
"Let no person, whatever his rank or condition, dare to follow the beautiful
Marcela, under pain of incurring my furious indignation" (1.14.156). After
impressing on everyone that they should continue on their way, Don Quijote
promptly does what he has just forbidden: «determinó de ir a buscar a la

pastora Marcela y ofrecerle todo lo que él podía en su servicio» "resolved to go and search for the shepherdess Marcela and to offer to serve her in any way that he could" (1.14.157). And topping off this case of blind hypocrisy, Cervantes then signals the animalistic ridiculousness of the mad knight's self-interested defense of Marcela by means of symbolic projection followed by poetic justice. At the beginning of the next episode, Rocinante attempts to have sex with a herd of mares and, as a result of the ensuing scuffle, the horse drovers leave him «malparado en el suelo» "laid out flat on the ground" and the knight and his squire «de mala traza y de peor talante» "looking poor and feeling worse" (1.15.160–61).

(2) AGRARIAN AND BOURGEOIS SKILL SETS: DOROTEA, DOÑA RODRÍGUEZ, AND SANCHICA

There is a type of idealized female character in *Don Quijote* who is adept at making, exchanging, and managing wealth. Initially, this idea is latent. But given Don Quijote's insanity and Sancho Panza's gullibility, at the beginning of part two, the hidalgo's niece and housekeeper as well as the squire's wife and daughter intervene and exert more influence on the would-be adventurers. Trying to reason with their men, these women articulate household virtues in response to feudal fantasy.

The novel's first formal presentation of the hybrid bourgeois-aristocratic ideal of financial realism and responsibility appears about halfway through part one in Dorotea's description of her role as manager of her family's estate:

> Y del mismo modo que yo era señora de sus ánimos, ansí lo era de su hacienda: por mí se recebían y despedían los criados; la razón y cuenta de lo que se sembraba y cogía pasaba por mi mano, los molinos de aceite, los lagares del vino, el número del ganado mayor y menor, el de las colmenas; finalmente, de todo aquello que un tan rico labrador como mi padre puede tener y tiene, tenía yo la cuenta y era la mayordoma y señora, con tanta solicitud mía y con tanto gusto suyo, que buenamente no acertaré a encarecerlo. (1.28.321–22).

> And in the same way that I was mistress of their hearts, so I was mistress of their estate: servants were hired and dismissed by me; the logic and accounting of what was sowed and harvested passed through my hands, the olive mills, the wine presses, the number of livestock, large and small, and the number of beehives; and thus, when it came to all that a rich peasant like my father could have ever wanted to have and did have, I was the accountant, stewardess, and mistress, with so much attention to detail on my part and such satisfaction on his, that I can never praise it enough.

Thus, Dorotea emerges from an agrarian and peasant context to become the first of many able and calculating feminine antidotes to Don Quijote's particularly anti-economical form of foolishness and unreason. Readers will recall that at the beginning of part one Don Quijote has read so many books of chivalry that he can no longer fulfill his basic social duties: «olvidó casi de todo punto el ejercicio de la caza y aun la administración de su hacienda» "he forgot almost entirely about the practice of hunting and even the administration of his estate" (1.1.37). We are meant to contrast Don Quijote's lurid failure with Dorotea's commonsensical, bookkeeping mode of successfully managing an agrarian estate. Similarly, Dorotea anticipates the harmonious male alternative represented by Don Diego de Miranda in *DQ* 2.16.

Women often press forward the same lesson about the virtues of commercial and fiscal reasoning and responsibility in part two. Both Don Quijote and Sancho must deal more directly with the women of their households than they did in part one. Don Quijote struggles to repress his housekeeper and his niece's skepticism about his adventures; Sancho has a lengthy debate with Teresa about his vision of their daughter's chivalric future. Part two elaborates on the symbolic depths of this conflict between fantasy and realism when Don Quijote has a vision of Dulcinea as a mirror of his own financial difficulties in the Cave of Montesinos. Echoing the economic stress experienced by many hidalgos, whose pensions lost purchasing power due to inflation, Dulcinea sends her maid to beg Don Quijote for a loan: «media docena de reales, o los que vuestra merced tuviere» "a half dozen *reales*, or as many as your grace might have" (2.23.827). Dulcinea's situation here is also compatible with the allegorical interpretation of both her and Don Quijote as Spain in fiscal decline. Her need for a loan alludes to the bankruptcies already experienced by the Crown in 1557, 1575, and 1597. Indeed, in his desperation to somehow become Dulcinea's personal banker, like a Fugger opposite her role as a Habsburg, Don Quijote returns from the Cave of Montesinos less four silver *reales*. Predictably materialistic, Sancho observes that this is the height of chivalric insanity.

After Don Quijote's cavernous quest for credit and collateral, both of which prove elusive, a series of episodes underscores the point that wealth is better when generated by investment, work, production, and trade. During her nocturnal conversation with Don Quijote, Doña Rodríguez notes her embroidery skills in *DQ* 2.48. While Sancho governs Barataria, the Duchess and Teresa Panza exchange a coral necklace for acorns in *DQ* 2.50. In order to save money for her dowry, Sancho's daughter makes bone lace items in *DQ* 2.52. In *DQ* 2.70, seeing eye to eye for a change, Sancho and Don Quijote offer stern bourgeois advice to the Duchess about what to do to cure her lovesick servant Altisidora: «sepa vuestra señoría que todo el mal desta doncella nace de ociosidad, cuyo remedio es la ocupación honesta y continua» "I'll have your ladyship know that all of the problems afflicting this maiden are born of idleness, the remedy for which is honest and continuous labor" and «las doncellas ocupadas más ponen sus pensamientos en acabar sus tareas que en pensar en sus amores» "maidens who are kept busy focus their thoughts on completing their work more than thinking about their love life" (2.70.1197). The irony attaches to the very foundations of Cervantes's masterpiece. *Don Quijote* begins as the story of a nobleman who suffers from idleness (*ociosidad*, Latin root: *otium*) and who has gone insane to the point that he no longer hunts and no longer manages his own household. But the novel soon turns our attention toward an exemplary blend of what are often feminist-leaning economics lessons about the division of domestic labor, respect for the property of women, and their capacity to produce income.

(3) CAMILA

A somewhat more cerebral form of feminism underwrites "The Tale of the Curious Impertinent," the interpellated novella in *DQ* 1.33–35. The abstract melodrama about a love triangle in early modern Florence descends into Freudian psychopathology as Camila falls victim to the jealousy and stupidity of her husband Anselmo and his friend Lotario.[1] We know that many readers in Cervantes's day objected to the novella on the grounds that it did not appear to them germane to the adventures of the mad hidalgo. Cervantes has the bachelor student Sansón Carrasco note the controversy early in part two: «Una de las tachas que ponen a la tal historia—dijo el bachiller—es que su autor puso en ella una novela intitulada *El Curioso impertinente*, no por mala ni por mal razonada, sino por no ser de aquel lugar, ni tiene que ver con la historia de su merced del señor don Quijote» "One of the faults that they attribute to the history—said the bachelor—is that its author inserted into it a novel entitled *The Curious Impertinent*, not because it was bad or poorly written, but because it is out of place there and has nothing to do with the history of his grace Sir Don Quijote" (2.3.652). Even a reader as sophisticated as Arturo Pérez-Reverte could not resist excising "The Curious Impertinent" from his recent edition of *Don Quijote*.

Nevertheless, literary critics like Edward Dudley, Javier Herrero, and Diana de Armas Wilson have shown how Cervantes's inset piece reflects on the similar impertinent curiosity in the love triangle in the Sierra Morena formed by Fernando, Dorotea, and Cardenio. Furthermore, Camila's name alludes to the Volsci warrioress who resists the Trojan invasion of Italy in Virgil's *Aeneid*. Metaphorically speaking, she's Amazonian and a devotee to the goddess Diana, and thus she shares military and mythological characteristics with Marcela. From a broader generic perspective, in terms of the era's shift toward the novel, Camila's name ironically signals a feminist response to the epic from which she sprang. In this sense, too, she echoes Marcela's rejection of the masculinist discourse deployed to define her by Grisóstomo and Ambrosio. In sum, from various perspectives the complaint that "The Curious Impertinent" is somehow out of place in *Don Quijote* reveals the carelessness of most readers, both then and now.

Due to its multiple perspectives on different sexual transgressions, it's easy to get distracted by the art and intrigue of "The Curious Impertinent." Still, Cervantes laces the text with some pretty sophisticated feminist lines. Camila's servant Leonela, for example, points out the natural problem of the different muscle sizes of the sexes: «Mira, señora, que somos flacas mujeres, y él es hombre, y determinado» "Be careful, my lady, for we are weak women and he is a man, and a determined one" (1.34.407). This story also contains a kind of dialectical, Hegelian lesson about the rhetorical and acting skills of women as natural responses to male domination. In other words, women's weakness leads to their ingenuity. With Anselmo watching from a hidden vantage point, Camila enacts a scene designed to extricate herself and Lotario from her husband's suspicions of adultery. The realism of her performance not only fools Anselmo, it surprises Lotario: «con una increíble fuerza y ligereza arremetió a Lotario con la daga desenvainada, con tales muestras de querer clavársela en el pecho, que casi él estuvo en duda si aquellas demonstraciones eran falsas o verdaderas, porque le fue forzoso valerse de su industria y de su fuerza para estorbar que Camila no le diese» "with incredible strength and swiftness she attacked Lotario with the unsheathed dagger, showing such indications of wanting to drive it into his heart that he was momentarily in doubt as to whether those demonstrations were true or false, because he was forced to employ skill and force in order to ensure that Camila did not stab him" (1.34.411).

Ultimately, "The Curious Impertinent" offers a theoretical critique of male desire as a function of a strange concoction of mimetic rivalry (see Girard, *Deceit, Desire, and the Novel*) and homosocial bonding (see Sedgwick), both of which occur between men and about a common love object as a point of reference. Everything ends badly, of course. Camila flees to a convent, Anselmo dies of rage, shame, and loss, and Lotario is killed in battle between the Spanish and the French for control of Italy. However, a namesake of the disgraced Anselmo appears in *DQ* 1.50, acting like a positive counterexample, like an idealized Anselmo resuscitated and cured of his previous condition. This new Anselmo's more angry rival Eugenio marvels at his tranquil refusal to be bothered by psychotic love triangles. The contrast is between a man who respects a woman's choice and one who vilifies her nature. Indeed, it would seem the very point of Cervantes's novel:

> Entre estos disparatados, el que muestra que menos y más juicio tiene es mi competidor Anselmo, el cual, teniendo tantas otras cosas de que quejarse, solo se queja de ausencia; y al son de un rabel que admirablemente toca, con versos donde muestra su buen entendimiento, cantando se queja. Yo sigo otro camino más fácil, y a mi parecer el más acertado, que es decir mal de la ligereza de las mujeres, de su inconstancia, de su doble trato, de sus promesas muertas, de su fe rompida y, finalmente, del poco discurso que tienen en saber colocar sus pensamientos e intenciones que tienen. (1.51.581–82)

> Among all these madmen, the one who shows that he has the least care and yet the most awareness about him is my rival Anselmo, who, while having so many other things to complain about, complains only of absence; and to the sound of a rebec, which he plays admirably, he sings his complaints with verses in which he reveals his good sense. I take an easier road, which seems to me more correct, which is to speak ill of the fickle nature of women, their inconstancy, their double dealings, their dead promises, their broken vows, and, finally, the lack of rationality they have when it comes to knowing how to direct the thoughts and inclinations they have.

A final note is in order here on "The Curious Impertinent." The geometry of triangles in *Don Quijote* signals a somewhat esoteric theoretical basis for the logic of the Counter-Reformation's response to what was viewed by many Catholics, especially after the Council of Trent (1545–63), as Protestantism's and Islam's respective attacks on women. Lotario criticizes Anselmo's jealous madness by comparing it to a Moorish obsession with women's virginity, the kind that demands nothing short of a mathematical demonstration, like Euclid's third common notion:

> Paréceme, ¡oh Anselmo!, que tienes tú ahora el ingenio como el que siempre tienen los moros, a los cuales no se les puede dar a entender el error de su secta con las acotaciones de la Santa Escritura, ni con razones que consistan en especulación del entendimiento, ni que vayan fundadas en artículos de fe, sino que les han de traer ejemplos palpables, fáciles, intelegibles, demostrativos, indubitables, con demostraciones matemáticas que no se pueden negar, como cuando dicen: «Si de dos partes iguales quitamos partes iguales, las que quedan también son iguales». (1.33.382)

> Oh Anselmo! It seems to me that you now have a mindset like that which always possesses the Moors, who cannot be convinced of the error of their sect by way of commentaries derived from Sacred Scripture, nor by arguments that

consist of speculation based on reason, or those derived from articles of faith, but, rather, must be presented with palpable, intelligible, comprehensible, demonstrable, and indubitable examples, with mathematical demonstrations that cannot be denied, such as when one says, "If from two equal parts we remove equal parts, then the remaining parts are also equal."

Even in his mathematical allusions, Cervantes is ironical. The third common notion is not a demonstration or proof but, rather, a premise. Another allusion to Euclid, this time interwoven with allusions to Protestantism, appears in the Countess Trifaldi's weird triangular dress:

> La cola o falda, o como llamarla quisieren, era de tres puntas, las cuales se sustentaban en las manos de tres pajes asimesmo vestidos de luto, haciendo una vistosa y matemática figura con aquellos tres ángulos acutos que las tres puntas formaban; por lo cual cayeron todos los que la falda puntiaguda miraron que por ella se debía llamar la condesa Trifaldi, como si dijésemos la condesa «de las Tres Faldas». (2.38.939)

> The tail, or skirt, or whatever it might be called, ended in three points which were carried along in the hands of three pages, who were similarly dressed in mourning and who made for a stylish mathematical figure with the three acute angles formed by the three points; by way of which everyone who saw the sharply pointed skirt understood that this must be the reason that the countess was named Trifaldi, as if we were to say the "Countess of the Three Skirts."

All of this triangulating fiction develops an overarching feminist moral in a way much like El Greco's *La huida a Egipto* (fig. 7), where the miracle of the virgin birth incorporates Joseph's ability to perceive a solitary mother's predicament. Additionally, by way of the symbolism of the bridge, the ass, and the conspicuous golden thread held aloft by Joseph which, like his staff, forms a right triangle with the earth, El Greco makes the acceptance of Mary and Jesus by Christianity's first saint in Matthew 2.13–15 analogous to the geometric proof known as the *pons asinorum* or "Bridge of Asses," which leads in due course to the triumphant proof of the Pythagorean theorem at the end of the first book of Euclid's *Elements* (see 1.5 and 1.47). In this way, El Greco grounds the gynocentric logic of Christian theology in the truth of mathematical reasoning, asserting as a unique feature of Catholic philosophy a principle we might describe as *in dubio pro femina*, or "when in doubt, respect women." For El Greco, the logic of Joseph's respect for Mary is the very *pons asinorum* of Counter-Reformation Christianity (see Graf, "El Greco's and Cervantes's Euclidean Theologies").

Figure 7.   El Greco, *La huida a Egipto*, c.1570 *Source*: Museo del Prado

(4) MISCEGENATION: MARITORNES, ALDONZA LORENZO, ZORAIDA, QUITERIA, ANA FÉLIX, AND ALTISIDORA

Cervantes's mockery of male desire hints at the solution to racism and ethnic conflict in southern Spain. Old Christians and institutions like religious confraternities and the Inquisition should relinquish their obsessions with sexual and blood purity and instead submit to the reality of centuries of miscegenation and assimilation.

Cervantes's perspectivism emphasizes realism over fantasy, but when we stop to consider Don Quijote's point of view, we confront frequent phantasmagoric projections of the novel's more specifically miscegenous goal. In *DQ* 1.2, the sometimes-puritan hero's first interlocutors in the novel are prostitutes. When defeated by the Toledan merchants in *DQ* 1.5, the knight mentally transforms Dulcinea and himself into the Moorish lovers Jarifa and Abindarráez. More allusions to sexual mixing are performed by the innkeeper Palomeque's daughter and the servant girl and prostitute Maritornes. These two young women are near simultaneous embodiments of racial hybridity. First, Palomeque's daughter confesses to having an hilariously recurrent and obviously sexual dream: «a mí me ha acontecido muchas veces soñar que caía de una torre abajo y que nunca acababa de llegar al suelo, y cuando despertaba

del sueño hallarme tan molida y quebrantada como si verdaderamente hubiera
caído» "it has often happened to me that I dream that I am falling down the
length of a tower and that I never manage to reach the ground, and when I
wake up from the dream, I find myself as thrashed and bruised as if I had truly
fallen" (1.16.169). Later that night, Don Quijote intrudes upon Maritornes's
sexual encounter with a certain mule driver who also signally happens to be a
relative of Cide Mahamete, a curious spelling of the original Arabic narrator
Cide Hamete. Maritornes's adornments cause the mad knight's imagination
to construct the kind of oriental and sexual fantasy found throughout the era's
chivalric novels.

> La asturiana, que toda recogida y callando iba con las manos delante buscando
> a su querido, topó con los brazos de don Quijote, el cual la asió fuertemente de
> una muñeca y tirándola hacia sí, sin que ella osase hablar palabra, la hizo sentar
> sobre la cama. Tentóle luego la camisa, y, aunque ella era de arpillera, a él le
> pareció ser de finísimo y delgado cendal. Traía en las muñecas unas cuentas de
> vidro, pero a él le dieron vislumbres de preciosas perlas orientales. Los cabellos,
> que en alguna manera tiraban a crines, él los marcó por hebras de lucidísimo oro
> de Arabia, cuyo resplandor al del mesmo sol escurecía; y el aliento, que sin duda
> alguna olía a ensalada fiambre y trasnochada, a él le pareció que arrojaba de su
> boca un olor suave y aromático; y, finalmente, él la pintó en su imaginación, de
> la misma traza y modo, lo que había leído en sus libros de la otra princesa que
> vino a ver el malferido caballero vencida de sus amores, con todos los adornos
> que aquí van puestos. (1.16.173–74)

> The Austurian girl, who went cautiously and silently with her hands before her
> in search of her lover, bumped into the arms of Don Quijote, who grabbed her
> firmly by the wrist and, pulling her towards him, and without her daring to say
> a word, forced her to sit down on the bed. He touched her blouse, and, even
> though it was made of burlap, to him it seemed to be of the finest and most sheen
> silk. On her wrists she wore some glass beads, but he imagined them to be pre-
> cious pearls from the Orient. Her locks of hair, which were more like a horse's
> mane, he saw as threads of shining Arabian gold, whose splendor eclipsed that
> of the very sun. And her breath, which doubtless smelt of the previous day's
> leftover salad, to him seemed to waft from her mouth with a sweet and aromatic
> scent. In the end, he painted her in his imagination according to the same form
> and appearance of another princess that he had read about in his books and who
> came to see the gravely wounded knight while overcome with love and wearing
> all the adornments we have just described.

Miscegenation has always been the rule in southern Spain due to its transi-
tory location at the margins of Europe and within reach of North Africa. The
transethnic lesson of Cervantes's novel targets Don Quijote and Sancho alike,
who each adopt various and often contradictory perspectives on the issue. For

example, in the Sierra Morena, or "Brown Mountains"—yet another hybrid symbol for mixed skin color—, Sancho Panza queries his master: «¿Que la hija de Lorenzo Corchuelo es la señora Dulcinea del Toboso, llamada por otro nombre Aldonza Lorenzo?» "So, the daughter of Lorenzo Corchuelo is my lady Dulcinea of Toboso, otherwise known as Aldonza Lorenzo?" (1.25.283). The squire instantly recognizes Aldonza as a local prostitute, «porque tiene mucho de cortesana» "because she has a lot of courtesan in her," and, moreover, she is very likely a Morisca since Sancho's memory of her shouting from the town's bell tower echoes the Muslim call to prayer: «se puso un día encima del campanario del aldea a llamar unos zagales suyos que andaban en un barbecho de su padre, y, aunque estaban de allí más de media legua, así la oyeron como si esuvieran al pie de la torre» "one day she climbed atop the town's bell tower to call some shepherds who were walking in one of her father's fields, and even though they were more than half a league away, they heard her as if they were at the foot of the tower" (1.25.283).

At first, Don Quijote casually discards the issue of Dulcinea's racial purity, admitting that Sancho has her identity right and even asserting that «es la que merece ser señora de todo el universo» "it is she who deserves to be queen of the entire universe" (1.25.283). But he contradicts himself in the very next chapter: «Porque mi Dulcinea del Toboso osaré yo jurar que no ha visto en todos los días de su vida moro alguno» "Because I dare say that my Dulcinea of Toboso has never seen a single Moor in all the days of her life" (1.26.291).

Given the heavy reverence for Aristotle among the late scholastics, this philosopher's appearance in Don Quijote's initial justification of his desire for Aldonza Lorenzo, by way of the anecdote about the aristocratic lady who has sex with a lowly monk, suggests Cervantes's more reasoned, liberal view of both feminine desire and interethnic copulation. When the monk's superior complains, the woman rebuffs him in a way that is both hilarious and suggestive of a feminist's cure to the insanity of racism: «para lo que yo le quiero, tanta filosfía sabe y más que Aristóteles» "considering what I want him for, he knows as much philosophy as Aristotle, more even" (1.25.285). This racy anecdote contrasts sharply with Don Quijote's subsequent squeamishness about Dulcinea's Morisca status in *DQ* 1.26, thereby suggesting a consciously formulated miscegenous remedy to the escalating conflict between Old Christians and Moriscos in Southern Spain circa 1600.

More symbolic figurations of the miscegenation that Cervantes beseeches of Old Christians follow. The arrival of the Algerian Princess Zoraida-María at the inn in the Sierra Morena reflects the similar transracial meaning of the metamorphosis of Dorotea into the African Princess Micomicona in *DQ* 1.37. Racial mixing also appears in the prophetic description of Don Quijote as a «león manchado» "the spotted lion" in *DQ* 1.46. Then there's the inset tale of the knight who leaps into a «gran lago de pez hirviendo a borbollones» "great lake of boiling and bubbling pitch" in conjunction with the sudden appearance of Eugenio's wandering «cabra manchada» "spotted she-goat" in *DQ* 1.50. Finally, penitent pilgrims arrive carrying the image of a black-clad Virgin in *DQ* 1.52.

A thick miscegenation message resurfaces dramatically in *DQ* 2.10 when Dulcinea rides atop a racialized parade of different beasts of burden.[2] In *DQ* 2.21, Quiteria marries Basilio, who dresses like a victim of the Inquisition. In *DQ* 2.41, Sancho frolics with multicolored she-goats who represent the Pleiades and Zoraida. In a remarkably picaresque inset narrative in *DQ* 2.48, Doña Rodríguez contrasts her Leonese husband's supposed racial purity with his expressly jet-black mule and a complex reference to the Morisca Saint Casilda of Toledo. In *DQ* 2.57, Altisidora inexplicably describes her legs as somehow both «blancas y negras» "black and white." Analogous to Zoraida-María at the end of part one, Ana Félix signifies racial hybridity at the end of part two; and echoing the role of Captain Viedma in love with the Algerian princess, the Old-Christian nobleman Don Gregorio is drawn to the daughter of Sancho's Morisco neighbor. Don Gregorio's reunion with Ana Félix in *DQ* 2.65 is the climax of the miscegenous theme in part two; and it's no coincidence that in the prior chapter, the symbolically Moorish Knight of the White Moon finally defeats Don Quijote, who is sometimes possessive and racist and other times ethnically liberal and sexually transgressive.

(5) THE DUCHESS

The most powerful female presence in the first modern novel is surely the Duchess. She synthesizes multiple feminist themes. Even more than Marcela, she recalls a martial goddess in the act of hunting, and like Camila, she directs imaginary scenes designed to fool her viewers. Moreover, like Jarifa, Maritornes, Zoraida, and Ana Félix, she signals miscegenation by way of her connection to Doña Rodríguez's picaresque. The Duchess even relates to a down-to-earth type of bourgeois feminism when she exchanges letters and gifts with Teresa. Given this last merchant-class consciousness, we cannot be surprised to find that she also expresses a version of the Protestant dictum *sola fide* which was censored as early as the Valencia edition of 1616.

The Duchess's initial impression is striking. With hunting falcon in hand, on horseback, and dressed in green, she embodies the noble caste, yet she also echoes the Knight of the Green Coat. If Don Diego de Miranda sounds Erasmian in his religious modesty; the Duchess is more radical still when she voices what comes close to an endorsement of Luther's criticism of the utility of charitable acts: «advierta Sancho que las obras de caridad que se hacen tibia y flojamente no tienen mérito ni valen nada» "be advised Sancho that works of charity that are performed in a lukewarm and indifferent way have no merit and are worthless" (2.36.930). Furthermore, like many nobles along the Spanish Mediterranean coast, her political advice to Sancho Panza reads like a call for moderation and assimilation regarding the Morisco problem: «Lo que yo le encargo es que mire cómo gobierna sus vasallos, advirtiendo que todos son leales y bien nacidos» "What I charge him with is that he take care in how he governs his vassals, remembering that all of them are loyal and wellborn" (2.33.908).

Most explicitly, however, the Duchess represents an overarching noble version of the feminist perspective already delivered in the reproaches to Sancho and Don Quijote delivered by Teresa Panza, the housekeeper, and the niece in *DQ* 2.5–6. After Sancho reveals his male chauvinism by way of an aggressive story about a Toledan pharmacist —«yo he oído decir a un boticario toledano, que hablaba como un silguero, que donde intervieniesen dueñas no podía suceder cosa buena» "I have heard it told by a certain Toledan apothecary, who always sounded like a goldfinch while speaking, that whenever mistresses are involved nothing good can come of it" (2.37.936)—, the Duchess then responds to him like a Medici queen, i.e., powerful, sophisticated, and quite sure in her view that women deserve far more respect than they have so far received from the future governor: «Mal estáis con las dueñas, Sancho amigo –dijo la duquesa–, mucho os vais tras la opinión del boticario toledano, pues a fe que no tenéis razón, que dueñas hay en mi casa que pueden ser ejemplo de dueñas» "'Sancho, my friend, you are in a bad way with duennas,' said the Duchess, 'you get too carried along by the opinion of that Toledan pharmacist, for, by my faith, you are wrong: there are duennas in my household who can be the very example of duennas'" (2.40.954).

The Duchess vindicates women everywhere by rising to the occasion in part two's running «coloquio dueñesco», meaning "duenna debate" or perhaps "mistress matter" (2.37.937). In concert with her objections, over the course of part two, Sancho gradually accepts the Duchess's lesson regarding the importance of respect for women: he submits to the Countess Trifaldi's pleas for help against Malambruno in *DQ* 2.40; he is erotically enchanted by the armed and dangerous Claudia Jerónima in *DQ* 2.60; and finally, he accepts martyrdom on behalf of Dulcinea in *DQ* 2.69.

The Duchess indicates that the feminism in *Don Quijote* is both radical and sustained. She also suggests, however, that its origins are aristocratic. Just as political liberalism arises among those nobles whose fortunes are most affected by kings and who therefore know full well that a king's power should be limited; so too with feminism, for it is powerful women who most directly realize that they can manage families, estates, cities, and even nation-states as well as any man. Aristocratic women are instinctively, empirically, and rationally at pains to reduce the arrogance of their powerful male counterparts.

(6) CLAUDIA JERÓNIMA

Claudia Jerónima is one of the first modern novel's most perplexing female characters. In *DQ* 2.60, she appears heavily armed, with a dagger, a short shotgun, and two pistols; she's a violent incarnation of the feminisms of Marcela, Dorotea, Camila, Teresa, the Duchess, and Altisidora. Moreover, readers accustomed to Cervantes's happy endings are often shocked and annoyed to find that, after Claudia Jerónima kills her fiancée in a fit of jealous rage, Don Vicente doesn't spring back to life via some industrious trick like Basilio's fake suicide in *DQ* 2.21. On some level, we've simply been set up as readers. On another level, though, Claudia Jerónima's misunderstanding allows that while guns might be a great physical equalizer between the sexes, this doesn't mean that immoral or irrational women won't commit horrific acts with them. There are still plenty of flawed and cruel women in the world, and some will murder people.

Still, Claudia Jerónima symbolizes much more than an extreme, ironical portrayal of feminism's potential for overreach. For starters, she's also a highly charged political figure in at least two ways. Early in *DQ* 2.60, Sancho rebels against Don Quijote. The knight tries to deliver the lashes the squire has promised in order to save Dulcinea. But Sancho performs a kind of Hegelian jujitsu and suddenly servant is master: «echándole una zancadilla, dio con él en el suelo boca arriba, púsole la rodilla derecha sobre el pecho y con las manos le tenía las manos de modo que ni le dejaba rodear ni alentar. Don Quijote le decía: −¿Cómo, traidor? ¿Contra tu amo y señor natural te demandas?» "throwing his leg behind him, he threw him to the ground face up, planted his right knee on his chest, and using his hands he pinned his arms such that he could neither move nor breathe. Don Quijote said to him, 'How now, you traitor? You dare to threaten your natural lord and master?'" (2.60.1117). Echoing the School of Salamanca, at last Sancho asserts his natural rights to his body and to self-defense. Notably, a few pages after this pivotal scene of rebellion, which overturns the novel's core relationship, Sancho considers that the armed and vindictive Claudia Jerónima was rather attractive: «no le había parecido mal la belleza, desenvoltura y brío de la moza» "the beauty, boldness, and braggadocio of the lass had not seemed at all bad to him" (2.60.1126). Beyond the silliness of Sancho's sexual attraction, Claudia Jerónima is clearly a projection of his own situation. A peasant laborer struggling for a salary from his occasionally abusive master instinctively likes the idea of an armed rebellious woman on horseback.

A second way gender parallels politics in the figure of Claudia Jerónima involves her links to the local power structure in places like Aragón and Cataluña, places inclined against the centralized Habsburg authority emanating from Madrid. On the one hand, Claudia Jerónima as well as her ally Roque Guinart highlight the problem of *bandolerismo* in the Catalan countryside; specifically, in the rivalry between the quasi-political criminal clans known as the Cadells and the Nyerros, they are partisans of the latter. On the other hand, and as Sancho can well attest, one person's brigand is another person's freedom fighter. Claudia Jerónima can be viewed positively, especially from an anti-Habsburg perspective. Her armed, erotic emergence from the no-man's land between Zaragoza and Barcelona also signals nostalgia for limits on the modern growth of imperial power. Indeed, late scholastics like Pedro Simón Abril (1540–91) and Juan de Mariana longed for such medieval checks on monarchical power, and, like Sancho, they would have approved of Claudia Jerónima. As capital of the Kingdom of Aragón, Zaragoza had its own laws, or *fueros*, and its own independent legal system, the last vestiges of which were crushed by Philip II in 1591. Similarly, around 1600, the parliamentary Courts of Barcelona hotly debated a Habsburg law banning a type of short shotgun used by the *bandoleros*. There was even drama over the final printed version of the law. Thus, on the road to Barcelona, the city which Cervantes later represents as the cosmopolitan focal point of an Erasmian printing press, Claudia Jerónima's unexpected appearance brandishing the elements of political and constitutional resistance has the effect of once again demarcating the limits of Habsburg tyranny.

Finally, I would argue that the asymmetrical case of Claudia Jerónima's extremely violent feminism relates to the looming limit encounter with Islam. Considered in the context of the interconnected chain of female figures in both parts of *Don Quijote*, Claudia Jerónima's enigmatic and tragic predicament in *DQ* 2.60 ushers in the final case of Ana Félix in *DQ* 2.63 and 2.65. Similar to the way that Zoraida-María opts for Spain and Captain Viedma over Algiers and her father Agi Morato toward the end of the 1605 novel, toward the end of the 1615 novel, Ana Félix hopes to marry Don Gregorio and gain reentry into Spain despite the recent expulsion ordered by Philip III. Just as big as the lines Cervantes draws in the sand against Habsburg tyranny are these climactic versions of *in dubio pro femina* leveraged against Islam at the Mediterranean shoreline. Perhaps now we understand how the lethality of Claudia Jerónima adds to the power of the proximate presentation of Ana Félix. Women fleeing Islam are crossing a line of no return, which means figuratively killing the patriarchy of their former cultures.

(7) ISLAM

Turning to Islam, we find Muslim and Morisca women throughout *Don Quijote*. Maritornes's relations with the mule driver who is also a relative of Cide Hamete in *DQ* 1.16; Dulcinea's connections to the Morisco population of El Toboso in *DQ* 1.25, 2.10, and 2.18; and Zoraida-María's and Ana Félix's flights from North Africa to Spain in *DQ* 1.41 and 2.63. The privileged positions occupied by these last two women at the international conclusions of each part of the novel indicate Cervantes's ultimate vision of Christianity as potentially winning over the hearts and minds of Muslim women. How modern is this? To this day, one of the most significant contrasts between the West and Islam is seen in their respective treatments of women.

Those who object to reading *Don Quijote* as a feminist novel take a negative view of its exceedingly young ideal of feminine beauty and its excessive enthusiasm for marriage plots. These objections echo the standard feminist reaction against the happy unions in the final scenes of Golden Age plays. Likewise, Cervantes's *Novelas ejemplares*, argues Theresa Sears, are not sufficiently feminist from a modern perspective. Too often they repair rape with marriage, for example. But this type of criticism says nothing about the fact that Dorotea fights off two rapists on her way to reclaiming Fernando as her husband. Many feminist critics will also sidestep the notion that Cervantes seeks to restrain hyperbolic men like Don Quijote, Anselmo, and Don Fernando. The repression of youthful lust and the contrast between rape and marriage are part of this process. Moreover, from the reclusive Marcela to the abusive Claudia Jerónima, Cervantes does indeed imagine other options besides marriage for exemplary female characters.

Feminism in *Don Quijote* has its natural-law components: Dorotea fights off two rapists; Leonela remarks on the physical advantages of men; and Princess Antonomasia faces the difficult prospect of an illegitimate pregnancy. This is simply to observe that Cervantes advances Christianity's "reason of women" against men throughout both parts of the novel and in many different countries. Zoraida risks inciting her father's violence in Algiers, but men also threaten the well-being of women in the Sierra Morena south of Toledo and even in Florence, Italy, the city that gave birth to the Renaissance. The effect of so many cases of abusive masculinity is similar to the novel's extreme religious relativism in support of the universal right to freedom of conscience. The essence of feminism transcends nationalities, and the novel underscores the importance of freedom for women everywhere.

Yet, just because feminism in *Don Quijote* is ancient and universal, and just because masculinist madness can break out in cosmopolitan Florence, doesn't mean that the feminist struggle is equally urgent everywhere. In the end, Zoraida and Ana Félix challenge the vague notion that Cervantes sustains the repressive patriarchy of Western Civilization, or that feminism is somehow cultural imperialism. The jujitsu of postmodern social theory is sometimes too clever by half. Skeptical feminist critics would do much better to recognize that the marriage plots that break down with Camila and Claudia Jerónima in *DQ* 1.35 and 2.60 inaugurate the respective plights of Zoraida and Ana Félix in *DQ* 1.37 and 2.63. If males are dangerously possessive and abusive in Renaissance Florence, such tendencies are greater still in the Muslim world. Historian Bernard Lewis has described this difference and its cultural consequences as follows:

> The women of Christian Europe were very far from achieving any kind of equality, but they were not subject to polygamy or legal concubinage. Even the limited measure of freedom and participation that they enjoyed never failed to shock a succession of Muslim visitors—all of them male—to Western lands. Western civilization was richer for women's presence; Muslim civilization, poorer by their absence. (24)

On its own, the feminist trajectory of *Don Quijote* indicates a way in which Cervantes endorses Christianity over Islam. To borrow a phrase, Cervantes recognizes a kind of "reason of women," or what I have called *in dubio pro femina*, as a major civilizing principle of Western Europe. To put it more bluntly, if feminism means cultural imperialism, then so be it. But this is more than a slogan. The aesthetic and philosophical precision of its articulation in Golden Age Spain is remarkable. As El Greco does in *La huida a Egipto* (fig. 7), Cervantes leverages a feminist preference for Catholic theology against the Islamic world. The novelist's allusions to Euclid's "bridge of asses" and his triangular presentations of characters like Camila, Zoraida, and the Countess Trifaldi echo the geometric symbolism of the Pythagorean theorem on display above the bridge in El Greco's *La huida a Egipto*.

A modern version of this combination of Catholic feminism and geometric symbolism can be seen in Salvador Dalí's surreal *Visage paranoïaque* (fig. 8). Dalí's perspectivism also challenges the familiar academic objection that feminism is somehow hegemonic and culturally repressive. He achieves this by advancing a feminist point of view against the Leninist and postcolonialist tendencies of Picasso's cubism. When a viewer rotates his head counterclockwise and ninety degrees to the left, he is eventually confronted by the cubist image of woman who emerges from the previously innocuous scene outside a tribal hut. To paraphrase: the more radical and leftist your defense of the Third World, the more you should be made to consider what to do about the repression of women there.[3]

Figure 8.   Salvador Dalí, *Visage paranoïaque*, c.1935 *Source*: Fundació Gala-Salvador Dalí

Like the art of El Greco and Dalí, the ancient history of the novel form also counters the idea that feminism is somehow cultural imperialism. Given *Don Quijote*'s multiple marriages among women and men of different ethnicities, and given the novel's consistent criticisms of slavery, it's easy to see how Cervantes paved the way for nineteenth-century narratives like Gertrudis Gómez de Avellaneda's *Sab* (1841), Cecilia Böhl de Faber's "La hija del sol" (1851), and Harriet Beecher Stowe's *Uncle Tom's Cabin* (1852). As it turns out, feminism, anti-racism, and abolitionism go together quite naturally in narrative fiction. *Don Quijote* reveals the early modern roots of this ideological alliance. In fact, *Don Quijote* reveals the ancient classical roots of the alliance. This is because Cervantes was also composing according to the proto-feminist and anti-slavery aspects of Apuleius's *The Golden Ass* (c.175), i.e., according to a trajectory from lust for Diana to respect for Isis, in conjunction with the discovery along the way that slaves are fellow human beings and not merely beasts of burden.

NOTES

1. For a review of Cervantes's influence on Freud as well as the utility of Freudian theory for understanding Cervantes, see the volume of essays entitled *Quixotic Desire* edited by Diana de Armas Wilson and Ruth Anthony El Saffar. See also Graf ("La antropología subversiva").

2. For more on Dulcinea and miscegenation, see Graf ("The Economy of Asses").

3. See Nieves Romero-Díaz for a similar, although opposite, argument against granting too much credit to María de Zayas's feminism. Romero insists that Zayas's feminism is insufficiently postcolonial.

Chapter Three

Don Quijote and Slavery

"'Very well,' thought I. 'Knowledge unfits a child to be a slave.'"

—Frederick Douglass, *Life and Times of Frederick Douglass* (91)

The theme of slavery is essential to any serious understanding of *Don Quijote de la Mancha*, and it's one that deserves more attention than it usually receives. Cervantes not only uses his novel to try to get readers to see that slavery is immoral, he suggests we consider that there are also good utilitarian reasons for favoring economic relationships over whips and chains. I argue that his objection is triple: slavery itself is wrong, the new racial justification of it is absurd, and any material advantage it offers over a free labor market is likely an illusion. Indeed, it is more likely that slavery is a competitive disadvantage. By signaling this last idea that remunerated work in the context of personal freedom and devoid of coercion might result in more efficient and productive outcomes than slavery, Cervantes anticipates a host of classical liberal thinkers, few of them as important as Adam Smith.

Scholars have focused on distinct elements of the slavery theme in *Don Quijote*, specific episodes, and related topics like labor (see Arrabal; Rossi; Redondo; Johnson, *Cervantes* 25). But in order to assess Cervantes's larger concerns, we need to trace out slavery's complex presence in the novel. I'll conclude by looking at a series of episodes that are transformed when we relate them to the theme of slavery, especially Sancho whipping himself in the woods in *DQ* 2.71 and the naval battle between the two galleys *La Loba* and *La Presa* at the beginning of "The Captive's Tale" in *DQ* 1.39.

First, let's review the five (5) basic reasons why we can expect the novel to attend to the topic of slavery in the first place. Cervantes's perspective on slavery can be divided according to five thematic categories (each with its own ideological and historical explanations): (A) aesthetic and amorous (novel form, Neoplatonism, courtly love); (B) personal and empirical (crime and war); (C) historical and socioeconomic (feudalism and merchant capitalism); (D) ethnic and racial (Moriscos and black Africans); (E) philosophical and theoretical (Aristotle and the School of Salamanca).

(A) SLAVERY AND THE NOVEL FORM

There are solid aesthetic reasons why slavery is a fundamental theme in the first modern novel. In an important essay entitled "Epic and Novel" (1941), Mikhail Bakhtin defined the novel as "a genre-in-the-making, one in the vanguard of all modern literary development" (11). He goes on to argue that the novel's resilience owes to the way it cannibalizes all other literary genres; the novel incorporates epic, myth, lyric, song, dramatic dialogue, carnivalesque ritual, philosophical discourse, example, folktale, etc.

One implication of Bakhtin's view of the novel as generically cannibalistic is as follows. Given that amorous passion is configured as an ennobling experience of spiritual enslavement in the mutually reinforcing modes of Neoplatonic philosophy and the courtly love tradition, and given that these two modes are at the heart of nearly all the various genres of early modern narrative fiction—from sentimental and pastoral novels, like Diego de San Pedro's *Cárcel de amor* (1492) or Jorge Montemayor's *La Diana* (1559), to satirical and urbane novels, like Fernando de Rojas's *La Celestina* (c.1499) or María de Zayas's *Estragos que causa el vicio* (1647)—, we can therefore expect that a master of the novel form should display a wide range of amorous slaveries. Indeed, the trope of amorous slavery makes a full circle in Cervantes's novel, beginning in *DQ* 1.1, when the hidalgo fantasizes about sending his victims in chains before his beloved Dulcinea, and ending in *DQ* 2.71, when Sancho undertakes to whip himself to secure her disenchantment. This amorous enslavement, for example, is the sense of Don Quijote's words to Rocinante when he unsaddles him before doing penance in the Sierra Morena: «Libertad te da el que sin ella queda» "Liberty is granted to thee by him who remains without her" (1.25.279).

So far so good. Modern readers, however, are inclined to miss the fact that leveraging narrative fiction against the institution of slavery was also a self-conscious aspect of both the ancient as well as the early modern novel form. Specifically, Cervantes inherited the abolitionist tradition from Apuleius's *The Golden Ass* (c.175) and from the anonymous *Lazarillo de Tormes* (c.1554). Just as he studied Heliodorus's byzantine epic *Aethiopica* (c.250 or c.363) before writing *Los trabajos de Persiles y Sigismunda* (1616), he studied models of the picaresque before writing part one of *Don Quijote*. Thus, direct references to the modern form occur throughout, especially in *DQ* 1.22, where the most dangerous galley slave, Ginés de Pasamonte, claims his autobiography will make an even better story than *Lazarillo de Tormes*. Cervantes overtly cites the classical model for picaresque fiction in his *Novela y coloquio que pasó entre Cipión y Berganza* (c.1605), when the witch Cañizares says she wishes she could help the dog Berganza return to his human form: «el cual modo quisiera yo que fuera tan fácil como el que se dice de Apuleyo en *El Asno de oro*, que consistía en solo comer una rosa» "the manner of which I wish were as simple as that told by Apuleius in *The Golden Ass*, which consisted of merely eating a rose" (337). The picaresque carries a host of philosophical, stylistic, symbolic, and thematic implications, among them very direct criticism of slavery on practically every level. It is no accident that Ginés de Pasamonte cites *Lazarillo de Tormes* during an episode populated by galley slaves. For his part, Lucius, the protagonist of *The Golden Ass*, recovers his human form precisely and ironically right after he recognizes the horror of slavery, which in effect turns his fellow human beings into beasts. In a similar manner, although opposite the trajectory of Lucius, Berganza's cruel abuse of a black African slave in *El coloquio de los perros* disqualifies him for redemption and so he never recovers his original human form (Graf, "La antropología subversiva" 36).

From another angle, race was already a major aspect of Heliodorus's *Aethiopica*, in which the African Princess Chariclea is born white because her parents have sex while gazing at a painting of Andromeda. If we think of the story told by the African Princess Micomicona as underscoring the theme of race in part one, then it is precisely in the form of a plot ripped from byzantine romance that the theme finds expression in *Don Quijote* (see Graf, "Heliodorus, Cervantes, La Fayette").

Indeed, a major Spanish innovation in early modern fiction was precisely to fold the themes of race and ethnicity into a picaresque satire against slavery. *Lazarillo de Tormes*'s author signals skin pigment as an issue at the outset. Lazarillo's mother had a dark lover, Zaide, clearly of Moorish descent, who cared for beasts of burden—i.e., the picaresque symbol *sine qua non*. Lazarillo confesses that he feared Zaide until he noticed that life got better whenever he visited. Finally, the future *pícaro* witnesses the tribal instincts of his half-brother, sired by Zaide, and concludes that racial hypocrisy is a universal problem:

> Ella y un hombre moreno de aquellos que las bestias curaban vinieron en conoscimiento. Éste algunas veces se venía a nuestra casa y se iba a la mañana; otras veces de día llegaba a la puerta, en achaque de comprar huevos, y entrábase en casa. Yo, al principio de su entrada, pesábame con él y habíale miedo, viendo

el color y mal gesto que tenía; mas de que vi su venida mejoraba el comer, fuile queriendo bien, porque siempre traía pan, pedazos de carne y en el invierno leños, a que nos calentábamos.

De manera que, continuando la posada y conversación, mi madre vino a darme un negrito muy bonito, el cual yo brincaba y ayudaba a calentar. Y acuérdome que estando el negro de mi padrastro trebajando con el mozuelo, como el niño vía a mi madre y a mí blancos y a él no, huía dél, con miedo, para mi madre, y, señalando con el dedo, decía:

–¡Madre, coco!

Respondió él riendo:

–¡Hideputa!

Yo, aunque bien mochacho, noté aquella palabra de mi hermancico y dije entre mí: «¡Cuántos debe de haber en el mundo que huyen de otros porque no se veen a sí mesmos!» (16–18)

She and a dark man, one of those who cares for beasts of burden, came to appreciate each other. This man sometimes visited our house and then left the next morning; other times he arrived at the door during the day, pretending to want to buy eggs, and he would come inside. At the beginning of his visits, I was made wary by him and was in fear of him, seeing his color and the ugly face that he had. But once I saw that his visits improved our meals, I started to love him well, because he always brought bread, pieces of meat, and, in the winter, firewood, in front of which we warmed ourselves.

And so, relations and his calling at our home went on, until one day my mother gave me a beautiful little black child, whom I bounced up and down and helped to keep warm. And I remember one day, while my black stepfather was playing with the little boy, and since the child saw that my mother and I were white and he was not, he ran in fear of him into the arms of my mother, and pointing with his finger, he said:

"Mother, bogeyman!"

And he responded, laughing:

"Son of a bitch!"

Even though I was very young, I noted that word from my little brother and said to myself: "How many are there in the world who flee from others because they do not see themselves!"

If the author of *Lazarillo de Tormes* subsequently reveals that Zaide was a thief, his point is not to reinforce the black muleteer's already marginal status but, rather, to further criticize the hypocrisy of the dominant culture. Note how religious orthodoxy is a key target of the following sentence, which also reveals that the slave Zaide is moved to steal by the particularly Christian emotion of love: «No nos maravillemos de un clérigo ni fraile porque el uno hurta de los pobres y el otro de casa para sus devotas y para ayuda de otro tanto, cuando a un pobre esclavo el amor le animaba a esto» "We should not be surprised by a cleric or friar because the one steals from the poor or the other steals from his own convent for devoted nuns and from other donations, when love drove a poor slave to do the same" (19).

Lazarillo de Tormes was written slightly prior to the rise of black African slavery in Spain, so its satire is still focused primarily on the misguided persecution of *conversos* and Moriscos, those Jewish and Moorish citizens who had converted to Christianity at the end of the fifteenth century in order to stay in the country. In sixteenth-century Spain, Old Christians and the Inquisition allied against these two ethnic minorities and used a combination of blood purity laws and accusations of religious heresy to marginalize them, exclude them from office, and sometimes even execute them and take their assets. Moriscos, in particular, were increasingly under threat of mass expulsion as the century waned. What we also witness in *Lazarillo de Tormes*, however, is that dark skin color has now become an added signifier of social subordination and exploitation.

His job caring for beasts of burden combines with his black skin and slave status to indicate Zaide's inferiority *vis-à-vis* ethnocentric religious purists. The novel's second symbolic deployment of a pack animal accentuates yet another criticism of the deception of the official belief system. Near the end of the novel's fifth *tractado*, Lazarillo witnesses a fraud staged by a town bailiff and a preacher who is his latest master. The preacher rails against sin and urges people to buy papal indulgences; the bailiff plays a skeptic who then pretends to be possessed by the devil and so very much in need of the mystical powers of one of the indulgences. The scene anticipates the fake beard miracle performed by the priest in *DQ* 1.29 as well as the reverberating cave into which Sancho falls in *DQ* 2.55. Note too how metaphorical "blackness" is worked into Lazarillo's description, adding another layer of irony to a description of a trick designed to make the public finance an increasingly racist form of orthodoxy:

> Apenas había acabado su oración el devoto señor mío, cuando el negro alguacil cae de su estado y da tan gran golpe en el suelo, que la iglesia toda hizo resonar, y comenzó a bramar y echar espumajos por la boca y torcella y hacer visajes con el gesto, dando de pie y de mano, revolviéndose por aquel suelo a una parte y a otra.
>
> El estruendo y voces de la gente era tan grande, que no se oían unos a otros . . . Finalmente, algunos que allí estaban, y a mi parecer no sin harto temor, se llegaron y le trabaron de los brazos, con las cuales daba fuertes puñadas a los que cerca dél estaban. Otros le tiraban por las piernas y tuvieron reciamente, porque no había mula falsa en el mundo que tan recias coces tirase. (119–20)

Scarcely had that devout master of mine finished his prayer, when that black bailiff falls from his seat and gives such a great thud as he hits the ground that he made the entire church resonate, and he began to groan and spew foam from his twisted mouth and to glare about, making faces, flailing his feet and hands, rolling about on the floor from one place to another.

The noise and the people's voices made so much noise that nobody could hear anybody . . . Finally, some who were there, and from what I could tell not without significant fear, approached him and grabbed his arms, with which he was raining heavy blows down upon those who were nearest him. Others pulled at his legs and held him fast, because there was not a false mule in all the world which delivered such solid kicks.

The anonymous author of *Lazarillo de Tormes* makes his final use of the picaresque's symbolic ass in the sixth *tractado*. After a stint working for a poor painter, Lazarillo finds his best master yet, a chaplain of the Cathedral of Toledo who lends him a donkey for the purpose of carrying water up from the Tagus River. Note three details here: (1) Lazarillo's initial task is mixing pigments, (2) followed by a financial arrangement that he makes with his new master *qua* business partner, (3) which allows him for the only time in his life to eat well and to save enough money to purchase for himself precisely the outer trappings of an hidalgo.

Después desto, asenté con un maestro de pintar panderos, para molelle los colores, y también sufrí mil males. Siendo ya en este tiempo buen mozuelo, entrando un día en la iglesia mayor, un capellán della me recibió por suyo; y púsome en poder un asno y cuatro cántaros y un azote, y comencé a echar agua por la cibdad. Éste fue el primer escalón que yo subí para venir a alcanzar buena vida, porque mi boca era medida. Daba cada día a mi amo treinta maravedís ganados, y los sábados ganaba para mí, y todo lo demás, entre semana, de treinta maravedís.

Fueme tan bien en el oficio, que al cabo de cuatro años que lo usé, con poner en la ganancia buen recaudo, ahorré para me vestir muy honradamente de la ropa vieja, de la cual compré un jubón de fustán viejo y un sayo raído de manga tranzada y puerta y una capa que había sido frisada, y una espada de las viejas primeras de Cuéllar. Desque me vi en hábito de hombre de bien, dije a mi amo que se tomase su asno, que no quería más seguir ese oficio. (125–27)

By that time, I was pretty well grown. And one day as I went into the main cathedral, a chaplain there offered me a job. He put me in charge of an ass, four earthen jugs, and a whip, and I began selling water about the city. This was the first step I took up the social ladder toward living the good life; my stomach was kept full for once. Weekdays, I gave my master thirty *maravedís* out of what I earned, keeping everything beyond that. And on Saturdays I got to keep all I earned.

I did so well in that office that after four years, always focused on my earnings, I saved enough to buy myself a good secondhand set of clothes. I bought a jacket of old cotton, a frayed coat with an open collar and braid on the sleeves, a cape that had once been of velvet, and an old sword—one of the first ones ever made at Cuellar. When I saw how sharp I looked in my gentleman's clothes, I told my master to take back his ass. I wasn't going to do that kind of work anymore.

In multiple ways, the passage reassesses the repressed potential of the slave Zaide. The overarching moral is that we should disregard the ethnic and religious differences underwriting slavery and instead attend to a market-based economy in which capital and work are harnessed to improve life. The fact that in the end Lazarillo returns the ass and renounces the only activity that improves his life in a way free of moral decrepitude only underscores the sad fragility of the bourgeois mentality in late sixteenth-century Spain, especially among the hidalgo caste. True to its literary genre, *Lazarillo de Tormes* deploys a transformative ass in order to satirize those Spaniards who reject the idea that wealth should be generated rather than coerced and conveyed.

These same themes of expropriation and slavery as well as their antidotes in private property, work, commerce, and thrift are fundamental to the classical urtext of the picaresque. According to modern translator Jack Lindsay, Apuleius's *The Golden Ass* examines the Roman Empire at a crossroads. The situation is not unlike that of late sixteenth-century Spain:

> The empire has spread over practically all that is known of the civilized world; there has been a steady growth of urbanization, trade, money-economy; local and tribal ways have gone down before the extension of Roman law with its strong emphasis in personal property . . . Yet under the impressive surfaces the corrosion was busily at work, sapping the urban bases, increasing instead of decreasing the differences between town and country, strengthening the big landlords and preparing the series of upheavals through the peasant-based army which led to the general crisis of the third century. (12)

That Apuleius intended *The Golden Ass* as criticism of emperors, generals, and patricians, who were corrupting the law to enrich themselves at the expense of the poor, is most obvious in book nine's rehearsal of a civil war between the peasantry and the military-backed gentry. Lucius the ass and his latest master, a humble gardener, are guests at the house of a farmer when news arrives that the latter's three sons have been massacred and had their land stolen from them by a plutocrat who is variously labeled "robber," "rich oppressor," "bloody man," "murderer," and "tyrant" (206–08). As Lucius's master heads home, "shaking his head over the catastrophic fate of his friend's house," an insolent Roman legionary restages the tyranny of the evil plutocrat by commandeering Lucius: "'Where are you taking that ass?' 'To the next village,' answered the gardener. 'But I happen to want him,' said the soldier, 'So I'm commandeering him . . .' With that, seizing my halter, he began to lead me off" (209). Lucius himself, then, is expropriated by Imperial Rome.

Alongside critical portrayals in *The Golden Ass* of Rome's caste conflict
and the military imperialism of the Principate period, we must consider Apuleius's analysis of the injustice of forced labor. The same book nine with its
mock civil war and its criticism of soldiers and plutocrats contains Lucius's
gruesome vision of slaves working at a bakery: "Their skin was striped all
over with scourge-scars . . . Their brows were branded; their heads were half-
shaved; irons clanked on their feet; their faces were sallow and ugly; the smoky
gloom of the reeking overheated room had bleared and dulled their smarting
eyes; and (like boxers who fight befouled with the dust of the arena) their
faces were wanly smeared with the dirtied flour" (192). It's crucial to see that
Lucius identifies with these slaves. Indeed, he describes them as the novel's
ultimate asses; like him they are alienated from their former selves: "But how
shall I describe the beasts, my comrades? . . . Dismayed at the graveyard-state
of these animals (perhaps foretelling my own future), I recalled the happy days
when I was Lucius; and hanging my head I mourned for this my final degra-
dation" (192). Lindsay makes the connection between the metamorphosis of
Lucius and the essential inhumanity of an expansionist empire based on slavery: "Here the beast-of-burden is revealed as one with the slave-worker; and
Apuleius' criticism penetrates to the heart of the social problem of antiquity.
Without this experience the 'fall' of Lucius would remain abstract; with it, it
is seen to express the totality of the inner contradictions and conflicts of the
ancient world" (22). Moreover, this is one of the only passages "in the whole
of ancient literature which realistically looks at and examines the conditions of
slave-exploitation on which the culture of the ancient world rested. And since
Apuleius . . . is also depicting the hellish state from within, he may claim the
proud position of being the only ancient writer with the courage, insight, and
humanity to look clearly and unflinchingly at the ugly thing" (22).

Apuleius meant for *The Golden Ass* to unleash a "moral earthquake"
(214) regarding forced labor. Because the protagonist Lucius identifies most
strongly with slaves, the novel's double metamorphosis of a man into an ass
and then back into a man again is the main metaphor of an attack on the institution of slavery as the key problem of the Roman Empire. This is why the
evil plutocrat of book nine is described as "master of an army of servants"
(206), and why, toward the novel's end, servants and slaves constantly and
dramatically intrude, hurtling themselves into dining-rooms, bolting up out
of cellars, and testifying at murder trials (185, 205, 217). This is also why the
novel hinges on the ability or inability to perceive the humanity of Lucius the
ass. A good example is the contradictory irony of a sales pitch made by one
of his last owners. At first, he jokes that Lucius can't possibly be "a true-born
Roman citizen" but then he insists that he's as docile as any human: "Why,
that's not an ass you're looking at; it's a lamb. He's not a biter, nor is he a

kicker. He's such a model of an ass that you'd think he was a godfearing man hiding under an ass's skin" (180). Soon thereafter, on the brink of being butchered and cooked like a stag to be eaten by a certain landlord, Lucius breaks his halter and escapes into a bedroom where he finds peace: "I slept the sleep of a human being as I had in the times long past" (186). In the end, Lucius manages to convince people that he isn't mad with rabies. Indeed, it's the other way around: "in point of fact, the madness was all on their side of the fence . . . I patiently submitted to being patted, and handled, and rubbed on the ears, and led by the halter, and put through any trial that they liked—till my mild demeanour shamed them one and all for their overeasy assumption of madness" (187).

A final point about Apuleius's novel. *Lazarillo de Tormes* criticizes a violently orthodox and racist Spanish public and makes gestures in the direction of the transformative, yet elusive, social palliatives of commerce and work. Likewise, Apuleius responds to the slave-based society of ancient Rome by making repeated references to money, pricing, and economic exchange. The very first line of the ancient picaresque—"Business directed me to Thessaly" (33)—ironically foreshadows the final pages in which Lucius the ass is sold for seventeen, twenty-four, fifty, and eleven pence (189, 191, 203, 220). The various sums that Lucius the man later spends on religious ceremonies are also detailed (247–49). Most suggestive is the gardener's comment upon purchasing Lucius at the very peak of his value: "Too much . . . but the two of us together, I trust, will help each other to keep alive" (203–04). Not slavery, this is a relationship of mutual advantage and respect: "both my master and myself had meals equal in size and substance" (204). Likewise, the gardener's generosity is the basis of his reciprocal friendship with the farmer who loses his sons to the evil plutocrat: "One night a householder of the next village lost his way in the glooms of a moonless night. Drenched to the skin with rain, he turned his tired horse into our little garden; and being hospitably received (all things considered) he was provided with a night's rest (the necessity he craved) though with no dainty extras. However, out of a grateful wish to remunerate his host, he promised to despatch from his farm some corn and oil, with two casks of wine" (204).

In the end, Apuleius underscores this prime virtue of honest commerce as the essence of his protagonist's redemption. The goddess Isis promises Lucius will regain human form; all he has to do is appear at a special ritual: "Tomorrow my priests will offer to me the first fruits of the year's navigation. They will consecrate in my name a new-built ship" (238). On the heels of his final metamorphosis back into a man, Lucius describes the ceremony's finale:

The spot chosen was the very beach where on the preceding day (while yet an ass) I had stabled myself. First, the images of the gods were orderly disposed; and then the high priest dedicated and consecrated to the Goddess a nobly built boat (scribbled all over with the peculiar Egyptian marks) after purifying its torch, flame, egg, and sulphur, and pouring solemn prayers from his sanctified lips.

The shining-white sail of this blessed ship bore a broidered inscription repeating the words of the prayer for this year's prosperous navigation . . .

All the people (initiate or lay) zealously piled up winnowing-fans with aromatic scents and other such offerings, and threw libations of milk mixed with crumbs into the sea, until the ship, cargoed with plentiful gifts and auspicious devotions, was let slip from her anchoring ropes. She put out to sea with a mild breeze; all her own; and after she had sailed out of sight into the distance of her course, the bearers of the holy things reassumed their burdens and began a lively return journey to the temple in the same order and propriety as they had come. (244–45)

Here the miracle of Lucius's transformation from an enslaved ass into a human being is one with the miracle of commerce. Apuleius's mercantile understanding of the cult of Isis offers a counterweight to ancient Rome's shameful dependence on expropriation and bondage. Perhaps the supreme allegorical gesture of *The Golden Ass*, also known as *The Metamorphoses*, is the way in which it geographically situates Lucius's final rediscovery of his humanity. X marks the spot. When he changes from an ass back into a man during the ritualized dedication of a ship at the port city Cenchreae on the Isthmus of Corinth, Lucius essentially embodies transit between the Ionian Sea and the Aegean Sea on the one hand and between mainland Greece and the Peloponnese on the other. Apuleius saw that the basis of a just and wealthy society, one that promotes social respect between individuals while also improving living standards, is blessed commerce. The anonymous author of *Lazarillo de Tormes*, many of the early economists of the School of Salamanca, and Miguel de Cervantes would reach the same conclusion some fourteen centuries later.

Apuleius's view in ancient Rome gets an update in sixteenth-century Spain. A global, historical reason to study early modern Spanish narrative is that the period coincides with the beginnings of a major shift toward the use of race to signify slavery. We see anxiety about this shift in other art forms, too, such as the paintings of El Greco (1541–1614), the poems of San Juan de la Cruz (1542–91), and the plays of Pedro Calderón de la Barca (1600–81). It's no surprise, then, that race is also one of Spain's self-conscious contributions to the picaresque genre, and, by extension, to the modern history of the novel form. *Lazarillo de Tormes* (c.1554) opens with a critique of racism when the narrator's black brother is frightened by the blackness of his own father. On the other hand, *Lazarillo de Tormes* also inherits a medieval trend. In Juan Ruiz's *Libro de buen amor* (1343), for example, the go-between Urraca, which means "magpie," symbolizes hope for a black and white combination.

A pigmentation-based outlook also informs the overtly picaresque "Example 32" of Juan Manuel's *El conde Lucanor* (1335), at the end of which it is a black servant who informs a prince that he wears no clothes. Hernando Díaz's edition of *El conde Lucanor* at Seville in 1575 added impetus in Spain to the notion that a modern conception of race was to be an integral aspect of picaresque fiction.

Along these lines, María de Zayas was one of the most thoughtful of Cervantes's early readers. Proper comprehension of the murder scene at the center of her short novel *Estragos que causa el vicio* (1647) hinges on our perception of the race of one of the household slaves. To sum up, via Apuleius's picaresque the Spanish Golden Age inherits slavery as a critical theme in narrative fiction; then, following Juan Manuel's picaresque, Spanish authors turn the era's racialized form of slavery into the new target of their satires. The long struggle against the pigmentary justification of slavery and other racialized acts of cruelty would go on to leave its mark on a large swath of the modern canon of narrative fiction, producing such abolitionist and anti-colonialist mainstays as Daniel Defoe's *The Life and Strange Surprising Adventures of Robinson Crusoe* (1719), Voltaire's *Candide* (1759), Gertrudis Gómez de Avellaneda's *Sab* (1841), Edgar Allan Poe's "The Gold Bug" (1843), Cecilia Böhl de Faber's "La hija del sol" (1851), Harriet Beecher Stowe's *Uncle Tom's Cabin* (1852), Mark Twain's *The Adventures of Huckleberry Finn* (1884), and Joseph Conrad's *Heart of Darkness* (1899).[1]

(B) SLAVERY AND AUTOBIOGRAPHY IN THE MEDITERRANEAN

Cervantes's personal experience of slavery in Algiers during the years 1575–80 also turned him against the institution. This is the clear sense of "The Captive's Tale" in *DQ* 1.39–41. Luis Andrés Murillo once noted that Captain Viedma's escape from slavery in Algiers was Cervantes's narrative and moral objective while writing part one of *Don Quijote*. Viedma is an autobiographical projection; he even mentions a certain Spaniard named Saavedra, which was Cervantes's second surname. Viedma's story includes the Battle of Lepanto (1571), in which Cervantes participated, and in which, as was always the case in galley warfare, slaves manning the oars bore the brunt of the casualties on both sides. Also sounding very much like Cervantes, Viedma voices criticism of the useless Habsburg military campaigns in North Africa in *DQ* 1.39.[2]

Thus, Cervantes was familiar with the brutal, volatile institution of Mediterranean slavery in the latter half of the sixteenth century. It targeted all faiths, ethnicities, and nationalities, and enemy captives in particular were obliged to row the era's war galleys. Historian Roger Crowley gives us a vivid picture of Barbarossa's rampage down the west coast of Italy in 1544. This was "slave taking on an enormous scale" driven along by "a combustible mixture of jihad, imperial warfare, personal plunder, and spiteful revenge," with the Ottomans taking "some six thousand captives from the coasts of Italy and the surrounding seas" (68–70). Crowley underscores that Christians displayed similar indiscriminate savagery toward defeated soldiers and civilian populations in enemy cities. Charles V's victory at Tunis in 1535, for example, was the apotheosis of his power, but it was also a bloodbath followed by pillage, "a fearful massacre" in which "thousands of surrendering Tunisians" were "cut down in the street," and after which "ten thousand more were sold into slavery" (53).

Finally, Cervantes was also jailed by Spanish authorities for brief periods, accused of embezzling public funds and at one point even suspected of murder. To sum up, the author of the first modern novel knew that being sent to row in the king's fleet often meant death, and he knew the experience of being a chattel slave and being imprisoned. On some level, simple biography explains why critical impressions of physical captivity related to crime and warfare dominate both parts of *Don Quijote*. Nevertheless, Cervantes gives indications of something more global and theoretical at work regarding this topic. Later in this chapter, we will pay special attention to the role played by the galley slaves who rebel in *DQ* 1.22, reappear in Viedma's tale in *DQ* 1.39–41, and take their revenge on Sancho in *DQ* 2.63.

(C) SLAVERY AND THE DECLINE OF FEUDALISM

Another way to view the recurring references to slavery in *Don Quijote* begins with the point that feudalism's obligations and bonds underwrote the courtly love narratives of the sixteenth century's chivalric and sentimental novels, i.e., precisely those narratives which Cervantes variously mocks, appropriates, and reworks throughout *Don Quijote*. Now, a basic and often illustrative move in Marxist literary criticism is to argue that aesthetic modes or styles are ideological projections of their historical circumstances. Thus, Cervantes's decimation of the chivalric novel is seen as dynamically related to the demise of feudalism based on serfdom. In other words, a change in the ideological superstructure of a society (the birth of the novel) reflects a change in the social relations at its material base (the rise of bourgeois capitalism). Accordingly, amorous sentiment in Cervantes's fiction evokes metaphors involving slavery simply because such poetry populates the chivalric romances of the feudal society undergoing dissolution under the skeptical gaze of the materialistic bourgeoisie. Author Mario Vargas Llosa offers a somewhat more nuanced version of the role of economic class in *Don Quijote*, pointing out that the era's popularity of chivalric fantasy also reflected the bourgeoisie's nostalgia for a pre-autocratic world in which merchants had once been far more autonomous than they were by the end of the sixteenth century.

I would only add to the Marxist view that the realist novel also records the self-conscious triumph of the bourgeoisie. Marxist literary critics usually analyze texts as projections of specific socioeconomic relations between the powerful and the weak at any given moment in history. Classics in the study of Spanish literature include Georg Lukács's vision of the disintegration of feudal loyalties in *Don Quijote* and Maravall's brilliant analysis of early modern class warfare in *La Celestina*. In each case, the old organic bond between lord and servant crumbles, with the lord losing out in the end. As for the agrarian world, just like Apuleius, Fernando de Rojas, and the anonymous author of *Lazarillo de Tormes*, Cervantes glimpses the end of serfdom. Moreover, the end of serfdom appears to have much to do with the early rise of industrial commerce. Juan Haldudo flogging the shepherd boy Andrés in *DQ* 1.4 is transformed into Sancho whipping himself for a fee calculated on a per unit basis in *DQ* 2.71. In this way, *Don Quijote* directs readers to critically contemplate one of the more reprehensible institutions of Western Civilization, one which would grow and persist for another three hundred years, until it was officially abolished in nations like Russia (1861), the United States (1863), and Brazil (1888). But is serfdom the same as slavery? There is a continuum, although most would agree that modern slavery is a more brutal institution.

(D) SLAVERY AND RACE

Due to certain racialized episodes in *Don Quijote*, however, Cervantes also writes something that anticipates the abolitionist novels of the United States during the nineteenth century. The novelist hits on Maravall's notion of class in *La Celestina*, but he adds the issue of race from *Lazarillo de Tormes*. *Don Quijote* mounts this particularly modern criticism of slavery because Cervantes composed the novel at a time when the transatlantic trade in black Africans was on the increase. So, not only does he target the institution of slavery as a kind of literary legacy of Apuleius, not only does he attack slavery from the vantage of his personal experience in Algiers, and not only does he perceive the end of slavery as the end of feudalism, Cervantes also manages to target the institution precisely when skin color was becoming the new main signifier of slave status.

José Luis Cortés López has traced the transition in Iberia away from dependence on mostly white slaves, during late antiquity and the medieval period, toward the use of slaves who were increasingly Moors, then Moriscos, especially after the Alpujarras Rebellion of 1568–71, and finally to black Africans, the latter becoming prominent in the second half of the sixteenth century, especially after the annexation of Portugal in 1580. When Philip II renewed the Spanish raids into Barbary in 1597, he alluded to the wealth generated by the capture of «moros y esclavos negros» "Moors and black slaves" (qtd. by Cortés López). At the margins of Europe, and easily accessible from North Africa, ancient, medieval, and early modern Iberia always involved encounters among very different skin colors. But then, towards the end of the sixteenth century, right when skin color finally didn't matter so much anymore, suddenly it did again. Allow me to explain.

On the one hand, Iberia's location implies the experience of more frequent racial contrasts between black Africans and white Europeans. We find hints of this pigmentation-based outlook in fourteenth-century texts by Juan Manuel and Juan Ruiz as well as sixteenth and seventeenth-century texts by Cervantes and Zayas. During these centuries, the arrival of lots of northern Europeans in Iberia accentuated perceptions of racial differences. Note, for example, the extreme contrasts in the German painter Andrés Marzal de Sas's early fifteenth-century vision of the Battle of the Puig, which took place between Aragonese and Valencian forces in 1237 (fig. 9).

On the other hand, Iberia also famously manifests a tendency away from racial differences by way of miscegenation and a general muddling of differences. A significant proportion of the population there is somewhere in the middle, that is to say, brown. And this is not simply a matter of geographical limits. When thinking about Iberia's potential for racial integration, the heavy presence of Islam during the medieval period was also a factor in two important ways. Philosophically speaking, Islamic doctrine tends to neutralize racial conflict. According to the Koran, the garden of Allah yields fruits that are "alike and different," thus providing "signs for true believers" (6.99). Demographically speaking, successive incursions brought all sorts of ethnicities from distant parts of the Islamic world. By 1600, nearly nine centuries after the first Arab incursion in 711, the differences between Moors, Moriscos, Jews, and Old Christians, especially in southern and eastern Spain, were oftentimes nothing more than a matter of custom or dress.[3]

Here is where things get slightly complicated, for medieval Spain's unique blend of philosophical harmony and demographic indeterminacy often worked paradoxically in the opposite direction, that is, against the grain of assimilation, which could have the perverse effect of exacerbating racial anxieties. As French sociologist René Girard reminds us, human beings are

Figure 9.   Andrés Marzal de Sas, *La batalla del Puig,*
c.1410–20 *Source*: Victoria and Albert Museum

so tribal in nature that oftentimes too much similarity among us can unleash a violent desire for distinctions again (see *Violence and the Sacred*). So, while Iberia's unique history at the blurry border between Africa and Europe suggests that race is a superficial illusion, the same phenomenon also produces serious and particularly absurd eruptions of interethnic violence. The rise of the Inquisition at the end of the medieval period is just such a return of the repressed need for clarifying differences (see Yerushalmi).

Furthermore, even this other type of racism, the one Girard describes as resulting from a *lack* of difference, was soon complicated by more waves of people arriving in Iberia who were once again very different. First, the epic scale of the struggle between the sizeable empires of the Spanish Habsburgs and the Ottoman Turks meant that early modern Mediterranean warfare one of history's most cosmopolitan clashes among disparate ethnic groups, who then became each other's slaves when defeated. In Spain, many slaves were domestic Moriscos captured during the repression of multiple uprisings in Andalucía, Valencia, and Aragón. There was also the constant influx of Moors plucked from the coastline during raids on North Africa. Farax de Terque and Andrés de Aragón, two of the leaders of the Alpujarras Rebellion of 1568–71, along with many of their guerrillas, were reportedly very black Africans. Finally, Philip II's annexation of Portugal in 1580 meant that more slaves were imported from colonial outposts like Guinea.

The great playwright Lope de Vega was of the same generation as El Greco and Cervantes. Lope's awareness of a moral contradiction and a fundamental injustice in the new racial status of slaves appears most overtly in his identification with the black African poet Juan Latino in *La dama boba* (publ.1613). A generation later, Pedro Calderón de la Barca fixes our attention on a transition between two types of slavery. In *El médico de su honra* (1637), he refers to the symbol of an 'S' crossed by a nail '/' branded into the face of a servant woman. In a perverse exchange of one form of brutality for another, this horrific phonetic pun in a scar meaning *ese-clavo* or *esclavo* "slave" was rendered unnecessary by the advent of the race-based system. In *El alcalde de Zalamea* (c.1642), Calderón likewise has the aptly named Crespo beg the rapacious Captain to brand his face and take him as his slave. It's no accident that at the play's conclusion, Philip II departs Zalamea on his way to claim Portugal with its growing trade in black Africans.

If we find this transitional moment in the history of slavery in novels like *Lazarillo de Tormes*, *El coloquio de los perros*, and *Estragos que causa el vicio*, as well as in plays like *El médico de su honra*, *El alcalde de Zalamea*, and *La dama boba*, we also spot it in the paintings of the two masters of late-Renaissance Spain: El Greco and Diego Velázquez. In his dark portrait of *San Francisco* (c.1567), three times in the *Tríptico de Módena* (c.1568), and throughout the ingenious "pigmentation puzzles" of pieces like *La curación del ciego* (c.1570), *Alegoría de la Liga Santa* (1577–79), and *San Martín y el mendigo* (1597–99), El Greco is one of the first modern painters to weave a racial component into his iconographic technique (fig. 10). Velázquez's perspectives on race in paintings like *La cena de Emaús* (c.1618–22) display similar agendas. In *San Martín y el mendigo*, El Greco deploys black straps and a white bandage and the contrasting skin colors of man and beast to signal the theme. In *La cena de Emaús* (fig. 11), Velázquez draws his viewer into an undulating meditation on race relations orchestrated among bright white everyday objects. The effect reorients the issue of the discernment of Christ in the resurrection tale of Luke 24.13–35, instead forcing viewers onto the perspective of a black African slave hard at work in the modern Spanish Empire.

Velázquez's *Retrato de Juan de Pareja* (1650) suggests this same recognition among the elite and educated that humanity transcends race. Other

Figure 10. El Greco, *San Martín y el mendigo*, 1597–99 *Source*: National Gallery of Art, Washington, DC

Figure 11. Diego Velázquez, *La cena de Emaús*, c.1618–22 *Source*: National Gallery of Ireland

early modern paintings of black Africans which transmit dignity include Jan Mostaert's *Portrait of an African Man* (1525–30), also known as *Portrait of a Moor*, apparently a member of the court of Charles V; and Cristofano dell Altissimo's *Portrait of Alessandro de' Medici* (c.1560–65), the Duke of Florence (r.1532–37), whose enemies were utterly uninterested in his race. In 1533, Charles V married his natural daughter Margaret of Austria to the Duke, known popularly as "il Moro," securing Florence for imperialists against republicans. It would seem the issue of race failed to take hold in the context of the early modern rivalry for control of Italy between Spain and France.

If only as an historical artefact, *Don Quijote* alludes to the new phenomenon of race-based slavery, which would evolve into a forced migration of gargantuan proportions (fig. 12). Cervantes returned from captivity in Algiers to find that, due to Philip II's annexation of Portugal in 1580, the trade in black Africans was now a fundamental aspect of the Spanish Empire. The future novelist would have witnessed these sociological changes in the Mediterranean port cities of Denia and Valencia, and even more so in Lisbon, where he visited the Habsburg court in 1581, and then for many years in Seville, where

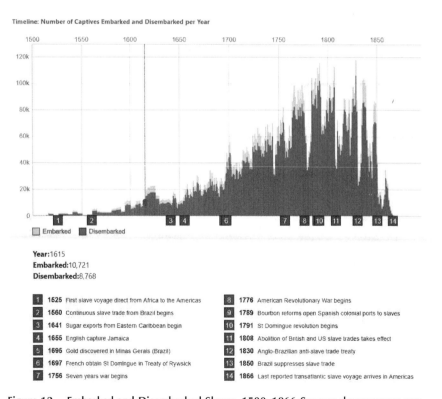

Figure 12.   Embarked and Disembarked Slaves, 1500–1866 *Source*: slavevoyages.org

Cervantes served as a requisitions officer for the ill-fated Armada of 1588. But as we see in El Greco and Velázquez, allusions to race-based slavery in *Don Quijote* are also likely to accompany significant moral commentary.

Cervantes experimented with a lot of genres. He eventually fell heavily into narrative satire, i.e., picaresque, around 1605 while writing *Don Quijote* and *El coloquio de los perros*. In the latter novel, the talking dog Berganza takes a bite out of a black female servant's leg. The lesson is that the merchants of Seville will not voluntarily relinquish their cut of the lucrative trade in African slaves. That will take instruction and a change in values. In *Don Quijote*, part one, this same abolitionist message is evident in the metamorphosis of Cardenio from *hombre salvaje*, or "savage man," back into a civilized gentleman, which occurs in tandem with the dissolution of Sancho's fantasy to get rich by selling the black African citizens of Micomicón as slaves. Like the merchants of Seville in *El coloquio de los perros*, Sancho Panza does not easily surrender the opportunity to profit from the suffering of others. Something must change his mind. Morally speaking, perhaps some slaves should confront him. Economically and politically speaking, perhaps there are better ways to get rich.

(E) SLAVERY, HUMANISM, AND THE SCHOOL OF SALAMANCA

The dueling students from the University of Salamanca in *DQ* 2.19 are a comical interlude, but they also signal that the intellectual context for Cervantes's criticism of slavery was the type of thinking modeled and advocated there. The institution of slavery has long had its apologists. Aristotle and Locke, for example, allow for it. The late classical list of justifications took slavery as a relatively natural consequence of war, crime, debt, or birth. A curious addition made by medieval Christians, Muslims, and Jews was the use of the Biblical story of Noah's curse of his youngest son Ham, the father of Canaan, as a way to justify black slavery: "Cursed be Canaan; a servant of servants shall he be unto his brethren" (Genesis 9.25).

But this last argument was doubly contradictory to many sixteenth-century observers. For starters, although skin does figure in Genesis 9, its color does not. Furthermore, humanists easily mocked the notion of racial distinctions as anathema to a Christian republic because Christianity itself depends on conversion. In his princely advice manual *Institución de un rey christiano* (1556), Felipe de la Torre, for example, heaps disdain on racial intolerance: «todos son miembros de un cuerpo, y en la religión unos, y hermanos de Jesucristo, en cuya presencia no hay diferencia de pueblos, ni naciones, de judíos, ni gentiles, de bárbaros, ni de escitas: porque su fe y religión quitó todos los intervalos y atajos que distinguían entre si los pueblos» "all are members of one body, and are the same in one religion, and are brothers of Jesus Christ, in whose presence there is no difference among peoples, nations, neither Jews nor Gentiles, neither barbarians nor Scythians, because His faith and religion removed all separations and fraudulent means of distinguishing among peoples" (f.85). Many humanists were also Neoplatonists, and so they tended to be already instinctively antiracist due to the metaphysical nature of their outlook. In deference to the soul, the body is an illusion in Neoplatonism. As William Kerrigan and Gordon Braden point out while describing how Marsilio Ficino's individualism fuses pagan Eros and Christian grace, "When one achieves a certain height in the Neoplatonic cosmos, distinctions become equivalences" (108).

The late scholastics of the School of Salamanca are perhaps more relevant than the humanists for understanding Cervantes's views on slavery, owing in particular to the legacy of the activist monk Bartolomé de las Casas (c.1484–1566). Las Casas was a student of Francisco de Vitoria, founder of the School of Salamanca. Vitoria and Las Casas, along with Domingo de Soto, Diego de Covarrubias, and Francisco Suárez, are founders of the modern fields of human rights and international law.[4] Soon after Columbus arrived in America in 1492, a seismic dispute arose over the status of the Amerindians. Were they slaves by definition or did they have rights? This was the essence of the climactic debate between Las Casas and Ginés de Sepúlveda at Valladolid in 1550–51. Soon after the debate, Las Casas evaded censors and rushed to publish *Brevísima relación de la destrucción de las Indias* (Seville, 1552), in which he advanced a markedly Aristotelian politics of international pluralism in defense of the indigenous populations of the New World. He argued that Amerindians had natural rights to their sovereignty, property, and person and that they therefore deserved protection from forced labor on the agricultural enterprises known as *encomiendas*. Implicit in all of this, of course, was the more general question of the rights of any non-European people. Thus, a tortuous irony still attends the fact that early in his campaign in defense of the Amerindians, Las Casas had asked Charles V to send black African slaves to labor in the West Indies in their stead.

Around 1547, however, during a visit to Lisbon, Las Casas appears to have experienced an epiphany which disillusioned him regarding the new institution of black African slavery (see Gutiérrez 319–30). When he previously had advocated replacing the Amerindians on the Caribbean plantations with black Africans, he had assumed that the slave status of the latter was the result of legitimate religious warfare. In Lisbon he learned that the Portuguese had advanced the lucrative trade in African slaves such that they paid one tribe to sell them the members of another, thus promoting warfare among African tribes not for any religious reason but simply as a means of obtaining slaves that they could then sell for profit. Las Casas did not publish the following passage in his lifetime; still, it indicates that the priest realized that black African slavery had crossed a moral line. Characteristically referring to himself in the third person, he admits to his error while doubting that his soul will be spared damnation:

> Deste aviso que dió el clérigo, no poco después se halló arrepiso, juzgándose culpado por inadvertente, porque como después vido y averiguó, según parecerá, ser tan injusto el captiverio de los negros como el de los indios, no fué discreto remedio el que aconsejó que se trujesen negros para que se libertasen los indios, aunque él suponía que eran justamente captivos, aunque no estuvo cierto que la ignorancia que en esto tuvo y buena voluntad lo excusase delante el juicio divino. (3.129.275)

> This advice, which the priest gave, he soon found that he regretted, judging himself inadvertently guilty. As he later learned and verified, it appears that blacks were enslaved as unjustly as the Indians had been. Imprudent was his previous remedy to turn to blacks in order to liberate the Indians. Even if he made the recommendation supposing that the blacks had been justly captured, it was not clear that this ignorance, nor the good will he proclaimed on behalf of the Indians, would be of any benefit to his soul before divine justice.

Two decades after Las Casas's *Brevísima relación de la destrucción de las Indias*, another distinguished jurist and historian from the School of Salamanca, Bartolomé de Albornoz (c.1519–73), published *Arte de los contractos* (Valencia, 1573). In this manual for theologians, confessors, judges, lawyers, scribes, and merchants, Albornoz condemned not just trade in slaves but the entire institution of slavery. *Arte de los contractos* eventually found its way onto the list of books banned by the Inquisition, a good indication of the text's radicality. We should also note that Albornoz dedicated his manual to the late scholastic Diego Covarrubias y Leiva (see the famous portrait by El Greco), arguably the most powerful man in all of sixteenth-century Spain. So, the School of Salamanca produced more than a sporadic set of contradictory opinions about slavery. Moreover, the political stature and global impact of figures like Covarrubias, Vitoria, and Las Casas indicate that the School of Salamanca provided an early impulse to a substantial line of abolitionist thinkers. Notice, too, that for both the Bishop of Chiapas and Albornoz, certain philosophical, ethical, moral, and theological considerations overlap economic ones. This is another characteristic of the School of Salamanca.

Given that important members of the School of Salamanca criticized slavery, recent speculation by Mercedes Agulló y Cobo that Diego Hurtado de

Mendoza (1503–75) authored the early picaresque novel *Lazarillo de Tormes* (c.1554) gains context and is even more compelling. If Professor Agulló is correct, Mendoza exemplifies that liberal combination of humanism and scholasticism that characterized the first half of the sixteenth century. One of the University of Salamanca's most remarkable graduates, Mendoza knew Latin, Greek, Hebrew, and Arabic, not to mention a handful of modern European languages. He was also a serious critic of the repression of the Moriscos. Mendoza voices open disgust in *Historia de la guerra de Granada* (publ.1610) about the handling of the Morisco uprising during the Alpujarras War of 1568–71. In sum, the anonymous *Lazarillo de Tormes* displays the kind of Erasmian and pro-Morisco satire we might expect from Mendoza. Just as importantly, given his expansive classical education, Mendoza would have understood that the picaresque genre of narrative fiction was by definition abolitionist via Apuleius.

Regardless of who authored *Lazarillo de Tormes*, the genre that Cervantes chose is fundamentally antislavery in both its classical and its early modern iterations. The chaos surrounding Sancho's ass in part one of *Don Quijote* accords with its deployment as an antislavery trope inherited from Apuleius. The same attitude appears in the elaborate Erasmian and pro-Morisco programs of part two. *Lazarillo de Tormes* and *Don Quijote*, then, are late-Renaissance texts that mediate between Apuleius's *The Golden Ass* and eighteenth- and nineteenth-century abolitionist classics by the likes of Voltaire, Poe, Böhl de Faber, and Twain. These are all examples of a specific type of satirical narrative that posits slavery as the moral issue of the day.

Any credible explanation of the significance of slavery in *Don Quijote* should note the allusions to the theme, assess its complications over the course of the novel, and then explain its overarching function. Let's now look at some of the prominent allusions to the slavery theme in *Don Quijote*. These may seem randomly distributed throughout the text; however, I will argue that Cervantes's reflections and impressions are woven together in a more purposeful way so as to ultimately have implications for theoretical economics.

(1) SLAVERY, LOVE, AND FEUDALISM

Inevitably, symbols and protocols in *Don Quijote* overlap. Love, for example, is a dominant theme which frequently directs our attention toward other themes. The idea that everything from carnal to conjugal desire in a text also signifies something else should not surprise students of literature and philosophy. In the classical epics by Homer and Virgil, and the anonymous

Poema de mio Cid (c.1200), Paris's abduction of Helen, Aeneas's affair with Dido, and the Cid's devotion to Ximena either cause, represent, or resolve major conflicts between Greece and Troy, Rome and Carthage, and Burgos and León. Similarly, picaresque, byzantine, chivalric, and sentimental novels from the classical and early modern periods deploy love stories while also voicing sophisticated social and political commentary. Examples useful for understanding these tendencies in *Don Quijote* include Apuleius's *The Golden Ass* (c.175), Heliodorus's *Aethiopica* (c.250 or c.363), Juan Ruiz's *Libro de buen amor* (1343), Boccaccio's *Decameron* (1353), Diego de San Pedro's *Cárcel de amor* (1492), Fernando de Rojas's *La Celestina* (c.1499), Garci Rodríguez de Montalvo's *Amadís de Gaula* (1508), and *Lazarillo de Tormes* (c.1554).

The same can be said of philosophy, theology, and lyric. Model texts for Cervantes would include Plato's *Symposium* (c.385 BCE), Dante's *Divina comedia* (1320), Petrarch's *Canzoniere* (1336), León Hebreo's *Diálogos de amor* (c.1502), Garcilaso de la Vega's *Obras completas* (1543), and San Juan de la Cruz's *Cántico espiritual* (c.1584), all of which posit love as a transcendental force that provides cosmic direction to the material universe.

Early in *Don Quijote*, Cervantes connects courtly love to the slavery theme via the metaphor of the feudal bond. The mad hidalgo grants Dulcinea «título de señora de sus pensamientos» "the title of mistress over his thoughts" (1.1.44). Later, in his silly flirtation with the innkeeper Palomeque's daughter, Don Quijote indicates that, like feudalism, courtly love is a mode of slavery: «plugiera a los altos cielos que el amor no me tuviera tan rendido y tan sujeto a sus leyes, y los ojos de aquella hermosa ingrata que digo entre mis dientes: que los desta fermosa doncella fueran señores de mi libertad» "if it were not the will of the heavens that love should hold me so defeated and subject to its laws, then, instead of the eyes of that beauteous ingrate whose name I pronounce between clinched teeth, those of the beauteous damsel of this castle would be the lords of my freedom" (1.16.170). In *DQ* 1.22, the hero puts in motion a metaphor for himself by unchaining the galley slaves and ordering them to go pay homage to Dulcinea. Similarly, the chain on Cardenio's valise signals his love for Luscinda in *DQ* 1.23. Five chapters later, Dorotea refuses to be Fernando's slave: «Tu vasalla soy, pero no tu esclava» "I am your vassal, but not your slave" (1.28.325). And eight chapters after that, she changes her mind: «admíteme por tu esclava» "accept me as your slave" (1.36.428). A common way to gauge men's gentlemanliness in *Don Quijote* is by way of women's relative willingness to subject themselves to them.

Beginning in *DQ* 1.29, all of these love stories occur against the backdrop of Sancho's nefarious fantasy to get rich by selling the black African citizens of Micomicón as chattel slaves in Spain. Likewise, love, slavery, and freedom are at the heart of the interethnic romance between Viedma and Zoraida in "The Captive's Tale" of *DQ* 1.39–41 (see Murillo). Yet another Christian-Morisca love story caps a series of contrasts between slavery and freedom in part two. At Camacho's wedding, the allegorical figure representing *Interest* attempts to steal a damsel from *Love* by throwing «una gran cadena de oro al cuello» "a great chain of gold over her neck" (2.20.798). Sancho later figures Basilio and Quiteria as if they were Jews escaping slavery in the Book of Exodus, leaving behind them «las ollas de Egipto» "the fleshpots of Egypt," (2.21.808). The Countess Trifaldi compares the love between Antonomasia and Don Clavijo to Samson's chains (2.38.945). Likely named after the slave in Aeschylus's *Persians*, Tosilos accepts Doña Rodríguez's daughter as «señora de su libertad» "mistress of his liberty" (2.56.1086). These love stories then climax in the interethnic romance between Ana Félix and Don Gregorio in *DQ* 2.64–65.

What's going on here? Cervantes exploits love stories in order to focus our attention on social and political problems. Erotic desire is the gateway to respect for one's fellow human beings. A Neoplatonic philosopher might say "*eros* leads to *agape*." Opposed to both black African slavery and the Expulsion of the Moriscos, Cervantes writes narratives of miscegenation and turns Don Quijote's love for Dulcinea into a lesson about miscegenation as well as a lesson on restraining imperialist and colonialist impulses. Thus, both parts of the novel end with symbolic cages related to Dulcinea. In part one, Don Quijote returns home in a cage, accepting the prophecy that he and Dulcinea will marry and procreate; in part two, Sancho places a small cage for crickets in Don Quijote's hands as the hidalgo agonizes over whether or not he will ever see Dulcinea again. And Cervantes's most memorable love story is also one of miscegenation. Like Zoraida and Ana Félix, the real Dulcinea is often figured as a Morisca (Aldonza Lorenzo). Like El Greco and Velázquez, Cervantes rejects the new racialist mode of slavery. Thus, Sancho's ugly fantasy of selling the citizens of the African Kingdom of Micomicón as slaves in *DQ* 1.29 and his poetic punishment in *DQ* 2.63 at the hands of another group of galley slaves.

(2) JOANNES LATINUS

The first Latin quote in the first prologue signals the theme of personal liberty in *Don Quijote*: «Non bene pro toto libertas venditur auro» "Liberty is not sold for all the world's gold" (1.pro.14). Confirming the importance of this Latin phrase, the next allusion to slavery is a reference to Joannes Latinus (1518–96) in the first of the dedicatory poems entitled «Al libro de Don Quijote de la Mancha, Urganda la desconocida» "To the Book *Don Quijote de la Mancha*, Urganda the Unknown." As the poem's voice, Urganda directs an apostrophe to the novel, telling it to stop presuming to be versed in Latin, «Como el negro Juan Lati[no]» "Like the black Juan Lati[no]" (v.43). Latinus was a black African slave in the household of the Duke of Sessa, who later rose to become a professor and poet of Latin at the University of Granada. Notice the overlap of abolitionist and feminist themes, for Latino is presented to us by way of the poem by Urganda, the chivalric witch and protectress of Amadís of Gaul. In this way, Cervantes anticipates the shared agendas of abolitionism and feminism in narratives by the likes of María de Zayas (1590–61), Gertrudis Gómez de Avellaneda (1814–73), and Cecilia Böhl de Faber (1796–1877).

By citing Joannes Latinus, Cervantes also alludes to the Battle of Lepanto (1571), as he will do again most prominently in "The Captive's Tale" (*DQ* 1.39). Latinus famously penned the epic poem *Austrias Carmen* (1573), which celebrated Don Juan de Austria's victory over the Turkish fleet in Latin hexameters. The reference to Joannes Latinus in the first prologue of *Don Quijote*—which Cervantes wrote last, i.e., as a reflection on part one— fuses together a contrast between two of the novel's major types of slavery: (1) slavery as a consequence of race, such as that at the crux of Sancho's Micomicón fantasy in *DQ* 1.29, and (2) slavery as a consequence of military defeat, such as that described in "The Captive's Tale" in *DQ* 1.39–41. Moreover, Latinus embodies the complexity of a black African slave with the literary pretentions of a new Virgil. He begins *Austrias Carmen* by lamenting the fate of the Moriscos defeated by Don Juan de Austria in the Alpujarras War (1568–71) just prior to Lepanto. He concludes the poem with the sons of the defeated Ottoman Admiral Ali Pasha bemoaning their new slave status.

More than irony, however, Cervantes's reference to Joannes Latinus likely contains criticism regarding a specific tactical advantage that Don Juan de Austria tried to exploit just prior to the Battle of Lepanto. According to Crowley, Don Juan "promised liberation for all the Christian galley slaves if they fought well, and ordered their shackles to be removed. It was in fact a promise that he could not guarantee, as only the oarsmen on his own ships were within his gift" (261). Writing in 1883, William Stirling-Maxwell described the same event by way of a dynamic contrast:

> Throughout the fleet the Christian slaves had their fetters knocked off and were furnished with arms, which they were encouraged to use valiantly by promises of freedom and rewards. Of the Muslims slaves, on the contrary, the chains which secured them to their places were carefully examined and their rivets secured; and they were, besides, fitted with handcuffs, to disable them from using their hands for any purpose but tugging at the oar. (1.404, qtd. by Hanson 258)

Likewise in Latinus's poetic version of the Battle of Lepanto, the Christian slaves are heroes, the promise of their liberty should be fulfilled, and captivity is more the destiny of the vanquished Ottomans. Himself a hero of the battle celebrated by *Austrias Carmen*, Cervantes appears to have recognized Latinus's critical take on the promise of freedom in the clash of civilizations off the coast of Greece on 7 October 1571.

(3) ANDRÉS AND HALDUDO

By contrast, Don Quijote's encounter with the shepherd boy Andrés and his peasant master Juan Haldudo in *DQ* 1.4 has an abstract tone to it. A struggle emerges from the primeval forest not unlike that of the master-slave allegory in Hegel's *Phenomenology of Spirit* (108–16). Haldudo is whipping Andrés. For his part, Andrés complains that he is owed back pay. So, although the scene suggests folkloric elements akin to the boy who cried wolf, Cervantes's materialism folds into the mix the decay of feudalism and the rise of the bourgeoisie. Finally, we should note that this type of peasant slavery serves as an early and basic form of coerced labor in *Don Quijote*. The serfdom imposed on Andrés by Haldudo in *DQ* 1.4 gives the novel a circular structure when Sancho later whips himself in these same woods of La Mancha in *DQ* 2.71.

(4) GALLEY SLAVES

Cervantes's allusions to Joannes Latinus and the Battle of Lepanto form part of a larger, coordinated series of reflections on galley slaves. The galley slaves who rebel in the Sierra Morena in *DQ* 1.22, the prominence of galley slaves in "The Captive's Tale" in *DQ* 2.39–41, and the final revenge of the galley slaves in *DQ* 2.63 underscore the mode of slavery that Cervantes ponders apart from the others. At first glance, there might not seem to be any racial component to galley slavery. Nevertheless, given the race of Joannes Latinus, given that Sancho's major sin in part one was his desire to enslave black Africans, and given that more galley slaves take revenge on him in part two, there's good reason to suspect that a racial element lurks alongside the galley slave theme. Moreover, when Ginés de Pasamonte explicitly cites *Lazarillo de Tormes*, a text in which race plays a big role, he mingles race into the galley slave motif. Still, Cervantes seems to focus more on galley slaves regardless of any racial affiliation, i.e., as if they belonged to their own special category. Their textual frequency argues that they differ from other types of slaves in the novel and that they carry greater theoretical significance for the author.

(5) THE KINGDOM OF MICOMICÓN

Overt satire of specifically race-based slavery is found in Sancho's nefarious fantasy of ruling over the legendary equatorial African Kingdom of Micomicón in *DQ* 1.29. Sancho is at one of his lower moral points in the narrative when he hits on the idea of getting rich by selling the future subjects of his kingdom as slaves:

> . . . solo le daba pesadumbre el pensar que aquel reino era en tierra de negros y que la gente que por sus vasallos le diesen habían de ser todos negros; a lo cual hizo luego en su imaginación un buen remedio, y díjose a sí mismo: «¿Qué se me da a mí que mis vasallos sean negros? ¿Habrá más que cargar con ellos y traerlos a España, donde los podré vender, y adonde me pagarán de contado? . . . y que, por negros que sean, los he de volver blancos o amarillos». (1.29.340)

> The only thing he regretted was the thought that the kingdom was in a land of blacks and that the people who were to be given to him as vassals would all be blacks; for which he then came up with an excellent remedy in his imagination, saying to himself: "What difference does it make to me if my vassals be black? Need I do anything more than load them up and ship them off to Spain, where I can sell them, and where they'll pay me cash? . . . for as black as they may be, I'll turn them back into white or yellow."

Here the narrator underscores Sancho Panza's satisfaction by referring again to his lost ass, noting that he no longer misses it: «Con esto andaba tan solícito y tan contento, que se le olvidaba la pesadumbre de caminar a pie» "With that he strutted about so eager and so satisfied that he forgot his regret at having to walk on foot" (1.29.340). It's a symbolic inversion for readers familiar with the metamorphosis in *The Golden Ass*, in which Lucius's return to bipedalism matches his rejection of the animalistic nature of the institution of slavery.

So, there are many layers of meaning in Sancho's slaver fantasy in *DQ* 1.29. First, the squire's strangely intermittent ass alludes to the major symbol of the picaresque (see Graf, "The Economy of Asses"). The squire adds a racial contrast by emphasizing the black skin of the citizens of Micomicón, whom he figuratively hopes to turn white (silver) and yellow (gold). Sancho's slaver fantasy from part one is reprised in part two in Doña Rodríguez's story about her husband's service to a particularly brutal duchess. Once again, Cervantes combines the theme of race and a figurative ass: «llevaba a mi señora a las ancas de una poderosa mula, negra como el mismo azabache» "he carried my Lady on the haunches of a powerful she-mule, as black as jet" (2.48.1019). *El coloquio de los perros* (c.1605) also folds the theme of race into a botched metamorphosis. Together, these three narratives told by

Sancho, Doña Rodríguez, and Berganza are good examples of the black and white racial dynamic that Cervantes understood to be a particular feature of the Spanish picaresque, especially *Lazarillo de Tormes*.

Sancho's slaver fantasy goes a step further, however, than Apuleius and the anonymous author of *Lazarillo de Tormes*. He expands the themes of race and slavery by linking them to the theme of monetary policy. Specifically, Sancho plans to turn black money, that is, coins that are oxidized due to their high copper content, back into gold and silver money, that is, those coins that preserve their value against the official policy of destroying the purchasing power of other coins by increasing their copper content. Again, Cervantes does the same thing in *El coloquio de los perros* by alluding to counterfeiters and alchemy in a tale that is all about ethnic confusion (see Graf, "La antropología subversiva"). Sancho's nefarious comment in *DQ* 1.29 even allows a link back to the brutality Haldudo shows Andrés in *DQ* 1.4, because silver and copper coins were at issue there too. Cervantes's triple trope of race, slavery, and monetary policy is a dazzling compounded Baroque criticism of the new copper coinage. Writing around the same time, Mariana offered two parts of this triangular metaphor by figuring monetary policy as a kind of tyranny and by figuring tyranny as a kind of slavery. Just as alchemy is a perversion of metallurgical laws, the hidden slavery induced by inflationary policy is a monstrous and tyrannical distortion of the laws of politics, economics, and nature (see this book's appendix).

(6) "THE CAPTIVE'S TALE," ANA FÉLIX, AND DON GREGORIO

According to Cervantes scholar Luis Andrés Murillo, the autobiographical aspects of "The Captive's Tale" indicate it was conceived as an early endpoint for part one of *Don Quijote*. Thus, Cervantes's personal experience is a major factor in his criticism of slavery. But there is also an important symbolic contrast between the former slave Captain Viedma and the novel's surplus of unstable male lovers. Viedma is an exemplary gentleman, sane and noble; opposite the series of imbalanced lovers of the Sierra Morena, especially Cardenio, Grisóstomo, Fernando, and Anselmo, but also the delusional Don Quijote. Viedma's personal liberation with the help of Zoraida in "The Captive's Tale" is reprised in part two in the adventures of Ana Félix and Don Gregorio. These are classic Mediterranean miscegenation tales, technically speaking, "interpolated byzantine romances," according to which a Mooress (Zoraida) and a Morisca (Ana Félix) are enamored of Old Christians (Viedma and Gregorio). And historically speaking, they function like amorous balms for the hatred and violence of the Alpujarras War. We should also keep in mind that significant passages in these stories involve galley warfare, and so galley slaves underwrite the major salvific love narratives of both parts of the novel.

(7) OLD SOLDIERS AND BLACK AFRICAN SLAVES

Don Quijote compares old forgotten soldiers to old manumitted slaves who are only freed when they can no longer work: «no es bien que se haga con ellos lo que suelen hacer los que ahorran y dan libertad a sus negros cuando ya son viejos y no pueden servir» "it is not right to deal with them like those who routinely cut their expenses by granting freedom to their blacks when they are old and can no longer serve" (2.24.835). This criticism of the new race-based slavery is a reprise of part one's criticism of black African slavery in the gradual dissolution of Sancho's Micomicón fantasy. The logic entails a recognition of injustice by Cervantes, and it is grounded in an autobiographical identification between the forgotten author-soldier and the black African slave. In addition to the slavery theme's consistent racial register, *Don Quijote* discloses a personal grievance, a sense that this new mode of slavery is a kind of national betrayal. Like the allusion to Latino, this passage provides a specific counterweight to the newest version of the ancient institution of bondage.

(8) SANCHO'S PAY

Professors Carroll Johnson and David Quint have fine-tuned Maravall's and Lucáks's earlier materialist approaches to *Don Quijote* by focusing respectively on the drama of Sancho Panza's quest for a salary from Don Quijote and on the novel's constant emphasis on bourgeois values. Accordingly, Don Quijote has to renounce his self-indulgent tendency to embrace violent pillage and learn instead to pay for goods and services. This simple idea is especially visible in the knight's relationship with his squire. Over the course of the novel, Don Quijote learns that an island governorship will not suffice when it comes to incentivizing Sancho Panza. When he first entices Sancho to accompany him, Don Quijote dangles before him future power and a share in the booty and conquest: «Decíale entre otras cosas don Quijote que se dispusiese a ir con él de buena gana, porque tal vez le podía suceder aventura que ganase, en quítame allá esas pajas, alguna ínsula, y le dejase a él por gobernador della. Con estas promesas y otras tales, Sancho Panza, que así se llamaba el labrador, dejó su mujer y hijos y asentó por escudero de su vecino» "Don Quijote told him, among other things, that he should prepare himself to go with him with enthusiasm, because perhaps an adventure would come upon them that would win, in the blink of an eye, some isle, and that he would grant it to him to be its governor. With these promises and others of a similar vein, Sancho Panza, for this was the name of the laborer, left his wife and children and agreed to be his neighbor's squire" (1.7.91). By the end of part two, the knight is forced to accept unit pricing and favorable terms for the lashes that Sancho agrees to give himself in order to free Dulcinea from enchantment. Thus, at least one specific type of slavery in *Don Quijote* becomes a labor market.

For his part, at the end of part two, Sancho embodies nothing short of an economic miracle. A man who repeatedly claims to be illiterate displays staggering mathematical skills when it comes to getting paid for his labor. Sancho is often misrepresented as mistreated and exploited, especially in part two, and yet, according to his various agreements with Don Quijote, and including the various sums of money he finds, steals, or receives from others, it has been calculated that the squire takes home some 5,264 *reales*, which is on the order of ten times his normal annual income as a peasant laborer (Graf, "The Economy of Asses" 280). It's not that critics of Cervantes like Johnson, Maravall, or Lucáks are necessarily off the mark when they read the early modern novel as a textual manifestation of the triumph of the bourgeoisie, it's just that they fail to acknowledge that the transition from serf status to independent contractor is actually quite good to Sancho.

(9) THE SHE-WOLF AND HER PREY: ECONOMICS AND SLAVERY IN CERVANTES AND SMITH

Cervantes weaves together so many perspectives on master-slave relationships in *Don Quijote* that inevitably he drifts toward abstract and speculative thinking on the topic. There's servitude as a metaphor for love, for example, whereby crazy men are captivated by their objects of desire. We see this in Don Quijote's devotion to Dulcinea in *DQ* 1.1 or Tosilos's enchantment by the daughter of Doña Rodríguez in *DQ* 2.56. In Torralba's fixation on Lope Ruiz in *DQ* 1.20 or Altisidora's obsession with Don Quijote in *DQ* 2.70, we see that women are also prone to a kind of amorous captivity. There are, however, more mundane forms of bondage, such as punishment for criminals or a consequence of naval warfare in the Mediterranean, which can be seen in the galley slaves in *DQ* 1.22, Captain Viedma's tale in *DQ* 1.39–41, or the story of Ana Félix in *DQ* 2.63–65.

A fourth type of slavery, the new transatlantic trade in black Africans, appears in three places in *Don Quijote*: Urganda's nod to the black African poet Johannes Latinus in the first dedicatory poem (v.43); Sancho Panza's plan to sell the black Africans of the Kingdom of Micomicón into slavery in *DQ* 1.29; and Don Quijote's angry remark about the mistreatment of old black African slaves in *DQ* 2.24. Cervantes's attitude against slavery is fairly explicit and consistent. Reserving slavery for criminals and prisoners of war allows for abuse and corruption, and the addition of the element of race adds another injustice.

In sixteenth- and seventeenth-century Spain, slavery and labor were topics studied and debated in technical and theoretical terms by intellectuals, theologians, jurists, and sometimes activists of the School of Salamanca. Bartolomé de las Casas's *Brevísima relación de la destrucción de las Indias* (1542, publ.1552) and Bartolomé Albornoz's *Arte de los contractos* (1573) are two good examples of late-scholastic texts that denounce the injustices of the institution of slavery. A century later, the Capuchin Francisco José Jaca wrote *Resolución sobre la libertad de los negros y sus originarios en estado de paganos y después ya cristianos* (Havana, 1681), which, in the words of Peruvian liberation theologian Gustavo Gutiérrez, "can be regarded as the most extensive and spirited abolitionist call of the time" (323). These texts represent the early modern stages of an abolitionist movement that would take three centuries to win out in countries like the United States (1863) and Brazil (1888). And the broad influence of this early modern Hispanic debate about human rights should not be underestimated. As Leonard Liggio once noted, "The expansion of rights theory which reached its heights from Locke to the American Revolution was founded on the rights debates which were introduced to Spain from the New World" (14).

Like Aquinas, the late scholastics of the School of Salamanca can be characterized by their deference to Aristotle, who was their preferred pagan philosopher, especially when making arguments based on natural law. Nevertheless, during the full flowering of the Renaissance, even Aristotle could be questioned, and often using Aristotle himself. For example, early modern theorists, many of them scholastics, recognized multiple and ancient justifications for slavery, including war, birth, debt, and crime—a list to which medieval Christian, Jewish, and Islamic doctrine had added heresy. Las Casas pointed out that most of these did not apply in the case of the Amerindians. But it's also true that Las Casas based much of his defense of the Amerindians on a pluralistic sense of international law, which, in turn, had its own roots in Aristotle's comparative survey in the *Politics* of the political regimes of different nations in the ancient Mediterranean world.

In his *De Indis* (1532) and *De Jure belli Hispanorum in barbaros* (1532), Francisco de Vitoria took particular aim at the more recent justification of slavery by way of heresy. He argued that since Christianity had not been properly demonstrated to the indigenous populations of the New World, the Amerindians were not heretics even if they still refused to accept the faith (Gutiérrez 244). Essentially, Vitoria allowed that Spanish cruelty and hypocrisy had sustained and amplified the notion of "invincible ignorance," whereby Amerindians who had not yet heard the gospel could not be condemned to the same degree as apostates, Jews, or Muslims. These are also the basic contours of Las Casas's more hyperbolic *Brevísima relación de la destrucción de las Indias*, written a decade later. Like Vitoria, Las Casas argues that the Amerindians have been alienated from Christianity by the barbarous and decidedly unchristian behavior of so many conquistadores and colonists.

Vitoria's and Las Casas's arguments take the last remnants of the medieval religious justification for slavery off the table, leaving international law as the only grounds for rational argument, the basis of which is natural law. Thus, Spaniards arriving in the New World could not assume sovereignty over the Amerindians, nor could they lay claim to their persons or their property.

A simple example of a natural law in *Don Quijote* is the right to self-defense. Sancho hints at this law early in the novel when, in the act of dismissing the chivalric laws of his master, he claims that divine and human laws have already granted him the right to resist force: «Bien es verdad que en lo que tocare a defender mi persona no tendré mucha cuenta con esas leyes, pues las divinas y humanas permiten que cada uno se defienda de quien quisiere agraviarle» "It is true enough that, when it comes to defending my person, I will not pay much attention to those laws, for laws both divine and human permit everyone to defend himself from whomever might wish to harm him" (1.8.99). Toward the end of part two, the squire resists his master's attempt to lash him by performing a jujitsu maneuver and pinning Don Quijote to the ground under his knee. He then proclaims his independence: «ayúdome a mí, que soy mi señor» "I help myself, for I am my own lord" (2.60.1118). Here we have the natural law of self-defense in action along with an assertion of individualism and autonomy.

Sancho's phrase borrows on the symbolism of the civil war between Pedro I, known as *el Cruel* "the Cruel" or *el Justo* "the Just," depending on your perspective, and Enrique II, known as *el Caballero* "the Gentleman" or *el Fratricida* "the Fratricide," again, depending on your perspective. Cervantes's allusion to the relativistic ethical contrast between opposing kings signals that Sancho's struggle for personal political autonomy is very much the question at hand as we near the novel's denouement. But it's more than that. Ultimately, Sancho's struggle articulates what is perhaps Cervantes's most theoretical criticism of the institution of slavery.

The squire's assertions of his natural right to self-defense can be better understood when we read them in conjunction with two of his other tendencies: (1) his constant requests for a contractual salary from Don Quijote and (2) his repeated difficulties with slaves. In the first case, Sancho plots a trajectory from medieval serf to free participant in the early modern labor market, indicating a shift in thinking about labor that moves away from coercion and toward voluntary negotiation. In the end, having pinned his master to the ground under his knee in *DQ* 2.60, Sancho subsequently repairs the relationship by negotiating a per unit labor contract in *DQ* 2.71. Note how this signals a connection between political and economic modes of autonomy.

With regard to the second case, simultaneous to Sancho's transformation of himself from a slave into someone who charges a just price for his services, he also has to learn that it is wrong to enslave others. His horrid plans for the citizens of the legendary equatorial African Kingdom of Micomicón combines with his encounters with aggressive groups of galley slaves in both parts of the novel in order to situate Sancho at the center of the slavery issue. Additionally, Andrés and Sancho make for a thematic narrative circle: master lashes slave in the woods of La Mancha in *DQ* 1.4 and then employee lashes himself and then trees for money in those same woods of La Mancha in *DQ* 2.71. This sequence is comical but also suggests something theoretical or primordial, not unlike Hegel's allegory of the master and the slave (see Kojève). In the context of Don Quijote's recent declaration on liberty—«uno de los más preciosos dones que a los hombres dieron los cielos» "one of the most precious gifts that the heavens gave to men" (2.58.1094)—, Sancho's struggle confirms Cervantes scholar Luis Rosales's observation that «la libertad es, justamente, el eje mismo del pensamiento cervantino» "liberty is, precisely, the very axis of Cervantes's thinking" (33). It also provides good supporting evidence for Luis Andrés Murillo's observation that "The Captive's Tale," with its heavy doses of slavery and autobiography, is the original endpoint of Cervantes's exemplary narrative. We are adding the element of salary to an already solid base of the theme of liberty in *Don Quijote*.

When thinking about *Don Quijote*, the School of Salamanca, Aristotle, and slavery, we cannot avoid Cervantes's early and fairly blatant references to the *Politics*. The premise—a mentally unstable noble is mismanaging his estate by selling off his property to buy chivalric novels—is a monstrous and imbalanced version of Aristotle's analogy between the political economy of a healthy city-state and the productive management of a gentleman's estate. It is in this same vein that Cervantes establishes a contrast in part two between two types of hidalgo: the arrogant, irrational, and impoverished Don Quijote versus the humble, methodical, and affluent Don Diego de Miranda. The idea is already in the first chapter of part one. Describing Don Quijote's insanity as adversely affecting his capacity to behave like a proper gentleman, i.e., to hunt and to manage his estate—«olvidó casi de todo punto el ejercicio de la caza y aun la administración de su hacienda» "he forgot almost every aspect of the exercise of the hunt and the administration of his estate" (1.1.37)—, the narrator next tells us that the old man's difficulties understanding certain intricate chivalric phrases place him beyond the assistance of even the greatest philosopher that ever lived: «ni las entendiera el mesmo Aristóteles si resucitara para solo ello» "nor could Aristotle himself have understood them even if he were to come back to life for just that purpose" (1.1.38). This second, explicit allusion to Aristotle the rhetorician echoes the only marginally disguised allusion to Aristotle the political economist.

Given Cervantes's heavy dependence on Aristotle's metaphor of the nobleman properly managing his estate, when we think more specifically about labor and servitude in *Don Quijote*, we cannot avoid Aristotle's problematical distinction between two types of slavery at the heart of book one of the *Politics*: "where the relation of master and slave between them is natural they are friends and have a common interest, but where it rests merely on law and force the reverse is true" (1.6). Modern readers often mistake Aristotle's point as somehow racist, as if he were arguing that non-Greeks deserved slavery more than the Greeks. What Aristotle means by natural slavery, however, is an economic relationship that is relatively devoid of coercion. As Michael Palmer notes, "the relationship between a 'natural master' and a 'natural slave' would be one of mutual advantage and friendship, which is not possible between a master and a slave of the other (i.e., 'conventional') sort" (4). What Aristotle means by natural slavery, then, is not slavery but, rather, voluntary exchange of labor for food, housing, military protection, etc. Aristotle envisions a cooperative scheme, a formal way of implementing what an economist might call "comparative advantage," all in the hopes of more efficiently managing an agricultural enterprise. Curiously, Aristotle's ideal estate is one that is self-sufficient via the proper employment of subordinates and slaves such that the owner can then dedicate himself to other pursuits, especially politics and philosophy (Palmer 4).

I would argue that Cervantes creates a fictional network of economic and political ideas in *Don Quijote* that we can organize in relation to Aristotle's fundamental contrast between natural and conventional slaveries. The ideas of later generations about labor and slavery are also helpful when describing Cervantes's perspective. Whereas Albornoz, Las Casas, and Aristotle are logical points of departure for approaching the novelist's understanding of slavery, later neoclassical and romantic liberals, like Thomas Hobbes,

Voltaire, Adam Smith, and David Ricardo, indicate directions the novelist anticipated.

Hobbes, for example, was a very careful reader of Cervantes in a number of respects, so it might be no coincidence that the English political philosopher described labor as market-priced like any other commodity (see Graf, "Martin and the Ghosts of the Papacy"). The lesson of Sancho's quest for a salary is echoed in Hobbes's harsh materialism: "The value or worth of a man, is as of all other things his price—that is to say, so much as would be given for the use of his power" (10.63).

Voltaire, too, was a close reader of Cervantes. Similar to key moments in *Don Quijote, Candide* drives home the particular shame of black African slavery in the West Indies: "they came on a Negro lying on the ground half-naked . . . missing his left leg and his right hand," at which point the double amputee declares, "This is the price you pay for the sugar you eat in Europe," at which point Candide finally renounces Pangloss's optimism (53–54). This stark depiction of a major moral pivot in Voltaire's satire recalls both the dissolution of the squire's slaver fantasy in part one of *Don Quijote* and the elderly hidalgo's empathy for old black African slaves in part two.

David Ricardo's thinking on slavery reveals that, like Voltaire, he was an abolitionist in reaction to the abuses of the Caribbean sugar plantations. In terms of his political economy, Ricardo extended Hobbesian realism about labor in pessimistic directions. His "iron law of rents," which John Stuart Mill once called the *pons asinorum* of economics (qtd. by MacLeod 96), seemed to have dark consequences for the compensation of human labor. In the gloomy company of his friend Malthus, who argued that populations constantly outrun their food supplies, Ricardo perhaps glimpsed how human beings might be turned into mere natural resources with rigidly predetermined values. However the case may have been, according to economic historian Peter Groenewegen: "befitting the husband of a Quaker, he confessed that 'he was inclined to blush with shame, to hide his face, when West-India slavery was mentioned'" (92n7). Ricardo deplored slavery as "infamous," "shocking" and "abominable" in his address of 19 March 1823 to the directors of the East India Company (*Works* 483). He also criticized slavery in a speech to Parliament during the 1823 debate on West and East Indian Sugar duties (297, 300).

In *Don Quijote*, we can see philosophical thinking about labor markets, slavery, and race beginning to converge in early seventeenth-century Europe. Later, Hobbes, Voltaire, and Ricardo make for good comparisons because they examined questions like those raised earlier by the novelist. But Cervantes's ultimate understanding of work and slavery might best be understood as resonating with the economic analysis of Adam Smith. Thinking about competing modes of labor, the Scottish philosopher was far more optimistic than Hobbes or Ricardo. *An Inquiry into the Nature and Causes of the Wealth of Nations* contains the following: "It appears, accordingly, from the experience of all ages and nations, I believe, that the work done by free men comes cheaper in the end than the work performed by slaves" (1.8.83). It might still be counterintuitive to some, but Smith reasoned that labor which is induced by compensation will generally be more efficient than labor which is coerced by force and violence. A carrot works better than a stick.

Cervantes directs readers toward a similar idea in "The Captive's Tale" of *DQ* 1.39–41. Of all the types of slavery on display in *Don Quijote*, there is a clear preponderance of galley slaves. This overweighting of galley slaves has specific moral and political implications. If we are to unravel the implications of this, it's worth recalling that just prior to the Battle of Lepanto (1571), Don Juan de Austria rashly promised freedom to more galley slaves than was his right. This helps explain why, textually speaking, Cervantes allows Viedma to voice disillusionment with Habsburg rule in the wake of the Battle of Lepanto. The moral cost of the victory was too high. In this light, the mutinous behavior of galley slaves throughout *Don Quijote* can read like a running poetic objection to Don Juan's betrayal of countless galley slaves at Lepanto. Moreover, many of the Christian galley slaves were captive Moriscos from the Alpujarras Rebellion (1570–71), which Don Juan had finally repressed earlier that year. A minority of intellectuals of the period, like Johannes Latinus and Diego Hurtado de Mendoza, would disapprove of the mistreatment of the Moriscos (see Gates and Darst). Cervantes, too, writes with a pro-Morisco agenda, deploying transethnic characters like Zoraida, Dulcinea, Ricote, and Ana Félix to repair a national rift (see Márquez Villanueva, "El morisco Ricote").

At one point in his narrative, however, Cervantes moves from a moral and political assessment of the racism and injustice of slavery onto a more theoretical critique that considers slavery in more utilitarian terms. The idea that Don Juan de Austria's promise to the galley slaves might have influenced the outcome at Lepanto implies two competing systems of incentives. Reinforcing the connection between victory and freedom in the epic engagement that pitted Constantinople against the alliance among Spain, Venice, and the Papal States known as the Holy League, Viedma subsequently narrates a precise allegory that expresses the same proposition in miniature. It's naval warfare reduced to exemplary combat: Spaniard versus Turk, Bazán versus Barbarossa, barbarity versus civilization, winner versus loser. Yet Viedma underscores that the outcome hinges on one thing: how the two opposing captains treat their respective galley slaves.

> En este viaje se tomó la galera que se llamaba *La Presa*, de quien era capitán un hijo de aquel famoso corsario Barbarroja. Tomóla la capitana de Nápoles, lla-

mada *La Loba*, regida por aquel rayo de la guerra, por el padre de los soldados, por aquel venturoso y jamás vencido capitán don Álvaro de Bazán, marqués de Santa Cruz. Y no quiero dejar de decir lo que sucedió en la presa de *La Presa*. Era tan cruel el hijo de Barbarroja y trataba tan mal a sus cautivos, que así como los que venían al remo vieron que la galera *Loba* les iba entrando y que los alcanzaba, soltaron todos a un tiempo los remos y asieron de su capitán, que estaba sobre el estanterol gritando que bogasen apriesa, y pasándole de banco en banco, de popa a proa, le dieron bocados, que a poco más que pasó del árbol ya había pasado su ánima al infierno: tal era, como he dicho, la crueldad con que los trataba y el odio que ellos le tenían. (1.39.455–56)

On this voyage the galley *The Prey*, the captain of which was a son of that famous corsair Barbarossa, was taken by the flagship of Naples, known as *The She-Wolf*, commanded by that lightning bolt of war, that father to his soldiers, that victorious and never defeated Captain Don Álvaro de Bazán, the Marquis of Santa Cruz. And I don't want to forget to tell about what happened to *The Prey* when it became our prey. That son of Barbarossa was so cruel and he treated his captives so poorly that as soon as those who were at the oars saw that *The She-Wolf* was closing on them and overtaking them, they all at once threw down their oars and seized their captain, who was at his post shouting at them to row faster, and they threw him from bench to bench, from stern to bow, biting him so many times that by the time he reached the mast his soul was already in hell, so cruel was his treatment of them, as I have said, and so great was their hatred of him.

In a vision that is perhaps even more radically global than Smith's, here Cervantes figures freedom as predator and slavery as its prey. *La Loba* overtakes *La Presa* due specifically to the latter's Achilles' heel: its crew of abused galley slaves. Note also how Captain Viedma's story boils down to the contrasting philosophies of two captains. The essential conflict on display in the brief episode functions like an abstract, theoretical rebuttal of all forms of slavery. All other factors being equal, Cervantes says, the winning captain is paternal and beloved, the losing captain is tyrannical and cruel. And like the Scottish moral philosopher, the Spanish novelist glimpses a natural law whereby societies based on freedom defeat those based on oppression.

We are beginning to see that Don Juan de Austria's broken promise of liberty to the galley slaves was particularly reprehensible to a novelist who later experienced slavery himself for five years in Algiers. The point is driven home again in Viedma's dramatic escape from captivity when the narrator emphasizes that the men at the oars are working for their own freedom, and so motivation is not a problem: «los que bogaban dijeron que no era aquél tiempo de tomar reposo alguno: que les diesen de comer los que no bogaban, que ellos no querían soltar los remos de las manos en manera alguna» "those who were rowing said that this was no time to rest, that those who were not rowing could feed them, for they did not want to let the oars out of their hands for any reason" (1.41.482). The same idea reappears in comical and grotesque fashion when a group of galley slaves abuses the sometimes-tyrannical Governor Sancho Panza off the coast of Barcelona in *DQ* 2.63. It's a reprise of *DQ* 1.39, with Sancho in the place of the son of Barbarossa killed by the galley slaves of *The Prey*.

In his book *Carnage and Culture*, historian Victor Davis Hanson argues that the struggle in the Mediterranean between the Ottoman Empire and the Holy League boiled down to one between slavery and freedom: "the two fleets at Lepanto represented opposite poles of political and religious organization—the Ottoman navy, an entire cadre of slaves of the sultan; the Christian fleet an alliance of autonomous states, a few of which were ruled by elected governments" (264–65). The difference extended to all actors at all levels of the social and military hierarchies that were engaged in the conflict: "The soldiers in the Christian fleet were not all free voting citizens—only Venice and a few Italian states were republican. Yet the crews of the Holy League were not exclusively servile either, as was true of the Ottoman armada, in which elite Janissaries and galley slaves alike were political nonentities. A Turkish galley slave was more likely to flee than a Christian, and European common soldiers were free persons and not the property of an imperial autocrat" (257–58). Hanson further argues that over the course of history the free markets and individualism that characterize Western Civilization have produced the most lethal fighting forces humankind has ever known. Thucydides understood this effect too, insisting in his *History of the Peloponnesian War* that autocratic systems cannot get the same effort out of soldiers nor raise the same funds for military machinery as can capitalist systems: "It must be a stock of money, not forced contributions, that support the wars . . . So that the Peloponnesians and their confederates, though for one battle they be able to stand out against all Greece besides, yet to maintain a war against such as have their preparations of another kind, they are not able" (1.141:146–47). And, of course, this is the military version of Adam Smith's dictum in *The Wealth of Nations* that "the work done by free men comes cheaper in the end than the work performed by slaves" (1.8). Cervantes's brief allegorical focus on the capture of *La Presa* by *La Loba* in *DQ* 1.39 indicates that he had the same basic insight as Hanson, Thucydides, and Smith.

To understand how Cervantes could have arrived at a point of view regarding the institution of slavery similar to the one articulated by Smith, we do well to return to Aristotle. Aristotle's theoretical contrast between natural and conventional types of slavery links mutual benefit to the first type and coercion to the second. Aristotle also allows that economic relationships in which exchange is voluntary are more just than those in which one party dominates another. Thus, Sancho's deepest moral depravity in *Don Quijote* is his dream of selling the citizens of Micomicón into slavery; and thus, Sancho's apotheosis at the novel's end occurs when he enters into a contractual agreement with his master by which he agrees to lash himself 3,300 times on a per unit basis, i.e., not like a slave because for a fee.

> Vengamos a los tres mil y trecientos, que a cuartillo cada uno, que no llevaré menos si todo el mundo me lo mandase, montan tres mil y trecientos cuartillos, que son los tres mil, mil y quinientos medios reales, que hacen setecientos y cincuenta reales; y los trecientos hacen ciento y cincuenta medios reales, que vienen a hacer setenta y cinco reales, que juntándose a los setecientos y cincuenta son por todos ochocientos y veinte y cinco reales. (2.71.1199–1200)

> Let's consider the three thousand and three hundred, which at a *cuartillo* each, for I will not accept less even if the whole world orders me to, amount to three thousand and three hundred *cuartillos*, and those three thousand make for fifteen hundred half *reales*, which come to seven hundred and fifty *reales*; and those three hundred make for one hundred and fifty half *reales*, which come to seventy-five *reales*, which together with the seven hundred and fifty make for a total of eight hundred and twenty-five *reales*.

A more bourgeois miracle has not been written. Sancho claims repeatedly to be illiterate, so this burst of mathematical skill is as astonishing as it is funny. It's also salvific. Don Quijote is joyful at being relieved of the burden of delivering the lashes—«¡Oh Sancho bendito, oh Sancho amable!» "Oh blessed Sancho, oh kind Sancho!"—; in fact, he's so relieved that he offers the squire a bonus: «Y mira, Sancho, cuándo quieres comenzar la disciplina, que porque la abrevies te añado cien reales» "And think, Sancho, about when you might wish to begin the lashings, for if you will make quick about them, I'll add one hundred *reales*" (1.71.1200). In this way, Cervantes signals the civilizing and even didactic effects of commerce and contractual labor. It's not just Montesquieu's notion of *doux commerce* but, rather, something more like an abolitionist's argument for *doux salariat*.

There are two principal implications of *Don Quijote* as a satire against slavery. First, *Don Quijote* fits into the long abolitionist tradition of realist novels stretching from Apuleius to Twain. In pushing the limits of the form, Cervantes, like Las Casas, progressively discards even other more plausible justifications of slavery. He satirizes the corruption involved in slavery for criminals in *DQ* 1.22, an episode in which the protagonist makes one of his more definitive statements on human liberty: «me parece duro caso hacer esclavos a los que Dios y naturaleza hizo libres» "it seems to me a harsh way to make slaves of those whom God and Nature made free" (1.22.244). Cervantes later shows the cruel abuse that occurs when using prisoners of war as slaves in *DQ* 1.40. Finally, he adds the factor of race, which is unaccounted for in Aristotle, criticizing it twice.

Figure 13.   Jocobo Cosmedi, *Signum Ordinis Sanctae Trinita-tis*, 1210 *Source*: Wikipedia

In light of the novel's consistent critique of slavery, Thomas Jefferson's intense interest in *Don Quijote*, which he often recommended to friends and family, begs the question of how exactly Jefferson understood *Don Quijote*'s references to that bitter topic. The third president of the United States adopted an aggressive foreign policy in the conduct of the First Barbary War of 1801–05, which suggests an uncanny relation to Cervantes's masterpiece. Jefferson appears to have even reached out to the Trinitarians (Kilmeade and Yaeger 16), the same religious order that had rescued Cervantes from Algiers in 1580.[5]

The second implication of the first modern novel's focus on slavery is more theoretical. Cervantes takes his place in a canon of liberal thinkers who criticized slavery in economic terms. We see this in *La Loba*'s capture of *La Presa* in *DQ* 1.39, according to which the incentive to be free is decisive in galley warfare. Ultimately, Sancho's calculated lashes in the woods of La Mancha in *DQ* 2.71 allow a negotiated contract to replace coercion. As in Smith, the utilitarian argument is that slavery fails to incentivize productivity. Even if Aristotle didn't hit directly on the idea of slavery as less efficient than remuneration, he subversively allowed that the type of slavery based on free association and mutual benefit is more just than the type of slavery based on whips and chains. W. L. Newman argued Aristotle was quite radical on this issue: "His theory of slavery implies, if followed to its results, the illegitimacy of the relation of master and slave in a large proportion of the cases in which it existed" (qtd. by Palmer 5).

To varying degrees, then, Aristotle, Cervantes, and Smith trace out a natural law of liberty as holding a major advantage over slavery. An economy based on free exchange will be more efficient than an economy based on limiting the worker's freedom. Whether or not to impose this law on those regimes that still repress their own workers is perhaps a separate question, although, for Aristotle and Cervantes, at least, the decision seems to be contingent on whether or not the slaves in question are willing to fight for their own freedom.

In the end, there is something still to be said for the theory that the early modern rebirth of the novel form gives voice to a roundly bourgeois reality. Lukács's view that *Don Quijote* dissolves epic heroism into market realism and Maravall's vision of early class warfare in Fernando de Roja's *La Celestina* (c.1499) are essentially correct. More recent critics of Cervantes, such as Carroll Johnson and David Quint, are also correct when they argue that *Don Quijote* highlights the importance of earning salaries and paying for services. I would simply stress the conscious improvement of living standards that bourgeois values denoted for the early modern merchant class as well as the degree of detail involved in novelistic representations of said values.

Nor can we be surprised to find that *Don Quijote* discloses a general work ethic as another bourgeois mainstay of the novel form. Dorotea, for example, is conscious that her own skills at managing her family's estate make her attractive: «por mí se recebían y despedían los criados; la razón y cuenta de lo que se sembraba y cogía pasaba por mi mano, los molinos de aceite, los lagares del vino, el número del ganado mayor y menor, el de las colmenas; finalmente, de todo aquello que un tan rico labrador como mi padre puede tener y tiene, tenía yo la cuenta y era la mayordoma y señora» "servants were hired and fired by me, the accounts of all that was planted and harvested passed through my hands, the olive and wine presses, the numbers of the livestock, large and small, and the beehives. In short, I kept the accounts of everything that a rich peasant like my father can and does have, and I was the administrator and mistress" (1.28.321–22). Similarly, right after his expression of empathy for the mistreated black African slaves in *DQ* 2.24, Don Quijote helps a mule driver and actually performs manual labor for the first and only time in the entire novel: «ahechándole la cebada y limpiando el pesebre» "sifting his barley for him and cleaning out the manger" (2.25.836). Later, according to Don Quijote's diagnosis of Altisidora's lovesickness: «todo el mal desta doncella nace de ociosidad, cuyo remedio es la ocupación honesta y continua» "all of the illness of this young maiden stems from idleness, the remedy for which is honest and continuous labor" (2.70.1197). And finally, as we have seen, the novel ends with the bourgeois miracle of a mathematically precise contract which Sancho and Don Quijote negotiate on a per unit basis. Indeed, Cervantes is all about teaching both his readers and his protagonists to pay for services, to earn what they receive, to settle their accounts, to compensate their victims for any losses, and even to help resolve payment disputes among others.

Orwell once claimed that modern creative fiction "is the product of rationalism, of the Protestant countries, of the autonomous individual" ("The Prevention of Literature," 171). Hispanic readers need not take offense; Orwell knew that the antiorthodox Erasmians of Renaissance Spain were advocates of rationalism and individualism. Radical texts like *Lazarillo de Tormes* and *Don Quijote* certainly count as monumental examples of the kind of prose literature Orwell had in mind. The Spanish picaresque was a potent combination of the ideas of Protestants and rebellious Catholics, i.e., both Erasmian and Salamancan dissenters, and therein it was an abolitionist and commercial institution which viewed slavery as analogous to tyranny.

Beyond the basic critiques produced in classical antiquity and the medieval period, a number of early modern Spanish intellectuals had two insights on slavery: (1) the race factor is absurd and unsustainable, and (2) remunerated work, or, in its crudest form, the mere promise of eventual freedom, is actually more efficient than slavery. The logic against slavery didn't win out for three hundred years, but the argument had been made that it was unjust, both in the galleys of the Mediterranean and on the plantations of the West Indies.

During the Sierra Morena episodes in part one of *Don Quijote*, the metamorphosis of Cardenio from a wild man back into a gentleman occurs parallel to the dissolution of Sancho Panza's fantasy about selling the citizens of Micomicón into slavery. As a savage man doing somersaults through the woods of the Sierra Morena, who occasionally calms himself enough to tell his story, Cardenio's intermittent state refers to the same topic at the heart of Sancho's fantasy, which was also at the heart of the debate between Las Casas and Sepúlveda at Valladolid in 1550–51. Cardenio raises complex questions. Can savages be civilized? Are we not more savage than the savages?

Precursors to Cervantes's subversive thinking about slavery include Aristotle, Apuleius, Las Casas, and Latinus. For his part, Cervantes's critique of slavery in early seventeenth-century Spain anticipated Hobbes's salaried worker and Smith's free laborer; it also contained the seeds of Rousseau's noble savage, Hegel's skillful slave, and Frederick Douglass's freedman philosopher.

NOTES

1. For the commonalities between Cervantes and Poe, see the respective essays by Hernán Sánchez Martínez de Pinillos and Fernando González de León.

2. This anti-imperialist jab also echoes the Senecan and Ciceronian stoicism of Garcilaso de la Vega's lyric production while in the service of Emperor Charles V (see Graf, "From Scipio to Nero to the Self").

3. Whereas María Rosa Menocal has focused on the cosmopolitan harmony of the Cordovan Caliphate (929–1031), historian David Nirenberg has argued, more convincingly I think, that much postmodern academic utopianism ignores the medieval period's very violent conflicts.

4. For more on the origins of international law in early modern Spain, see the essay by Scott and the review by Gómez and Soto.

5. Madison would pursue a similarly aggressive foreign policy in the conduct of the Second Barbary War (1815). Opposing this tendency, in his speech to Congress of 4 July 1821, John Quincy Adams, at that time still Secretary of State, warned in quixotic terms against going abroad "in search of monsters to destroy."

Chapter Four

Don Quijote and Politics

"The fact is that certain themes cannot be celebrated in words, and tyranny is one of them. No one ever wrote a good book in praise of the Inquisition."

—George Orwell, "The Prevention of Literature" (170)

Politics in *Don Quijote de la Mancha* often receive whimsical and anachronistic analysis by commentators with other agendas. Readers can rightly suspect me of having my own. But regardless of our points of view, it's worth noting that political ideas are *ipso facto* important for understanding Cervantes's novel due to the proliferation of princely advice manuals during the sixteenth and seventeenth centuries. And the popularity of Nicolò Machiavelli's *Il principe* (1513, publ.1532), Jean Bodin's *Les Six livres de la République* (1576), or Thomas Hobbes's *Leviathan* (1651) reflected the astonishing level of political discourse across early modern Europe. The topics in these manuals are still debated today: taxation, courtly expenditures, religious policies, marketplace regulations, censorship, corruption, forms of government, the advisability of wars, definitions of tyranny, assassination, how to educate kings, and the relative talents, characters, and powers of leaders and advisors. Important Spanish authors of such manuals include Antonio de Guevara (c.1481–1545), Felipe de la Torre (1500s), Sebastián Fox Morcillo (1526/28–c.1559), Fadrique Furió Ceriol (1527–92), Pedro de Ribadeneyra (1526–1611), Juan de Mariana (1536–1624), Francisco de Quevedo (1580–1645), and Diego de Saavedra Fajardo (1584–1648). Of course, political theorists can also be idiots; thus, parallel to the proliferation of princely advice manuals, the comical *arbitrista*, a species of quack political commentator, became a fairly stock figure in early modern Spanish culture.

It should come as no surprise that Cervantes attended to the political issues of his day. Moreover, he was quite familiar with the specific genre of books by way of which these issues were debated. One of his most enigmatic texts, *El coloquio de los perros* (c.1605), concludes with a conversation among a group of patients in a hospital in Valladolid, the capital at the time. An alchemist, a poet, a mathematician, and an *arbitrista* are in turn frustrated by tasks particular to their respective professions. The *arbitrista*, of course, fancies that he has finally come up with a perfect actuarial scheme in order to solve Spain's ongoing fiscal crisis.

A similar scenario opens *Don Quijote*. The narrator notes in *DQ* 1.1 that not even Aristotle could have helped the mad hidalgo recover his sanity. As per Aristotle on rhetoric, aesthetics, or poetry, Don Quijote cannot make sense of the convoluted chivalric phrases penned by Feliciano de Silva; by implication, however, as per Aristotle on political economy, Don Quijote has strayed from the proper administration of his estate. The early theme of a nobleman's struggle to maintain his household soon morphs into attention to the master-slave relationship, which appears when the wealthy peasant Juan Haldudo whips the shepherd boy Andrés in *DQ* 1.4 and again when Don Quijote recruits Sancho Panza as his squire in *DQ* 1.7.

Concern about a gentleman's administration of his estate and subsequent attention to contrasting master-slave relationships are key aspects of Aristotle's *Politics*, an indispensable text for understanding *Don Quijote*. Aristotle's theoretical subtext allows for a simple allegorical reading of Cervantes's masterpiece, according to which the protagonist's insane mismanagement of his estate mirrors the maladministration of Spain by the Habsburgs. This is not unexpected in a novel influenced by the late scholastics of Renaissance Spain. Among the educated elite of the so-called School of Salamanca, Aristotle's *Politics* was near the top of the reading list.

Political topics are just as overt in the second part of *Don Quijote*, and once again this is clear from the outset. In *DQ* 2.1, the priest, the barber, and Don Quijote debate each other's utopian ideas. Cervantes presents all three of these characters as *arbitristas*: they ponder the logic of «razón de estado» "reason of state," they consider «modos de gobierno» "modes of government," they propose laws as if each were «un Licurgo moderno o un Solón flamante» "a modern-day Licurgus or a sparkling new Solon," and they even make specific «arbitrios» "policy recommendations" (2.1.626–27).

These comical touches are also overt invitations to read *Don Quijote* as a political text. Having invented so many other narrative genres, a strong case can be made that Cervantes also penned the first modern political novel. In this chapter, we will attend to significant passages which address political topics that were important to early modern Spanish readers: monetary inflation, rebellious Morisco populations along the Mediterranean coast, a string of national bankruptcies, endless wars against Protestantism and Islam, increasingly burdensome tax and tariff policies, etc. Again, even though the political issues Cervantes addresses in *Don Quijote* were specific to sixteenth- and seventeenth-century Spain, today's and tomorrow's readers will recognize many of their arguments and implications.

Before considering the politics of *Don Quijote*, let's make two qualifications that will help us to avoid a lot of confusion: (A) as was the case in classical antiquity, the theoretical aim of the art of politics was understood to be that of avoiding and limiting the destructive effects of factionalism; (B) due to the forces and conflicts unleashed by the Protestant Reformation, early modern politics were often inseparable from a frenetic array of doctrinal disputes and competing religious identities, and indeed, 99% of prohibited books were religious in nature (Bass 151).

(A) FACTIONALISM

Spain experienced its share of factionalism during its Golden Age. Historians like José Antonio Maravall (*Las Comunidades*) and Stephen Haliczer (*The Comuneros*) have argued that the uprising of the Castilian townships known as the *Comuneros* Rebellion of 1520–21 was in many ways the first modern revolution. The Alpujarras War of 1568–71 was a different kind of rebellion involving the Morisco population in the area south of Granada and reproducing the medieval ethnic conflicts of the Reconquest. Spain annexed Portugal in 1580, when Philip II took advantage of a crisis of succession in the nation-state next door. In 1591, the *Alteraciones* or "Troubles" in Aragón were a local nobility's last-ditch effort at checking the authoritarian and imperial aspirations of the Habsburgs. A half century later, two decades of upheaval in Cataluña during the years 1640–59 expressed familiar regional discontent with Habsburg power. There was also a lot of factionalism at the international level; Spain seemed perpetually at war with England, France, the Netherlands, the Barbary States, and the Ottoman Empire.

Factionalism is omnipresent in *Don Quijote*, signaled by allusions to a long list of tribal, national, and ethnic rivalries: Christians versus Moors in *DQ* 1.5; Castilians versus Basques in *DQ* 1.8; clan tensions in Andalucía in *DQ* 1.24–37; internecine struggles in Florence in *DQ* 1.33–35; Spaniards against Algerians and Turks in *DQ* 1.39–41. The theme becomes more absurd and then turns historically specific again in the novel's second part: university students engage in a fencing match in *DQ* 2.19; opposing families draw swords at Camacho's wedding in *DQ* 2.21; two towns go to war over the art of braying like asses in *DQ* 2.27; Baratarians fight off a mysterious invasion in *DQ* 2.53; Roque Guinart's bandits are partisans in a guerrilla-style clan war between Nyerros and Cadells in *DQ* 2.60; Old Christians (Sancho) and Moriscos (Ricote) get drunk together in *DQ* 2.54 and then attempt to resolve their differences in *DQ* 2.65.

Factionalism from Cervantes's day is supplemented by the novel's allusions to ancient struggles between Greeks, Trojans, Romans, Carthaginians, Jews, and Egyptians. Atop Clavileño in *DQ* 2.41, for example, Don Quijote fears there might be Greek warriors hidden inside the wooden horse's belly. The allusion to the Trojan War simultaneously expresses the Old Christian view of the Moriscos as a dangerous fifth column that might assist the Ottomans.

With Nyerros and Cadells on the narrative horizon, one of the novel's most complex allusions to factionalism and civil wars is when Sancho resists Don Quijote's attempt to lash him. Sancho pins his now former master under his knee and declares independence: «Ni quito rey ni pongo rey –respondió Sancho–, sino ayúdome a mí, que soy mi señor» "'I remove no king, I install no king,' responded Sancho, 'rather, I help myself, for I am my own lord'" (2.60.1118). In the first phrase, the rebellious peasant refers to an ironic proverb attributed to the medieval French mercenary Bertrand du Guesclin, who intervened in a knife fight between Pedro I (House of Ivrea) and Enrique II (House of Trastámara) at Montiel in 1369. But instead of Guesclin's next expression, «ayudo a mi señor» "I help my lord," Sancho says he helps himself, adding «que soy mi señor» "for I am my own lord." This distortion of Guesclin's phrase bridges two kinds of civil war: medieval dynastic struggles that often ended in fratricide and modern-day national and class struggles that emphasize the rights and liberties of citizens.

There's often little difference between factionalism and something we might consider politically sophisticated. Confronting factionalism, for example, we expect Cervantes's satire to investigate the alliance between the monarchy and the populace against the nobility, a dynamic that was also very common in the era's theater. When a peasant (Sancho) triumphs over a low noble (Don Quijote) and then articulates his victory in terms of a choice between rival medieval kings, we have factionalism. We also have a grotesque echo of the Struggle of the Orders of the Roman Republic, which pits the masses (Plebeians) against the landed aristocrats (Patricians) for control of the powerful consulships (see Polybius, *Histories* 6.11–13). According to medieval estates theory, Sancho is the peasant arm of the third estate rising up against a low noble of the second estate. In many ways, Sancho's declaration of personal sovereignty invokes thinking about the power claimed by monarchs as well as the tensions among the various factions of a nation's citizenry.

(B) RELIGIOUS IDENTITY

In sixteenth- and seventeenth-century Europe, partisan politics were deeply involved in rival notions of religious faith. Modern theorists as diverse as Carl Schmitt, Sigmund Freud, Leo Strauss, Eric Hoffer, René Girard, and Fredric Jameson have indicated ways in which politics is another form of religion and *vice versa*. It's a strong maxim for the early modern period, when the Protestant-Catholic schism meant that religious affiliation was a matter of national allegiance and a defining aspect of struggles among political coalitions at courts across Europe. Even so, assessing the social significance of early modern religious strife is precarious. Most sects could turn fanatical. A group of Calvinists burned Michael Servetus at the stake in Geneva in 1553. But most sects also manifested enlightened tendencies. Members of the same Calvinist creed advocated city-state republics, freedom of the printing press, and political assassination.

The politics of religion are prevalent in *Don Quijote*, and Cervantes was clearly familiar with many radical points of view regarding subtle doctrinal differences. The major examples are found in the novel's multiple allusions to Erasmism: Cervantes satirizes the Inquisition's *auto de fe* in *DQ* 1.6–7 and 2.73; attacks the entire hierarchy of the Roman Catholic Church in *DQ* 1.19; mocks public displays of faith with vulgar rosaries in *DQ* 1.26 and 2.46; and rejects attempts at censorship in relation to the Expulsion of the Moriscos in *DQ* 1.32 and Erasmism in *DQ* 2.62 (see Duffield, Castro, *El pensamiento*; Bataillon, Forcione, Herrero, "Sierra Morena as Labyrinth"; Vilanova, and Johnson, *The Quest*).

Keeping in mind these two qualifications—(A) the art of early modern politics was to avoid factionalism and sustain the state, and (B) politics and religion were often one and the same—here are ten (10) ways that we might consider relating *Don Quijote* to politics.

(1) DEMOCRACY

It's best to remove our postmodern type of democracy from consideration. Cervantes was not impressed by the *vulgo* or "commoner," or by what Ortega y Gasset would call the rebellious "masses," i.e., the Greek *demos*. Cervantes's aristocratic and individualistic bias accords well with the first modern novel as the creative fiction preferred by classical liberals, who also worried about the unruly mob. It's not that Cervantes opposed the masses outright; it's just that, as anyone who has read *Don Quijote* can attest, at some deeply moral level, the author found any and all appeals to authority deserving of mockery, including when they accompanied the tendency to locate and expand authority by way of popular vote.

The first modern novel's most overt representation of democracy in action is, at best, comical, and, at worst, cynical. Late in part one, Don Fernando conducts a vote in order to discover if the second barber's common pack-saddle might not be a more exotic caparison for medieval warhorses. Don Fernando directs himself to each voter as if lobbying: «hablándolos al oído para que en secreto declarasen si era albarda o jaez aquella joya sobre quien tanto se había peleado» "whispering to each of them in his ear so that they would declare in secret whether that jewel that had been so fiercely fought over was an ass's packsaddle or a warhorse's caparison" (1.45.523). Cervantes indicates that a characteristic of democracy is its tendency to subject reality to silly referenda that are easily corrupted. Few of the Salamancan theorists of the day were democrats in our own sense of voting booths for everyone and votes on everything. Like most of their classical and medieval precursors, late scholastics were skeptical about the power of the masses. Moreover, the major examples of democracy in this period—the election of the Pope by a College of Cardinals and the election of the Holy Roman Emperor by a council of princes—were notoriously corrupt affairs in which the winners just bribed the voters.

A negative symbolic representation of democracy in *Don Quijote* occurs when a group of boys tie thorny shrubs to the tails of Sancho's ass and Rocinante as Don Quijote and Sancho make their triumphant entrance into Barcelona, «de manera que, dando mil corcovos, dieron con sus dueños en tierra» "in such a way that, bucking a thousand times over, they threw their masters to the ground" (2.61.1132). This reads like a cynical amplification of Plato's metaphorical description of the democratic regime in book eight of the *Republic*: "there come to be horses and asses who have gotten the habit of making their way quite freely and solemnly, bumping into whomever they happen to meet on the roads, if he doesn't stand aside, and all else is similarly full of freedom" (242). Echoing Plato's skepticism, Cervantes signals the anarchical dangers of democracy in the direction of the unruly Principality of Cataluña.

Finally, when plotting Cervantes's vision of democracy, we do well to keep in mind a type of thinking exemplified by Hobbes and Thucydides. These historians were philosophically down-to-earth realists rather than utopian populists. Moreover, their skepticism regarding the incompetence of the masses extended to their perception that a rise in linguistic distortion is a barometer for the destruction sought and wrought during seditious times.

Hobbes published his translation of Thucydides's *History of the Peloponnesian War* in 1629. In one famous passage, Thucydides describes how language erodes in concert with the instability of popular uprisings:

The cities therefore being now in sedition, and those that fell into it later having heard what had been done in the former, they far exceeded the same in newness of conceit, both for the art of assailing and for the strangeness of their revenges. The received value of names imposed for signification of things, was changed into arbitrary. For inconsiderate boldness, was counted true-hearted manliness: provident deliberation, a handsome fear: modesty, the cloak of cowardice: to be wise in everything, to be lazy in everything. A furious suddenness was reputed a point of valour. To re-advise for the better security, was held for a fair pretext of tergiversation. He that was fierce, was always trusty; and he that contraried such a one, was suspected. He that did insidiate, if it took, was a wise man; but he that could smell out a trap laid, a more dangerous man than he. But he that had been so provident as not to need to do the one or the other, was said to be a dissolver of society, and one that stood in fear of his adversary. In brief, he that could outstrip another in the doing of an evil act, or that could persuade another thereto that never meant it, was commended. (3.80.348–49)

Something on par with Thucydides's connection between democracy and linguistic topsy-turvy permeates *Don Quijote*, albeit in lighter and more comical tones. The most famous example is the debate at the second inn over the nature of the donkey trappings that Sancho and Don Quijote robbed from the first barber back in *DQ* 1.21. The result is an excess of linguistic distortion: a grotesque compromise, a hybrid of the barber's basin fused with the helmet of Mambrino appears in Sancho's «baciyelmo» "bashelmet" in *DQ* 1.44; then, in *DQ* 1.45, an everyday «albarda» "packsaddle" undergoes a metamorphosis into an exotic and chivalric «jaez de caballo» "warhorse's caparison." Note that this last transformation takes place right before the original owner's eyes. It also takes place by way of the mockery of a popular vote conducted by Don Fernando.

In other words, *DQ* 1.45 manifests a conservative's fear of democratic egalitarianism and a vision of the eventual absurdity of holding plebiscites on definitions of things. Readers from today's democracies will recognize that odd words born of populist and propagandistic brushes with Orwellian "Newspeak" are not particular to communist dictatorships. A Spanish view in keeping with Hobbes's and Thucydides's cynicism toward democracy is found in Guevara's partiality to the countryside in lieu of life at court in his *Menosprecio de corte y alabanza de aldea* (Valladolid, 1539). Guevara, too, links linguistic lunacy and political decay: «¡Oh quán difficultoso es de conoscer el coraçón del hombre, lo qual paresce muy claro, porque muchas vezes nos haze entender que la hipocresía es devoción, la ambición que es grandeza, la escaseza que es grangería, la crueldad que es celo, la dessemboltura que es eloqüencia, la extrañeza que es vanidad, la locura que es gravedad y la disolución que es diligencia!» "Oh how difficult it is to know the heart of a man, which seems quite clear, because many times it makes us believe that hypocrisy is devotion, ambition is greatness, scarcity is surplus, cruelty is zeal, meandering is eloquence, strangeness is vanity, insanity is gravity, and dissolution, diligence" (2.18).

(2) COMMUNISM

Cervantes appears to consider communism no more viable than democracy. Like the pejorative representation of the act of voting under Don Fernando's guidance, and like Plato's derogatory equivalence between rule by the masses and freely roaming equines, the famous Golden Age speech that Don Quijote delivers to the goatherders in *DQ* 1.11, and in which he longs for ancient, agrarian, and property-less harmony, is not flattering to the communist system. Still, many modern readers conclude that Don Quijote's nostalgia for a utopian world lacking any concept of *yours* and *mine* (i.e., private property) must reflect Cervantes's own view (see Pérez de Antón and Byrne). Instead, I would argue that the problem is the misguided communist nostalgia of Don Quijote, not that of Cervantes. At this relative early point in the novel, the author is still mocking Don Quijote's idealism *vis-à-vis* the world as it really is. Technically speaking, Don Quijote's communist Golden Age occurs too soon to be Marxist; rather, it is essentially Platonic. Nevertheless, the mindset is the same to the degree that statist utopias are often portrayed as fantastically bountiful in a vaguely agrarian manner.

Signaling theoretical gravity, *DQ* 1.11 discloses the first case of physical conflict between master and servant. The squire would rather drink wine and eat by himself than sit «a par de un emperador» "next to an emperor," but the hidalgo obliges him to join him: «Y asiéndole por el brazo, le forzó a que junto dél se sentase» "And grabbing him by the arm, he forced him to sit next to him" (1.11.120). Sancho responds to the hidalgo's idealism by noting his master's disregard for the time preferences of the goatherders: «el trabajo que estos buenos hombres tienen todo el día no permite que pasen las noches cantando» "the work that these good men have all day long does not permit them to pass the nights singing" (1.11.127).

Sancho defends the point of view of peasant labor and remains skeptical of his master's communist rhetoric. He's noting that Don Quijote represents what economists call the "free-rider" problem, which occurs when someone benefits from resources, goods, or services without contributing to their procurement. While one could argue that he voices a syndicalist point of view because he constantly requests compensation for his services, free-rider works too for Sancho, who elsewhere steals 100 *escudos* from Cardenio, receives 200 *escudos* from the Duke, accepts a tip of 10 *escudos* from Roque

Guinart, and negotiates 825 *reales* from his master for lashes he doesn't produce. Sancho is too much of a *pícaro* to be a communist.

The School of Salamanca's focus on the ancient problem of "*mine* and *yours*" is the likely source for the Golden Age speech against property. However, if Cervantes's "criticism of that system is stinging and mordant" (Byrne 42), it runs counter to most Salamancan theory. Most of the late scholastics, although not all of them, related individual liberty to private property, not collectivist fantasy. Such realism anticipated Frédéric Bastiat's point that the law exists because property exists, and not the other way around. On a more popular level, there's the medieval Spanish proverb: «Cuando un asno es de muchos, los lobos se lo comen» "When an ass belongs to many, the wolves eat it." The blowhard of *DQ* 1.11 is not the author but, rather, the character: an idealistic knight dropped into a pastoral setting where he survives by consuming the fruits of the labor of others. Don Quijote is nostalgic for what authorities foist on the rest of us, namely, their right to take what they want, which they then justify by appealing to the "greater good." All of us see through the knight's ruse, especially Sancho, perhaps because his character is relatively more exploited for his labor.

After mocking a property-less communist fantasy in the Golden Age speech of *DQ* 1.11, Cervantes drops the topic, until the end of part two. The parodies of the pastoral genre in *DQ* 2.58, 2.67, and 2.73 resurrect the Golden Age fantasy. One brutal counterpoint to the communist agrarian fantasy is represented by Roque Guinart and his bandits in *DQ* 2.60. Guinart rules according to absolute distributive justice, that is, all share equally in the community's wealth. And yet, when one of the bandits complains that the payouts in Guinart's syndicate are meager, he draws his sword and splits his head open: «le abrió la cabeza casi en dos partes, diciéndole: –Desta manera castigo yo a los deslenguados y atrevidos» "he almost split his head in two, saying: 'This is how I punish insubordinates who talk too much'" (2.60.1128). Guinart represents the reality of a sadistic, repressive regime that uses egalitarianism to justify a terror that keeps citizens poor and weak. It's an awful, brutish existence because paranoid dictators seduce us with the allure of extracting wealth from others rather than producing it ourselves. Cervantes not only rejects communism because of the free-rider problem, he anticipates Karl Popper's view that utopian egalitarianism often leads to barbaric, predatory tyranny.

(3) REPUBLICANISM

By republicanism, I refer broadly to classical and medieval notions of government as parliamentary or conciliar in nature, as opposed to the absolutist governments of monarchs or emperors. Here I think we have a perspective that offers possibilities for understanding Cervantes's most likely political views. The author of the first modern novel contemplates various articulations of anti-imperialist republicanism. For example, his protagonist's desire to visit Zaragoza expresses nostalgia for the independent parliamentary and judiciary bodies of the Kingdom of Aragón. Similarly, his turn toward Barcelona expresses an uneasy infatuation with the urban unruliness of a port city and perhaps a longing for an even older independent parliament, the *Corts Catalanes* of the Principality of Cataluña.

In *DQ* 2.52, Teresa tells an anecdote that suggests Cervantes's antimonarchic attitude and alludes to the *Comuneros* Rebellion against Charles V. She reports that a local man was ordered to paint «las armas de Su Majestad, sobre las puertas del Ayuntamiento» "the coat of arms of His Majesty above the doors of the town council," but in the end, «no pintó nada y dijo que no acertaba a pintar tantas baratijas» "he didn't paint anything, saying that he was no good at painting such trash" (2.52.1059). When the painter returns the money and takes up farming, Teresa's story hints at the Cincinnatus myth of republican virtue (cf. Guevara, *Menosprecio de corte*): «ya ha dejado el pincel y tomado el azada, y va al campo como gentilhombre» "he has abandoned the brush and taken up the hoe, and he goes into the fields like a gentleman" (2.52.1060).

Let's be more specific about Cervantes's republicanism. Towards the end of *Don Quijote*, part two, we find a series of grand, nostalgic gestures toward Zaragoza and Barcelona. These, in turn, invite us to interpret somewhat more obscure references to radical city-states like Ragusa in the first prologue, La Rochelle in *DQ* 1.41, and Mainz in *DQ* 2.38–39. Here, I think, is a brush with the cosmopolitan spirit of the radical townships of early modern Europe. Antonomasia's mother is named Maguncia (Mainz), which is the city of Gutenberg's fantastic invention. The first modern novel's only overt Calvinists are an odd group of pirates headed for the port of La Rochelle, a radical Huguenot republic on the French Atlantic. Cities like La Rochelle, Mainz, and Barcelona appear to form a kind of urban retinue in *Don Quijote*, one which simultaneously suggests Cervantes was intrigued by the political liberty advocated by radical Protestantism.[1]

Ragusa was a maritime republic centered on the city-state of Dubrovnik on the Dalmatian coast of the Adriatic. Noteworthy for enduring 450 years (1358–1808), Ragusa was already two and a half centuries old in Cervantes's day. Ragusa was also unique for being early to ban the slave trade in 1416. The first modern novel references Ragusa by citing its motto in the first prologue: «Non bene pro toto libertas venditur auro» "Liberty is not sold for all the world's gold" (1.pro.14). In a novel written by a former slave that

Figure 14.   Fernando II of Aragón with Catalan Court,
1495 *Source:* Biblioteca Virtual de Derecho Aragonés

criticizes slavery and contains an interpolated autobiographical novel which also criticizes slavery, we might think of the Republic of Ragusa as a guiding light for slaves like Latino, Aesop, the citizens of Sancho's Micomicón, and Captain Viedma.

La Rochelle was a commercial republic, an intermittently independent Huguenot refuge north of Bordeaux on the Bay of Biscay during the French Wars of Religion. Modeled after Geneva, it declared itself a Reformed Republic in 1568. The Huguenots were French Calvinists, an ethnoreligious group who, among other ideas, embraced regicide, popular sovereignty, and a radically free press. In 1572, they were crushed during the Saint Bartholomew's Day massacre, but they were eventually granted substantial autonomy by the Edict of Nantes in 1598. The only Huguenots in *Don Quijote* appear as odd pirates headed for La Rochelle. They intercept Viedma and Zoraida near the Straights of Gibraltar during their dash from Algiers to Spain. Curiously, they respect

Zoraida's virginity, although, according to Viedma, they are gentlemanly pirates for a particular reason: «los deseos de aquella gente no se estienden a más que al dinero» "the desires of those people do not extend to anything beyond money" (1.41.488). It's a serious joke. An obsession with money is a Calvinist stereotype, but it's also a bourgeois ideal. A Protestant might claim that, much like Viedma, these pirates are actually proper gentlemen.

The city of Mainz, near Frankfurt, was synonymous with political autonomy and the unruliness of the printing press. Comparable in its revolutionary impact to Luther's *Ninety-five Theses* at Wittenberg in 1517 was the Gutenberg Bible at Mainz in the 1450s, which began the age of the printed book in the West. Cervantes's use of Mainz in *DQ* 2.38–39 is ludic on one level. He deploys the Spanish name for the city, Maguncia, as the pseudo-chivalric name of the Queen mother of Princess Antonomasia in the Kingdom of Candaya.

But there's subversion here too. The struggle between Maguncia's kingdom and that of her cousin Malambruno, an evil and jealous sorcerer, is an allegory for the struggle between the Protestant Reformation and the Catholic Counter-Reformation, and the parallels are not always flattering for the Spanish side. The menacing giant Malambruno «aunque es encantador, es cristiano» "although an enchanter, is a Christian" (2.41.958). The Mainz clan are the heroes of the tale. As an Erasmian novelist, we can expect Cervantes to favor the site of Gutenberg's invention. We also note that Mariana, conceivably in order to evade a direct confrontation with authorities in Spain, chose Mainz to publish his 1605 edition of *De rege et regis institutione* with its added chapter on monetary policy. To sum up, the Antonomasia episode reads like a Protestant, although also a radical Jesuit, allegory about resisting the extreme abuses of orthodox Catholicism. According to this allegory, when Mainz resists Malambruno, the more Western, realistic, and pro-free press side resists the more Oriental, supernatural, and authoritarian side.

Cervantes orchestrates these geopolitical and ideological details with precision. Just prior to the appearance of the gentlemen pirates of La Rochelle, Viedma's renegade friend describes Zoraida as «tan contenta . . . de verse en este estado como el que sale de las tinieblas a la luz» "as happy . . . to see herself in this state as one who comes out of the darkness into the light" (1.41.484). He alludes to Job 17.12: *Post tenebras spero lucem* "After darkness, I hope for light." The sentence from Job happens to be the motto of Calvinism and the Protestant Reformation. This situates Zoraida, herself a convert from Islam to Catholicism, on a broader sliding scale of religious freedom that now includes the Calvinism of the Republic of La Rochelle.

Mainz also signals a dogmatic issue in *Don Quijote*. First, let's attend to the dogma. Near the end of part one, Cervantes comically mingles the official

Counter-Reformation position in favor of moral acts of charity with Luther's opposing view that only faith gains one entry to heaven: «el pobre está inhabilitado de poder mostrar la virtud de liberalidad con ninguno, aunque en sumo grado la posea, y el agradecimiento que solo consiste en el deseo es cosa muerta, como es muerta la fe sin obras» "the poor man is incapable of displaying the virtue of liberality with anyone, even if he possesses it in the highest degree, and gratitude that consists of no more than desire is a dead thing, just as faith without works is dead" (1.50.572).

It's an hilariously meandering contradiction. Sounding Lutheran, Don Quijote points out that the poor man who has a liberal character, but who cannot display it because he is poor, is through no fault of his own denied the salvation to be obtained by performing charity. But then, in the same breath, and via an awkward comparison, he voices the Catholic view that works of faith are as important as intentions and beliefs. It's only a hint of Protestant rebellion, from which Don Quijote retreats. By contrast, the Duchess's Lutheran remark in part two is more confrontational: «advierta Sancho que las obras de caridad que se hacen tibia y flojamente no tienen mérito ni valen nada» "be advised Sancho that works of charity that are performed halfheartedly or casually have no merit and are worthless" (2.36.930). We know the Duchess's reference to Luther's assertion that faith trumps acts (*sola fide*) irked Spanish religious authorities because her sentence was censored for the 1632 edition of the novel. And two chapters later, in *DQ* 2.38, a messenger from Doña Maguncia (Mainz) appears in the Duchess's garden seeking Don Quijote. Thus, Cervantes pushes Protestant allusions to the limit, allowing his leading Lutheran to direct a spectacle in which Don Quijote aligns himself with Gutenberg. It's an allegory for the Protestant Reformation with another note of urban power.

Many of the freedoms associated with places like Ragusa, La Rochelle, and Mainz find their domestic Spanish parallels in *Don Quijote*, especially in part two's emphasis on Zaragoza and Barcelona. By far the most mentioned city in Cervantes's novel is Zaragoza, capital of the neighboring Kingdom of Aragón. Throughout most of part two, Don Quijote's objective is to participate in its annual jousting tournament. From the perspective of intellectuals anxious about Habsburg power like Abril and Mariana, Aragón symbolized a vital tradition of resistance to monarchical tyranny (Graf, "The Politics of Renouncing Zaragoza"). In his princely advice manual of 1598, Mariana admired the Aragonese practice of limiting the power of their kings:

Como refiere Aristóteles, entre los griegos, los lacedemonios sólo confiaron a sus reyes la dirección de la guerra y el cuidado y el ministerio de las cosas sagradas. Y de la misma forma pensaron en un tiempo más reciente los aragoneses

en España, tan celosos de su libertad que creen que las libertades se amenguan
cuando se hace alguna pequeña concesión. (93–94)

As Aristotle reports, among the Greeks, the Lacedemonians only confided in
their kings the direction of war and the administration of sacred things. And
more recently, the Aragonese of Spain thought along the same lines, being so
vigilant of their liberty that they believe that liberties are reduced even when the
slightest concession is made.

Ultimately, Aragón represents nostalgia for the medieval *fuero* tradition
of local legal codes in opposition to the early modern reality of centralized
Habsburg authority emanating from Castile. During the *Alteraciones*, the
Aragonese nobility had risen in support of a formal legal challenge to the authority of Philip II. The rebellion was triggered by the Antonio Pérez Affair,
which, for its part, began with the murder of Don Juan de Austria's secretary
Juan de Escobedo in Madrid in 1578. Philip II soon had his own secretary
Antonio Pérez arrested for the murder in 1579, but he waited until 1587 to
formally charge him. Pérez eventually escaped to Aragón, where he claimed
citizenship. After some military skirmishes in 1591, Juan de Lanuza, the chief
justice of Aragón who had arranged political asylum for Pérez, ended up with
his head on a stake in a plaza in Zaragoza. The nobility in Aragón and any
lingering medieval chivalric sense of judicial or political independence were
crushed by an early modern version of the state as war machine. This is why
Mariana uses Aragón to lament by way of analogy a similar loss of popular
sovereignty and parliamentary power in Castile:

Nuestros antepasados previeron, como hombres prudentes, este peligro y san-
cionaron muchas y muy sabias medidas para que los reyes se contuvieran en
los límites de la moderación y templanza y no pudieran ejercer una potestad
excesiva de la que derivara un daño público. Entre otras cosas, establecieron
con gran prudencia que no se resolviera ningún negocio importante sin el con-
sentimiento de los nobles y del pueblo, a cuyo efecto se convocaban a cortes
del reino a representantes elegidos por todos los brazos, esto es, a los prelados
con plena jurisdicción, a los nobles y a los procuradores de las ciudades. Esta
costumbre se conserva en Aragón y en otras provincias y ¡ojalá que nuestros
príncipes volvieran a restablecerla! (101)

Our ancestors anticipated, like prudent men, this danger and they approved
many most wise measures such that kings would be contained by the limits of
moderation and temperance and would not be able to exercise excessive power
from which would derive public harm. Among other things, they established
with great prudence that no major concern should be resolved without the consent of the nobility and the townships, to which ends were invited to the kingdom's *Cortes* representatives from all the estates, that is, bishops with clear ju-

risdiction, nobles, and deputies from the townships. This custom is preserved in Aragón and other provinces, and would that our princes look again to restore it.

We might read Don Quijote's quest for Zaragoza as a ridiculous version of Philip II's invasion of Aragón in 1591 in order to overthrow the local legal system there and have his way with Antonio Pérez. But we have reasons to suspect more aggressive satire. First, Don Quijote constantly claims to defend justice, which would presumably include Aragonese judges and defendants like Lanuza and Pérez.

Second, consider the irony that Don Quijote seems to reach for political representation in Aragón. The Castilian *Cortes* system allowed representation of the three traditional medieval estates: clergy, nobility, and townships. By contrast, the Aragonese system had a quaternary structure. As in Castile, the assembly included clergy, townships, and high nobility; but it also included a group of low nobles known as *infanzones*, analogous to the hidalgos of Castile ("Cortes de Aragón"). Moreover, the Habsburgs were inclined toward repressing all such representative institutions. Like Abril and Mariana, Don Quijote's nostalgia for his caste's political standing in the Aragonese past carries concern about Habsburg tyranny in the present.

Cervantes can be read as expressing some sympathy for the rebels of the insurgency at Zaragoza in 1591. In *DQ* 2.59, Don Quijote avoids Zaragoza in order to spite Avellaneda's apocryphal continuation. Given Cervantes's satirical tendencies, and given the more tragic tone of part two, on another level Don Quijote's original trajectory reflects darkly on the recent military adventure to repress Aragón, thereby exposing another political blind spot in Castilian nationalism. It's worth recalling that Philip II was at his most Machiavellian during the Antonio Pérez affair. It took an experienced and manipulative prince to turn Pérez into a scapegoat by accusing him of a political murder that his majesty likely ordered. Also, in the end Philip II repressed local Aragonese parliamentary and legal traditions, giving every indication of being an opportunistic tyrant directing the soldiers of Castile against his rivals.

But if *Don Quijote* satirizes the Habsburg monarchy, does it conversely endorse the Aragonese aristocracy? Modern critics of Cervantes tend to dislike the Duke and Duchess characters, falling more or less in line with the 1957 Soviet film directed by Grigori Kozintsev. They have a point in that the landed aristocrats behave cruelly towards both Don Quijote and Sancho Panza. The idea that Cervantes intended to offend important Aragonese nobles is further confirmed by the fact that Zaragozan literary critic Baltasar Gracián in his *Arte del ingenio, tratado de la agudeza* (Huesca, 1648) excluded *Don Quijote* from his canon of Spanish masterpieces. Gracián had close ties with the Dukes of Villahermosa, the apparent models for the vacuous Duke and

Duchess, and he had ties with an Aragonese soldier named Jerónimo de Pasamonte, whom Cervantes mocks in the figure of Ginés de Pasamonte. Then there is the fact that *Don Quijote* was never printed in Zaragoza during the seventeenth century (Pérez Lasheras 152). The Aragonese nobility were not amused by their treatment in *DQ* 2.

Nevertheless, to the degree that the novel's nobles are flawed, they are like every other character, and a rigidly negative view of the Duke and Duchess risks ignoring their positive aspects. The Duchess, for example, has good advice for Governor Sancho and her rational brand of aristocratic feminism accords with Cervantes's general regard for women. For his part, the Duke practices the art of hunting near Zaragoza, and he sends letters of introduction on behalf of knight and squire to his friends in Barcelona. In other words, as an echo of medieval nobility, the Duke represents the second estate, and as a more modern noble, he communes with the republican bourgeoisie of the third estate. He bridges landed and urban gentry, allies driven together by the ascendancy of Habsburg autocracy.

We know that criticism of Philip II's invasion of Aragón existed at the time due to variations in the wording and tone of certain political treatises. In their respective translations of a passage from Aristotle's *Politics*, Abril and Mariana disclose negative assessments of Philip II's maneuvers against Aragón. First, note Aristotle's original and relatively neutral description of the only way to control tyrants, namely, by checking their monopoly on force. As an example, he relates that this wise reasoning nearly prevented the rise to power of the tyrant Dionysius:

> He himself should have a certain force, but the force should be such that it is superior to individuals both by themselves and taking many of them together, but inferior to the multitude. It was thus that the ancients gave a bodyguard whenever they selected someone to be what they called dictator or tyrant of the city; and when Dionysius requested a bodyguard, someone advised the Syracusans to give him a bodyguard of this size. (*Politics* 3.15.112–13)

As the Escobar crisis at court evolved into the *Alteraciones* of Aragón, Abril adapted his translation of 1584 to the reality of his readers, inserting an allusion to Zaragoza and inventing a senator to signal a tyrant's repression of a parliamentary body: «I quando Dionysio en Çaragoça de Sicilia pidió guarda, cierto senador aconsejaua a los Syracusanos que no le diessen mas guarda de aquella» "And when Dionysius of Zaragoza of Sicily asked for a bodyguard, a certain senator counseled the Syracusans that they should not give him more than that" (98v–99r).

Nearly a decade after the invasion of Aragón and the execution of Lanuza, Mariana translated the same passage. He shifted the emphasis to mean that it is really the tyrant Dionysius against whom the people should have armed protection: «Y cuando Dionisio reclamó tropas para su custodia, alguien respondió que era a los siracusanos a quienes debía dárseles protección» "And when Dionysius required troops for his safety, someone responded that it was the Syracusans who needed to be given protection" (103–04).

An overarching irony here is that medieval Aragón maintained a similar confrontation with potential tyrants via a famous oath that the kingdom required of its monarchs dating from the reign of Pedro II (1196–1213). A triumphant expression of the formalist medieval political tradition, the sovereign had to make a public declaration of his allegiance to the kingdom, at which point the nobility would respond with the following formula: «Nos, que cada uno de nosotros somos igual que vos y todos juntos más que vos, te hacemos Rey si cumples nuestros fueros y los haces cumplir, si no, no» "We, who are each equal to you and who together are more than you, make you king so long as you comply with our laws (*fueros*) and enforce them; if not, then we refuse" ("El juramento de los Reyes de Aragón"). Note how well this formula echoes Aristotle's assessment of the response by the Syracusans to Dionysius's request for a bodyguard in the *Politics*. Such moments are struggles between a people's right to freedom from tyranny and a king's desire for absolute power.

Where does Don Quijote go upon renouncing Zaragoza? Republican Barcelona, an even more radically independent place than Zaragoza, and one with a printing industry to boot. A kind of hybrid of La Rochelle and Mainz, Barcelona is a major endpoint in the political trajectory of the first modern novel. The episodes in Barcelona are thick with acts of circling, presenting, and naming, as if Cervantes wished to signal his hidalgo's true purpose. *DQ* 2.62 stands out among these chapters as intensely personal and confessional in nature. The narrator cites Juan de Jáuregui, who once painted Cervantes's portrait. And Antonio Moreno's enchanted head is an elaborate and provocative symbol, as if the author were saying, "Here's what I think about how they suppress thinking," or "We should be free to think," or "Idle reader, please think."

In Barcelona the mad hidalgo is doubly marked as a figure associated with the invention of printing at Mainz. First, Moreno parades Don Quijote through the city with a sign on his back that reads «Este es don Quijote de la Mancha» "This is Don Quijote of La Mancha" (2.62.1136). In yet another reflexive and metanarrative gesture, Cervantes takes his protagonist inside a printer's shop where he observes the mechanical reproduction of texts and discusses several of *Don Quijote*'s sources and tropes. To top it all off, Don Quijote recommends printing Meneses's Erasmian catechism. Whereas Aragón allows Cervantes to allude to republican and parliamentary resistance to Habsburg rule; with Barcelona he signals the Protestant Reformation. The cosmopolitan freedom of an armed, semi-autonomous city-state that can maintain a reformist printing press seems worth the risk of unleashing anarchy or factionalism.

(4) ARISTOTLE OVER PLATO

A good way of thinking about Cervantes's preference for city-state republics over autocratic kings is to note that he constantly leverages empirical Aristotelian realism against speculative Platonic utopianism. In another of his masterpieces of literary criticism, *Utopía y contrautopía en El Quijote*, Maravall pointed out that the protagonist's fantasy recalls the chivalric idealism of the court of Charles V. In short, as an anti-chivalric novel, *Don Quijote* is by definition anti-utopian and anti-Platonic. Early in book seven of Plato's *Republic*, within the allegory of the cave the puppet show is the major metaphor for the false reality projected onto the wall opposite the unenlightened prisoners. This helps us to see how Cervantes twice marks utopian thinking as Platonic by mocking chivalric idealism in the Cave of Montesinos in *DQ* 2.23 and then again in Maese Pedro's puppet show in *DQ* 2.26.

In his book *Cervantes, Literature, and the Discourse of Politics*, Anthony Cascardi indicates a range of Platonic political tropes in part two of *Don Quijote*. For example, the flight atop Clavileño in *DQ* 2.41 recalls Scipio's walk in the clouds with his ancestors as told by Cicero in *Somnium Scipionis*. It's a Platonic trope, but note that it's also republican, due to Cicero's political fame. Cervantes even allows that the essence of republicanism is its anti-Caesarism. In *DQ* 2.43, when the hidalgo tells his squire to attend to his personal appearance, his example of a leader negligent in this area is Julius Caesar. This echoes Cicero's famous warning that Caesar's slovenly appearance reflected his tyrannical character. Cervantes alludes yet again to Cicero when Sancho notes justice among thieves in *DQ* 2.61. The squire's capacity for tyranny as a sovereign is the issue and allusions to Cicero are republican ways of maintaining the theme.

Early modern tension between Platonists and Aristotelians can be overstated. They can be mildly indistinguishable, perfectly compatible even. But in political terms, there are differences. Quentin Skinner has argued that the demise of medieval republics and the rise of transatlantic super-states in sixteenth-century Europe explains the intellectual turn toward the tradition of educating princes by way of the light of reason as revealed in utopian curriculums of study ("Political Philosophy" 441–52). Princely advice manuals by the likes of Machiavelli, Bodin, and Hobbes leaned authoritarian, endorsing the view held by Plato's Thrasymachus that might makes right. By contrast,

Skinner locates the origins of more modern political theory in Salamancan neo-Aristotelians like Francisco de Vitoria, Domingo de Soto, Luis de Molina, Francisco Suárez, and Juan de Mariana (*The Foundations of Modern Political Thought* 173–74).

Early modern novelists were interested in citing as many of the great Greek and Latin political philosophers as they could, and *Don Quijote* certainly abounds with references to the likes of Xenophone, Diogenes, Cicero, and Augustine. Nevertheless, Cervantes seems intent on maintaining a particularly aggressive dialogue with Plato, whose philosophy he dismantles on multiple occasions. Libraries and their curriculums are burned, allegorical caves remain dark dreamscapes, and despite Sancho's best efforts on the Isle of Barataria, there's no utopian paradise where educated guardians can rule over a harmonious society.

In *Don Quijote*, the fantasy of Plato's *Laws* cannot salvage a crumbling version of Plato's *Republic*. One of the novel's more meaningful Latin phrases occurs in the hidalgo's last letter to Governor Sancho Panza: «Plato amicus, sed magis amica veritas» "Plato is a friend, but a greater friend is the truth" (2.51.1050). We can hear the antimonarchic, neo-Aristotelian, empiricism of the late scholastics. On the other hand, it's difficult to accept Countess Trifaldi's endorsement of Plato's disdain for poets in *DQ* 2.38. Cervantes was a poet, playwright, and novelist, so Trifaldi's allusion reads like a joke aimed at fumbling attempts at censorship by the Habsburgs and the Inquisition: «he considerado que de las buenas y concertadas repúblicas se habían de desterrar los poetas, como aconsejaba Platón» "I have concluded that from good and harmonious republics poets must be banished, as Plato advised" (2.38.943). This is classic Cervantine irony. And the metanarrative contradiction implies sarcasm, for Cervantes's own satire can only have its desired political effect if poetry is allowed to circulate freely.

Cervantes's most overt criticism of Plato, however, appears in the novel's series of caves. The effect highlights the absurdity of Plato's contention in the *Republic* that political knowledge is found in the sunshine outside the cave of ignorance, with the latter revealed as nothing but beguiling shadows and puppet shows. Much of *Don Quijote* operates by subverting Plato's trope. There's no ideal political insight to be found outside the caves of *Don Quijote*, only more caves and more puppet shows. Don Quijote is himself a puppet when Maritornes leaves him hanging by a chord against a wall in the mysteriously absent *DQ* 1.43. Later, in *DQ* 2.22–23, the knight enters the Cave of Montesinos, where he stages a projection of his chivalric imagination. After he emerges, presumably into the light of reason but just as deluded as ever, he next attacks a puppet show, which, for its part, was again in the process of projecting his chivalric fantasies.

Cervantes's anti-Platonic satire of chivalric idealism accords with the ideas of Skinner and Maravall. His neo-Aristotelian postures against princes confirm Skinner's view of the surplus of sycophantic humanists cranking out advice manuals for sixteenth-century autocrats. His mockeries of the knight's fantasies in the Cave of Montesinos and Maese Pedro's puppet show confirm Maravall's vision of the novel's attack on chivalric idealism as the fading ideology of Habsburg Spain (*Utopía y contrautopía*). Accentuating this anti-Platonic trend, the outcome of Don Quijote's adventure in the Cave of Montesinos is not a guardian's triumph but, rather, the discordant tragedy of Dulcinea's moral and financial bankruptcy.

By the way, Cervantes's broad displeasure with imperialism and colonialism in *Don Quijote* anticipates Voltaire's satire of the foolish spirit of conquest in *Candide*, a novel that directs readers to tend to their own gardens. Don Quijote's niece Antonia Quijana floats this idea early in part one: «¿No será mejor estarse pacífico en su casa, y no irse por el mundo a buscar pan de trastrigo, sin considerar que muchos van por lana y vuelven tresquilados?» "Would it not be better to stay at home peacefully, and not to go around the world looking for bread made from something finer than wheat, never understanding that many who seek wool return shorn?" (1.7.90). In part two, the Ecclesiastic voices a graver version: «Y a vos, alma de cántaro, ¿quién os ha encajado en el celebro que sois caballero andante y que vencéis gigantes y prendéis malandrines? Andad enhorabuena, y en tal se os diga: ‹Volveos a vuestra casa y criad vuestros hijos, si los tenéis, y curad de vuestra hacienda›» "And you, you vapid soul, who has gotten it into your head that you are a knight-errant and that you defeat giants and capture villains? Go now in peace, and in going let it be said unto you: 'Return home, rear your children if you have any, and tend to your estate'" (2.31.888).

The political differences between Plato and Aristotle are not difficult, and Renaissance simplifications need not be obstacles to our comprehension. There is truth, for example, in the autocratic stereotype about Machiavelli's prince. If we are to talk about princes at all, then to some degree we have admitted the point of view of Thrasymachus in Plato's *Republic*, i.e., justice is the value system imposed by he who has power. The next steps are logically devoted to how to go about securing power before one's enemies do. Louis Althusser's *Machiavelli and Us* exhibits the attraction that "reason of state" thinking has always held for Marxists. For many of the same reasons, the effect of Machiavelli in Spain was traumatic. After all, Machiavelli's final arch example of a brutal prince who uses religion to foment a nationalist military campaign is none other than Ferdinand II of Aragón, who founded the Spanish state with Isabella I of Castile.

In Aristotelian fashion, however, Cervantes challenges absolutist princes, starting with the "reason of state" thinking mocked in the *arbitristas* of *DQ* 2.1 and extending to Governor Sancho Panza's resignation in *DQ* 2.53. In contrast to Platonists, Aristotelians are not overly interested in the characters of princes. They're focused on the idea that monarchs always fall into caves, i.e., men like Caligula, Commodus, and Caracalla are sure to come along and commit arrogant acts of ignorance and violence. Better to set aside the reading curriculums of princes and find ways to limit their monopoly on power so as to reduce the damage of their tyrannies. Abril, Mariana, and Cervantes read Aristotle's passage on the ascent of Dionysius at Syracuse in the *Politics* as a warning to nobles across Spain: tyrants will take your power unless you check theirs (Graf, "The Politics of Renouncing Zaragoza"). Finally, this explains the roles of the two major cities in *Don Quijote*, part two: Zaragoza, the capital of the Kingdom of Aragón repressed by Philip II in 1591, and Barcelona, the site of the *Corts Catalanes* of the Principality of Cataluña, Spain's oldest parliament with its written constitution dating from 1283. These cities evoke Aristotelian nostalgia for the medieval legal codes and conciliar institutions threatened by the Habsburgs (see Liggio). Similar longing for the political freedom and contractual institutions of Aragón appears in the work of historian Jéronimo de Blancas, for example, his *Aragonesium rerum comentarii* (1588) written at the height of the Antonio Pérez Affair.

(5) MONARCHOMACHS

Driving towards Zaragoza and Barcelona, then, *Don Quijote* orchestrates a philosophy of republicanism in opposition to Habsburg acts like beheading the chief magistrate of Aragón and banning specific firearms in Cataluña. In fact, Cervantes figures republicanism according to the same anti-imperialist logic found in Garcilaso de la Vega's lyrical allusions to Scipio, Cicero, and Seneca. This posture is summed up in Don Quijote's anecdote about Charles V's visit to the Pantheon of Rome, also known as the Rotunda. A Roman gentleman accompanies the Holy Roman Emperor on his tour, which includes a view down from the open skylight in the middle of the dome. Afterward, the gentleman confesses that he had experienced a strange urge: «Mil veces, Sacra Majestad, me vino deseo de abrazarme con vuestra majestad y arrojarme de aquella claraboya abajo, por dejar de mí fama eterna en el mundo» "A thousand times, your Sacred Majesty, I was seized by the desire to put my arms around your majesty and fling myself down from that skylight, so as to gain eternal fame in the world" (2.8.690).

But we can be even more specific regarding Cervantes's politics. Constraints on kings characterized much medieval and early modern political thought, i.e., ideas like the popular origins of sovereignty and the need for conciliar institutions and formal limits on royal power. The Monarchomachs, however, were a group of Huguenot theorists who went a step further and advocated the use of regicide as a political weapon. Spanish Jesuit philosopher Juan de Mariana can be considered a Catholic version of the same political philosophy.

In chapters five through eight of the first book of *De rege et regis institutione* (1598), Mariana is very much concerned with qualifying the legitimacy of regicide. Requirements must be met in order to define the king as a tyrant, and then other authorities should be consulted and the king given a chance to change course. Mariana also emphasizes that the assassin must be prepared to die in the act. In the end, however, he underscores the ultimate utility of political assassination. Jacques Clément's murder of Henry III of France in 1589 was a lamentable spectacle, yes, but Mariana grants it legitimacy because «los príncipes pueden comprender que no pueden quedar impunes sus audaces e impías maldades» "princes will comprehend that their arrogant and impious ways cannot remain unpunished" (1.6.71). More aggressive still, Mariana sees regicide as a way to prevent tyranny over the long term: «Es, sin embargo, saludable que estén persuadidos los príncipes de que si oprimen al reino, si se hacen intolerables por sus vicios y por sus delitos, pueden ser privados de vida, no sólo con derecho, sino hasta con aplauso y gloria de las generaciones venideras» "It is, nevertheless, salutary for princes to be persuaded that if they oppress the realm, if they make themselves intolerable due to their vices and their crimes, then they can have their lives taken from them, not only by right but also even to the applause and glory of future generations" (1.6.81). Like Mariana, Don Quijote's anecdote about Charles V's risky tour of Rome's Rotunda signals both the condition of suicide and the enticement of glory.

It's important to see that Cervantes's hostility against kings echoes both the Huguenots and the late scholastics. The first were a besieged group of French Protestants who held out in cities like La Rochelle: in *DQ* 1.41, 2.36, and 2.68 we find Calvinist pirates and allusions to Protestant mottos such as *sola fide* and *post tenebras spero lucem*. The second group were the neo-Aristotelian intellectuals of the School of Salamanca who tried to yoke the power of the Spanish Habsburgs: Don Quijote's desire to visit Aragón, where his caste once enjoyed political representation, parallels Abril's and Mariana's nostalgias for Castile's lost conciliar traditions. Another overtly late-scholastic reference to autocratic overreach occurs when Don Quijote warns Sancho Panza not to provoke his future citizens, who will rebel like the *Comuneros* against Charles V: «te han de quitar el gobierno tus vasallos o ha de haber entre ellos comunidades» "your vassals will have to remove you from government or else they will form rebellious communities" (2.43.977).

The Monarchomachs and late scholastics both opposed the Machiavellian logic that justified violent and immoral actions by the prince so long as they were means of preserving or advancing the state. By contrast, "reason of state" thinking predominated in the era's Platonic princely advice manuals (Skinner, "Political Philosophy"). Cervantes specifically mocks the concept in the opening scene of part two: «en el discurso de su plática vinieron a tratar en esto que llaman ‹razón de estado› y modos de gobierno» "over the course of their conversation they came to discuss that which is known as 'reason of state' and modes of government" (2.1.626). According to Márquez Villanueva, *Don Quijote* is criticism of the Spanish use of "reason of state" to justify the Expulsion of the Moriscos. Characters like Zoraida, Ricote, and Ana Félix offer Cervantes's antidotes of miscegenation, assimilation, and transculturation in lieu of isolation, expulsion, and persecution.

It's also important to recognize that Monarchomach thinking led Mariana and Cervantes to add menacing melodies to their philosophical and literary treatments of princes. Cervantes found the notion of assaulting kings vital enough to signal in each of *Don Quijote*'s prologues: «debajo de mi manto, al rey mato» "beneath my cloak, I kill the king" and «como si hubiera hecho alguna traición de lesa majestad» "as if he had committed some treasonous *lèse-majesté*" (1.pro.10, 2.pro.618). These lines anticipate long antimonarchic shadows in both parts: criticism of the Inquisition in *DQ* 1.6–7 and 2.69, freedom for the king's galley slaves in *DQ* 1.22, condemnation of the trade in black Africans in *DQ* 1.29, censure of Philip II's policies in North Africa and the Low Countries in *DQ* 1.39, a riposte to Caesarism in *DQ* 2.8, and disapproval of Philip III's inflationary monetary policy in *DQ* 1.29, 2.17, and 2.45. There's also a lot of remorse over the Expulsion of the Moriscos, the lost political independence of Aragón and Cataluña, and corruption among so many priests, judges, governors, and tax collectors.

Nor should Monarchomach thinking be overlooked as a passing fad. At the height of salon culture, the famous dictum attributed to Voltaire that the best government is "a benevolent tyranny tempered by an occasional assassination" repeats the Monarchomach perspective for modern readers. Likewise, there's Monarchomach logic in Thomas Jefferson's famous pronouncements in favor of political violence: "The spirit of resistance to government is so valuable on certain occasions, that I wish it to be always kept alive. It will often be exercised when wrong, but better so than not to be exercised at all. I like a little rebellion now and then. It is like a storm in the Atmosphere" ("Letter to Abigail Adams, February 22, 1787," Capon 172). Similarly: "The tree of liberty must be refreshed from time to time, with the blood of patriots and tyrants. It is its natural manure" ("Letter to William Stephens Smith, November 13, 1787," Boyd 356). Cromwell, surely England's most radical republican, cited Mariana to justify beheading Charles I. Ironically, Locke, who had copies of Mariana's *History of Spain* (*Historia de rebus Hispaniae*, 1592) and *On Weights and Measures* (*De ponderibus et mensuris*, 1599), probably had Cromwell in mind when he noted that even antimonarchic republics spawn tyrants.[2]

(6) CONSTITUTIONALISM

Followers of Aristotle see tyranny as a structural problem, not a matter of cultivating character or recommending the right books. Alternative traditions and forms of government attract pragmatic realists, not utopian idealists. Anticipating modern conservativism, Aristotle's point of view was popular throughout the medieval period and from the Renaissance to the Enlightenment. Mariana and Cervantes would have agreed with Jefferson regarding the vitality of killing kings. Their nostalgia for Aragón locates formalism and constitutionalism as further antidotes to princely tyranny. Authors of the Spanish Golden Age, who were anxious about the growth of an Atlantic super-state with an increasingly authoritarian monarchy ruling a global empire, understandably preferred the rational constitutionalism of Aristotelians to the utopian autocracy of Platonists. Later, classical liberals formulated similar political ideas because they experienced the apogee of the absolutist monarchies of the eighteenth and nineteenth centuries. The late scholastics simply saw those absolutist monarchies forming like clouds on the horizon.

The oath of loyalty to their local laws that the Aragonese nobility famously required of their new kings was an anti-absolutist tradition that Mariana and Abril could well appreciate. Technically speaking, Mariana and Abril represent what we would call formalism. Nevertheless, the oath indicates a collection of local laws known as *fueros*, which, in theory at least, cannot be violated by the monarch. Mariana taps into this medieval type of proto-constitutionalism when he praises the Aragonese for fiercely defending their *fueros* and chastises Castilians for sacrificing theirs before the altar of Habsburg power.

With his usual combination of mockery and contradiction, Cervantes pens a provocative meditation on the idea of a written political constitution in *Don Quijote*, part two. When Sancho cites a mysterious employment contract, which Don Quijote significantly cannot remember, it sounds rather like an assertion of freedom of speech: «debiérase acordar de los capítulos de nuestro concierto antes que esta última vez saliésemos de casa: uno dellos fue que me había de dejar hablar todo aquello que quisiese» "you should remember the articles of our agreement that we drew up before we left home this last time: one of them was that you were to permit me to talk all that I might want" (2.20.792).

Later, when Don Quijote invests Sancho with political knowledge in *DQ* 2.42–43 so that the squire will know how to govern Barataria, the knight recalls both the princely advice manuals and the "reason of state" thinking announced at the outset of *DQ* 2.1. Additionally, however, written records of laws now become a conspicuous problem. Don Quijote discloses two different definitions of the word «documentos» "documents." At first, the term appears to mean simply verbal advice: «Esto que hasta aquí te he dicho son documentos que han de adornar tu alma; escucha ahora los que han de servir para adorno de tu cuerpo» "What I have explained to you so far are documents that should adorn your soul; listen now to those that should adorn your body" (2.42.972). In response to Don Quijote's second list of "documents," however, Sancho loses heart: «será menester que se me den por escrito» "it will be necessary that they be given to me in written form" (2.43.976). When the squire finally arrives to govern Barataria in *DQ* 2.45, someone has to read to him what is written on the wall opposite his throne. The theme of written traditions reaches its apex when Governor Sancho *qua* Moses bestows a collection of laws upon the citizens of Barataria in *DQ* 2.51. These documents are overtly called a constitution: «Las constituciones del gran gobernador Sancho Panza» "The Constitutions of the Great Governor Sancho Panza" (2.51.1053). Sancho's laws, ironical and contradictory, offer us a case study of the relative feasibility of written constitutions.

Topics that drew the attention of early modern formalists and modern constitutionalists alike included freedom of religion, the right to free speech, freedom of the press, and the right to self-defense. The freedoms of religion, speech, and press were eventually recorded in the First Amendment to the US Constitution. Mariana and Cervantes manifest earlier Hispanic versions of concern for these same rights. Mariana shocked many when he approved publication of Benito Arias Montano's edition of the polyglot *Biblia regia* (1572). And any number of episodes in *Don Quijote* protest religious repression by linking the abuse and censorship of books to the persecution of human beings: the burning of the hidalgo's heretical library (1.6–7), the defense of a similar sect of books by the innkeeper Palomeque (1.32), criticism of the Inquisition in the printer's shop of Barcelona (2.62), Altisidora's vision of devils torturing books in Hell (2.70), and Sancho Panza's return home with his ass bound in buckram like a book or a victim of the Holy Office (2.73).

Among the connections between Mariana and Cervantes, the presence of «la reina doña Maguncia» "the Queen Doña Maguntia" in *Don Quijote* 2.38

alludes to the same German city where the second edition of *De rege et regis institutione* was published in 1605. That Maguntia edition of *De rege* contained a single new radical chapter on money, which would later serve as the basis for the polemical *De monetae mutatione*, which, for its part, had to be published at Cologne in 1609. None of this worked, by the way; Habsburg authorities still put Mariana on trial for *lèse-majesté*. It seems that writing novels was an easier way around the censors.

Turning to self-defense, the Second Amendment of the US Constitution enshrines "the right of the people to keep and bear arms." Two centuries earlier, a similar right preoccupied Spaniards like Mariana and Cervantes. Mariana complained that the Castilian aristocracy had allowed itself to be neutered by the Habsburg monarchy, urging nobles to recover their right to military training. Cervantes was even more specific in *Don Quijote*, alluding to a type of firearm that the Habsburgs tried to prohibit in Cataluña. In fact, towards the end of part two, there's an uncanny confluence of constitutionalist allusions to the right to bear arms and the freedoms of religion and the press. Sancho sets the tone in *DQ* 2.60 when he rebels against his master. Declaring his independence, he also cites the fourteenth-century civil war between the Houses of Ivrea (Pedro I) and Trastámara (Enrique II). The subsequent appearances of Roque Guinart and Claudia Jerónima establish a kind of secret alliance among rebellious partisans. Sancho, for example, is enamored of Claudia Jerónima and he later accepts ten gold *escudos* from Guinart. Furthermore, Guinart and Claudia Jerónima are conspicuously armed. Guinart carries «cuatro pistoletes (que en aquella tierra se llaman *pedreñales*)» "four pistolettes (which in that land were called *petronels*)"; Claudia Jerónima carries «dos escopetas» "two shotguns" and «dos pistolas» "two pistols" (2.60.1119–21).

From the novel's outset, the hidalgo's status implies the obligation to carry arms (see Lloréns). Mariana saw the right to bear arms as a matter of the nobility protecting itself against tyrannical kings: «El tirano teme necesariamente a los que le temen . . . y para evitar que éstos preparen su muerte, suprime todas sus posibles garantías y defensas, les priva de las armas» "The tyrant necessarily fears those who fear him . . . and so as to avoid that these should plot his death, he suppresses all their possible defenses and guarantees, he denies them arms" (*La dignidad real* 68). The Duke expressly signals the boar hunt as practice for war in *DQ* 2.34. The issue resurfaces in the guns of Guinart and Claudia Jerónima, signaling political tension in the countryside of Cataluña. Guinart will arrange to have Don Quijote conveyed to Barcelona in *DQ* 2.61, so the bandit's short-handled shotguns (*pedreñales*) in *DQ* 2.60 direct our attention toward a constitutional crisis that took place there around 1599. The Habsburgs wanted to impose a law banning the *pedreñal*;

but local deputies insisted that they first gain the proper approval of the *Corts Catalanes*. There was even controversy surrounding the final printed version of the law, which took more than a year and a half to produce.

At the end of this increasingly militant sequence of constitutionalist issues, we shouldn't be surprised to find that Barcelona becomes nothing less than the site of a declaration in favor of religious freedom in a printer's shop in *DQ* 2.62. All these struggles between a monarchy and a parliament over who controls things like guns and printing presses are the last gasps of medieval republicanism. They also anticipate many of the behaviors, attitudes, and ideas that would drive revolutionary struggles against absolutist monarchies in the eighteenth century. The right to a personalized religious conscience, for example, would become a pillar of modern revolutionary freedom, as would the right to self-defense.

Another effect of Cervantes's politicized road to Barcelona is that what first appears to be a matter of violent brigands extorting travelers increasingly looks like a border dispute between competing states. This is why different modes of classical justice are explicitly addressed in Guinart's episode: commutative, distributive, and legal. This is not to erase the episode's factionalism. In a kind of return of the politically repressed, Guinart and Claudia Jerónima are on one side in a struggle for power in the Cataluña countryside between two competing clans. As quasi political guerrilla groups, Nyerros and Cadells faced off in a drama not unlike Guelphs and Ghibellines in Dante's Florence (see Rico 2.60.1121n31). But Cervantes writes in the era of the princely authority of Medici and Habsburgs. Like Mariana's nostalgia for Aragón, Don Quijote's move toward Barcelona suggests that political stability had come at a cost.

Finally, when gauging *Don Quijote*'s treatment of constitutionalism, it's interesting to consider that the founders and revolutionaries of the United States were serious readers of both Cervantes and Mariana. George Washington had multiple copies of the novel. Thomas Jefferson sent Mariana's *History of Spain* to his friend James Madison. Jefferson also held *Don Quijote* in high esteem. The author of multiple drafts of the right to bear arms for the Virginia Constitution often recommended Cervantes's novel to family and friends alike. In the saga of La Mancha, Jefferson might have found inspiration for his skepticism regarding statist monetary policy, his aggressive response to the Barbary pirates, his fondness for violence against political tyranny, his resurrection of medieval republican constitutionalism, his belief in the right to self-defense, and even his lifelong struggle with the issue of slavery.

Jefferson's friend Madison also makes for an interesting comparison with Cervantes. Take Madison's view in *Federalist 51* that since men are not angels, government is a necessary evil, and that since government is made up of these same men who are not angels, it should therefore be limited and divided against itself: "If men were angels, no government would be necessary. If angels were to govern men, neither external nor internal controls on government would be necessary." Governor Sancho Panza makes repeated use of a similar metaphor when overstating his lack of corruption: «he gobernado como un ángel» "I have governed like an angel" (2.53.1067). True or not, the comment voices the Platonic myth of beneficent tyrants. Aristotelians would rather submit princes to limitations. Not surprisingly, in the same passage in which Sancho claims angelic altruism, he refuses for the second time to submit to the procedure known as the *juicio de residencia* or "review of time in office" (2.53.1066), claiming that only the Duke can judge whether or not he is corrupt. It's one of many tyrannical gestures by Governor Sancho that require more attention.[3]

(7) CORRUPTION AND CYNICISM

Murray Rothbard once described the state as nothing more than the social formation arrived at when a group of people who sustain themselves by raiding others realizes that their piracy would be more efficient if it were presented as politically mandated protection in need of further funding (*Anatomy of the State* 13–17). Irrespective of his ties to Catalan republicanism, Guinart's extortion of travelers in *DQ* 2.60 encapsulates Rothbard's idea of the state as a stylized form of highway robbery. Don Quijote's attack on an innocent barber in *DQ* 1.21 does likewise. Moreover, due to the overt injustice of the knight's theft of Mambrino's helmet, the subsequent review of the petty crimes committed by the galley slaves in *DQ* 1.22 makes the king's justice an improper monopoly on force. Worse, the Spanish state uses justice as a way of manning the oars against its foreign enemies.

Cervantes's pessimism in the face of tyranny should not surprise us. In 1598, he wrote a sonnet mocking Philip II's catafalque in Seville (see Lezra). In *DQ* 1.39, he criticizes the same king's forays into North Africa. In *DQ* 2.16–17, he attacks Philip III and Lerma's use of monetary adulteration as a way to tax Spanish citizens without their consent. The political denouement of *Don Quijote*, part two, is Baroque politics as systematic cynicism. A grotesque cave and a ridiculous puppet show in *DQ* 2.25 and 2.26 make a kind of *tabula rasa* reference to Plato's *Republic*. In *DQ* 2.27, politics are revealed—*reductio ad absurdum*—as wars between idiots over their respective abilities to imitate asses. More Platonic frame is provided by the cosmic journey atop Clavileño in *DQ* 2.41 and the princely advice in *DQ* 2.42–43. Cervantes then presents the two pillars of Habsburg tyranny circa 1600: the cases at Sancho's court allude to monetary manipulation in *DQ* 2.45, and Sancho's neighbor Ricote delivers a painful report on the Expulsion of the Moriscos in *DQ* 2.54. We then witness extreme corruption in Guinart's shakedown of travelers outside Barcelona in *DQ* 2.60, implying a kind of Rothbardian frontier where two criminal regimes face off against one another.

Nevertheless, Cervantes does not wallow in cynicism as merely a mode of pessimism. His cynicism is both less traumatic and more sophisticated. First, there's light at the end of the tunnel on the other side of the frontier occupied by Guinart. In Barcelona, we find one of the most affirmational sequences of the novel. In one chapter, *DQ* 2.62, Cervantes takes his protagonist to a printing press, alludes to an artist who once painted his portrait, and concludes with another of his characteristically Erasmian slaps at the Inquisition. Second, in *DQ* 2.63, Cervantes offers an antidote, a powerful counterexample to the Expulsion of the Moriscos, when Don Antonio Moreno befriends Ricote and Ana Félix.

Don Quijote, part two, then, draws readers past pessimism. The political lesson discloses a deeper, more philosophical and ethical point. For anarcho-capitalists like Rothbard, the right to property is the cornerstone of all other rights (*The Ethics of Liberty*). Guinart's monopoly on force is immoral precisely because the property that he so generously redistributes has been stolen. Another way to think about this is that Guinart's brand of distributive justice, which addresses the allocation of goods in a community, ends up short-circuiting the possibility of commutative justice, which would address reciprocal obligations among individuals.

A third form of justice is also at issue on the road to Cataluña. Legal justice addresses a community's obligations to individuals. At first glance, Guinart's bandits operate beyond the reach of any state; on closer examination, they operate just like a state in their own right. For example, opposite tyrannical Habsburg monetary policy which Cervantes assails in the lion episode and again in Sancho's first cases on the Isle of Barataria, the paramilitary Catalan bandit makes natural and prudent use of money as a portable and universally recognized store of value. In other words, Guinart acts, or governs, very much according to Salamancan neo-Aristotelian teachings about money: «volviendo lo no repartible y reduciéndolo a dineros, lo repartió por toda la compañía, con tanta legalidad y prudencia, que no pasó un punto ni defraudó nada de la justicia distributiva» "gathering together that which was not divisible and converting it into money, he divided it among the company, and with such legality and prudence that he did not exceed nor withhold distributive justice in any way" (2.60.1124). If Guinart's monetary policy is oddly rational and ethical, that's because it's the Habsburg bandits masquerading as monarchs who should learn from his example. After Guinart divvies up the wealth he has expropriated from the travelers, former Governor Sancho Panza sarcastically cites Cicero: «es tan buena la justicia, que es necesaria que se use aun entre los mesmos ladrones» "justice is such an important good that it's necessary to use it even among thieves" (2.60.1125). Of course, "justice among thieves" cuts both ways. What if the state is nothing more than a syndicate that robs us with monetary policy instead of guns? Sancho Panza, after all, who is a thief in part one and supposedly a governor in part two, exhibits much the same dexterity as Guinart when shuttling between robbery and justice.

From Rothbard's perspective, Governor Sancho Panza and highwayman Roque Guinart are one and the same. Don Quijote himself often proves little more than a bandit, as when he attacks a Basque hidalgo in *DQ* 1.8, runs down a barber in *DQ* 1.21, or just blocks the road for everyone in *DQ* 2.58. But political corruption is more obvious to modern readers in Cervantes's references to tax policy and outright bribery. As Adam Smith observed in *The Wealth of Nations*: "There is no art which one government sooner learns of another than that of draining money from the pockets of the people" (2.346). And prominent among the arts of taking money from citizens on display in *Don Quijote* is the art of taxation. In her letter to her husband upon learning that he has been made a governor, Teresa neatly summarizes the idea that the power to tax leads to the personal wealth of political appointees: «no pienso parar hasta verte arrendador o alcabalero, que son oficios que aunque lleva el diablo a quien mal los usa, en fin en fin, siempre tienen y manejan dineros» "I don't plan on stopping until I see you made a revenue or sales tax collector, which are offices in which, after all is said and done, and even though the devil does carry away those who abuse them, one is always controlling and directing the flow of money" (2.52.1059).

With Teresa's vision of a government's power to extract wealth from its citizens in mind, Guinart's extorsion of travelers outside Barcelona reads like another calque on taxation. Guinart pays his men, but then he gives much of the money back to the travelers. The pilgrims even come out ahead, as does Sancho, whom the robber tips ten *escudos* so that he will speak well of him. In other words, government policies not only favor the Church or the rural poor, they also try to influence the public discourse in some way. Note how the travelers approve of Guinart like citizens celebrating a refund on a tax to which they never agreed in the first place: «teniéndole más por un Alejandro Magno que por ladrón conocido» "seeing him more like Alexander the Great than a notorious thief" (2.60.1128). Also, when the archcriminal distributes the proceeds of an earlier robbery, he does so «con tanta legalidad y prudencia, que no pasó un punto ni defraudó nada de la justicia distributiva» "with such prudence and legality that he adhered strictly to distribute justice and defrauded nobody" (2.60.1124).

Another wry look at taxation and corruption surfaces in the weird story of the «doncella curiosa» "curious damsel" in *DQ* 2.49. The excess romance and intrigue acts like a school of red herring. The identities of the girl and her brother, why they are crossdressing, and just what they are doing in the street at night might seem like good questions. The oddest detail, however, is that the young woman forgets the name of her own father. This astonishing mistake calls attention to the fact that, regardless of which is her father, the man who collects taxes in the area frequents the house of a rich hidalgo. The girl's confusion hints that they are in collusion. We further suspect corruption because Sancho's butler is attracted to the girl and because Sancho considers marrying his daughter Sanchica to her brother. Part of the pair's attraction would seem to be that they represent guaranteed income: either, like the tax collector, they'll get rich off those who produce wealth, or, like the rich hidalgo, they'll bribe the tax collector to enforce policies that will benefit them.

The reason we can so often attribute ulterior motives to Sancho Panza is that, generally speaking, he is a rent-seeker. This is not always a bad thing. He displays entrepreneurial instincts in *DQ* 1.10, for example, when he asks Don Quijote to give him the formula for the Balm of Fierabrás so that he might market it. But it's not always a good thing either. In keeping with his wife Teresa's vision of government as corrupt, and rather like a free-rider, Sancho just as instinctively imagines political power as a means of obtaining wealth: «y el señor se está a pierna tendida, gozando de la renta que le dan, sin curarse de otra cosa» "and the lord puts his feet up, enjoying the rents they pay him and not worrying about a thing" (1.50.572). This idea is echoed early in part two: «será bien dar con mi cuerpo en algún gobierno provechoso que nos saque el pie del lodo» "it will be good for me to land myself a lucrative governorship which will lift me out of the mud" (2.5.667). When he imagines the wealth he will generate for his wife, Sancho's triplet of Arabic textiles discloses the medieval perspective of a crusader who gets rich by reconquering the Moorish South: «verás como te llaman a ti ‹doña Teresa Panza› y te sientas en la iglesia sobre alcatifa, almohadas y arambeles, a pesar y despecho de las hidalgas del pueblo» "you'll see how they'll call you 'Doña Teresa Panza' and you'll sit in church on a carpet, with cushions and tapestries, all regardless of and in spite of our town's *hidalgas*" (2.5.667). Later, Sancho fantasizes about getting rich off income from financial instruments, as if this were the inevitable outcome of being a monarch: «echo censos y fundo rentas y vivo como un príncipe» "I'll pitch leases and collect rents and live like a prince" (2.13.730). In his letter to Teresa, where he joyfully announces that he has finally obtained political office, Sancho also reveals his view that this means rents: «De aquí a pocos días me partiré al gobierno, adonde voy con grandísimo deseo de hacer dineros, porque me han dicho que todos los gobernadores nuevos van con este mesmo deseo» "From here, in a few days, I will depart for my governorship, and I go there with a very great desire to make money, for they have told me that all the new governors have this same desire" (2.36.931). He then equates his theft of money from Cardenio to what it will be like to govern: «No ha sido Dios servido de depararme otra maleta con otros cien escudos como la de marras, pero no te dé pena, Teresa mía, que en salvo está el que repica, y todo saldrá en la colada del gobierno» "God has not seen fit to grant me another case with another hundred *escudos* like before, but don't let that trouble you, my Teresa, for he who makes noise gets help, and it'll all come out in the wash of this governorship" (2.36.932). The risk of rent-seeking, unethical behavior also figures among the Duchess's political advice to the squire: «la codicia rompe el saco, y el gobernador codicioso hace la justicia desgobernada» "greed rips the sack, and a greedy governor will dispense injustice" (2.36.932). Finally, we should recall that in *DQ* 1.29 Sancho translates his rent-seeking into the ultimate injustice of selling the citizens he governs into slavery, as if the people of Micomicón were a natural resource to be harvested toward his personal enrichment.

The flipside of Sancho's tendency to embrace governance as personal wealth is his frequent claim that he does the opposite. But he protests too much to be believed. For instance, upon learning of a gift that Teresa has sent to the Duchess, he nervously declares: «Lo que me consuela es que esta dádiva no se le puede dar nombre de cohecho, porque ya tenía yo gobierno cuando ella las envió» "I am consoled by the fact that this gift cannot be called a bribe, because I was already governing when she sent them" (2.57.1089). Again: «En efecto, yo entré desnudo en el gobierno y salgo desnudo dél, y así podré decir con segura conciencia, que no es poco: ‹Desnudo nací, desnudo me hallo: ni pierdo ni gano›» "In effect, I entered government naked and I leave it naked, and thus I will be able to say with a clear conscience, which is no small thing: 'I was born naked, and naked I still am: I have neither lost nor gained'" (2.59.1090). Eventually, the Duke's payment to Governor Sancho undercuts all his assertions of innocence: «Estaba Sancho sobre su rucio, con sus alforjas, maleta y repuesto, contentísimo porque el mayordomo del duque, el que fue de la Trifaldi, le había dado un bolsico con docientos escudos de oro para suplir los menesteres del camino, y esto aún no lo sabía don Quijote» "Sancho was atop his ass, with his saddlebags, case, and provisions, and overjoyed because the Duke's majordomo, the one who had been Trifaldi, had given him a small purse with two hundred gold *escudos* to cover the costs of the trip, and Don Quijote still knew nothing of this" (2.57.1090). What does it mean that Sancho previously turned down this exact sum from Ricote? Is unknowing Don Quijote still complicit in Sancho's corruption? No matter which way we incline to answer these questions, it's difficult to take the measure of politics in *Don Quijote* apart from human greed.

The darkness of the Spanish Baroque is often thought to reflect the austerity of the Counter-Reformation. We see Philip II's palace at San Lorenzo de El Escorial, like we do his wardrobe, as grim and without accoutrement. Late-Renaissance Spain also consciously embraces disillusionment (*desengaño*), and the idea gains momentum as the grandiose vision of the noble, stoic defender of Catholic Europe begins to unravel. Once heroic, chivalric Spain under Emperor Charles V—whom historian Fernand Braudel called "the least unpleasant and perhaps the most attractive of those who sought hegemony in Europe" (*A History of Civilizations* 418)—starts to lack conviction by the second half of the sixteenth century. Even before Lepanto (1571), there was cause for pessimism as Spanish *tercios* had already wandered into the quagmire in the Low Countries that would become the Eighty Years War (1568–1648). The invasion of Portugal in 1580 and seething unrest in Cataluña during the sixteenth and seventeenth centuries accentuated a sense of imperial overreach. The loss of the *Armada Invencible* in 1588 added more weight to the sense of decline. In the philosophical terms of the era's manuals for princes, during the Antonio Pérez Affair and the *Alteraciones de Aragón* in 1591, Philip II had proven to be as Machiavellian as any of the era's other monarchs. Many deemed Spain's destiny tarnished.

One can imagine how such disillusionments might lend credence to what American economist and philosopher Thomas Sowell calls the "tragic view" of human existence, one skeptical of utopian schemes and chivalric idealism. On the one hand, there is surely something dark and disheartening about *Don Quijote*, especially part two. It's the same aesthetic and moral shadow found in Quevedo's famous sonnet «Miré los muros de la patria mía» "I looked at the ramparts of my country," in which the poet ponders his nation's defenses, «ya desmoronados / de la carrera de la edad cansados» "crumbling now / exhausted by the passage of the years" (vv.2–3), likewise his staff, «más corvo y menos fuerte» "more bowed and less sturdy" (v.11), and finally his sword, «vencida de la edad» "defeated by age" (v.12).

Quevedo's sonnet shows that the shadow of the Spanish Baroque still carried a dose of nationalist ideology. In key texts by Cervantes, this nationalist component is rendered pessimistic in ways that anticipate Rothbard's cynicism about the state. We see this in the coercive violence of Don Quijote's attack on the barber or Guinart's highway robbery. But there's an even more strictly classical form of cynicism lurking in the first modern novel. Written simultaneous to *Don Quijote*, Cervantes's exemplary novel *El coloquio de los perros* alludes to the ancient origins of the philosophy of cynicism, from the Greek *kynicos* and its root *kynos* or "dog." The founding figure here is

Diogenes the Cynic of Sinope (412–323 BCE), famous for preferring the company of dogs to that of men, carrying a lantern in broad daylight in search of a good man, and telling the Emperor Alexander to step aside and stop blocking the sunlight. In the context of Cipión and Berganza, the talking dogs of the exemplary tale, the dogs in *Don Quijote*'s second prologue make for another allusion to classical cynicism. Then we have the dogs mentioned by Sansón Carrasco at the end of the novel when the Salamancan student tries to animate his friend with a new pastoral fantasy: «ya tenía comprados de su propio dinero dos famosos perros para guardar el ganado, el uno llamado Barcino y el otro Butrón, que se los había vendido un ganadero del Quintanar» "he had already bought with his own money two famous dogs to guard the flock, one named Barcino and the other Butrón, which a herder from Quintanar had sold to him" (2.74.1216). All this canine symbolism, I think, reinforces an anti-imperialist, Monarchomach attitude against Caesarian expansionism, corruption, and repression, as well as pre-Imperial nostalgia for the constitutional limitations of smaller republics. And evidence is again provided by Mariana, who identifies with Diogenes in the prologue to his *De monetae mutatione* of 1609.[4]

Together with heroic restraint in *Don Quijote*, we find an agrarian ideal that acts like a refuge against metropolitan corruption. This echoes the *beatus ille* theme in Horace and the vision of country as antidote to court in Guevara's *Menosprecio de corte y alabanza de aldea*, and it anticipates the Cincinnatus myth so popular among the American founders. The idea appears in the lifestyle of Don Diego de Miranda, who maintains a productive and peaceful estate, thus serving as an Aristotelian exemplar in *DQ* 2.16. The same idea reappears in Sancho's resignation as Governor of Barataria. The peasant declares his preference for a life free of governance, and so he retreats to the farm, the locus of his «antigua libertad» "ancient liberty": «Mejor me está a mi una hoz en la mano que un cetro de gobernador» "I'm better off with a sickle in my hand than a governor's scepter" (2.53.1065). The anti-federalists of the revolutionary period of the United States are often mocked as ingenuous, especially when compared to their more urbane counterparts. Brazilian political scientist José Guilherme Merquior, for example, saw Jefferson as "dreaming of agrarian virtue within autarky" while his colleagues proceeded in more responsible ways: "Hamilton was deepening the psychological grasp of liberalism and Madison was devising a republican machinery that suited the manifold morals of a commercial society" (44). But the psychology and political machinery of republican liberalism seek geographical checks to the impulsive masses of cities. For many, an agrarian, autarkic aristocracy offers refuge against the tyranny of urban bribery.

(8) SANCHO TYRANT?

If Cervantes composed a universal satire from a broadly disillusioned perspective, his work also had its targets. Gauging Sancho's capacity for specific tyrannies is a major aspect of *Don Quijote*. A lot of symbolism suggests it, especially in part two. In *DQ* 2.1, the debate over things like "reason of state," different "modes of government," and laws to reform the "republic" foregrounds politics. Later, prior to Sancho's governorship, the flight with Don Quijote atop Clavileño in *DQ* 2.41 deploys the classical ritual of cosmic perspectivism designed to instill political humility (Cascardi, *Cervantes, Literature, and the Discourse of Politics*). Subsequently, there's the overt sequence of "princely advice" in *DQ* 2.42–43. In *DQ* 2.45, when Sancho assumes power over Barataria, he struggles to make out writing on the wall opposite his throne, referring to the Biblical judgment against the tyrant Belshazzar (see Daniel 5.1–31). Sancho's time as governor then involves a series of royal judgments and decrees rendered with varying degrees of prudence and despotism.

Also calling our attention to Sancho's capacity for tyranny, like Thrasymachus in Plato's *Republic* or Machiavelli in *The Prince*, Sancho often equates might with right. In the matter of the rivalry between Basilio and Camacho, for example, he's at once metaphorical and direct about whose side he prefers: «El rey es mi gallo: a Camacho me atengo» "My cock's the king: I'm with Camacho" (2.20.799). Don Quijote is not surprised by Sancho's vulgar attraction to power, and he sums up the squire's view with emphasis on force: «eres villano y de aquellos que dicen: ‹¡Viva quien vence!›» "you are a peasant, and one of those who shout, 'Long live the victor!'" (2.20.799). John Acton (1834–1902) is an iconic liberal for having underscored the tragedy that power corrupts human beings. Right before Sancho departs to govern Barataria, the Duke observes that power is above all else tempting: «Si una vez lo probáis, Sancho –dijo el duque–, comeros heis las manos tras el gobierno, por ser dulcísima cosa el mandar y ser obedecido» "'Once you try it, Sancho,' said the Duke, 'you will be licking your fingers to be governor again, for it is a very sweet thing to command and to be obeyed'" (2.42.968).

After he is made governor, Sancho twice refers to the Spanish custom of putting office holders on trial at the end of their terms. And as we would expect of a tyrant, he twice rejects the idea. It's notable that in the first case, by way of a Machiavellian "reason of state," Sancho also considers the idea of directing political violence against his own doctor: «pídanmelo en residencia, que yo me descargaré con decir que hice servicio a Dios en matar a un mal médico, verdugo de la república» "let them ask me about it during the review of my time in office, and I'll justify my actions by saying that I did service to God by killing a bad doctor who would murder the republic" (2.47.1007). Sancho articulates the classical view of political philosophy and medicinal healing as overlapping fields of knowledge. Werner Jaeger indicates this overlap in his book on ancient Greek education and Jacques Derrida analyzes the same idea in Plato's vision of the sovereign who must know how to use the *pharmakon*, which can be either medicine or poison ("Plato's Pharmacy"). In sixteenth-century Spain, Guevara described political appointments to government offices as being like «la rosa del campo de la qual haze su miel el abeja y aun su ponzoña la araña» "the rose in the field from which the bee makes his honey but also the spider her venom" (*Menosprecio de corte*, ch.2). The same continuity between politics and medicine allows us to grasp the irony of Governor Sancho turning on Pedro Recio. Again, he can be a loveable sidekick, but as a sovereign Sancho often acts like Nero discarding Seneca or Dionysius disappointing Plato.

The squire-governor as a potential tyrant in the novel's second part also explains Sancho's fearful mania regarding beards while at the Duke and Duchess's palace. Sancho is horrified at the idea of submitting to the humiliation of having his beard cleaned like his master's in *DQ* 2.32. He's equally traumatized by his vision of the bearded faces of Countess Trifaldi and her ladies-in-waiting in *DQ* 2.39. Finally, he is punished by having to present his face and beard to abuse by a series of mourners at Altisidora's funeral in *DQ* 2.69. This is all in reference to the tyrant Dionysius of Syracuse, who trimmed his own beard with hot coals out of fear of being assassinated by barbers. Mariana noted the popular example in *De rege et regis insitutione*: «Qué vida tan triste y miserable la de quien se ve obligado a quemar sus cabellos y sus barbas con ascuas por temor a la mano de un barbero, como sucedía al tirano Dionisio» "What a miserable and sad life is that of he who finds himself obligated to burn his hair and beard with hot coals out of fear for the hand of a barber, as was the case with the tyrant Dionysius" (1.6.86; see Cicero, *Tusculanae disputationes* 5.20). Sancho's beard anxiety is another way by which Cervantes underscores Ciceronian concern for limits on tyrants in lieu of Platonic education of princes.

Here is a case, however, in which the binary opposition between Plato and Aristotle advanced by critics like Skinner ("Political Philosophy") and Maravall (*Utopía y contrautopía*) loses some of its validity. This is because Cicero can be a mediating figure, Neoplatonist by way of his interest in the celestial character of Scipio and neo-Aristotelian due to his defense of the Roman Republic under assault by Caesars. We see this admixture even in a Jesuit like Mariana. Normally formalist, analytical, and historical (Aristotelian), in one passage of his *De rege et regis institutione*, for instance, he also emphasizes an ancient fable about princely education (Platonic): «pues se dice que Aquiles fue entregado para su educación al centenauro Quirón, que era un monstruo horrible, pero tenía cara de hombre y de la cintura abajo tenía cuerpo de toro o caballo» "for it is said that Achilles was delivered for his education to the centaur Chiron, who was a horrible monster, but who had the face of a man and from the waist down had the body of a bull or a horse" (2.10.213). Sancho says to Ricote that he has ruled Barataria «como un sagitario» "like a Sagittarius" (2.54.1075), referring to the same mythical teacher of Achilles. Neoplatonism plays a role even in mostly Aristotelian texts like *Don Quijote* and *De rege et regis institutione*.

Despite the political gamut of *Don Quijote* from ancient myths to modern advice manuals, Cervantes's survey of the potential tyranny of Sancho circles back to two main sources of disillusionment: (1) the exploitation and the religious and ethnic persecution of Moriscos in southern and eastern Spain, and (2) the use of inflationary monetary policy by Habsburgs as a way to finance wars and courtly extravagance. Sancho's reign opens with allusions to monetary theory and climaxes with the Morisco question. Echoing *DQ* 2.17, where the mad knight figuratively attacks one of Philip III's money carts, Sancho's rule begins in *DQ* 2.45 with a nod to a famous scriptural passage on monetary adulteration in the Book of Daniel (the Bible's "writing on the wall" refers literally to measures, weights, deficiencies, and divisions, all elements of debasement). His rule ends with the haunting invasion of Barataria in *DQ* 2.53, followed by Sancho's brushes with Ricote in *DQ* 2.54 and then Ana Félix in *DQ* 2.63–65. Pro-Morisco sentiment is perhaps most focused in the figure of Don Antonio Moreno, who welcomes Don Quijote to Barcelona and vows to assist the Félix family.

(9) MORISCOS

Márquez Villanueva's vision of *Don Quijote* as criticism of Spain's "reason of state" approach to the Morisco problem in 1609–14 is spot on. Cervantes had already come to the defense of Moriscos in part one, especially when the innkeeper Palomeque objects to his books being burned like members of a sacrilegious sect: «Pues ¿por ventura –dijo el ventero– mis libros son herejes o flemáticos?» "'So, somehow my books,' said the innkeeper, 'are heretics or unrepentant?'" (1.32.371). Pro-Morisco sentiment also appears in the novel's syncretic and transethnic program: Dulcinea is a Morisca, the Algerian Zoraida represents the Virgin Mary, Ana Félix loves Don Pedro Gregorio, etc.

But criticism of the tyranny of the Expulsion of the Moriscos reaches a feverish pitch in part two, especially in its series of anti-Platonic caves. The Cave of Montesinos sets the tone by mocking the aesthetic and ideological preferences of the Habsburg court (see Maravall, *Utopía y contrautopía*). Upon resigning as Governor of Barataria, Sancho refuses for a second time to submit to the traditional *juicio de residencia* or "review of time in office" (2.53.1066); and subsequently, the narrator identifies Sancho with the arch tyrant Nero by citing a popular ballad «Mira Nero de Tarpeya / a Roma cómo se ardía» "From Tarpeia Nero does gaze / at Rome consumed and set ablaze" (2.54.1070n26). The exile of the Moriscos as a case of imperial tyranny is suggested because Sancho adopts Nero's perspective precisely in the presence of his Morisco neighbor Ricote, whom he refuses to assist in his efforts to recover his fortune and evade the Inquisition's flames. In other words, Sancho embodies an anti-Morisco attitude toward Ricote, and this even though he happily partakes of his desperate neighbor's rather expensive food and drink (cf. *DQ* 1.11). This sets the stage for politically charged poetic justice when Sancho falls into yet another of the novel's caves in *DQ* 2.55. In *DQ* 2.63–65 the ex-governor's reencounter with Ricote, along with daughter Ana Félix, is further evidence of an anti-expulsion agenda.

The Félix family allows Cervantes to contextualize the fallen governor with the great moral and political issue of the day, i.e., the Expulsion of the Morisco population from southern Spain between 1609 and 1614. Now we understand the reason for the oddly late date of 20 July 1614 at the end of Sancho's letter to Teresa way back in *DQ* 2.36. According to the novel's internal chronology, the first part takes place well before 1605 and the second starts soon after the end of the first. But Cervantes is not concerned with maintaining temporal coherence in his already chaotic novel; he's signaling a political, economic, and cultural sea change that has occurred in Spain via the ethnic cleansing that was coming to a close while he was writing.

Having established the Morisco question, Cervantes adds criticism of the Inquisition and an attack on censorship as he brings the novel's politics to a climax in *DQ* 2.62. First, Don Antonio Moreno discloses the existence of his enchanted head to «los señores inquisidores» "our lords the inquisitors" (2.62.1142), who order him to dismantle it. Then, Don Quijote visits a printer's shop. Finally, at the end of *DQ* 2.65, Moreno offers to plead at the court of Philip III for a pardon on behalf of his new Morisco friends. The surname Moreno, meaning "brown," underscores his mediating ethnicity and makes him function like the symbolic Sierra Morena in part one. Furthermore, by agreeing to defend Moriscos from unfair persecution, Moreno adopts an anti-inquisitorial posture and models the ancient legal principle *in dubio pro reo* ("[when] in doubt, [decide] for the accused"), the same principle at the heart of the fable of the bridge in *DQ* 2.51. This series of episodes, then, specifies mercy and empathy toward the Morisco population as antidotes to the aggressive "reason of state" logic that had driven the policy of expulsion and according to which *in dubio pro estado* ("[when] in doubt, [decide] for the state").

(10) MONEY

Biographer William Byron's intuition that much of Cervantes's experience of disillusionment was fiscal and financial is also spot on. The Crown's policy of debasing the currency carried the same "reason of state" justifications as the Expulsion of the Moriscos. Indeed, since debasement paid the Crown's debts, it therefore carried virtually all of their statist justifications. Cervantes's satire of the policy is savage, likely due to inflation's overarching consequences, both as a means of funding other objectionable polices and as a tax that weighed most heavily on the poor, who spent a greater percentage of their income on everyday needs.

How do we know Cervantes was concerned about this topic? There are clues already in part one. The first metaphor of the first modern novel describes Rocinante's rotting hooves as having «más cuartos que un real» "more quarter cracks than a piece of eight" (1.1.42). Sancho Panza finds a ragged valise containing 100 *escudos* in the Sierra Morena in *DQ* 1.23, and he later fantasizes about turning the black citizens of Micomicón into gold and silver in *DQ* 1.29 (see Graf, "Sancho Panza"). All these tropes signal that Cervantes understood the phenomenon—studied previously by Oresme, Copernicus, and Gresham—according to which bad money floods the marketplace and good money disappears. We should add that Sancho's Micomicón trope also hints at Mariana's argument that unauthorized inflationary monetary policy is a kind of tyrannical theft because, ultimately, it's also a kind of slavery.

Even clearer evidence that Cervantes objected to Philip III and the Duke of Lerma's policy of raising funds this way is found in two sets of chapters in *Don Quijote*, part two. First, at the end of *DQ* 2.16, and in one of his more sagacious moments, the mad knight finishes his praise for the profession of creative writing by lauding Horace and Ovid, specifically, two classical satirists. Don Quijote encourages the writing of «sermones al modo de Horacio» "sermons [satires] in the manner of Horace" and then expresses awe for Ovid's willingness to assume the risk of exile: «hay poetas que, a trueco de decir una malicia, se pondrán a peligro que los destierren a las islas de Ponto» "there are poets who, as a consequence of uttering spite, will put themselves in danger of being exiled to the Black Sea" (2.16.758–59). If we recall that Cervantes embraces the art of satire in the second prologue, then this exaltation of Horace and Ovid shifts our reading into a more critically political mode.

The knight's confrontation with the lions in *DQ* 2.17 subsequently specifies the target of the novel's satire, namely, Philip III and Lerma's inflationary monetary policy. *DQ* 2.17 is shot through with references to this policy:
(1) Diego de Miranda initially thinks the lion cart carries the king's money;
(2) as symbols of the Kingdom of León, images of lions frequented the royal
coinage; (3) Don Quijote appears to warn commoners to avoid copper money
when he gives the lion keeper and the cart driver each a gold *escudo* to compensate them for their time; (4) the lion keeper intends to report the victory to
Philip III and Lerma: «prometióle de contar aquella valerosa hazaña al mismo
rey, cuando en la corte se viese» "he promised him to relate that valiant deed
to the king himself, as soon as he arrived at court" (2.17.768). This also explains the episode's other emphatic aspects, such as Don Quijote's flashy new
moniker when he declares himself «el Caballero de los Leones» "the Knight
of the Lions" (2.17.768). Then there's Cide Hamete's booming praise: «¡Oh
fuerte y sobre todo encarecimiento animoso don Quijote de la Mancha, espejo
donde se pueden mirar todos los valientes del mundo!» "Oh, most strong and
above all estimation courageous Don Quijote de la Mancha, mirror in which
are reflected all the other valiant men of the world!" (2.17.765).

The second set of chapters that focus on Habsburg inflationary monetary
policy starts with *DQ* 2.45, precisely when Sancho assumes the throne of
Barataria. The political apotheosis of Governor Sancho opens with "writing
on the wall," thus, establishing the Biblical frame of both the tyranny and the
monetary adulteration attributed to King Belshazzar in the Book of Daniel. In
the remainder of *DQ* 2.45, all three cases that Sancho must adjudicate involve
monetary manipulation or inflation in one way or another. The theme is so
persistent that the sequence appears to counsel readers not to be fooled by
the irregular qualities and quantities of the different metals in the coins now
being minted by the authorities.

In the first case, a dispute between a tailor and his client affirms that you
cannot get more for less. When the client demands more caps from the same
cut of cloth, the tailor responds by producing tinier caps, i.e., less useful caps.
It's an elegant actuarial view of the effect of inflation as a currency's loss of
purchasing power. Simply put, the quantity and quality of what a currency
can buy diminishes. The second case reveals the injustice that inflationary
monetary policy represents within a moral or legal framework that forbids
the charging of interest on loans. Under such circumstances, a creditor will
be penalized for his generosity because a debtor will steal the time value of
the money he has lent. The third and final case is that of a swineherd, who is
literally on his way home from paying his taxes, and who then gets robbed by
a prostitute who tricks him into paying twice for her services, the first time
legally and the second time with the assistance of Governor Sancho Panza.

Informed readers will also note that she is quite concerned with the metallic content of the coins paid her. As in other casuistic scenes, here Sancho plays both roles, first that of a tyrant (say, Belshazzar) and then that of a beneficent judge advocate (say, Solomon). The initial concord between the justice system of Barataria and the prostitute suggests they're one and the same. Also, since the swineherd is already on his way home from paying taxes, the state appears to be "double dipping," so to speak. First, the state shakes down her citizens through taxes, perhaps offering short-term pleasures; then she does so again by way of the hidden tax of inflation, which leverages the law and monetary policy to rob citizens.

Viewed in political terms, the money scenes of *DQ* 2.45 also evoke the corruption and decay of Republican Rome. Lucius Junius Brutus, the founder of the Roman Republic, carried gold in his cane to remind himself to keep his thoughts secret so as to avoid the wrath of the tyrant Tarquin. When Tarquin's son raped Lucretia, Brutus and his allies rebelled, afterwards pledging to never again accept monarchical rule. In *DQ* 2.45, given that the man who carries gold in his cane is exposed as a deceitful debtor, and given that a prostitute lies about being raped, Cervantes has figured the corruption of classical republican ideals, reinforcing the ancient insight that monetary adulteration often coincides with the rise of Caesarism.

The cat attack that follows in *DQ* 2.46 complements *DQ* 2.45 by reworking Don Quijote's previous victory over Philip III's debased money in the lion episode of *DQ* 2.17. This time felines win, scratching Don Quijote so severely with their claws that it takes him a week to recover. Whereas in *DQ* 2.17 the hero's tip of two *escudos* indicates that a personal victory over inflation can be had by saving gold; in *DQ* 2.46, the shredded hero and his agonizing recovery are metaphors for hidalgos who receive a fixed stipend paid according to the Crown's unit of account. The purchasing power of his pension falls away as the prices of everyday goods rise.

As with other reading strategies, stressing the presence of specifically political topics in *Don Quijote* affects how we interpret the novel's symbolic content. On multiple occasions in *Don Quijote*, serious political issues, such as taxation or the right to own specific firearms, lie in wait just below the surface of what might seem like little more than comical or lascivious story-telling. No matter how Governor Sancho rules, for example, in any of the Solomon-like cases of *DQ* 2.45, the chapter's run of narrative gestures at inflation, the time value of money, and the hidden status or questionable metallic content of coins still calls attention to the Habsburg crime of debasing the nation's currency. Another example can be seen in the continuity between the lion episode of *DQ* 2.17 and the cat adventure of *DQ* 2.46, which in addition to felines now includes the effects of rising prices. Likewise, Sancho's quip in *DQ* 1.29 that he will turn black Africans into silver and gold satirizes Habsburg monetary policy and, by adding the element of slavery, articulates moral criticism of said policy. Upon inspection, we find that the first metaphor of the first modern novel is Cervantes's pathetic description of Rocinante's rotting hooves having «más cuartos que un real» "more quarter cracks than a piece of eight" (1.1.42).

Imagine we were to follow Miguel de Unamuno's suggestion that we read *Don Quijote* like a national Bible, or at least a cultural artefact that offers detailed, if comical and convoluted, advice about what to consider when thinking about sociopolitical practices and institutions. If we were to focus on those passages in *Don Quijote* most related to governance, then, in a stricter sense, we would be reading the novel as a kind of constitution. At which point, a case could be made that we should consider the novel's warnings regarding what happens when a nation allows its political authorities to monopolize money. The temptation to raise funds by debasing the currency is too powerful, and the consequences of this insidious form of taxation without representation are nearly always destructive (see this book's appendix).

Finally, among the uncanny results of reading *Don Quijote* as a political document are the multiple ways in which early American politics echo aspects of the first modern novel. Jefferson alone makes for a wide-ranging case study. His agrarian idealism, his disdain for central banks, and his struggle with the institution of slavery all correlate with ideas found in Cervantes's masterpiece. Even more curiously choreographed is the contrast between the foreign policies advocated by Jefferson and John Quincy Adams. The contrast reads like the struggle between the adventurous Don Quijote and those characters who would restrain him. Jefferson's and Madison's aggressive prosecutions of the Barbary Wars (1801–05, 1815) seems inspired by the captivity of Viedma and Cervantes; whereas, in his speech of 4 July 1821, the younger Adams sounds more like Antonia Quijana or the Ecclesiastic when he insists that America abstain from foreign wars, that she go not abroad, "in search of monsters to destroy."

NOTES

1. For Cervantes's deep interest in the unruliness of urban life, see the study by Piñero and Reyes of the role played by Seville in his novels. For Spanish cities as sites of struggle between liberty and tyranny under the Habsburgs, see Nader.

2. For the continuities between the antimonarchical radicalism of the late scholastics and the classical liberal response to authoritarianism, see Rothbard (*Economic Thought* 117–22, 314), Skinner (*The Foundations of Modern Political Thought*

173–74), Calzada, Fernández Álvarez (39n24, 42), and Graf ("Juan de Mariana"). For a review of political theories of tyrannicide, see Brincat.

3. The connections between early modern Spain and the early United States are likely more extensive than most care to admit. John Adams refers to the medieval "fuero" tradition of Spain in Letter IV, "A Defence of the Constitutions of Government of the United States of America" (1787): "This extraordinary people have preserved their ancient language, genius, laws, government, and manners without innovation, longer than any other nation of Europe."

4. For the contours and targets of Cervantes's philosophical cynicism in *El coloquio de los perros*, see Graf ("La antropología subversiva").

Chapter Five

Don Quijote and Economics

". . . the laborer is worthy of his hire."

—Luke 10.7

A good example of the theme of politics overlapping with that of economics in *Don Quijote de la Mancha* surfaces near the end of part two, when Sancho Panza resists his master's attempt to lash him in *DQ* 2.60. Sancho's refrain «Ni quito rey ni pongo rey» "I remove no king; I install no king" (2.60.1118) recalls the fourteenth-century civil war between those loyal to Pedro I and Enrique II. But in more modern terms, Sancho represents the peasant-laborer faction of the third estate rebelling against the impoverished low-ranking nobility of the second estate. Given this basic contour of the Ancient Regime, Sancho's political defiance suggests a crisis in what Marxist historians refer to as the relations of production. The economic relations that characterize the old feudal order are in decline and those of the new bourgeois capitalist society are on the rise. After all, Sancho is a serf rebelling against the local gentry. This transpired quite often in the late medieval and early modern periods, and under complex circumstances. Historian Joseph Pérez, for example, notes that the turning point of the *Comuneros* Rebellion came in September of 1520 when the urban elite got dragged by the peasants of Dueñas into their conflict with the landed aristocracy (170–77). Sancho's self-centered rebelliousness is an early version of Lenin's most persistent problem, namely, peasants who dream of owning land and collecting rent more than they do of fighting for any revolution.

A classical-liberal perspective on Sancho's political independence in *DQ* 2.60 would accentuate his status as a mercenary, that is, his desire to sell himself to the highest bidder. It's a climactic moment in what Carroll

Johnson once called "the drama of Sancho's salary" (see *Cervantes* 15–36), and its successful resolution coincides with the novel's exhibition of what David Quint calls "the gentler, wiser Don Quijote" (see 93–130). From a market-oriented perspective, Sancho's free agency anticipates his miraculous calculation of just how many *reales* his master will pay him for the labor of his lashes in *DQ* 2.71. In this sense, Sancho's declaration of individual sovereignty in *DQ* 2.60 exposes one of the pillars of classical liberalism, found in thinkers from Aristotle to Adam Smith. To wit, freedom, that is, uncoerced labor, is not only morally but also economically preferable to slavery. In the direction of classical liberalism, Sancho's economic type of individualism at the end of *Don Quijote* foreshadows any number of nationalist and revolutionary struggles that emphasize the rights and liberties of citizens.

But there's a more precise economic meaning lodged in Sancho's allusion to the medieval civil war between Pedro I and Enrique II. The late-scholastic philosopher Juan de Mariana was a giant among the Golden Age intellectuals known as the School of Salamanca. Famous for his down to earth *Historia general de España* (1601), he was also known for his public confrontations with the Habsburgs over their inflationary monetary policy. In two of his essays, the "De moneta" chapter of the 1605 edition of *De rege et regis institutione* (see this book's appendix) and the more elaborate *De monetae mutatione* of 1609, Mariana essentially charged Philip III and the Duke of Lerma with tyranny on the grounds that their debasement of the money supply was an unauthorized tax and therein a type of slavery. Furthermore, in all three of these texts, Mariana allows the traditional hero, Enrique II "the Honorable," and the traditional villain, Pedro I "the Cruel," to momentarily exchange monikers precisely according to the metallic content of their respective coinages. By way of archeology and metallurgy, and even earlier than the Latin edition of *Historiae de rebus Hispaniae Libri XXX* (1592), the great Jesuit historian had discovered that the coins of Pedro I were superior to those of his rival Enrique II. In other words, if viewed strictly in terms of their monetary policies, the historical record ironically reveals Pedro to be more honorable and less cruel than Enrique.

Just as John Maynard Keynes would argue three centuries later, Mariana fully recognized that existential emergencies might call for monetary debasement. However, during the decades either side of 1600, he gradually became convinced that a scientific understanding of the Crown's manipulation of the money supply carried grave ethical and political consequences. The different qualities of their respective coinages did not prevent the more inflationary Enrique II from taking his brother Pedro I's throne. But this only means that additional forces were at work that outweighed the contrast between their monetary policies. In other words, Enrique II got away with minting bad money either because someone intervened (as did Bertrand du Guesclin) or because supporters were willing to assume the material and social costs of his inflated money.

In the fluid situation of a civil war, military interventions and economic sacrifices abound. Nevertheless, Mariana also saw that in the absence of existential threats, monetary debasement's negative consequences tend to outweigh its benefits. And he would grow increasingly radical on this score, eventually turning monetary policy into his personal litmus test for loyalty to the Spanish Crown. By 1609 he was so confrontational that the Habsburgs burned all the copies of *De monetae mutatione* that they could find and had its author arrested and put on trial by the Inquisition for *lesa majestad*, i.e., treachery against the king. Clearly, criticism of the Crown's monetary policy carried risk.

Given all the other critical references to Habsburg monetary policy in *Don Quijote*, especially *DQ* 1.1, 1.29, 2.17, and 2.45, it is likely that Sancho's appropriation in *DQ* 2.60 of Guesclin's witticism at the end of the fight between Pedro I and Enrique II insinuates Mariana's monetary analysis of the same contest. My thesis here is that Cervantes incorporated early modern economic ideas into the casuistic puzzles of multiple passages in *Don Quijote*. Specifically, I'll argue that Cervantes's novel voices a weighty and systematic, albeit dissembling and coded, criticism of the harm caused by the Habsburg policy of monetary debasement at the beginning of seventeenth century.[1]

A key historical factor in the economic backdrop to *Don Quijote* was rapid globalization during the Renaissance. New sea routes opened to the New World and the Orient, international networks of trade were established, and merchants began to service growing domestic and foreign markets. During this trade revolution in early modern Europe: (a) larger banking and financing needs arose; (b) there was an explosion of complex financial instruments; (c) states were increasingly drawn to monetary debasement as way to raise revenue; and (d) there was everywhere a deluge of currencies, counterfeiters, tariffs, tax collectors, and marketplace meddling by authorities of all stripes. In Spain, public deposit banks had been established at Barcelona in 1401 and Valencia in 1407, and by the middle of the sixteenth century, due to the massive importation of New World silver, "the fairs at Medina del Campo became the focus of a new financial network in Western Europe" attended by "as many as two thousand merchants who were served by fifteen or so bankers for the settlement of transactions" (D'Emic 221).

A narrower frame explains the presence of so many topics related to economics in *Don Quijote* by way of the huge influx of gold and silver from the New World. These precious metals added momentum to the new economic reality and also raised the theoretical specter of inflation supposedly induced by the sudden presence of so much money. Scholars still debate its effects, but the influx appears to have caused inflation of around 1.5% per year, although not without the occasional spike (Bernholz and Kugler 2). That would sound enviable to a central banker of the twenty-first century, but after a mostly deflationary medieval period, it came as something of a shock to many. Then there were the sovereign bankruptcies of 1557, 1575, 1597, 1627, 1647, 1656, and 1662. Given the enormous amounts of gold and silver entering Spain at this time, these bankruptcies also came as a shock. In his book *Art and Money*, Marc Shell relates that Philip II called the gold and silver from the New World "ghost money" because it didn't seem to produce any real wealth (133).

A more subtle historical justification for an economically-inflected inter-pretation of *Don Quijote* is allowed because many economic concepts, both ancient and modern, were the subject of much analysis by the theologians of the School of Salamanca. Why should this be so? At the turn of the fif-teenth century, the Catholic Monarchs, Isabel I of Castile and Fernando II of Aragón, forced the conversions and expulsions of the Jews and Muslims of Spain. Before that time, during the Reconquest period, financially lucra-tive activities had been left largely to Jews and Moors because business was held to be inherently sinful. It's sociologically realistic that Sancho's exiled Morisco neighbor Ricote should be a shopkeeper. Theoretically, a theologian or parish confessor could assume that Christians worried about the fate of their souls would not shoulder the moral hazard of becoming merchants or bankers. After the expulsions and conversions, however, the late-scholastic thinkers of Spain were forced to attend to the rules of commerce and finance. This is because their congregations now rather abruptly teemed with *con-versos* and Moriscos, that is, New Christian merchants and bankers worried about the fates of their souls given their professions and the anti-capitalist tone of Church authorities.

Due to these New Christians, as well as Old Christians assuming ventures vacated by exiled merchants, a lot of complex financial activities now came under the purview of the late-scholastic theologians of Spain. In 1517, a group of Spanish merchants in Antwerp approached Francisco de Vitoria directly and asked him about the moral legitimacy of their profession (Grice-Hutchinson, *Early Economic Thought* 98). Subsequent generations of stu-dents at Salamanca would have to think deeply about commerce and finance. Add printing presses in the major urban centers of Spain, and you have the makings of a "school" of economic thought. A flood of manuals around the middle of the sixteenth century, such as Cristóbal de Villalón's *El provechoso tratado de cambios y contrataciones de mercaderes y reprobación de usura*

(Valladolid, 1541), Luis Saravia de la Calle's *La instrución de mercaderes muy provechosa* (Medina del Campo, 1544), and Tomás de Mercado's *Suma de tratos y contratos* (Sevilla, 1571), offers a good barometer of the scale of both academic and public interest in the details of intricate merchant practices involving unusual financial instruments. Put simply, both confessors and their flocks required guidance through this increasingly labyrinthine sector of society that still seemed so fraught with moral danger. The authors of these manuals sought to meet that need, but they also ended up in a lot of theoretical debates with each other.

These dramatic and often agonizing social transformations in Golden Age Spain and the consequent birth of early modern economic theory are why so many of the Austrian School argue that the free-market mentality, which reached its pinnacle during the eighteenth and nineteenth centuries, can trace its own origins back to the late scholastics of the sixteenth and seventeenth centuries. Men like Domingo de Soto (1494–1560), Juan de Medina (1490–1547), Martín de Azpilcueta (1491–1586), Diego de Covarrubias (1512–77), Luis Saravia de la Calle (1500s), Tomás de Mercado (1525–75), Luis de Molina (1535–1600), Juan de Mariana (1536–1624), Jerónimo Castillo de Bobadilla (c.1547–c.1605), Juan de Salas (1553–1612), Juan de Lugo (1583–1660), and Felipe de la Cruz Vasconcillos (1600s?) truly were keen to study, explain, and debate phenomena like interest rates, prices of goods and services, theories of value, currency exchange rates, monopolies, inflation, monetary policy, and relations among supply, demand, scarcity, and abundance. The intellectual debts owed by Austrians to the School of Salamanca and the historical continuities between the economic ideas of Renaissance Spain and those of Enlightenment France, early Industrial England, and revolutionary North America have been documented by the likes of Carl Menger ("History of Theories"), Bernard Dempsey, Joseph Schumpeter (*History of Economic Analysis*), Raymond de Roover, Marjorie Grice-Hutchinson, Murray Rothbard (*Economic Thought*), Jesús Huerta de Soto, and Darío Fernández-Morera.

Now, in addition to drawing on his empirical experience of late sixteenth-century economic reality, and in addition to drawing on his direct or indirect knowledge of the ideas of late-scholastic thinkers like Mariana, Molina, and Mercado, it's also quite clear that Cervantes drew on his detailed understanding of Apuleius's *The Golden Ass* (c.175 CE). Indeed, many have argued that this ancient classical precursor to the modern picaresque influenced the content, structure, and morality of *Don Quijote* (see Graf, "The Economy of Asses"). This is important because it is precisely thanks to Apuleius that the novel has long been a consciously mercantile form of creative narrative fiction that displays a lot of interest in things like commerce and monetary policy. "Business directed me to Thessaly," says Lucius in the opening lines of the great classical *urtext* of the picaresque (33).

Towards the end of *The Golden Ass* in "The Tale of the Wicked Step-mother," Apuleius develops a spectacular allegorical critique of the monetary adulteration perpetrated again and again by generations of lawless Roman emperors. What Apuleius calls the "moral earthquake" (214) of the step-mother's murder of her stepson is solved by way of circumstantial evidence provided by an apothecary who testifies that one of the stepmother's servants had purchased from him the poison used in the crime. Heavy political symbolism attends the apothecary's story about how he preserved this evidence: "I did not at once accept the proffered price. I said to the man, 'Lest any of these goldpieces that you produce should turn out to be lightweight or base-metal, put them in this bag and seal it with your own seal, till they are examined tomorrow by a competent banker'" (218). Translation: to solve the real mystery of *The Golden Ass* is to discover that inflationary monetary policy is the true felony of the ages committed by the very same emperors who inscribed their debased coins with their names and images. Both the crime and the criminal, says Apuleius to his present and future readers, are easily found in your own pocket.

By contrast, the happy ending to *The Golden Ass* involves the hero joining the cult of Isis, which is basically a community of traders. The final ceremony near Corinth at the port town of Cenchrae coincides with Lucius's transformation from an ass back into a man. A collective sacrifice in honor of Isis is performed by merchants offering the goddess "the first fruits of the year's navigation" (238). A "blessed ship" with a "shining-white sail" bearing "a broidered inscription repeating the words of the prayer for this year's prosperous navigation" is filled with commercial goods and sent to sea: "the ship, cargoed with plentiful gifts and auspicious devotions, was let slip from her anchoring ropes. She put out to sea with a mild breeze, all her own; and after she had sailed out of sight into the distance on her course, the bearers of the holy things resumed their burdens and began a lively return journey to the temple in the same order and propriety as they had come" (245). The cosmic lesson of *The Golden Ass* is that a stable, rational monetary policy facilitates commerce, and that since commerce facilitates the well-being of all citizens, we should all give thanks for this state of affairs.

In addition to Apuleius's humanizing and transformative visions of money and trade, Cervantes drew on the importance played by merchant capitalists in major works of medieval and Renaissance creative fiction, especially Boccaccio's *Decameron* (1353), Fernando de Rojas's *La Celestina* (c.1499), and the anonymous author's *Lazarillo de Tormes* (c.1554). This last text displays an astonishing amount of bourgeois savvy. Lazarillo describes several complex business arrangements and displays an abstract appreciation for the natural law of *necessitas magistra* as the ancient basis for a theory of incentives: «Como la necesidad sea tan gran maestra, viéndome con tanta, siempre, noche y día, estaba pensando la manera que ternía en sustentar el vivir; y pienso, para hallar estos negros remedios, que me era luz la hambre, pues dicen que el ingenio con ella se avisa y al contrario con la hartura, y así era por cierto en mí» "Since need is so great a teacher, and finding myself in so much of it, I was always thinking, day and night, about how I would stay alive; and I think that, in order to discover these black remedies, hunger was my guiding light, for they say that she advises invention and to the contrary in the case of satiety, and so it certainly was in my case" (tratado 2; see Plato, *Republic* 2.369c; Aesop, "The Crow and the Pitcher").

Finally, we should note that Cervantes's biography is roundly bourgeois and that his other works treat these same themes (see Byron and Canavaggio). Over the course of his life he acquired tangible micro- and macro-economic knowledge about things like tax laws, the quality of different coins, and the gain, loss, and risk of a range of debt and credit arrangements. His parents suffered financial difficulties throughout his childhood. His mother's family were peasant farmers. His father was a petty barber-surgeon whose father and grandfather were, respectively, a lawyer trained at Salamanca and a junk dealer. Cervantes himself was variously a soldier, ambassador, and tax collector. But, largely due to the success of *Don Quijote*, he finally approached the brink of financial stability as one of history's first professionally independent writers of creative fiction. Perhaps his most ironic reaction to Avellaneda's apocryphal sequel to *Don Quijote* is expressed by way of Sancho's shock at the spurious author's pursuit of financial gain: «¿Al dinero y al interés mira el autor?» "The author's interested in money and profit?" (2.4.659). But of course he is!

Cervantes knew quite well that, as fellow picaresque novelist Quevedo put it: «Poderoso caballero es don Dinero» "Sir Money is a mighty knight." His sonnet «Al túmulo del rey Felipe II en Sevilla» "At the Tomb of Philip II in Seville" (1598) criticizes the monetary debasements and bankruptcies of the Habsburgs (see Lezra). Significant passages in *El licenciado Vidriera* and *Don Quijote* (2.62) disclose the wheelings and dealings of the printing business, and the plot of *La española inglesa* hinges on the same bills of exchange that drew the attention of Gresham (see Johnson, "*La española inglesa*"). Then we have the famous words of another thinker associated with Salamanca, Martín González de Cellorigo, whose take on the Spanish economy circa 1600 sounds like the materialist satire of *Don Quijote*: «No parece sino que se han querido reducir estos reinos a una república de hombres encantados que viven fuera del orden natural» "It plainly seems that these kingdoms have wanted to reduce themselves to a republic of enchanted men who live beyond the natural order of things" (qtd. by Maravall, *La oposición política* 231).

Two additional texts, written around the same time as part one of *Don Quijote*, also focus on economic matters. *El coloquio de los perros*, which contains Cervantes's most overt reference to Apuleius's *The Golden Ass*, cites the covert minting of counterfeit money made profitable by the Habsburgs' recourse to debasement. It then hints that debasement, itself a statist form of counterfeiting, is akin to both alchemy and the starvation of Spanish citizens. *El coloquio de los perros* also intimates that the absence of price controls on Seville's meat industry explains the absence of shortages of this product in that city. Similarly, in his *Novela de Rinconete y Cortadillo*, which the innkeeper actually gives to the priest in *DQ* 1.47, Cervantes offers a critique of the state's parasitic control over commerce via the *Casa de Contratación* in Seville.

So, according to Cervantes's historical, economic, and intellectual milieu, according to his main classical model for the picaresque genre, and according to his wide-ranging personal and professional business experiences, we shouldn't be surprised to find that the first modern novel exhibits critical meditations on financial and commercial matters. Such a reading of *Don Quijote* posits that a specific set of politically charged economic issues are at the foundations of the modern novel. In some cases, Cervantes even anticipates theories about these issues later proffered by classical liberals like Locke, Montesquieu, Jefferson, and Bastiat. No doubt, these and other Enlightenment thinkers based their ideas on ancient and universal theories of human nature. Nevertheless, it can be helpful to remember that, like many Enlightenment thinkers, all four men were also careful readers of *Don Quijote*.

Most readers take the first modern novel in one of two ways: (1) the inspirational story of a Romantic hero who struggles against all odds to "dream the impossible dream," (2) a comedy of errors that deploys slapstick humor in the adventures of a senile madman and his silly sidekick. But these interpretations only scratch the surface of the Baroque masterpiece. *Don Quijote* also contains a significant set of sophisticated casuistic lessons about liberty as an economic science of unusual complexity. Exceptional among these lessons are Cervantes's recurring meditations on the politics of money. In this chapter we'll survey evidence in *Don Quijote* that the novelist understood abstract concepts like Gresham's Law and the subjective theory of value, and that he grasped the folly and immorality of authoritarian decrees like price controls, penalties for usury, and compulsory exchange rates. What reader wouldn't benefit from a few of life's ancient economic rules of thumb? For starters: avoid debt, verify the quality of currency, loans shouldn't be free, inflation is bad, economic activity is good, save gold coins and spend copper ones, some jobs pay more than others, and it wouldn't kill you to learn some math.

A warning is in order in that not all of the examples are obvious. Take *DQ* 2.20, for example, where the modern romantic urge to marry for love instead of money might cause readers to identify with Basilio instead of Camacho. That Basilio has copper *cuartos* and Camacho has silver *reales*, however, are worrying signs that Quiteria might have made the wrong decision regarding whom to marry. The truth is that, even though these are not difficult ideas once we perceive them, they're still not necessarily intuitive to most people; ergo, the need for novelists and literary critics.

Let's define some basic notions by way of what neo-Marxist philosopher Louis Althusser once called "descriptive theory" (see "Ideology and Ideological State Apparatuses").

Students of economics learn pretty quickly that price controls, monetary debasement, and laws against usury require authoritarian rule and that they're socially and economically unwise to boot. Such policies distort more natural and subjective market activities and mechanisms. Oftentimes, laws against usury were designed and enforced in order to ensure that creditors would lend to princes on more favorable terms. In addition to penalizing savers and creditors while benefitting spenders and debtors, monetary debasement and interference in the value of things tends to create asymmetrical information, which in turn favors those who have the power, wealth, and knowledge to navigate and profit from exotic financial instruments, labyrinthine market regulations, and artificial economic crises. In short, select groups of financiers, politicians, and merchants will benefit; less informed, less agile actors will lose, especially commoners. Also, by distorting credit markets, these kinds of policies often stifle adequate investment in sectors that would better satisfy more people's needs.

Finally, according to a common pattern of governance, corrupt, expansionist, and wasteful authorities turn to debasement of the coinage in order to generate revenue by literally extracting wealth from the coins of their citizens. This causes price inflation, which then forces the same authorities to institute price controls, which then cause shortages and lower the quality goods and services. This last phenomenon occurs because producers and merchants either go out of business or else they sell their better-quality items into freer markets where they can fetch higher prices, while reserving their cheaper, lower-quality items for controlled markets. Many of the early modern economic theorists of Spain understood these mechanisms very well. More generally, many of them grasped that interventionist economic policies are usually bad ideas that only wreak havoc on commerce and diminish the well-being of citizens.

These are not difficult concepts or patterns, but neither are they at the front of everyone's mind. Once they are incorporated into our view of early modern history, however, we can begin to recognize how policies like debasement and laws against usury affected the behavior of market participants in odd, if rational, ways. For example, complex financial instruments and payment mechanisms evolved in order to cloak interest payments and thereby avoid getting caught by political and moral authorities (see D'Emic). Likewise, the use of different types of coins at different stages of loans allowed for ways of escaping notice. Such examples reveal the ingenuity of merchants and bankers; but all this sophisticated financial evasion had its costs.

For its part, the hidden tax of inflation sustained what many historians now regard as some of the more defining aspects of Baroque culture around 1600. For example, the Duke of Lerma's enormous collection of artifacts from around the world and his aggressive patronage of painters like El Greco evince an insider's ability to anticipate the effects of inflation. Meanwhile, the social decay represented by the era's mostly idle and impoverished hidalgo caste, basically an enormous group of pensioners, was one prominent effect of inflation's gradual erosion of the purchasing power of their fixed incomes. As usual, disillusionment is probably overreported by the era's intellectuals, but to the degree that the purchasing power of money was measurably on the decline, optimism must have been difficult to maintain. Quevedo's cynical poem about powerful Don Dinero isn't just a satire of people's materialistic desires in the familiar sense that money corrupts people; it's also an ironic political jab, because it was thanks to the Habsburgs that so much of the nation's money supply was now precisely nowhere near as mighty as before.[2]

Here, then, is a list of topics in the field of economics about which Cervantes seems to have been quite conscious while writing *Don Quijote*. I have attempted to provide some analysis of those key passages in the novel which most relate to economic topics, paying special attention to those that were of interest to the School of Salamanca.

(1) SUBJECTIVE VALUE AND JUST PRICE

The subjective theory of value is a cornerstone of both classical liberal and Austrian economic analysis. As Carl Menger, founder of the Austrian School, put it: "The measure of value is entirely subjective in nature, and for this reason a good can have great value to one economizing individual, little value to another, and no value at all to a third, depending upon the differences in their requirements and available amounts. What one person disdains or values lightly is appreciated by another, and what one person abandons is often picked up by another" (*Principles of Economics* 146; see also Gómez, "La teoria del valor"). Joseph Schumpeter was among the first to credit the School of Salamanca as pioneers in the field of economics. Schumpeter noted that the late scholastics understood that scarcity and utility are the true sources of value. He also credited them with having rejected the objective theory of value, which mistakenly alleges that material and labor costs determine the prices of goods and services: "the late scholastics, particularly Molina, made it quite clear that cost, though a factor in the determination of exchange value (or price), was not its logical source or 'cause'" (*History of Economic Analysis* 94).

After considering the alternatives, many of the Salamancans concluded that a corollary to the subjective theory of value is that the only morally «precio justo» "just price" of a good or service is the one determined by the free market as an aggregate expression of its utility and scarcity. Some, like De Soto, placed heavy qualifications on this insight; others vaguely opined that price controls might be made to reflect the just price. Still others, however, like Saravia, Molina, and Lugo, were unyielding about the availability of something in combination with its utility being the only true determinants of prices. Lugo and Salas even reasoned that a market is by definition always a dynamic process incapable of obtaining any true equilibrium. Schumpeter points to the groundbreaking nature of the Salamancan emphasis on subjective value, utility, and individual preference: "they adumbrated with unmistakable clearness the theory of the utility which they considered as the source or cause of value. Molina and Lugo, for instance, were as careful as C. Menger was to be to point out that this utility was not a property of the goods themselves or identical with any of their inherent qualities, but was the reflex of the uses the individuals under observation proposed to make of these goods and of the importance they attached to these uses" (*History of Economic Analysis* 94). In sum, utility is not an inherent characteristic of things but, rather, a function of the uses that individuals have for them in conjunction with the relative importance that they give to these uses.

One ethical implication of the subjective theory of value is that despite our urge to make life fair, market interference is wrong. If both of us leave an exchange happy, then any "true" value of what we exchange matters less than the fact that we make an exchange. Moreover, subjective factors like tastes, wants, and needs are precisely why we produce things and trade them. Without elemental differences in our desires, we would all still be poor, starving brutes. In sum, more suffering is alleviated by a policy of non-interference in most market activities.

As advocates of subjective value theory, the Salamancans sometimes arrived at the counterintuitive insight that voluntary exchange vindicates behavior many considered immoral. Prostitution, for example, might be wrong, but to outlaw it could be more so because it would repress a woman's right to feed herself. Then there's Saravia's momentarily hellish vision of commercial transactions in the form of what modern economists would call "lemon" markets. Buyers and sellers might always be unethically attempting to gain advantage over each other, but the result can still be positive (see D'Emic 126–27).

The free-market view echoes the late-scholastic concept of the commonwealth as a *corpus mysticum politicum* "mystical body politic," except in the field of economics. In the political sphere the public must be consulted before a monarch levies new taxes; likewise, no authority can fairly dictate the prices at which citizens must buy and sell their goods and services. The only moral alternative is to revert to the natural law of the market, or, to paraphrase in Jesuit terms, the *corpus mysticum economicum* "mystical economic body." This leads us to Friedrich Hayek's notion of the marketplace as a mechanism for expressing a dispersed form of knowledge that governments are unable to comprehend and should not attempt to control ("The Use of Knowledge"). In his Nobel Prize lecture, Hayek explained what the late scholastics meant in their market analysis by the *pretium iustum mathematicum* "just mathematical price," which, in his words, "depended on so many particular circumstances that it could never be known to man but was known only to God" ("The Pretense of Knowledge").

The notion that the value of something must be subjective since quantity, usefulness, and choice vary according to time, place, and personal preference remains uncomfortable to many people due to its counterintuitive consequences. For example, if value is subjective, determined by the aggregate demand of the market's participants, then the prices people pay for things determine their production costs and not the other way around. Marxists, mercantilists, and moralists have similar problems with this idea, preferring the less-grounded idea that value is determined by the costs of labor and materials used in production. But labor and materials are themselves priced according to the dynamics of supply and demand. Protectionist and mercantilist policies, like minimum prices and minimum wage laws, countervail subjective value theory and burden consumers with costs that they would not assume under free-market conditions. Inflationary monetary policy is a version of the same because it operates by overvaluing money relative to its demand; and Gresham's law describes the public's response, which is to shun bad money and horde good. Natural, subjective, and market-value theorists hold that prices should be determined by those who exchange money for goods and services free of coercion, i.e., that scarcity alone, not laws enforced by authorities, should determine what people pay. Note that subjective value theory does not assert that prices are arbitrary *per se* but, rather, that they depend on the aggregate of the marginal utilities asserted by market participants.

A few late-scholastic Salamancans, like De Soto and Villalón, worried about dismissing the objective or labor theory of value; but most, including Vitoria, Medina, Saravia, Covarrubias, Molina, Mariana, Suárez, and Lugo, insisted that value is based on the utility that people perceive for goods and services (from St. Bernardino's and St. Antonino's *complacibilitas* or "capacity to satisfy"). A few of these men had rather obscure reasons for maintaining their view, ranging from complex theological notions of free will (e.g., Molinism) to the sheer power of Scripture (e.g., the "Parable of the Talents" in Mt. 25.13–40). But we would be wrong to underestimate the modernity, sophistication, and theoretical importance of their insights. In the late nineteenth century, Karl Marx's updated version of the labor theory of value became radically popular, but then the subjective theory of value would be resurrected by Carl Menger and Eugen Böhm von Bawerk in their refutations of Marx's logic.

DQ 1.21—Mambrino's helmet, subjective value, and violence

In *DQ* 1.21, the hidalgo is again insane and violent, instantly ruthless over what seems like a trifle, much like when he had attacked the Basque hidalgo and lost the better part of his left ear at the end of *DQ* 1.8. And much like at the beginning of *DQ* 1.9, when the narrator buys the lost manuscript in the Toledan marketplace, in *DQ* 1.21 the hidalgo alludes to the subjective theory of value and asymmetrical information in his assessment of Mambrino's helmet. There is, of course, a big difference. In Toledo, the narrator purchases his prized manuscript; here Don Quijote takes Mambrino's helmet by force. An important upshot of subjective value theory is that exchanges of money, goods, and services are only just when they're voluntary.

Beyond Don Quijote's violent robbery of the barber, the hypocrisy of statist monetary policy is also on display here, for he claims that an item made from base metals is actually made of gold. As elsewhere, the novel's allegorical approach to debasement hinges on a clash between the different perspectives of characters as well as readers. The hidalgo sees gold—«¿no ves aquel caballero que hacia nosotros viene, sobre un caballo rucio rodado, que trae puesto en la cabeza un yelmo de oro?» "do you not see that knight coming toward us, mounted on a dappled gray and wearing on his head a helmet of gold?"—, but the squire remains unconvinced: «no es sino un hombre sobre un asno pardo, como el mío, que trae sobre la cabeza una cosa que relumbra» "nothing but a man riding on a donkey that's gray like mine, and wearing something shiny on his head" (1.21.223). The narrator confirms Sancho's view, noting that the barber wears a shaving basin on his head due to the rain: «venía el barbero y traía una bacía de azófar; y quiso la suerte que al tiempo que venía comenzó a llover, y porque no se le manchase el sombrero, que debía de ser nuevo, se puso la bacía sobre la cabeza, y, como estaba limpia, desde media legua relumbraba» "the barber was traveling and carrying a brass basin; and as luck would have it, as he was traveling it began to rain, and to keep his hat from being stained, for it must have been new, he put the basin on his head, and since it was clean, at a distance of half a league, it glistened" (1.21.224).

Rothbard described the state as what happens when gangsters articulate their robbery as a politically mandated protection racket (*Anatomy of the State*, 13–17). Don Quijote's attack on the innocent barber suggests the same, with the added wrinkle that the government's game of misrepresenting the metallic value of coins is an even more insidious form of civilized piracy. As we see in the mandated exchange rates of early twenty-first century Argentina and Venezuela, in order for inflationary policies to benefit the state, they require the force of law. The same is true in the United States, where the state requires that taxes be paid in fiat dollars and reaps further revenue by taxing the capital gains that citizens earn on non-fiat money like, say, gold or bitcoin.

DQ 1.22—Galley slaves and subjective value adrift

In the most famous episode dealing with justice in *Don Quijote*, one of the galley slaves reports that he has been condemned to five years at the oars of the king's fleet because he lacked ten gold ducats. When Don Quijote empathizes with him and offers to help—«Yo daré veinte de muy buena gana ... por libraros desa pesadumbre» "I should gladly give you twenty ... to free you from this sorrowful burden" (1.22.238)—, the man responds with a lesson about the temporally and geographically contingent nature of value, which changes according to scarcity and utility. The money that the hidalgo offers him is as useless to him now as if he were a rich man starving to death on the open sea: «como quien tiene dineros en mitad del golfo y se está muriendo de hambre, sin tener adonde comprar lo que ha menester» "like a man who has money in the middle of the ocean and is dying of hunger and doesn't have a place where he can buy what he needs" (1.22.238).

The galley slave's comment refers overtly to the uselessness of money when nothing is available to buy, but it also contains a more subtle reference to a classic expression of the value problem. Until Menger resolved it, the "diamond-water paradox" was one of the great dilemmas of economics, challenging thinkers from Plato to Copernicus to Locke. If water is so vital for life and diamonds have far fewer uses, then why do diamonds cost so much more than water? In fact, the galley slave's comment even brushes up against Menger's concept of "marginal utility," which states that the first quantum of any desired good is worth more than the second, which is worth more than the third, and so on. The explanation of the diamond-water paradox is that the unit price of something is determined by its least valuable use, which is found as far as possible beyond the margin of what is vital. Since there is typically so much water available that people use it for all sorts of things, we say that its marginal utility is low, i.e., its desirability at the margin tends toward zero. Meanwhile, diamonds are so rare that they are useful as a way of preserving wealth and so people will not tend to find many uses for them beyond that.

Schumpeter credited the Salamancans with perceiving all of the elements of Menger's theory in the factors of preference, scarcity, and utility. They only fell short of formulating it in terms of marginal increments of satisfaction. The example in *DQ* 1.22 of the rich man starving in the middle of the ocean alludes to the paradox of the almost valueless status of water. Cervantes adds an ironical wink to readers who know that saltwater oceans are deserts to humans, which, in turn, increases the utility of freshwater far above that of food. The irony of the rich man's mis-prioritized hunger derives from rational thinking about the utility of these similar types of goods (the only difference being the amount of salt in the water). Indeed, if the reader gets the irony, he can potentially grasp the incremental nature of valuation. Similarly, the metaphor of the starving man at sea places the needed food beyond the horizon of his existence. This links satisfaction to distance, i.e., value derives from a gradient between abundance and scarcity, which for its part is hooked to another gradient between indifference (lots of freshwater) and desperation (lots of saltwater). Finally, note that the food beyond the horizon is right where it should be; both figuratively and relatively speaking, the concern must be finding water before food.

When describing how close the late scholastics came to Menger's thinking, Schumpeter might as well have been talking about Cervantes's ironically concatenating stories about people trying to get what they need or want: "the late scholastics, though they did not explicitly resolve the 'paradox of value'—that water though useful has normally no exchange value—obviated the difficulty by making their utility concept, from the first, relative to abundance or scarcity; their utility was not utility of goods in the abstract, but utility of the quantities of goods available or producible in the individual's particular situations" (*History of Economic Analysis* 94).

DQ 2.pro.—Author's work, subjective value, and the novel

In the prologue of *Don Quijote*, part two, Cervantes parries an attack on the sloppiness of his novels by his pseudonymous rival Alonso Fernández Avellaneda by turning a generic insult into a compliment, a badge of honor:

«le agradezco a este señor autor el decir que mis novelas son más satíricas que ejemplares» "I thank the gentleman for saying that my novels are more satirical than exemplary" (2.pro.618). One man's generic preferences will differ from those of another. Lope de Vega had the same insight when he argued that what's tragic from one perspective can be comedic from the next (see *El arte nuevo*). Subjective value again.

At the end of this same prologue, the narrator describes the novel's second part as «cortada del mismo artífice y del mesmo paño que la primera» "cut by the same artisan and from the same cloth as the first" (2.pro.621). So it is, and especially in terms of economic themes. Moments later, the narrator proclaims that this time he'll bring about a definitive end to Don Quijote's adventures, thereby increasing their value. Having established subjective value, Cervantes now turns to one of its expressions: the law of supply and demand. Let it be enough, the narrator says, «que un hombre honrado haya dado noticia destas discretas locuras, sin querer de nuevo entrarse en ellas: que la abundancia de las cosas aunque sean buenas, hace que no se estimen, y la carestía, aun de las malas, se estima en algo» "that an honorable man has recounted these clever follies and does not want to take them up again: for abundance, even of things that are good, makes people esteem them less, and scarcity, even of bad things, lends a certain value" (2.pro.621).

Cervantes ingeniously deploys this object lesson on the value of his own novel as a way to signal yet again that he has all along been performing precisely these kinds of ironical textual demonstrations of the economic reasoning practiced by the School of Salamanca. Since he christens part two with the conceptual foundations of late-scholastic value theory, i.e., subjective value in combination with relative scarcity, we can expect the rest of the text to weave together more allusions to economic matters of this sort. In fact, long considered the first man to have read *Don Quijote*, the Licentiate Francisco Márquez Torres alludes to economic theory in the novel when he incorporates the ancient topic of necessity being the mother of invention (*necessitas magistra*) into his anecdote about the French diplomat who approves of Cervantes's poverty: «Si necesidad le ha de obligar a escribir, plega a Dios que nunca tenga abundancia, para que con sus obras, siendo él pobre, haga rico a todo el mundo» "If necessity is required to oblige him to write, then may it please God that he never have abundance, so that with his works, he being poor, he shall enrich the whole world" (2.apr.612).

DQ 2.2—Sancho and just price theory

When Sancho first appears in *Don Quijote*, part two, the housekeeper and niece block his entrance into their master's home and accuse him of causing the hidalgo's adventurousness. Sancho counters that he is the one who has been tricked, observing that the two women are off by half the just price: «Ama de Satanás, el sonsacado y el destraído y el llevado por esos andurriales soy yo, que no tu amo: él me llevó por esos mundos, y vosotras os engañáis en la mitad del justo precio» "Housekeeper from hell, the one who's lured and led astray and taken to godforsaken places is me, not your master; he led me everywhere, and you two are deceived by half the just price" (2.2.640). Colloquially, the squire means that they are way off the mark, but the term also alludes to the era's heated debate over whether the free market or governing officials should set prices. Indeed, the "just price" issue is but another form of the objective (mandated) versus subjective (market) value debate.

Two points here. First, in contrast to subjective value theory, objective value theory opposes the free market. Cristóbal de Villalón, for example, argued that production costs should be used to establish minimum prices while also holding that market participants who took advantage of asymmetrical information were immoral and should be penalized. Note Cervantes's irony as Sancho argues that the women have been misled about a price about which he himself has been misled. There's not much pretense of certainty when it comes to the value of things in *Don Quijote*, and laborers are not unique in this regard.

Second, since a major component of production costs is usually labor, it makes sense that Sancho should bring up the just price debate in the presence of the housekeeper, i.e., his master's principal domestic employee. The phrase clearly alludes to his own quest for a salary from Don Quijote, which remains a major theme throughout part two (Johnson, *Cervantes*). Moreover, in the presence of two of the knight's employees, Sancho's reference to the *justo precio* transcends its ordinary meaning and signals economic thinking in the first modern novel. As Hayek noted in his Nobel Prize speech, the late scholastics favored the *pretium iustum mathematicum* as the only equivalent of anything approaching a "true" price, precisely because it is dynamic and "known only to God" ("The Pretense of Knowledge"). The just price as the free-market price is the ethical corollary to subjective value. If the only fair price in any given transaction is that agreed to by the uncoerced participants, then it follows that the market price is even fairer to the degree that it reflects an even larger aggregate of uncoerced transactions.

(2) SWEET COMMERCE

So, am I saying Cervantes was a capitalist? An Austrian? A free-market Randian? A libertarian? An English classical liberal? In a general sense, yes, and probably to a greater degree than most readers recognize. Critics who insist

that Cervantes was only a precursor to modern views are unnecessarily hedg-
ing their bets. When it comes to the spread of free-market thinking, there's
an intellectual feedback mechanism that amplifies the influence of the first
modern novel. The economic ideas of the Salamancans influenced Cervantes;
later, classical liberals, who were also reading the Salamancans, could vali-
date their ideas while reading *Don Quijote*. Locke, Jefferson, and Bastiat had
good political reasons for being fans of the first modern novel, but they also
had good economic reasons.

This ethical vision of the free market makes it a virtue in its own right.
Because it's observably pacific, economical, civilizing, productive, empow-
ering, etc., at different moments and places in history the free market has
been viewed as beneficial to human society. Montesquieu's notion of *doux
commerce* "sweet commerce" has found similar expression in the work of
such luminaries as Adam Smith, James Madison, David Ricardo, Norbert
Elias, Friedrich Hayek, Steven Pinker, Pedro Schwartz, Matt Ridley, and
Niall Ferguson. Milton Friedman described how the free market ensures both
social stability and a free society:

> The widespread use of the market reduces strain on the social fabric by render-
> ing conformity unnecessary with respect to any activities it encompasses. The
> wider the range of activities covered by the market, the fewer are the issues on
> which explicitly political decisions are required and hence on which it is neces-
> sary to achieve agreement. (24)

Anticipating Montesquieu's *doux commerce*, of course, were the late
scholastics. Subjective value theory and just price theory led many of them
to conclude that the free market was preferable and palliative. Mariana, for
instance, left some impressive formulas along these lines. First, commerce
civilizes us by requiring social cohesion and respect: «Nada hay en la vida
humana más excelente que la buena fe, con la cual se establecen las relaciones
comerciales y se constituye la sociedad entre los hombres» "There's nothing
more excellent in human life than good faith, according to which commercial
relations are established and society among men is constituted"; and second,
commerce simply makes life better: «Si el comercio se suprimiera, ¿qué
habría más triste ni más infeliz que la vida humana?» "If commerce were to
be suppressed, what would be more sad or unhappy than human life?" (*La
dignidad real* 216, 389).

Don Quijote signals these lessons at every turn. Its trajectory is a modern
bourgeois baptism for a medieval crusader knight. This is why the protagonist's aggressive madness dissipates over the course of the novel as he
comes to terms with the new materialism. In *DQ* 1.1, he is mismanaging his
domestic economy so badly that by implication not even Aristotle can help

him. In *DQ* 1.2, he's faced by the fact that, unlike chivalric novels, the real world requires payment for goods and services. In *DQ* 1.3, the first innkeeper knights him by pretending to read biblical Latin from an accounting ledger. In *DQ* 1.4, the protagonist backtracks twice, fumbling an opportunity for justice in a labor dispute and then attacking a group of silk merchants on their way from Toledo to Murcia. By *DQ* 1.7, he at least grasps that he must finance his adventures: «Dio luego don Quijote orden en buscar dineros, y, vendiendo una cosa y empeñando otra y malbaratándolas todas, llegó una razonable cantidad» "Then Don Quijote set about finding some money, and, by hawking one thing and pawning another, and all for less than he should have, he came up with a reasonable amount" (1.7.92). By the same token, the battle between Basque and Manchegan hidalgos at the end of *DQ* 1.8 is interrupted by the quest for the missing manuscript, which takes place precisely in the Alcaná marketplace of Toledo in *DQ* 1.9. Recall, too, that Cervantes's Christian narrator refers to the presence of Hebrew before eventually contracting a Morisco translator. In this way, the narrative about the narrator's quest for the missing text unites the religious ethnicities of Spain (cf. Boccaccio's third novella in the *Decameron*).

The bourgeois transformation continues at the second inn. Unlike Don Quijote's first outing, this time the narrator reports meticulous payment for everything. His stay at Palomeque's inn includes room and board for hidalgo and squire, water and hay for their mounts, and a lavish dinner for multiple guests over which the hero presides in *DQ* 1.38. The formerly mad knight is at his most bourgeois in *DQ* 1.44 when he quietly resolves a violent payment dispute between the innkeeper and two mysterious guests: «Ya a esta sazón estaban en paz los huéspedes con el ventero, pues por persuasión y buenas razones de don Quijote, más que por amenazas, le habían pagado todo lo que él quiso» "By this time the guests were at peace with the innkeeper, for by way of the persuasion and good arguments of Don Quijote, more than by threats, they had paid him all that he demanded" (1.44.518). The principle of *doux commerce* is similarly at work when the priest makes right the damages incurred by the second barber: «le dio por la bacía ocho reales, y el barbero le hizo una cédula del recibo» "he gave him eight *reales* for the basin, and the barber made out a receipt for him" (1.46.530). Subsequently, we learn that Don Fernando pays everyone's expenses at the inn, «y de tal manera quedaron todos en paz y sosiego» "and in this way everyone was made calm and at peace" (1.46.531). Here's the realist's cornucopia, the true Golden Age from a bourgeois perspective. Thus too, at the end of life, Don Quijote's cure is symbolized by his return to financial responsibility, as from his deathbed he pays his employees and transfers his wealth to his niece Antonia in *DQ* 2.74.

Figure 15. Hispaleto, *Discurso que hizo don Quijote sobre las armas y las letras*, 1884
Source: Museo del Prado

Consider, too, the mutually reinforcing themes of love and economics, specifically the extent to which love stories dovetail with economic exchange in *Don Quijote*. Analogous to good love on a personal level, commerce can bring tranquility, wealth, progress, and stability on a social level. Thus, an array of currencies and merchants are needed for Zoraida and Viedma to escape to Spain in *DQ* 1.39–41. This offers bourgeois confirmation of Luis Andrés Murillo's thesis that the byzantine love story in "The Captive's Tale" is the exemplary endpoint of *Don Quijote*. In *DQ* 1.44, Don Quijote's resolution of the payment dispute between the innkeeper and two anonymous guests parallels the imminent union between Don Luis and Doña Clara. In *DQ* 2.26, Don Quijote destroys the puppets used in the love story between Gaiferos and Melisenda but then agrees to pay Maese Pedro for damages. And after that he buys everyone dinner: «todos cenaron en paz y en buena compañía, a costa de don Quijote, que era liberal en todo estremo» "everyone dined in peace and in good company, and at Don Quijote's expense, for he was liberal in the extreme" (2.26.854). Love and economic exchange also overlap in the relations among the principal husbands and wives of part two. In *DQ* 2.57, the Duke pays Sancho Panza 200 *escudos* for his services as Governor of

Barataria. The Duchess and Teresa exchange coral and acorns in *DQ* 2.50 and 2.52. In *DQ* 2.64–65, the Morisco Ricote pays handsomely for the rescue of his daughter Ana Félix's Christian lover Gregorio. Fortunately for the idealized interethnic couple, Ricote is also a wealthy shopkeeper.

DQ 1.3, 1.4, 1.17, 1.44, 1.46, etc.—Don Quijote versus innkeepers and merchants

One of the mad hidalgo's earliest lessons is given to him by the first inn-keeper, who notes that even though the chivalric novels don't mention it, all knights-errant needed money to cover expenses, and so, «llevaban bien herradas las bolsas» "carried heavily laden purses" (1.3.56). But it's a hard lesson to absorb. In *DQ* 1.17, when Don Quijote refuses to compensate the innkeeper Palomeque, it's Sancho who pays the price by getting blanketed by other guests. Nevertheless, the lesson appears more or less learned by *DQ* 1.44, when Don Quijote resolves the payment dispute between the innkeeper and two mysterious guests. Soon thereafter, in *DQ* 1.46, Don Fernando echoes the example when he pays Palomeque for all expenses incurred by Don Quijote and all the other guests. The message is repeated late in part two: «Pagó Sancho al ventero magníficamente» "Sancho paid the innkeeper handsomely" (2.59.1115).

Standing out among the many victims of Don Quijote's irrational out-bursts of aggression are the merchants of Toledo, «que iban a comprar seda a Murcia» "who were on their way to Murcia to buy silk" (1.4.67). Like so many others, especially innkeepers, the Toledan merchants suffer the consequences of Don Quijote's lack of understanding about how things work in the modern world. Ultimately, the hidalgo loses the battle, but in the process Cervantes establishes the orthodox nature of his hero's anti-merchant tendencies (cf. Mises). More specifically, at the end of *DQ* 1.4 the furious knight prophetically encapsulates the way in which Catholic zeal was threatening to destroy the silk trade of southeastern Spain by repressing *converso* merchants and expelling Morisco laborers. The expulsion of the latter took place in 1609–14, and it was every bit as devastating to the silk industry as many had predicted.

DQ 1.8—Don Quijote versus windmills

The adventure of the windmills in *Don Quijote* has come to symbolize the mad knight's desire to "dream the impossible dream." History's first reading of the machines, however, will always belong to Sancho Panza, who confirms that Don Quijote's state of mind is at issue: «¿No dije yo a vuestra merced que mirase bien lo que hacía, que no eran sino molinos de viento, y no lo podía ignorar sino quien llevase otros tales en la cabeza?» "Did I not tell your grace to consider well what you were doing, that those were in reality windmills, and that only somebody whose head was full of them wouldn't know that?" (1.8.96). We have every right to ask, then, what is Don Quijote thinking that would cause him to attack windmills?

On a literary level, Cervantes transforms the famous metaphor at the end of the *Inferno*, whereby Dante initially mistakes Satan for a giant windmill. Like a Dantesque Luddite, Don Quijote also attacks monstrous mills. But we can be more specific if we keep in mind that the windmill episode occurs near a border between two territories governed by competing military orders. Here, at least, Don Quijote is still a feudal lacky operating in the name of privilege. His action defends a monopoly on milling held by the Prior of the Order of San Juan against the opportunistic builders of windmills located just over the border in the territory of the Order of Santiago (Román 5–6). This makes the famous windmill episode in *Don Quijote* analogous to something like the members of a public employees' union in New York City attacking a cigarette vendor in New Jersey, where taxes on tobacco are half what they are in New York.

Subjective value theorists favor free markets and reject monopolies, oligopolies, and market interference by authorities. In his *Política para Corregidores* (1597), for example, late scholastic Jerónimo Castillo de Bobadilla insisted that barring someone entry into a market was immoral. Cervantes clearly considered the contrast between free and closed markets. He paints a picture of surplus in the unregulated meat industry of *El coloquio de los per-*

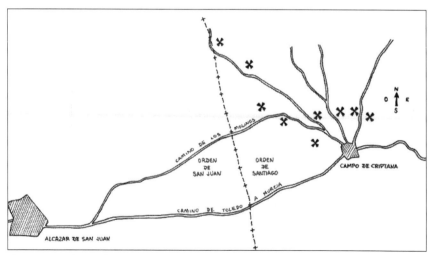

Figure 16.   Sixteenth-Century Windmills in La Mancha and Territories of the Orders of San Juan and Santiago *Source*: Luis Román

ros. In *Rinconete y Cortadillo*, he sarcastically represents a crime syndicate in Seville as a monopoly operating in the shadow of the protectionist *Casa de Contratación*, which imposed a 20% tax on all goods imported from the New World. In other words, there's little difference between extortion and mercantilism. Sancho himself gives us the first figurative interpretation of the windmills as projections of Don Quijote's insanity. Valid and compelling interpretations of the quintessential Cervantine symbol include everything from Dante's Satan to the Pythagorean Theorem (Fajardo; Graf, "The Economy of Asses"). To this list we can add that the windmills were a disruptive technology that wrought Schumpeter's "creative destruction" as they replaced older, less efficient mills (see *Capitalism* 82–83). And their location in late sixteenth-century La Mancha, near Campo de Criptana to the east of a territory controlled by the Order of San Juan, suggests that they posed the greatest threat to the monopoly on milling there held by that order's prior.

DQ 1.9, 2.62—Manuscripts and markets

The second narrator's discovery of the lost manuscript in the Toledan marketplace is one of many episodes in *Don Quijote* that anticipate the metatextual experiments of modernist novels like Galdós's *El amigo Manso* (1882) or Unamuno's *Niebla* (1914) by three centuries. But note, too, the degree to which the subjective theory of value underwrites the discovery:

> Cuando yo oí decir «Dulcinea del Toboso», quedé atónito y suspenso, porque luego se me representó que aquellos cartapacios contenían la historia de don Quijote. Con esta imaginación, le di priesa que leyese el principio, y haciéndolo ansí, volviendo de improviso el arábigo en castellano, dijo que decía: *Historia de don Quijote de la Mancha, escrita por Cide Hamete Benengeli, historiador arábigo*. Mucha discreción fue menester para disimular el contento que recebí cuando llegó a mis oídos el título del libro, y, salteándosele al sedero, compré al muchacho todos los papeles y cartapacios por medio real; que si él tuviera discreción y supiera lo que yo los deseaba, bien se pudiera prometer y llevar más de seis reales de la compra. (1.9.108)

> When I heard him say "Dulcinea of Toboso," I was astounded and filled with anticipation, for it occurred to me that those volumes contained the history of Don Quijote. With this thought in mind, I urged him to read the beginning, which he did, extemporizing a translation of the Arabic into Castilian and saying that it said: *History of Don Quijote of La Mancha. Written by Cide Hamete Benengeli, an Arab Historian*. I needed a good deal of cleverness to hide the joy I felt when the title of the book reached my ears; moving more quickly than the silk merchant, I bought all the papers and notebooks from the boy for half a

real, but if he had been astute and known how much I wanted them, he certainly could have demanded and received more than six *reales* for their purchase.

A fantastic irony involving commerce in *Don Quijote* is the fact that the marketplace rescues the novel from its own violence against itself. The bundles of paper that the narrator spies in Toledo's Alcaná marketplace require asymmetrical information in order to appreciate their true worth. He underscores that he paid half a *real* instead of the six *reales* he admits the manuscript would have been worth to him. Moreover, the purchase results in the subsequent employment of a local Morisco to translate the papers. Think about this. In theory, we couldn't read the novel past *DQ* 1.8 were it not for the miracle of a multiethnic marketplace for goods and services. Readers who doubt that Cervantes consciously wove economic analysis into *Don Quijote* face a noteworthy challenge in the bundle of papers that the narrator buys in the Alcaná marketplace of Toledo, and which, by the way, we know were intended to feed the silkworms of an industry under threat of extinction circa 1605.

Similar detailed knowledge about the book industry surfaces late in the novel's second part. In the printer's shop in Barcelona in *DQ* 2.62, the remarkably sane hidalgo engages in conversation with a man who plans to get rich selling Italian novels in translation. Given that one *ducado* equals eleven *reales*, Don Quijote instantly realizes that if the printer expects to pocket 1,000 *ducados* by selling 2,000 copies at six *reales* each, then he means to clear 11,000 *reales* profit on sales of 12,000 *reales*. But that leaves only 1,000 *reales* for production costs and commissions to dealers. The same hidalgo who was unable to administer his own household in *DQ* 1.1, who couldn't tell a Bible from a ledger in *DQ* 1.3, and who miscalculated Andrés's salary in *DQ* 1.4, has finally risen to the bourgeois challenge, revealing himself to be remarkably quick with numbers and value judgments. He even takes a sarcastic swipe at the printer's business model: «¡Bien está vuesa merced en la cuenta!» "You've got it all figured out!" (2.62.1145).

DQ 1.16, 1.22, 1.26, 2.45, etc.—Prostitution

Don Quijote's interactions with innkeepers, booksellers, and millers explore the limits of what is permissible in the new commercial environment. The knight's early defeats underscore his ignorance of the ethics of the marketplace. Another limit case in early modern thinking about economics was prostitution. While still holding that prostitution is immoral, some Salamancans argued that depriving a woman of her means of sustaining herself was worse (Chafuen 116). We see prostitution throughout Cervantes's prose and *Don Quijote* is no exception. In *DQ* 1.16, Maritornes visits a client in the attic, and heavy irony attends the knight's declaration of loyalty to Dulcinea while he essentially refuses to allow the young woman to leave his bed. In other words, the prostitute's choice is very much at issue in this encounter and the mad hidalgo again tilts against the grain of voluntary exchange.

In *DQ* 1.22, Cervantes uses humor to push the limits of acceptable prostitution further. When an old galley slave is revealed to be an *alcuahuete* or "pimp," Don Quijote heaps praise on the man: «por solamente el alcahuete limpio no merecía él ir a bogar en las galeras, sino a mandallas y a ser general dellas. Porque no es así como quiera el oficio de alcahuete, que es oficio de discretos y necesarísimo en la república bien ordenada» "for the mere act of pimping, he would not deserve to row in the galleys, but rather to command them and to be their admiral. The office of a pimp is not like all the others, for it is an office of persons of discretion, and one of vital necessity in a well-ordered republic" (1.22.239). We laugh, but the episode situates the oldest profession among the substantial list of petty crimes that do not deserve the death sentence of manning the oars in the Mediterranean.

Similarly, in the third case of *DQ* 2.45, Sancho finds a prostitute guilty of perjury, and fraud, whereas her profession is not at issue. In the end, the Governor of Barataria even directs a bit of advice to her victim that reflects a liberal view of the marketplace: «Buen hombre, andad con Dios a vuestro lugar con vuestro dinero, y de aquí adelante, si no le queréis perder, procurad que no os venga en voluntad de yogar con nadie» "My good man, God speed and go home with your money; and from now on, if you don't want to lose it, make sure you don't follow the urge to lie down with anybody" (2.45.998). *Caveat emptor*: "buyer beware." Cervantes taps common knowledge about how the world really works, and prudish idealism yields to a view that participants in voluntary exchanges are responsible for their actions.

DQ 1.4, 1.9, 1.22, 2.38, etc.—Textiles

Among the first modern novel's economic morals is that activities which promote specialization, productivity, and trade create more wealth than pillage and conquest. When we view late-Renaissance Spain through the prism of *Don Quijote*, the industry that seems to offer the most opportunity for wealth and progress is textiles (see Postrel, *The Fabric of Civilization*). This makes perfect sense. Spain at the time was a major producer of silk and wool. The silk came mostly from Andalucía, Murcia, and Valencia with their large laboring Morisco populations; the wool came from the large herds of sheep maintained by the powerful association of transhumant livestock herders in Castile known as the *Mesta*. Cervantes makes loaded allusions to the silk industry by way of the merchants in *DQ* 1.4 and the dealer who nearly purchases the lost manuscript to feed his worms in *DQ* 1.9. He makes allusions to the wool industry by way of the fulling mills beating cloth in *DQ* 1.22 and the garish flannel worn by the Countess of Trifaldi in *DQ* 2.38. Such passages accord with the novel's descriptions of every conceivable manner of dress. When it comes to the clothes of his characters, Cervantes obsesses over the fabrics, cuts, weaves, textures, and colors of the latest fashions in veils, handkerchiefs, stockings, gowns, jackets, shirts, pants, and underwear. At the end of part two, for example, Altisidora describes the devils she sees in Hell with an hilarious attention to detail: «todos en calzas y jubones, con valonas guarnecidas con puntas de randas flamencas, y con unas vueltas de lo mismo que les servían de puños, con cuatro dedos de brazo fuera, porque pareciesen las manos más largas» "all in breeches and doublets, with large collars trimmed with Flemish bone lace, and ruffles of the same that served them for cuffs, with four fingers' length of the arms exposed in order to make their hands look longer" (2.70.1194).

One might variously argue that this reflects the aesthetic preferences of the late Renaissance, that it's just a literary technique designed to help readers visualize each new character, that it expresses the ancient metaphor for the art of writing as weaving, or even that it points up the prominent role played by women in the early modern evolution of the novel form. Nevertheless, the scale and location of textiles in *Don Quijote* suggests something more along the lines of Montesquieu's appreciation of the wondrous effects of "sweet commerce."

The fulling mills episode of *DQ* 1.22 merits particular attention. The mill's hammers pound away in the middle of the night, cleansing, softening, and thickening wool for trade at Medina del Campo or perhaps export to Flanders or Italy. Meanwhile, Sancho cowers in fear of some monster that will surely kill his master and leave him defenseless. As eerie emblems logged three hundred years before Schumpeter's "creative destruction," the fulling mills are another of the novel's many mechanical marvels that underscore the knight's futile struggle against early industrial capitalism. Rocinante's paralysis before these machines adds to his master's sense of helplessness. Another economic irony surfaces when Sancho takes precisely this opportunity to ask Don Quijote what kind of salary a squire could expect from a knight. In other words, as industrialization looms, the organic nature of the traditional feudal relationship falls apart. Machines manned by salaried employees now siphon off the viability of poor peasants working aristocratic estates.

This theme only grows in part two. Readers will recall the turn of phrase in the second prologue when Cervantes tells us that the sequel is cut «del mesmo paño que la primera» "from same cloth as the first" (2.pro.621). After Cide Hamete says in an aside that he would have given «la mejor almalafa de dos que tenía» "the best haik of the two he had" to have witnessed their dialogue, Doña Rodríguez brags to Don Quijote about her service to a certain noblewoman: «mis padres me acomodaron a servir de doncella de labor a una principal señora; y quiero hacer sabidor a vuestra merced que en hacer vainillas y labor blanca ninguna me ha echado el pie adelante en toda la vida» "my parents placed me as a seamstress in the service of a noblewoman, and I want you know that when it comes to hemming and sewing I have never been surpassed by anyone in all my life" (2.48.1018). In her letter to Sancho, Teresa says their daughter is now earning money: «Sanchica hace puntas de randas; gana cada día ocho maravedís horros, que los va echando en una alcancía para ayuda a su ajuar» "Sanchica is making bone lace; she earns eight *maravedís* a day, which she puts into a moneybox to help grow her dowry" (2.52.1060). When Don Quijote and Sancho assert that only honest labor can cure Altisidora's hyper imagination, the Duchess makes a promise: «yo haré que mi Altisidora se ocupe de aquí adelante en hacer alguna labor blanca, que la sabe hacer por estremo» "I will make sure that my Altisidora employs herself henceforward in needlework of some sort, for she is extremely good at it" (2.70.1197).

Finally, we should attend to one of Cervantes's most spectacular formulations of the civilizing effects of commerce in textiles. The narrator's explication of the meaning of Countess Trifaldi's surname in *DQ* 2.38 contains a curious contrast: «de su propio apellido se llamó la condesa Lobuna, a causa que se criaban en su condado muchos lobos» "according to her real last name, she was called the Countess Lupine, because so many wolves roamed her county," which then yields to a metamorphosis: «empero esta condesa, por favorecer la novedad de su falda, dejó el Lobuna y tomó el Trifaldi» "but this countess, to signal the innovation of her dress's tail, dropped the name Lupine and adopted that of Trifaldi" (2.38.939). What can turn vicious wolves into fantabulous triple-tailed flannel dresses? Like Altidisora's vision of Flemish collars in Hell, here we have an emblem for the humanizing effects of the wool industry as opposed to the dehumanizing effects of the "wolf" industry.[3]

On the one hand, Cervantes echoes the line from Plautus's *Asinaria* about the nature of human relations: *lupus est homō hominī, nōn homō, quom quālis sit nōn nōvit* "A man is a wolf, not a man, to another man which he hasn't yet met" (line 495). On the other hand, he anticipates sociologist Franz Oppenheimer's view of the two mutually exclusive ways humans attain wealth. In his book *The State*, Oppenheimer calls these "economic" and "political." American economist Murray Rothbard explained that the first way is more efficient since "through the process of voluntary, mutual exchange, the productivity and hence, the living standards, of all participants in exchange may increase enormously." This is "the path of 'property rights' and the 'free market' of gift or exchange of such rights," by which "men have learned how to avoid the 'jungle' methods of fighting over scarce resources so that A can only acquire them at the expense of B and, instead, to multiply those resources enormously in peaceful and harmonious production and exchange." The second way is "seizure of another's goods or services by the use of force and violence," in effect, "the method of one-sided confiscation, of theft of the property of others." Honing ideas that link Aristotle to Mariana to Locke, Rothbard argues that "the coercive, exploitative means is contrary to natural law" because it "siphons production off to a parasitic and destructive individual or group; and this siphoning not only subtracts from the number producing, but also lowers the producer's incentive to produce beyond his own subsistence" (*Anatomy of the State* 13–15).

Readers will recall that when Teresa says that Sanchica is earning money, she ominously notes that this is no longer necessary: «pero ahora que es hija de un gobernador, tú le darás la dote sin que ella lo trabaje» "but now that she is a governor's daughter thou wilt give her a portion without her working for it" (2.52.1060). Cervantes's continuous exploration of the contrast between productive work and rent-seeking behavior underscores that the prior is perpetually at risk of being siphoned off by the latter, that the unethical means of generating wealth, those that are essentially parasitic, exploitative, and political in nature, are always a threat to the ethical generation of wealth that takes place through industry and exchange.

DQ 1.46, 2.6, 2.38, and 2.73—Fabricating cages

Cervantes's novel contains multiple allusions to cages that merit attention. First, we have the image of Don Quijote placed in a cage by his friends at the end of part one: «hicieron una como jaula, de palos enrejados, capaz que pudiese en ella caber holgadamente don Quijote» "they made a kind of cage, with crisscrossed beams, large enough to hold Don Quijote comfortably" (1.46.536). This was a standard way of transporting the insane during the early modern period. Next, Antonia marvels at her uncle's skills as an artisan prior to his first sally in part two: «yo apostaré que si quisiera ser albañil, que supiera fabricar una casa como una jaula» "I wager if he wanted to be a bricklayer, he'd know how to build a house as easily as a cage" (2.6.677). Then we have the caged lions that the knight defeats on the road to Zaragoza: «En el espacio que tardó el leonero en abrir la jaula primera estuvo considerando don Quijote si sería bien hacer la batalla antes a pie que a caballo» "In the time it took the lion keeper to open the first cage, Don Quijote was considering whether it would be better to do battle on foot or on horseback" (2.17.765). Later, in one of the novel's many interpolated tales, the Countess Trifaldi describes Princess Antonomasia's lover Don Clavijo as follows: «sabía hacer una jaula de pájaros, que solamente a hacerlas pudiera ganar la vida, cuando se viera en estrema necesidad» "he knew how to make such a bird cage that, if he ever found himself in extreme necessity, he could have earned a living making them" (2.38.943). Finally, Sancho purchases a cage and places it in Don Quijote's hands at the end of part two: «Sacó Sancho cuatro cuartos de la faltriquera, y dióselos al mochacho por la jaula» "Sancho took out four quarter coins from his pocket and gave them to the boy in exchange for the cage" (2.73.1211).

The cage motif supports the view that Cervantes's novel concerns an attempt to confine the lingering ferocity of the crusader knights of medieval Spain, but it's also all about the social benefits of labor, commerce, and wealth. Don Quijote and the lions in their respective cages represent the containment of violence; by contrast the other cages indicate a preference for cottage industry and economic exchange. Most remarkable, however, is the way that Cervantes appropriates the ancient framing concept of *mise en abîme* in order to advance bourgeois values and market principles. Once again, the first modern novel does more than comically restrain chivalric fantasy with everyday realism; it advances the idea that economic activity, which involves work, specialization, improvisation, and trade, is far preferable to conquest.

DQ 2.44—Materialisms

Materialism, in both senses of the term, characterizes *Don Quijote*. In the first case, though he was writing at the height of the Counter-Reformation, Cervantes's fiction is remarkably lacking in references to metaphysical existence. On the one hand, Cervantes echoes Averröes's insistence that the material universe operates according to natural, physical laws and not divine will. This reflects the Andalusian philosopher's vital role in the conveyance of Aristotle to medieval Spain and Italy. On the other hand, Cervantes's anticipations of Hobbes's and Hume's rejections of miracles and spirits might entail some degree of direct influence, since each of these English atheists were avid readers of his novel (see Graf, "Martin and the Ghosts").

One of the most salient scenes that indicate an anti-metaphysical type of materialism in *Don Quijote* is the resurrection of Basilio at the wedding of Camacho and Quiteria in *DQ* 2.28. When Basilio jumps back to life, the crowd shouts «¡Milagro, milagro!» "Miracle, miracle!" His response: «¡No milagro, milagro, sino industria industria!» "Not miracle, miracle, but rather industry, industry!" (2.21.806). Likewise, the exchange between Don Quijote and Montesinos during the encounter with Dulcinea foreshadows Hobbesian ridicule. The knight asks: «¿Es posible, señor Montesinos, que los encantados principales padecen necesidad?» "Is it possible, Sir Montesinos, that enchanted high-born people suffer from want?" Montesinos's hilarious response disallows any metaphysical escape from the facts of life: «Créame vuestra merced, señor don Quijote de la Mancha, que esta que llaman necesidad adondequiera se usa y por todo se estiende y a todos alcanza, y aun hasta los encantados no perdona» "Your grace should believe me, Sir Don Quijote of La Mancha, that this thing called need occurs everywhere and extends to all places and reaches everyone, and even the enchanted are not exempt" (2.23.827). Note how this is also uncannily similar to the modern rendering of economics as the science of scarcity and the persistence of opportunity costs.

In the second case, Cervantes's fiction foregrounds people's natural desire for material things. Hinting at Averröes's philosophy as the grounds for this other type of materialism, it is precisely the Moorish narrator Cide Hamete who voices the most passionate case for greed being good. When the hidalgo laments a run in his stocking in *DQ* 2.44, Hamete emphatically intrudes a second time in the same chapter. His words are a sophisticated critique of the notably Christian disciples of the cult of poverty. He doesn't complain about the existence of poverty *per se* but, rather, the weird tendency among Christians to embrace poverty as a virtue. In particular, he questions the logic of the great medieval Spanish poet Juan de Mena: «¡Oh pobreza, pobreza! ¡No sé yo con qué razón se movió aquel gran poeta cordobés a llamarte ‹dádiva santa desagradecida›! Yo, aunque moro, bien sé, por la comunicación que he tenido con cristianos, que la santidad consiste en la caridad, humildad, fee, obediencia y pobreza; pero, con todo eso, digo que ha de tener mucho de Dios el que se viniere a contentar con ser pobre» "Oh poverty, poverty! I do not know the reason that great Cordovan poet was moved to call you 'sacred and unwelcome gift!' I, even though I am a Moor, know all too well, through the interactions that I have had with Christians, that saintliness consists of charity, humility, faith, obedience, and poverty; but, even so, I say that he who manages to make himself content with being poor must have a lot of God in him" (2.44.984).

Finally, coupled with force, a materialistic outlook on life has negative social and political consequences. In particular, Cervantes viewed the Inquisition as a shameful matter of land grabs and confiscations of wealth. Early in part two, the barber's tale of the madman who escapes from an insane asylum in Seville underscores the corrupt methods of the Holy Office: «sus parientes, por gozar de la parte de su hacienda, le tenían allí, y a pesar de la verdad querían que fuese loco hasta la muerte» "his relatives, in order to enjoy his portion of the family estate, were keeping him there, and, in spite of the truth, they wanted him to be considered insane until his death" (2.1.630). Sancho's encounter with his exiled neighbor Ricote indicates the same, i.e., that stealing the wealth of others is the real motive driving the policy of religious persecution: «Ahora es mi intención, Sancho, sacar el tesoro que dejé enterrado, que por estar fuera del pueblo lo podré hacer sin peligro, y escribir o pasar desde Valencia a mi hija y a mi mujer, que sé que están en Argel» "It is my present intention, Sancho, to recover the treasure that I left buried, which I will be able to do without danger because it is outside of town, and to write or go from Valencia to my daughter and my wife, for I know that they are in Algiers" (2.54.1073).

In such moments, Cervantes walks a fine line in the context of the Counter-Reformation, but the results are spectacular. My favorite example is Sancho's disarming quip about the curiously selfish kind of charity practiced by Saint Martin. The squire intimates that a truly materialistic miracle is to be found in mutually advantageous events made possible by commerce: «para dar y tener, seso es menester» "to give and to withhold require wisdom untold" (2.58.1096). One way of interpreting this proverbial expression is that in a non-coercive exchange between two people, both of them are better off than before (see Ayau; Ricardo, "An Essay on Profits").

DQ 2.51—Constitutions and economic policy

The ordinances for the Isle of Barataria found in «*Las constituciones del gran gobernador Sancho Panza*» "*The Constitutions of the Great Governor Sancho Panza*" (2.51.1053) were common in Cervantes's day. This does not, however, mean they were considered reasonable by all or that they were easily enforced. A comical aspect of Sancho's laws derives from the way they reflect what the picaresque governor knows from experience: beware of free-riders! But there's something inherently futile about many of them. How can a law, for example, ensure the verification of miracles sung about by blind beggars?

Along similar lines, Sancho's economic edicts are a mess. Late-scholastic economists would have noted that his ban on speculating is likely an attempt to counter a side effect of the inflation caused by his own meddling. Rising prices caused by debasements force authorities to turn to price controls, which then bring about shortages and bans on hoarding. Notice, too, how Sancho's decrees regarding wine, shoes, and the salaries of servants reflect the desperation of princes who meddle with markets and money. We can also ask whether or not Sancho favors free markets at all. For wines, he mandates they should trade «según su estimación, bondad y fama» "according to their value, quality, and reputation" (2.51.1053), but when it comes to footwear and salaries, he mandates price controls. The ironies of these policies are compounded by what we know about Sancho. He loves wine, so the first law makes sense because it favors quality through competition. But Sancho also wants a salary from Don Quijote and his wife wants good shoes for their children, so why does he decree artificially low prices for these?

We see the ironical genius of Cervantes in his juxtaposition of a free market for wine and a regulated market for shoes. If readers favor one policy, logically they should oppose the other. Which is it going to be? Do readers want freedom and well-being or control and depravation? Sancho's laws are a case of Cervantes's tendency to construct casuistic puzzles for his readers. Thus, Sancho is only intermittently like King Solomon. His policies will cause shortages, reduce labor productivity, and lower the quality and availability of shoes. The salary cap for servants might reflect Sancho's quest for wealth without effort, but bad shoes hurt the well-being of his own children. Moreover, Sancho's price controls on footwear add meaningful pathos to the hidalgo's decision in *DQ* 2.46 to wear his squire's boots so as to hide the run in his stocking. To grasp the tragicomedy of such cases requires knowledge about economics and human nature. For all his princely advice, Don Quijote never manages to transmit to Sancho one of Mariana's most crucial insights: meddling in a republic's economy almost always harms most of its citizens.

(3) USURY, INTEREST, AND THE TIME VALUE OF MONEY

The early modern period inherited a long tradition of deeming interest, or "usury," both greedy and immoral. Classical and medieval thinkers like Aristotle and Aquinas argued that it was "unnatural" to use money to make more money. Dante placed usurers in the inner ring of the seventh circle of Hell. However, to borrow the words of eighteenth-century Tory jurist William Blackstone: "money is lent on a contract to receive not only the principal sum again, but also an increase by way of compensation for the use; which generally is called *interest* by those who think it lawful, and *usury* by those who do not so" (1336).

Protestant reformers and secessionists like John Calvin and Henry VIII began eroding laws against usury around 1550. In Spain, the issue was hotly debated around the same time by the late scholastics. Examples of a new assessment included Saravia's *Instrución de mercaderes* (1544), which marked a transition between antithetical ways of thinking about business loans; Medina's *Codex de Restitutione et Contractibus* (1546), which defended the legitimacy of compensating creditors for repayment risk; Mercado's *Suma de tratos y contratos* (1571), which articulated an open-minded view of interest for a popular audience; and Vasconcillos's *Tratado único de intereses* (1637), which smashed the logic of laws against usury by disclosing "the fundamental injustice of expecting to borrow money for free" (D'Emic 159).

Perhaps above all else, laws against usury distort the time value of money. Like inflation, they benefit debtors at the expense of savers. When the market for loans is allowed to operate free of interference by authorities, the time value of money reflects the choices of market participants. We say that debtors, who focus on their near-term well-being, have a "high time preference," whereas creditors, who focus on their well-being in the future, have a "low time preference." Interest rates reflect the intersection of these preferences in the aggregate.

DQ 1.4—Andrés's back pay

In *Don Quijote*, Cervantes's critique of usury laws first surfaces in the subtle dialogue between the hero and the rich farmer Juan Haldudo. At issue is the back pay the farmer owes the shepherd boy Andrés. When Haldudo finally agrees to pay the boy, he lets slip that he also owes him interest, metaphorically figured as a kind of supplemental perfume (*sahumerio*). Don Quijote recognizes this interest, but he appears to excuse it, so long as Haldudo agrees to pay Andrés with silver *reales* instead of debased billon coins, which now contained only copper. In other words, the debased coins distorted labor contracts to the benefit of employers. By expropriating the wealth of those who were paid with billon coins, Habsburg monetary policy turned normal employment into a kind of slavery. Haldudo whipping Andrés is analogous to the state's inflationary abuse of Spain's poorest citizens.

Note, however, Don Quijote's hilarious miscalculation of Andrés's salary. His conclusion that «nueve meses, a siete reales cada mes» "nine months, at seven *reales* a month" makes for «setenta y tres reales» "seventy-three *reales*" (1.1.36), requires us to think in terms of both debasement and the time value of money. Business-oriented readers will see that Don Quijote has, in fact, not excused the interest Haldudo owes Andrés. It's another Cervantine game of perspectives: if we laugh at Don Quijote, we endorse official policy; if we accept his calculation, then we are thinking like informed market participants who would object to both debasement and laws against usury. By the way, a surcharge of ten *reales* for the use of sixty-three *reales* for nine months, or 21% annually, was a reasonable rate around 1600.

DQ 2.45—Debtors versus creditors

At the beginning of his reign as Governor of Barataria, Sancho Panza must adjudicate a case involving a creditor who accuses a debtor of not repaying a loan. If readers don't understand credit risk, they can learn about it here (see Medina). But there's more. Much like the hidalgo's miscalculation of Andrés's back pay in *DQ* 1.4, which seems wrong but, in fact, is correct if we allow for the time value of money, Sancho's detection of the creditor's coins hidden in the debtor's cane seems like justice, but it isn't. Why? As benevolent as Sancho seems, his ruling still favors the deceptive debtor. We know this because the creditor says that he waited for a while before approaching the debtor for repayment of the coins: «Pasáronse muchos días sin pedírselos» "Many days went by without my asking for them" (2.45.994). This information undercuts Sancho's ruling because, in the end, he only orders the return of the original sum of ten gold *escudos*. Though the governor rightly finds the debtor guilty, he still shortchanges the creditor because he doesn't allow for the time value of money. An obvious lesson about credit risk contains a more subtle lesson about the interest that ought to be paid as a result. Justice on Barataria is never what it seems.

There's more. The episode hints at the variable metal content of the era's coins. As in the case of Cardenio's 100 *escudos* that go missing in the Sierra Morena, the fact that ten more of these rare gold coins are hidden away reflects Gresham's law. Moreover, when the creditor states that he lent «diez escudos de oro en oro» "ten gold *escudos* in gold" (2.45.994), his pleonasm stresses that the loan contract is valued in gold instead of *maravedís*, the era's abstract unit of account that might have allowed repayment in silver *reales* or, worse still, debased copper coins.

Beyond Gresham's law and debasement, the episode alludes to the theme of usury in at least two ways. The contract is oral, so there's likely more than meets the eye. The loan, for example, could have originated in another denomination, with only its repayment specified in gold. If the debtor received part of the loan in coins with inflated face values, then the creditor would later receive adequate compensation by way of repayment in gold coins. Sancho doesn't punish either man, so it's even possible that they have outwitted laws against usury and gained perverse approval for their transaction. Again, Cervantes's "perspectivism," which obliges us to consider the motives and actions of his characters, often takes the form of an economic riddle.

(4) INFLATION

Among the economic topics in *Don Quijote*, Habsburg monetary policy looms large, especially in part two. Like Keynes, Salamancan theorists understood the utility of debasement in a time of crisis. But even then, the citizens whose wealth is coopted in the conduct of a war, for example, must still be repaid. If not, it's tyranny. Cervantes appears to have agreed.[4]

Inflation is a multifaceted phenomenon, and its effects vary depending on which part of the economy we consider. Named after sixteenth-century Tudor financier Sir Thomas Gresham (c.1519–79), who was shocked by the absence of gold currency in Seville, Gresham's law states that bad money drives out good. Think of bad money as money that loses its purchasing power relative to good money. Fiat money is notoriously bad because it generally overstates the value of the metals used to mint it, whereas good money maintains a more honest correlation. As market participants grow wise to its false status, they'll prefer to use it in their everyday transactions while withdrawing good money from circulation as a way to preserve their wealth. This ancient phenomenon's most common cause is monetary adulteration by political authorities, i.e., princes whose policies "magically" enrich the state at the expense of citizens in three principal ways:

i.   Wholesale extraction: authorities order commoners to exchange purer gold and silver coins for coins that are either debased with higher copper content or re-stamped with higher face values.
ii. Fiat financing: authorities force their creditors to accept debased or re-stamped money as legal repayment of previously incurred debt.
iii. Asymmetrical information: authorities who control the production of adulterated money, as well as insiders with early access to it, take advantage of the delayed effects of price inflation to purchase goods and services for the state and themselves at a discount.

Throughout recorded history this practice has been railed against by Judaic, Christian, and Muslim moralists, mocked by classical authors like Aristophanes (*The Frogs*, 405 BCE) and Plautus (*Casina*, c.185 BCE), and formally scrutinized by medieval and Renaissance theorists like Oresme (*De moneta*, c.1360) and Copernicus (*De monetae cudendae ratione*, 1526). Renaissance thinkers clearly understood the mechanics of debasement and re-stamping and their inflationary results. They also understood that such practices represented an illegal tax, i.e., a form of theft used to finance irresponsible fiscal policies, thus benefiting authorities and insiders at the expense of citizens. Except in extreme cases of national emergency, the consequences of inflation are market fragility, on the one hand, and, on the other hand, the decimation of the personal wealth of commoners, most especially the poor, who are unable to protect their wealth by shifting it into more reliable assets.

Furthermore, the havoc extends to the social realm, for as prices rise, frustration and resentment grow. The most famous modern proponent of monetary debasement was John Maynard Keynes (1883–1946). Even Keynes, however, recognized that the policy should only be used in the case of an existential emergency; otherwise, the results are poisonous. In Keynes's own words: "Lenin was certainly right. There is no subtler, no surer means of overturning the existing basis of society than to debauch the currency. The process engages all the hidden forces of economic law on the side of destruction, and does it in a manner which not one man in a million is able to diagnose" (236).

In late-Renaissance Spain, Jesuit philosopher Juan de Mariana was the most widely known source of insight on royal monetary shenanigans and their harmful effects. Key passages in his monumental *Historia de España* (1592/1605) unveiled damning contrasts between the bad and good monies minted by medieval Spanish kings. Subsequently, the chapter "De moneta," which he added to the second edition of his princely advice manual, *De rege et regis institutione* (1598/1605), and which he later expanded into a formal treatise, *De monetae mutatione* (1609), condemned the debasements and re-stampings ordered by Philip II and Philip III (see this book's appendix). Mariana exposed the Spanish state's Machiavellian expropriation of the wealth of its citizens as a form of theft, even slavery. *De monetae mutatione* led to Mariana's arrest for *lèse-majesté* and his prosecution by the Inquisition. It's easy to see why this should have happened, for his sarcasm was scathing even in the earlier "De moneta" (see this book's appendix):

> In order to fill a gap in the budget, which is never not a problem, especially in a sprawling empire, certain smart and clever men propose that it would be helpful in many difficult situations if something were to be pulled out of the weight of the coinage or from its quality, by debasing the metal while still retaining its original value. The prince gets to keep whatever is deducted from the quality or the weight of the currency. And what is more amazing, in the absence of harm or complaint on the part of the provincials. This wonderful technique is not a secret, but rather a useful method by which an incredible amount of gold and silver is redirected into the public treasury without the imposition of any new burden. I have always typically thought of those men who promise to transform metals by some magical method—to make silver out of bronze and gold out of silver—as being the most untrustworthy sort, like itinerant snake oil salesmen. Now I see that metals are rendered more valuable without any effort; that they are doubled in value without any smelting, controlled merely by the edict of the prince, as if multiplied by some sacred touch or higher power; that the subjects are getting back from the economy what they had before at full value; that there is public utility in the fact that what is left over is handed over to the prince for his use. Who is so unreasonable, or, if you prefer, so insightful, that he would

begrudge this happy state of affairs—especially when no innovations are being introduced? [p.268]

Mariana then lays out the immorality and illegality of the practice of monetary debasement:

First off, I assert that neither the portable possessions nor the land of subjects is under the legal control of the prince to the degree that he can take these things for himself at his own discretion or hand them over to someone else on a whim. Those who argue otherwise are blowhards and yes-men of the sort that are numerous in the halls of the powerful. Because of this, it is the case that he cannot order new taxes upon his nation without the consent of the people. For he should get his subjects to pay by asking openly, not by cheating them, nor should he capriciously take a cut on a daily basis whereby they are reduced from a state of abundance and prosperity to a state of need. For that would be to behave like a tyrant who measures everything by his own desires, who takes possession of everything for himself, not a king who restrains the power that he has received from willing people with law and reason, and who does not extend his power all over the place. [p.270]

. . . a king cannot debase the coinage arbitrarily and without the consent of the people. It, too, is a kind of tax by which an amount is extracted from the possessions of subjects. Who would agree to exchange gold for an equal weight of silver, or silver for an equal weight of iron? Generally speaking, why would anyone agree to accept a silver coin for a gold one or a copper coin for a silver one? This happens every time the money is debased. [p.270]

Finally, Mariana describes the economic and social effects of debasement:

The first consequence will be the high cost of all commodities and food—doubtless not less than the amount that will have been subtracted from the quality of the currency. For people do not value a currency any more than the quality and amount of metal allows—not even if there are strict laws against doing this. Indeed, at that point the people will bemoan the fact that they have been tricked by an illusion, and they will sense that the new currency that has been substituted for the old one is not worth as much as the former currency when they need much greater resources than they used to in order to feed their families. [p.274]

Another problem flows from the first: commercial activity that for the most part makes up both public and private wealth is slowed down by a debased coinage. The low quality of the currency clearly frightens shopkeepers and their customers; the high prices that follow on from this problem also frighten them. But if the prince were to set prices for things by fiat (as always seems to happen), instead of a cure, the problem will get much worse since there is no one who will agree to sell for that price, which is so clearly unfair and not

squared with commonly recognized valuation. Once commercial activity has
stopped, there is no category of problem which does not befall such a people.
Certainly, the provincials will be of necessity stretched thin in two ways: first,
due to the slowdown in buying and selling, the income from which the majority
of the population lives will grind to a halt. These people are craftsmen for the
most part and people whose hopes for a meal lie in their hands and in working
every day—which is most people. Second, the prince will be forced either to
completely withdraw the bad currency which is the cause of the problem or to
issue a currency that is worse with its previous value reduced. [p.276]

Technological innovation and political power underwrote the Habsburgs'
schemes. In 1580, Philip II founded the *Real Casa de la Moneda* at Segovia,
which employed a machine invented in Austria in 1550. Amidst protests by
the Cortes, now but a weak conciliar relic of medieval Castile, as well as by
intellectuals like Mariana, an experiment designed to make minting small
denominated coins more efficient soon became a means of financing wars,
courtly extravagance, and corruption. The Spanish *monedas de vellón*, copper
billon coins completely denuded of their silver content, were the modern era's
first industrial attempt at compulsory fiat money. The result was twofold: (1)
a withdrawal from the marketplace of coveted silver *reales* and gold *escudos*,
and (2) price inflation, as those forced to accept adulterated coins in their
commercial activities raised the nominal values of their goods and services.
The inflationary chaos unleashed by the Habsburgs was a factor in the fall of
the Spanish Empire, which is usually marked by the Treaty of Westphalia in
1648 (fig. 17; see Velde; Velde and Weber).

The Baroque aesthetic of *Don Quijote* signals this web of problems:
governmental corruption and wars combined with fiscal and monetary deceit, resulting in inflation, which in turn caused impoverishment and social
disintegration. Cervantes's biographer William Byron is to be credited for
underscoring the predominance of fiscal themes in his fiction. The inflation
motif is so consistent in *Don Quijote* that it infiltrates episodes traditionally
thought to deal with different topics. For example, Andrés's back pay in *DQ*
1.4 insinuates a preference for silver over copper. The same occurs in Don
Quijote's evaluation of Mambrino's helmet in *DQ* 1.21, which turns an item
made from base metals into one made of gold. Why does Quiteria chose
Basilio over Camacho in *DQ* 2.21? It sure can't be money, for Basilio is
associated with copper coins and Camacho with silver *reales*. In the case of
the creditor versus the debtor in *DQ* 2.45, the injustice of flouting repayment
risk and the time value of money is aggravated by a hoax designed to make
gold coins vanish, which, in turn, becomes yet another of the novel's many
figurative representations of the phenomenon described by Gresham's law.

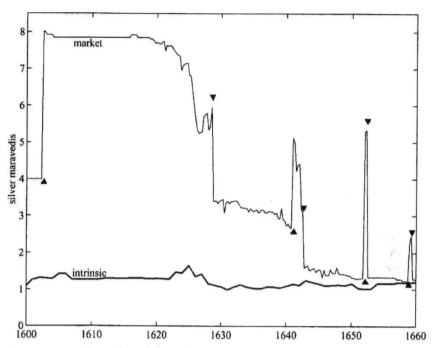

Figure 17. Market Value of *Cuartillo* Billon Coin Versus Intrinsic Value of Copper, 1597–1659 *Source*: Federal Reserve Bank of Chicago

DQ 1.1—Rocinante's debased hooves

The first simile in history's greatest work of narrative fiction describes Rocinante's hooves as having «más cuartos que un real» "more *cuartos* than a *real*" (1.1.42). The word *cuartos* indicates a disease which afflicts neglected horses by fracturing their hooves. But by way of a homonym, the term also alludes to inflationary monetary policy, which made smaller denominated copper billon coins, especially *cuartos*, lose purchasing power with respect to silver *reales*. Officially, thirty-four *maravedís*, a bit more than eight *cuartos*, each with a face value of four *maravedís*, equaled a *real*. In reality, however, circa 1605, may people began to avoid receiving payment in *cuartos* because government officials were extracting their silver content. As the Habsburg policy took effect, and as counterfeiters began flooding the Spanish economy with even more copper coins, the odds of finding quarter coins that still contained grains of silver decreased, and so it took more and more *cuartos* to buy a *real*. The first description of Rocinante seems casual, comic; it is, however, a grave reference to the corrosive effects of debasement. The ultimate symbol of chivalric heroism is rotting at its base: national ruin, in the form of an economic disease, hobbles the crusading warhorse before the Manchegan knight can sally forth.

DQ 1.11—Don Quijote's "Golden Age"

Many scholars cite Don Quijote's most famous speech as indicative of Cervantes's nostalgia for a kind of prehistoric communist utopia (Pérez de Antón; Byrne 42). But given Rocinante's debased hooves, Andrés's back pay, and the discounted Toledan manuscript, we might consider a different perspective. In the context of the ideas of the School of Salamanca, it's the hidalgo's ignorance on display in *DQ* 1.11, not Cervantes's. As Mariana demonstrated, debasement enslaves citizens by stealing their wealth and it thus represents a tyrant's violation of the principle of private property. Like a tyrant, Don Quijote happily consumes the food and drink of his hosts, and like a rent-seeking governor, he justifies his policy by attacking the very idea of ownership. There's further irony in the hidalgo's nostalgia for something golden, because gold was one of the few mechanisms by which citizens might guard their wealth from the Habsburgs. Don Quijote should have known this as much as anyone, because the fixed income hidalgos received from the state lost its purchasing power at an accelerated rate in the early seventeenth century. If Habsburg ideology fashioned the monarchy's political power as the restoration the mythical golden age of pre-classical antiquity (see Tanner), in reality its policy of debasement and forced exchange rates violated this ideal. The scene of the Golden Age speech seems peaceful, in contrast to the mad knight's direct attacks in *DQ* 1.8 and 1.21; nevertheless, the goatherders see their wealth eroded in ways they perhaps could not have anticipated.

DQ 1.23—Adultery and adulteration in the Sierra Morena

On their surface, the Sierra Morena episodes involve a series of more or less interpolated tales of sexual lunacy. Cardenio, Don Fernando, and Anselmo must reject their erotic appetites and learn to appreciate the vitality of more mature and more rational marital relationships with Luscinda, Dorotea, and Camila (see Herrero "The Beheading of the Giant"). But the Sierra Morena also contains an economic allegory that hinges on a subtle metaphor. Adultery is analogous to bad monetary policy. The infidelity of *adulterio* (Latin, *adulterium*) and the falsification of *adulterar* (Latin, *adulterare*) are linked etymologically and governed by narcissistic corruption: monetary authorities and unfaithful lovers benefit from deceiving their contractual partners. Thus, Sancho's discovery of Cardenio's 100 gold *escudos* in *DQ* 1.23 inaugurates the adulterous Sierra Morena episodes.

The unruly desires in the Sierra Morena dissolve by the end of part one of *Don Quijote*, leaving readers only with the eternal problem of Sancho's theft of Cardenio's *escudos*, a problem that resurfaces in part two. Cardenio's chained valise containing those gold coins is itself a concatenating metaphor for the action of Gresham's law by which market participants secreted away good money as a store of value against unbridled inflation. Likewise, both the tyrannical behavior of the arch-adulterer Don Fernando and the base thievery of the arch-picaroon Sancho parallel the tyranny of Habsburg monetary authorities. Also, the squire's discovery of 100 *escudos* in spite of Cardenio's chain recalls the chained galley slaves in the previous chapter and anticipates Don Quijote's filthy rosary and Sancho's awful slaver fantasy in *DQ* 1.26 and 1.29. Translation: monetary adulteration is a political tyrant succumbing to the moral corruption of exploiting and enslaving his subjects. This metaphorical structure prods us to imagine how monetary inflation functions, i.e., a sequence of corrupt transactions trickles through society, enslaving and stealing from everyone involved in economic exchange. Authorities who control the production of adulterated money benefit most by being the first who use it, i.e., they set loose Gresham's law on society and reap profits from those most ignorant of the phenomenon.[5]

DQ 1.29—Sancho turns copper into silver and gold

¿Qué se me da a mí que mis vasallos sean negros? ¿Habrá más que cargar con ellos y traerlos a España, donde los podré vender y adonde me los pagarán de contado, de cuyo dinero podré comprar algún título o algún oficio con que vivir descansado todos los días de mi vida? ¡No, sino dormíos, y no tengáis ingenio ni habilidad para disponer de las cosas y para vender treinta o diez mil vasallos en dácame esas pajas! Par Dios que los he de volar, chico con grande, o como pudiere, y que, por negros que sean, los he de volver blancos o amarillos. ¡Llegaos, que me mamo el dedo! (1.29.341)

What difference does it make to me if my vassals are blacks? All I have to do is put them on a ship and bring them to Spain, where I can sell them, and I'll be paid for them in cash, and with that money I'll be able to buy some title or office and live on that for the rest of my life. No flies on me! Who says I don't have wit or ability to arrange things and sell thirty or ten thousand vassals in the wink of an eye? By God, I'll sell them all, large or small, it's all the same to me, and no matter how black they are, I'll turn them white and yellow. Bring them on, then, I'm no fool!

Assisted by Dorotea, the priest and the barber create the backstory of the besieged equatorial African Kingdom of Micomicón in order to entice the mad hidalgo to cease his penance in the Sierra Morena. Striking here is Sancho's moral depravity when he imagines getting rich by selling the black citizens of Micomicón into slavery in Spain. His slaver fantasy alludes to the counterfeit coin industry that sprang to life in response to the Crown's monetary adulterations (see Lea). Due to its higher copper content, debased money oxidizes and turns black. Mariana analyzed this phenomenon in his history of 1592, his princely advice chapter of 1605, and his treatise of 1609. So, when Sancho says that, as black as they be, he'll turn his future citizens into silver or gold, he refers to more than skin color. His business plan will take advantage of Gresham's law to profit from the Habsburg policy of stamping an inflated value on their new copper coins. By dumping so-called black money in Spain, Sancho will arbitrage the difference between official and market values, offering Spanish citizens a discount on the overvalued coins while pocketing the margin above his production costs.

DQ 2.3—Don Quijote versus counterfeiters

Early in part two of *Don Quijote*, we find an explicit analogy between the writing of false history and the minting of false money. Ironies ripple out from the hidalgo's assertion that historians who promulgate lies should be burned like counterfeiters: «los historiadores que de mentiras se valen habían de ser quemados como los que hacen moneda falsa» "historians who deploy lies ought to be burned like those who make false money" (2.3.653). Novels are false histories, so Don Quijote's hyperbole is more of part two's mockery of the complaints made by the confused readers of part one. But monetary policy is also in play. The illegal practice of counterfeiting money was made profitable by the official and far more pervasive practice of debasing it. Don Quijote's censure of historians is also ironic because Mariana's attacks on the Habsburgs, published in 1605 and 1609, resulted from the Jesuit's investigations of the monetary policies of medieval kings as early as 1592. On the one hand, Mariana confirmed that history's greatest counterfeiters are the political authorities themselves; on the other hand, he showed that these same adulterating authorities have a vested interest in falsifying history, both their own and that of their precursors and rivals. By false histories, of course, Cervantes also means novels, and so in pre-modernist fashion his own character condemns him. The simile with counterfeiters, however, allows for an ingenious case of *tu quoque* "you do it too!" aimed at the Habsburgs.

Don Quijote's comment also relates to the metaphor for Gresham's law exhibited by Sancho's theft of the 100 gold *escudos* found in Cardenio's valise. This is because later in this same chapter Sansón Carrasco cites those same vanishing gold coins in the adulterous Sierra Morena as a serious problem in the reception of part one: «También dicen que se le olvidó poner lo que Sancho hizo de aquellos cien escudos que halló en la maleta en Sierra Morena, que nunca más los nombra» "They also say that he forgot to put in what Sancho did with the hundred *escudos* he found in the traveling case in the Sierra Morena, for he never mentions them again" (2.3.655). Gresham's law underwrites the activities of counterfeiters and monetary authorities alike, because each arbitrages the artificial value gradient created by bad money circulating in the presence of good. Thanks to the hidalgo's hostility toward counterfeiters in *DQ* 2.3, the same chapter's comical reflections on the textual problem of Cardenio's gold further insinuate inflationary monetary policy. And all of this confirms at the outset Cervantes's claim in the second prologue that his novel's sequel is cut from the same economic "cloth" as part one.

DQ 2.17 and 2.46—Don Quijote versus debased lions and inflationary cats

Don Quijote's confrontation with lions involves a more elaborate metaphor than most readers realize. Critics note that his new friend Diego de Miranda, also known as the «Caballero del Verde Gabán» "Knight of the Green Coat," is an Erasmian figure whose humble lifestyle countervails the irrational excesses of Don Quijote. Here, however, his initial observation that the cart containing the king's feckless lions looks like a vehicle transporting money hints at neo-Aristotelian treatises on money: «tendió la vista por todas partes y no descubrió otra cosa que un carro que hacia ellos venía, con dos o tres banderas pequeñas, que le dieron a entender que el tal carro debía de traer moneda de Su Majestad, y así se lo dijo a don Quijote, pero él no le dio crédito, siempre creyendo y pensando que todo lo que le sucediese habían de ser aventuras y más aventuras» "he looked all around and could see nothing but a wagon coming toward them, with two or three small flags on it, which led him to assume it was carrying currency that belonged to His Majesty, and he told this to Don Quijote, but he did not give credit to what he said, for he always believed and thought that everything that happened to him had to be adventures and more adventures" (2.17.760).

We have yet another allegory for Habsburg monetary policy, and, as with fiat money itself, perception is key. At first, Miranda seems mistaken about the cart's contents, but if we read his view as a metaphor, then Don Quijote's mad act is a valiant assault on the deceptive practice of minting debased currency. In the end, the knight tips the driver and lion keeper with gold coins, indicating the era's best defense against bad money. Cide Hamete's enthusiasm for this episode makes sense. The hidalgo's gesture is bold and flippant, akin to Mariana's exposure of the Crown's attempts to enslave citizens by extracting their wealth. The lion keeper even promises to report the hidalgo's feat to Philip III and the Duke of Lerma: «besó las manos el leonero a don Quijote por la merced recebida y prometióle de contar aquella valerosa hazaña al mismo rey, cuando en la corte se viese» "the lion keeper kissed Don Quijote's hands for the received favor and promised to retell that valiant deed to the king himself when he arrived at court" (2.17.768). The common man is indebted to Don Quijote for showing him the truth, i.e., traditional gold coins are far preferable to the king's new money.

The lion episode also hints at an ironic awareness of the economic cycle exacerbated by bad monetary policy. Artificial inflation leads to credit and speculative bubbles, as excess money flows through the system chasing investment opportunities with ever diminishing returns. In the context of the politics of money, when Don Quijote doesn't give "credit" to Miranda's warning, believing instead that "adventures" always lead to "more adventures," his insanity reflects uninformed faith in the inevitability of economic growth. The idea that asset prices deviate dangerously from their usual values during debasement-driven outbreaks of inflation is not the lonely insight of nineteenth- or twentieth-century economists. Indeed, the novel coincided with the early years of "Tulip Mania." An edict banned short selling of tulip futures in the Low Countries in 1610 but the bubble finally burst in 1637. *Don Quijote* also anticipated the Holy Roman Empire's "Kipper und Wipper" crisis of 1619–22, which was set in motion by attempts to raise funds with debased coinage at the beginning of the Thirty Year's War (1618–48).

It's risky to argue for the primacy of a particular episode in a Baroque masterpiece like *Don Quijote*. Still, there are clues indicating that *DQ* 2.17 carried a certain weight in the author's mind. First, we note that the hidalgo adopts his third and final moniker before returning to sanity as Alonso Quijano at the end of part two. Unlike *DQ* 1.19, where Sancho christened him as the pathetic «Caballero de la Triste Figura» "Knight of the Sorrowful Face," this time a new and self-chosen name reflects the hero's defiant individualism against the Crown: «Pues si acaso Su Majestad preguntare quién la hizo, diréisle que el Caballero de los Leones» "Well, if by chance His Majesty should ask who did this, tell him it was the Knight of the Lions" (2.17.768). More importantly, *DQ* 2.17 signals the nub of the novel's political satire. There are two reasons we know this: (1) in the second prologue, Cervantes wears Avellaneda's description of his novel as satire as a badge of honor, and (2) while at Diego de Miranda's house in *DQ* 2.16, Don Quijote praises the satires of Horace and Ovid as a prelude to the encounter with the lions.

Finally, the lion episode has implications for the novel's other symbols. Reflecting back on Don Quijote's journey in a cage at the end of part one,

Figure 18. Billon Coin from the Reign of Philip III, 1604 *Source*: Gabriel Calzada

the role reversal in *DQ* 2.17 allows us to better imagine an interconnected metaphor for inflation's attenuation of the purchasing power of poor hidalgo pensioners. If the lion episode represents criticism of Habsburg monetary policy, then the cat episode in *DQ* 2.46 represents the effects of inflation on daily life, as a hidden tax on every purchase slices away at the wealth of Spanish citizens. More debilitating than his combat with a lion, the cumulative result of so many tiny claws is analogous to today's senior citizens facing increases in the prices of basic necessities. Note that Don Quijote's hopelessly «desigual pelea» "unequal battle" (2.46.1003) against the Duke and Duchess's felines follows his attempt to conceal the shame of his ripped stocking by wearing Sancho's boots: «se calzó sus botas de camino, por encubrir la desgracia de sus medias» "he put on his traveling boots in order to hide the misfortune of his stockings" (2.46.999). Note, too, that at the height of the novel's critique of inflation at Sancho's court in *DQ* 2.45, when the whore who also checks the quality of her silver *reales* tells the governor that she's too strong to be robbed of her purse, she links the lions of *DQ* 2.17 to the cats of *DQ* 2.46: «¡Otros gatos me han de echar a las barbas, que no este desventurado y asqueroso! ¡Tenazas y martillos, mazos y escoplos, no serán bastantes a sacármela de las uñas, ni aun garras de leones!» "You'll have to throw other cats at my beard, not this miserable and filthy man! Pliers and hammers, clubs and chisels, would not be enough to pry it from my fingers, not even the claws of lions!" (2.45.998).

The lesson is that gold affords protection against the broad effects of fiat money (lions), but that the poor are always decimated by the inflated prices of those small items required for everyday life (cats). And in much the same way as the hidalgo's praise of satire in *DQ* 2.16 sets the stage for the debased lions in *DQ* 2.17, the inflationary cats of *DQ* 2.46 allow Cervantes to reiterate the inflationary theme running through the three cases resolved by Governor Sancho in *DQ* 2.45. We should now look closely at those cases.

DQ 2.45—Inflation and the Governor of the Isle of Barataria

As the great French liberal Frédéric Bastiat well understood, Cervantes's most ornate meditation on political economy in *Don Quijote* appears in the first three cases adjudicated by the Governor of Barataria. These cases focus on money, trade, credit, and taxes. Via mounting stages of economic reflection, they reinforce and recycle the themes they put in play. Sancho's desire to govern an ínsula has been persistent throughout the novel starting with the squire's first appearance in *DQ* 1.7. On its surface, the fulfillment of his dream in *DQ* 2.45 reads like a series of comical rulings meant to transform the poor, ignorant peasant into an enlightened ruler like Solomon. Nevertheless, the tripartite episode is literally cut from the same economic "cloth" as the rest of the novel, and when we analyze it in the context of late-scholastic economists, its lessons are subtle and problematic for both princes and their citizens.

Sancho's reign begins when he finally sits on his throne and ponders the writing on the wall opposite him: «estaba él mirando unas grandes y muchas letras que en la pared frontera de su silla estaban escritas, y como él no sabía leer, preguntó que qué eran aquellas pinturas que en aquella pared estaban» "he was looking at a number of large letters written on the wall facing his throne, and since he did not know how to read, he asked what was painted there on the wall" (2.45.992). This refers to King Belshazzar in the Book of Daniel. Recall that the words on the wall that Daniel read for the Baby-lonian king were monetary weights and measures, which the prophet then interpreted as verbs to mean that the king's days had been "measured," that he had been "weighed" and found "lacking," and that his kingdom was to be "divided" among his enemies. In other words, the allusion to Daniel in the writing on the wall across from Sancho is itself an allusion to the relation between inflationary monetary policy and the blasphemous rule of tyrants.

DQ 2.45.a—Inflation and a tailor's cuts

Sancho's first case in *DQ* 2.45 revolves around a fixed amount of cloth or *paño*. This same term in the second prologue's definition of the novel should alert us to what amounts to Cervantes's clearest description of a currency's loss of purchasing power. Recall that political authorities use debasement to raise revenues, hoping nobody notices that their substitution of bad money for good money causes the prices of goods and services to rise while lowering their quality. The case of the peasant versus the tailor cuts straight to the lesson that, all things being equal, you cannot get more for less. When the peasant demands the production of first one, then two, then three, four, and five caps, all from a fixed amount of fabric, the tailor produces smaller and smaller caps until they only fit fingers instead of heads. When Sancho punishes both men by taking both the cloth and the money, we read a metaphor for inflation's destruction of everyone's wealth. Then, when he orders the tiny caps to be distributed to the nation's prisoners, it's more than criticism of the conditions of early modern jails. Inflation and the government largesse it funds force everyone to accept less. By raiding the general economy, governments worsen economic conditions while claiming to ameliorate them, not to mention the fact that government always takes its own "cut" from the wealth that it pretends to hand out.

DQ 2.45.b—Inflation and debtors versus creditors

In Shakespeare's *The Merchant of Venice* (c.1599), Antonio defaults on Shylock's loan and the state and society proceed to penalize the creditor instead of the debtor. By contrast, in the first case of *DQ* 2.45, Cervantes potentially models how two parties who want to complete a loan might fake a repayment issue as a red herring that will distract certain authorities from penalizing the sin of usury. In this regard, the novelist pens a lyrically provocative description of the credit arrangement. Notice how phonetic confusion between time (*días* or "days") and quantity (*diez* or "ten") accompanies redundancy about quality (*oro en oro* or "gold in gold"): «le presté días ha diez escudos de oro en oro» "some days ago, I lent him ten *escudos* of gold in gold" (2.45.994). Due to the tale's focus on the lack of circulation of hidden gold coins, it's also difficult to avoid the issue of Habsburg monetary policy. Complementing this, the debtor's oath that he has already paid the creditor echoes how the very same authorities who penalized usury also used debasement to steal the wealth of their citizens, while maintaining the illusion of officious honesty. Finally, given that the quality of coins and the diminishment of their purchasing power are essential aspects of the two other cases in *DQ* 2.45, we can add inflation risk to Cervantes's lesson about the factors involved in the calculation of interest on loans.

DQ 2.45.c. Inflation and the lost Golden Age

The beginning of the fable of the prostitute and the swineherd alludes to the same Golden Age lauded by the mad knight in his speech in *DQ* 1.11. The prostitute fashions herself as Astraea, the last immortal to ascend to heaven in order to escape humanity's turn to injustice at the onset of the Iron Age: «¡Justicia, señor gobernador, justicia, y si no la hallo en la tierra, la iré a buscar al cielo» "Justice, Lord Governor, justice, and if I cannot find it on earth, I'll go looking for it in heaven!" (2.45.996). Once again, however, a literary topic blurs with an economic one. As in the Sierra Morena's admixture of adultery and adulteration, sexual deceptions and contaminations coincide with monetary issues in the final case of *DQ* 2.45.

The devil is in the details. The swineherd loses most of the initial value of his pigs to taxes; then the prostitute checks the quality of the silver coins she receives upon Sancho's initial ruling in her favor; and still another abstract unit of account, the *ducado* or "ducat," complicates the calculation of relative values across the board. Furthermore, as with the hidalgo's ambivalent tip to the lion keeper and the cart driver in *DQ* 2.17, Sancho's last words to the swineherd serve as a bit of friendly advice for the common man: «Buen hombre, andad con Dios a vuestro lugar con vuestro dinero, y de aquí adelante, si no le queréis perder, procurad que no os venga en voluntad de yogar con nadie» "My good man, go with God to your home with your money, and from now on, if you don't wish to lose it, make sure to refrain from your desire to lie with anybody" (2.45.998). Knowledge of Gresham's law resolves the lesson. If you don't want the state to steal your wealth like the lying whore that she is, then don't play her game, i.e., stick to precious metals and other assets in lieu of adulterated coins.

The cumulative effect of the three casuistic fables strung together in *DQ* 2.45 makes it difficult to avoid thinking about the mechanics and dynamics of inflation at the beginning of Sancho's rule over Barataria. Not surprisingly, in the very next chapter we read about how ruthless inflationary cats carve up an old man with a run in his stocking. Perspective is crucial when reading Cervantes's fiction. As with cats, so with inflation: what makes for inconsequential amusement to wealthy dukes and duchesses is a matter of life and death for a poor hidalgo.

DQ 2.54. Gresham's law and Ricote's treasure

Given his theft of Cardenio's 100 gold *escudos*, the irony of Sancho's response to his friend Ricote's entourage in *DQ* 2.54 is that once again he doesn't understand Gresham's law in action right before his eyes (see Liu). The pilgrims cry «¡Guelte! ¡Guelte!», which is German for "Gold! Gold!" But Sancho doesn't get it: «No entiendo» "I don't understand" (2.54.1068). Furthermore, if the pilgrims seek gold just like Gresham, then Sancho has none just like the citizens of the city of Seville visited by Gresham.

More amazing, Cervantes deploys Gresham's law as a metaphor for the consequences of the Expulsion of the Moriscos between 1609 and 1614. In Cervantes's day a major issue, on par with the failing Spanish economy, was what to do about the rebellious Morisco populations along the Mediterranean coast. In the same way that the author advocates free market exchange (see Quint), he rejects the racism and expropriation that drove the statist and Inquisitorial policy of expulsion (see Márquez Villanueva, "El morisco Ricote"). If, on the one hand, Sancho's governorship of Barataria traces the tragic costs of bad economic policies like monetary inflation, usury laws, and price fixing; on the other hand, his subsequent refusal to help his Morisco neighbor recover his treasure highlights the immorality of Philip III's ethnic cleansing. The irony is that Sancho, the embodiment of greed, now inexplicably refuses Ricote's offer of 200 *escudos* for his assistance, adding that he would not help his friend even if he were to offer him 400 *escudos*, that is, exactly double what the squire stole from Cardenio in part one. Note also that Sancho's point includes a clear sense of the time value of money:

> . . . si tú, Sancho, quieres venir conmigo y ayudarme a sacarlo y a encubrirlo, yo te daré docientos escudos, con que podrás remediar tus necesidades, que ya sabes que sé yo que las tienes muchas.
> –Yo lo hiciera –respondió Sancho–, pero no soy nada codicioso, que, a serlo, un oficio dejé yo esta mañana de las manos donde pudiera hacer las paredes de mi casa de oro y comer antes de seis meses en platos de plata; y así por esto como por parecerme haría traición a mi rey en dar favor a sus enemigos, no fuera contigo, si como me prometes docientos escudos me dieras aquí de contado cuatrocientos. (2.54.1074)

> "Sancho, if you want to come with me and help me to dig it up and hide it, I'll give you two hundred escudos, and with that you can meet all your needs, for you know that I know you have a good many of them."
> "I'd do it," responded Sancho, "but I'm not a greedy man, because just this morning I left a post where in six months' time I could have had gold walls in my house and been eating off silver plates; and for this reason, and because I

think it would be treason against my king to assist his enemies, I wouldn't go with you even if you gave me four hundred *escudos* in cash right here and now instead of promising me two hundred later."

With Gresham's law as context, Cervantes's criticism of the Expulsion of the Moriscos is more profound than Sancho's betrayal of the obligations of friendship. When Sancho rebuffs his neighbor's offer to pay him, he's refusing to participate in the growth of the Spanish economy. The fact that Ricote is a «tendero» "shopkeeper" (2.54.1069) adds momentum to the idea that the failed economic policy of the Habsburgs is tantamount to their failed social policy, and *vice versa*. Analogous to monetary manipulation, ethnic expulsion brought a short-term boon for the Crown and its allies, who expropriated the wealth of their victims. In the long run, however, the removal of around 300,000 citizens from Aragón, Valencia, and Andalucía would impoverish everyone, especially poor people like Sancho (see 2.54.1069n12). Cervantes understood that the involuntary seizure of wealth turns life into a zero-sum game; whereas non-coercive economic exchange improves life for all involved (cf. Ayau).

With Ricote in part two, as with Sancho's slaver fantasy in part one, Cervantes weaves the metaphorical potential of Gresham's law into his larger criticism of Habsburg tyranny. In the context of inter-ethnic relations, the coerced movement of money is analogous to the coerced movement of black African slaves and Moriscos. This suggests a more liberal and uplifting view of the humanizing effect of economic exchange than many at the time were prepared to admit. Theorists like González de Cellorigo and Mariana, for example, endorsed expulsion.

(5) LABOR MARKETS

We've attended to the first modern novel's economic lessons on subjective value, sweet commerce, interest on loans, and monetary debasement. There remains the thorny matter of labor. Once again, I would argue that Cervantes anticipates a lot of modern thinking on the topic due to the confluence of the history of the novel form and the history of theoretical economics.

First, it's important to realize that the novel has always been a veritable commercial institution in the broad sense of a traditional practice devoted to the promotion of social ideals related to commerce. A proto-liberal perspective on labor, for example, appears in the sixth chapter of *Lazarillo de Tormes*, where a detailed contractual arrangement to deliver water to the center of Toledo lifts the hero out of poverty for the first time in his life, so much so that he can finally afford to feed and clothe himself. It's all there:

incentive, hard work, capital and labor satisfying demand, a share in the profits, the accumulation of wealth, and even the promise of social ascent. For its part, the anonymous Spanish picaresque draws on the classical model of Apuleius's *The Golden Ass* (c.175), where satirical criticism of the moral and economic decay wrought by slavery parallels Lucius's symbolic transformation back into a human being after a ceremony performed by merchants near Corinth. These two archetypes of narrative fiction go a long way toward explaining why Cervantes's masterpiece traces out an overarching trajectory from slavery to work.

The issue of labor in *Don Quijote*, however, is more complex than narrative imitation. Early modern economic theory adds an innovative impetus to the history of the novel. Recall that at the beginning of part two, Sancho brings up just price theory in the context of his salary dispute with Don Quijote (2.2.640). This shows how crucial subjective value theory was to late-scholastic thinking about labor, echoing the basis of Saravia's assault on the objective theory defended by Villalón. Given the primacy of subjective value theory for the Salamancans, it should come as no surprise that the vast majority of them objected to using positive human law as a means of guaranteeing anyone the right to a minimum wage (Chafuen 106–07).

The sixteenth-century debate between subjectivists and objectivists carried over to its modern variants in the contrast between advocates of the free market (classical liberals and Austrians) and advocates of protectionism or revolution (mercantilists and Marxists). Carl Menger, for example, founder of the Austrian School, in his book *Principles of Economics* (1871), lays out an objection to Marxist theory that the Salamancans would have recognized:

> There is no necessary and direct connection between the value of a good and whether, or in what quantities, labor and other goods of higher order were applied to its production. A non-economic good (a quantity of timber in a virgin forest, for example) does not attain value for men if large quantities of labor or other economic goods were applied to its production. Whether a diamond was found accidentally or was obtained from a diamond pit with the employment of a thousand days of labor is completely irrelevant for its value. (146)

For their part, Karl Marx and Friedrich Engels, arguably the modern era's most important materialists, credited Thomas Hobbes as a major precursor of their view of how the world really works. On the one hand, they worshipped Hobbes's critique of metaphysical thinking, and on the other hand, they lauded his understanding of labor as but another commodity subject to the law of supply and demand.[6]

Now, Austrians and Marxists are not at odds on everything. They would agree, for example, that a fundamental aspect of the transition from feudalism to bourgeois capitalism involved an expanding cultural awareness that employers should compensate their employees for their work. We see this same evolution throughout *Don Quijote*, especially in those moments when the squire and the hidalgo negotiate Sancho's salary. The issue surfaces very early in the fulling mills episode: «querría yo saber, por si acaso no llegase el tiempo de las mercedes y fuese necesario acudir al de los salarios, cuánto ganaba un escudero de un caballero andante en aquellos tiempos, y si se concertaban por meses, o por días, como peones de albañir» "I would like to know, in case we never get around to the matter of rewards and we are obliged to turn to that of salaries, just how much did a squire make from a knight-errant in those days, and also whether they were paid on a monthly basis or daily like common bricklayers" (1.20.221–22). The theme appears again in the prophecy delivered by the barber when Don Quijote is placed in a cage for his return home. The barber tells Sancho that his salary will be paid and then Don Quijote confirms it: «por lo menos su salario no podrá perderse» "at least his salary will not be lost" (1.46.538–39).

In *DQ* 2.17, before opening the cage so that Don Quijote can do battle with the lion, the lion keeper makes special legal use of his own salary. He turns it into an asset consisting of the sum of its parts, and he further proclaims that liability for this asset is now being assumed by the mad knight, and that all present are witnesses to this effect:

> Séanme testigos cuantos aquí están como contra mi voluntad y forzado abro las jaulas y suelto los leones, y de que protesto a este señor que todo el mal y daño que estas bestias hicieren corra y vaya por su cuenta, con más mis salarios y derechos. (2.17.764)

> Let all present be made witness to the fact that, against my will and forced, I open these cages and let loose the lions, and that I declare to this gentleman that all the damage and harm that these beasts might cause is on his account and will be accounted for by him, with my salary and fees included.

Later in part two, aspects of Sancho's anxiety about his salary are projected again by Doña Rodríguez's story: «Quedé huérfana y atenida al miserable salario y a las angustiadas mercedes que a las tales criadas se suele dar en palacio» "I remained an orphan and subjected to the miserable salary and the anxiously awaited mercies" (2.48.1018–19).

One of the key differences between classical liberals and Marxists arises when Sancho threatens to go on a labor strike in *DQ* 2.7. In response, Sansón Carrasco, whom Don Quijote calls «perpetuo trastulo y regocijador de los patios de las escuelas salmanticenses» "perpetual diversion and delight of the courtyards of the schools of Salamanca," offers his services, and suddenly Don Quijote perceives a labor market: «¿No te dijo yo, Sancho, que me habían de sobrar escuderos?» "Did I not tell you, Sancho, that I would be inundated with squires?" (2.7.683). Marxists find this situation unacceptable; by contrast, late scholastics, classical liberals, and Austrians begin to imagine additional, more liberating possibilities, such as a salary as collateral, or an employee's claim to future earnings as an asset, or even the creative and competitive advantages unleashed by allowing better work to fetch higher prices.

For classical liberals, both laborers and their employers should be free; for Marxists, labor takes absolute and dictatorial primacy to the point that it is syndicated by the state, and as a result neither labor nor capital are free to act as they see fit. Beyond the relatively obvious immorality of slavery, the forced syndication of labor rewards wastefulness and inadaptability throughout a given economy. This is a major reason why so many repressive "people's" republics, such as the Soviet Union, East Germany, China, North Korea, Venezuela, and Cuba have struggled so mightily to keep up with the free states of Western Europe and North America.

Classical liberals like John Locke, Adam Smith, Frédéric Bastiat, and Frederick Douglass recognized that coercion is a far less efficient means of production than a system based on pay for work. They understood that what Schumpeter would call capitalism's "creative destruction" took place in the labor market too. Modern expressions of the same idea would be Friedrich Hayek's vision of how liberal societies promote "dynamic efficiency" (see *Law, Legislation, and Liberty*) or Nasim Taleb's idea that the short-term messiness of a free economy grants it a certain "antifragility" that allows it to produce and preserve more wealth over the long-term. Cervantes illustrates the same insight in the engagement between the galleys *La Loba* and *La Presa* at the beginning of "The Captive's Tale" in *DQ* 1.39. Captain Álvaro de Bazán overtakes Captain Mahomet Bey because, all things being equal, a free system will defeat a tyrannical one.

Now, classical liberal philosophers also emphasize that individualism, i.e., personal liberty, underwrites a free economy. For Locke, the ultimate foundation of personal property is proper possession of one's self. For Douglass, freedom from slavery is a right, but in order for it to come to pass, it also requires rational respect for one's own personhood. For Rothbard, all freedom departs from economic freedom, that is, the rights to work, produce, and possess are an inseparable trinity. Here again, Cervantes's fiction seems far ahead of its time. Perhaps the most salient example is the ultimate bourgeois miracle of Sancho's evaluation of his physical labor in *DQ* 2.71. It's a spectacular demonstration of the late-scholastic notion of the *pretium iustum mathematicum* "just mathematical price" in the full glory of a free market for labor. Illiterate Sancho embodies the ultimate bourgeois lesson when he places a price on himself, articulating the following equation: 3,300 *cuartillos* = 3,000 *cuartillos* + 300 *cuartillos* = 1,500 half *reales* + 150 half *reales* = 750 *reales* + 75 *reales* = 825 *reales* (2.71.1199–1200).

American abolitionist and essayist Ralph Waldo Emerson wrote an essay entitled "Montaigne; or, the Skeptic" (1850), in which he made the following observation: "Things always bring their own philosophy with them, that is, prudence. No man acquires property without acquiring with it a little arithmetic also." For classical liberals, Austrians, and libertarians alike, the key to overcoming slavery is to make the mental leap toward individual liberty, i.e., each of us must take conscious possession of ourselves. Rothbard once called Mariana "pre-Lockean" in his insistence on the need to place limits on monarchical authority (*Economic Thought* 314). In a remarkably similar way, Locke is post-Cervantine in his sense of economics as first and foremost a calculated ownership of the self.

To conclude, the Baroque and casuistic type of irony in *Don Quijote* usually signals far more problems than it does solutions. So, I'm content if readers grasp that Cervantes wrote down sophisticated thoughts about the economic issues of his day and that he crafted striking textual maneuvers so as to model and elicit such thoughts. Both parts of the novel contain early overt examples: Rocinante's hooves, Andrés's back pay, the second prologue's relation between scarcity to value, Sancho's nod to the "just price" debate,

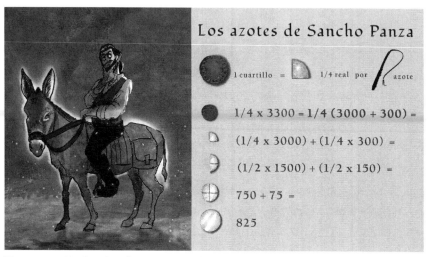

Figure 19. Sergio Miranda, *Los azotes de Sancho Panza*, 2015
Source: donquijote.ufm.edu

and Don Quijote's anger towards counterfeiters. Once we recognize these formulas, we can then grasp more subtle metaphors, especially those pertaining to the manipulation of money. The Sierra Morena's adultery theme, Cardenio's vanishing gold *escudos*, and Sancho's counterfeiting plans for the citizens of Micomicón turn the heart of part one into an allegorical meditation on Habsburg monetary policy. Similarly, the feline episodes and the first three cases of Sancho's governorship of Barataria in part two offer a detailed and coordinated critique of the effects of inflation. Finally, Ricote's treasure represents Cervantes's vision of the Expulsion of the Moriscos as morally analogous to the phenomenon described by Gresham's law.

I have further argued that *Don Quijote* articulates criticisms of economic errors and fallacies like debasement, price fixing, laws against usury, and the obstinate view that commerce is a zero-sum game. Skeptics will make three objections: (1) I'm forcing the ideas of eighteenth- and nineteenth-century Englishmen on a writer from sixteenth-century Spain; (2) the novel might conjure vaguely economic concepts, but these are random commonplaces; (3) since Cervantes's incessant irony muddles his ideological intentions, his actual point of view could just as well be tyrannical, statist, or collectivist in nature. I simply argue that it's foolish to separate Cervantes's ideas from those of other sophisticated Renaissance thinkers like Copernicus, Gresham, Saravia, Mercado, Mariana, and Vasconcillos. The greater error lies in believing that Cervantes was less conscious than us.

Finally, the author's emphasis on personal freedom and his radical undecidability suggest the same counterintuitive, tragic, and fragmentary visions of human knowledge that would later characterize classical liberal and Austrian thinking about economics (see Hayek, *The Fatal Conceit*; Sowell). Thus, the essential attraction of Cervantes's great novel for the likes of Locke, Hume, Jefferson, and Bastiat, all of whom emphasized individualism, private property, stable money, and free markets in lieu of market intervention and control.[7] Again, there are logical explanations for this. On the one hand, Bernard Dempsey, Joseph Schumpeter (*History of Economic Analysis*), Marjorie Grice-Hutchinson, and Murray Rothbard (*Economic Thought*) have shown that the Salamancans who influenced Cervantes also laid the foundations of modern economics. On the other hand, as Apuleius's *The Golden Ass* reveals, criticism of monetary inflation and a basic, if also cultish, intuition regarding the social benefits of commerce are essential aspects of the novel form as it was inherited from classical antiquity.

Mario Vargas Llosa has argued that *Don Quijote* nostalgically salvages from the novels of chivalry a moral code based on the personal virtue of the idealized medieval subject, who now found himself locked in a struggle against the early modern caste system and the growing tyranny of the statist Habsburgs.

However, the novel also brandishes a slew of loaded technical phrases that indicate gold *escudos* and silver *reales* as the best means of countervailing the Crown's new copper-based monetary policy. We can stipulate that Cervantes also expresses nostalgia for freedom from the specifically economic tyranny of inflated fiat money. And to the degree that he configures monetary debasement as the effective enslavement of the Spanish citizenry, *Don Quijote* represents the novelization of the scrupulous complaints made by Juan de Mariana against the wicked activities of Philip III and the Duke of Lerma.

NOTES

1. For a range of economic approaches to *Don Quijote*, see Johnson (*Cervantes*), Liu, Quint, Fernández-Morera, Brewer, Graf ("The Economy of Asses" and "Sancho Panza"), and the spectacularly detailed study by Fernández-Flores.

2. For the chaos created by differing denominations of coins in late-Renaissance Spain, see Lea. For a study of the general anxiety caused by the Spanish importation of specie from the New World, see Vilches. For the complex financial instruments that arose in response to moral and economic interference by Spanish authorities, see D'Emic.

3. For a discussion of Plato's "wolf-tyrant" in book eight of the *Republic*, see Jacques Derrida's *The Beast and the Sovereign* (88–101).

4. For the modern evolution of monetary theory from the School of Salamanca to classical liberalism to the Austrian School, see Menger ("History of Theories"), Grice-Hutchinson (*The School of Salamanca*), Rothbard (*Economic Thought*), and Grabill. For Mariana's monetary theory, see Laures, Calzada, and Graf ("Juan de Mariana").

5. In essence, Cervantes anticipates by more than a century the effects of the non-neutrality of money as first described by Richard Cantillon in his *Essai sur la Nature du Commerce en Général*, which was written around 1730 and published in 1755.

6. Engels writes in his letter to Joseph Bloch: "Hobbes was the first modern materialist" (Marx 764).

7. Maravall is rightly credited for having demonstrated the disillusioned, anti-utopian tendencies of Cervantes's great novel (*Utopía y contrautopía*). Still, Frédéric Bastiat's creative gloss of the episodes on the Isle of Barataria is evidence of *Don Quijote* as a specifically pre-classical liberal text that takes special aim at the folly of market interference by political authorities (see Hart).

Epilogue

Pigs, Asses, Cats, and Humility *in* Don Quijote

". . . how shall I describe the beasts, my comrades?"

—Apuleius, *The Golden Ass* (192)

". . . what was cruelty to a cat *might* be cruelty to a boy, too."

—Mark Twain, *The Adventures of Tom Sawyer* (108)

Orwell, I think, is to be credited for recognizing the essentially political nature of great narrative fiction. At first glance, however, his novels often seem so simple, and so painfully germane to the brutal experience of the twentieth century, that most readers remain oblivious to how they relate to the history of the novel form. Ancient classical Menippean satire, the chief legacy of which is Apuleius's *The Golden Ass* (c.175), was always a political form of narrative due to its mutually reinforcing criticisms of imperialism and slavery. The early modern Spanish picaresque inherits these generic contours, combining surveys of societal decay with symbolic contrasts between humans and animals, often by way of interspecies transformations or else dreams and hallucinations of these transformations.[1]

The episodic complexity of Menippean satire makes it difficult to direct toward specific ideological ends, but given Apuleius's criticisms of the emperors and landed aristocrats of Roman society circa 175 CE, subsequent novelists have often felt compelled to make similar attempts. At an overtly Lutheran moment in *Lazarillo de Tormes* (c.1554), that is, at a politically charged antipapist moment in response to the sale of indulgences, a *pícaro* brays like an ass. In Cervantes's *El coloquio de los perros* (c.1605), a pair of dogs share stories focused on the injustices of late-Renaissance Iberia. One of them is named after the Portuguese House of Breganza and the other after Scipio, a favorite classical exemplar of the Spanish Habsburgs.

Among the great political novels of the modern era, George Orwell's *Animal Farm* (1945) and Fyodor Dostoevsky's *Devils* (1872) are comparable in several ways. Both draw on Menippean satire for their overarching metaphorical structures and both are highly critical of the rise of communism in Russia. At the end of *Animal Farm*, the beasts on the revolutionary farm watch in dismay as their masters, the pigs, stand upright and begin to look like their capitalist human counterparts. Orwell embraced many of socialism's misguided criticisms of capitalism, but he also saw that political liberalization could be coopted by tyrants like Stalin. As for Dostoevsky, at the conclusion of *Devils*, the character Stepan Trofimovich explains that the Marxist madness now muddling the minds of so many young Russian aristocrats has made them like the herd of swine possessed by the devils that Jesus casts out of the man from a city near Galilee in Luke 8.26–39. Dostoevsky wants no truck with the political liberalization emanating from Geneva, Paris, and St. Petersburg; he wants a return to religious and agrarian purity. In *DQ* 2.68, Don Quijote and Sancho are overrun by a heard of pigs on their way back to La Mancha from Barcelona. We might think of this as a symbolic baptism, a purging of all remaining fanatical and irrational demons before we turn to the novel's commonsensical denouement.

Pointing out the obligation to alleviate the suffering of fellow human beings is moral; but as soon as we start to consider what actions we should take, things get political. Just where the demarcation lies is always a matter of debate. What if, for example, a mixture of economic and political liberty alleviates more human suffering than Dostoevsky's calls for a return to religion or even Orwell's calls for a more humane type of socialism? What if freedom trumps the tyranny of charity when it comes to making life better for the most people? I think Cervantes had in mind something analogous to this combination of limited government, freedom of conscience, and the free market when he rejected the Spanish Crown and the Catholic Church's violent imposition of religious orthodoxy via censorship and *autos de fe* as well as their expropriation of private property via monetary debasement and ethnic expulsion.

In this book I have emphasized Cervantine cases for privatization of religion, respect for women, abolition of slavery, resistance to tyranny, and economic freedom. There are, of course, other social virtues on display in the first modern novel, such as laughter, dialogue, beauty, creativity, work, and life in the country. Moreover, the topics I have chosen often overlap in extreme ways. Freedom of religious conscience, for example, also entails each of the other categories of freedom in one way or another. Religious freedom in *Don Quijote* also means respect for a woman's right to choose

Christianity over Islam, rejection of the policy of expelling Spain's minority Morisco population, antagonism toward the anti-Erasmian censors of the Counter-Reformation, and mockery of the economic ignorance and deception underwriting official attitudes against usury.

Still, broadly conceived, it is liberty that most efficiently unites the five overlapping themes that I have analyzed in this book. A corollary, however, is that if liberty is to continue to be a universal ideal, then we all must practice humility on occasion. Humility is also the essence of much late-scholastic thinking about economics and politics; and it's a major virtue of the Austrian School of economics. Beyond its utility as the basis for ancient morality's "Golden Rule" of treating others as we wish to be treated ourselves, humility has serious consequences when it comes to imagining governing practices and economic policies.

This last lesson remains so counterintuitive to so many people that it merits repeating. As Friedrich Hayek put it: "The peculiar character of the problem of a rational economic order is determined precisely by the fact that the knowledge of the circumstances of which we must make use never exists in concentrated or integrated form but solely as the dispersed bits of incomplete and frequently contradictory knowledge which all the separate individuals possess" ("The Use of Knowledge"). Matt Ridley, in "Friedrich Hayek and the Collective Brain," has eloquently described the political consequences of this idea: "central planning cannot work because it is trying to substitute an individual all-knowing intelligence for a distributed and fragmented system of localized but connected knowledge, much of which is tacit." Ridley goes on to argue that this insight is the essence of anti-elitism and liberal-leaning populism. And classical-liberal and Austrian versions of humility are not merely a matter of respecting the dispersed nature of human knowledge. As Jeffrey Tucker points out, the problem of an elusive rational economic order is further complicated by the exigencies of time: "Even under the best circumstances, the planners would only be planning the past." There are multiple risks, then, posed to us all by those economists and politicians who suffer from the pretense of thinking that they can know and provide for our individual needs.

In the same Nobel Laureate speech in which he mentioned the *pretium mathematicum iustum* "just mathematical price" of the late scholastics, Hayek underlined humility as the true antidote to tyranny:

> The recognition of the insuperable limits to his knowledge ought indeed to teach the student of society a lesson of humility which should guard him against becoming an accomplice in men's fatal striving to control society—a striving which makes him not only a tyrant over his fellows, but which may well make him the destroyer of a civilization which no brain has designed but which has grown from the free efforts of millions of individuals. ("The Pretense of Knowledge")

Given the impossibility of absolute knowledge about such dynamic things as desires, talents, resources, and uses, Hayek, Ridley, and Tucker emphasize that the implementation of economic planning leads inevitably toward madness and brutality. Moreover, planners cannot resist the urge to fix what they break, which often leads to more coercive intervention, which leads to shortages and poverty, which bring more calls for even more radical degrees of political authority and economic planning. *Don Quijote* provides similar lessons about the lack of ideal perspective, and thus the need for humility. In the Clavileño adventure, soon-to-be Governor Sancho Panza claims to have gazed down upon the earth in its entirety. But the Duchess objects: «por un ladito no se vee el todo de lo que se mira» "one does not view the entirety of what one contemplates from just one side" (2.41.965). The Duchess already has her reasons for doubting the squire's princely abilities; but when he justifies himself by way of pretensions to absolute knowledge, she has reason to fear his tyranny.

This notion of respecting the vitality of economic and political uncertainty is akin to the intentionality problem in the study of literature. The unavailability of so many dead authors whom we might wish to interrogate regarding the intentions of their creative work requires humility on the part of literary critics. We can never know for certain the true meaning of any sufficiently complex work of fiction from the past. Indeed, the author himself might not be aware of its meaning. At best, we speculate, debate, and hope to someday arrive at a consensus view. Moreover, it's the nature of imaginative discourse to eschew monolithic answers. Basic literary tools like symbols, for example, require humility to be appreciated as such. If a "rose" simply means "love," then it's a substitution, not a symbol. As a symbol it must carry multiple and often highly subjective senses. Roses have pleasant colors and scents and layers of soft petals, but they are also ephemeral and thorny, all of which imply different aspects of the experience of love.

The case for the experience of literature as one of uncertainty is an idea amplified by the animal protagonists of Menippean satire. The already difficult problem of identifying with fictional characters is made more difficult when those characters metamorphose into animals. This difficulty, however, is not unrelated to the moral trajectories of the genre. On the one hand, an animal is often less limiting for identification purposes than a person, and, on the other hand, if I can empathize with a zebra or a dog, then, at least in theory, empathizing with another human being should be easier.

Two symbolic animals stand out for readers interested in understanding the overlapping moral, political, and economic specificity of *Don Quijote*. Asses and felines are at the centers of the author's respective criticisms of the problems of race-based slavery and imperialistic monetary policy.

Orwell understood the symbolic purpose of the ass as a means of advocating for the alleviation of the suffering of one's fellow human beings. On two different occasions, first in his essay "Inside the Whale" (19) and then again in the preface to the Ukrainian edition of *Animal Farm* (112), Orwell cites Balaam's ass from the Book of Numbers 22.21–34 as the inspiration for his novel. In Numbers, the ass speaks, asking Balaam why he beat him on the three occasions that the animal had bowed down before the angel of the Lord. For political effect, Orwell coopts Balaam's ass's point of view and transforms it into that of workers exploited by the rich and powerful. This is possibly a case of a modern novelist refusing to acknowledge the influence of similarly symbolic and sociological asses in *The Golden Ass*, *Lazarillo de Tormes*, and *Don Quijote* (cf. Harold Bloom's *tessera* and *askesis*). Or it might be that Orwell wishes to indicate the Bible as the source of inspiration for the roles of still other animals in the novel, pigs, for example. But Orwell's broader point is easier to grasp: *Animal Farm* signals human suffering in the tradition of Menippean satire. To put it another way, when humans view others as animals, then we have a social problem. In Cervantes's great novel, Sancho's intermittent ass signals this with respect to black African slaves in *DQ* 1.29 and 1.44–46 and then again with respect to expelled Moriscos in *DQ* 2.10 and 2.53–55 (Graf, "The Economy of Asses").

The felines of *DQ* 2.17 and 2.46 signal the debilitating effects of the currency debasement unleashed by Philip III. The American novelist Mark Twain, as good a reader of Cervantes as Orwell, appears to have sensed the Spaniard's mingling of a certain trio of issues: monetary policy, race, and slavery. In chapter twelve of *The Adventures of Tom Sawyer* (1876), the famous episode of Aunt Polly's cat hints at Cervantes's influence. This time, however, it's the cat who suffers instead of the protagonist. Whereas Don Quijote is attacked by cats in *DQ* 2.46 and then must convalesce at the ducal palace on the Ebro for five days, Tom Sawyer gives one of Aunt Polly's quack remedies to her cat, which then results in the animal's spectacularly agonizing death. The sickness of race-based slavery provides the social context for nearly everything Twain wrote. On its surface, Aunt Polly's lethal medicine highlights the problem of overcoming one creature's sadism toward another. Treating Tom like the cat would be cruel, just like treating Lucius or the citizens of Micomicón like asses.

In a later essay entitled "Corn-Pone Opinions" (1901), Twain describes his youthful enthrallment with the rhetorical skills of a black preacher, and then he turns to address the fickle nature of the general public, one good example of which are the competing lobbies for silver and gold as the proper metallic bases for money in late nineteenth-century America. When read together, and especially when read in the context of Cervantes's fiction, Twain's "Aunt

Polly's Cat" and "Corn-Pone Opinions" alert us to the inflation experienced by both sides of the American Civil War fought to liberate black slaves.[2]

For Cervantes scholars, Twain's ambivalence about monetary inflation is a curious and important detail. Mariana and Cervantes had, respectively, argued and fictionalized the idea that increasing the supply of money reduces its relative purchasing power, basically stealing people's wealth without their consent. Mariana and Cervantes even saw inflation as analogous to slavery. But what if the mass enslavement of debasement is itself necessary? Winning wars and fixing the effects of wars can justify almost anything. Why shouldn't the government subsidize silver production in the Western territories after the Civil War? Why not press for bimetallism? Or is that just another means of carrying out the nefarious policy of debasement?

After the Civil War, Twain inclines toward avoiding fanaticism on either side of an issue that has likely plagued humanity since the evolution of money in the place of barter. Even in the debate over monetary policy, about which my libertarian friends often hold fanatically strong points of view, Twain stresses in "Corn-Pone Opinions" that there's plenty of tribal foolishness on both sides: "half of the nation passionately believed that in silver lay salvation, the other half as passionately believed that that way lay destruction. Do you believe that a tenth part of the people, on either side, had any rational excuse for having an opinion about the matter at all?"

From Twain's perspective, it's as if the American Civil War has been sublimated into an ensuing political battle over money. Reader, which do you prefer, a lot of death and destruction or a lot of lost purchasing power? Winning the war in the first place required the massive tax of debased money on both sides. Perhaps Twain now thought that healing the nation's wounds, or paying for its sins, as it were, mattered more than maintaining the fiction of a righteous monetary policy. Of course, neither does this mean that postmodern Keynesians, who regularly insist on perpetual inflation as the solution to all sorts of social problems, aren't themselves guilty of producing what Twain called "a mush of mutilated morals."

Hayekians would likely agree with Cide Hamete Benengeli's praise of Don Quijote when he hardly hesitates to attack a cart that might contain Philip III's already notoriously debased money in *DQ* 2.17. But Hayek's emphasis on economic humility implies political humility. The knowledge problem is not unique to economics; neither can there exist any perfect, all-knowing political action, even when it comes to the wicked policy of debasement. Furthermore, even if we were to agree that existential threats might justify debasement, how are we to agree on a proper definition of what constitutes an existential threat?

Cervantes's genius lies in his perspectivism, which complicates symbols like pigs, asses, and cats because he is always pushing them to their metaphorical limits. His inflationary felines, which take the contrary forms of harmless lions and nearly lethal cats, suggest that even Hayekians could use humility now and again regarding this issue. In Twain's fiction, on some level it's nothing but "curiosity" that kills Aunt Polly's cat.[3] However, given Cervantes's inflationary cats, and given Plato's vision of politics as the application of a social medicine, which in the wrong doses can become a fatal poison (see Derrida, "Plato's Pharmacy"), Twain's episode can read a lot like a surreal meditation on one of the most difficult and most common problems faced by governments wherever and whenever they have been attempted. Namely, once it has been proposed to inflate a currency, for whatever reason, whether to finance social engineering or to cover the costs of war, where can we ever find the political will, the constitutional medicine, so to speak, necessary to place the cat back into its bag?

A final memo on my overt political motives for writing *Anatomy of Liberty*, which I hope have not overly enervated the book's capacity to provide interested readers with insights derived from close readings of particular episodes. Why presume to read *Don Quijote* as a proto-liberal text? Aside from understanding Cervantes's fiction in order to appreciate the subtleties of other masterpieces like Dostoevsky's *Devils*, Orwell's *Animal Farm*, or Poe's "The Black Cat" or "The Gold-Bug," we might consider that there are consequences to the ways in which great literature is taught at institutions of higher learning. If literature is taught at all nowadays, it's generally not according to anything resembling a liberal perspective. Plato, Gramsci, and Althusser understood that politics is ultimately a struggle to control education. Likewise, John Dewey, the darling of the progressive American left, once urged that "liberalism must now become radical," arguing that liberals should recognize "the necessity of thoroughgoing changes in the set-up of institutions and corresponding activity to bring the changes to pass" (qtd. by Levin 32). Over the course of the twentieth century, Dewey and his ilk successfully transformed liberalism into radicalism, and they won near absolute control of academia in the process. One lesson to draw from this history is that when conservatives and entrepreneurs concede the arts and humanities to Marxists and post-Marxists, as we have essentially done since 1968, then the study of the complexity of human life falls to people with more neurotic and dogmatic answers to society's problems, i.e., to people who are more willing to indoctrinate students with the new religion of revolt. Another not-so-inconsequential result is a general intellectual inability to confront the persistent tyranny and poverty that still threaten far more people around the world than they should.

NOTES

1. As is the case with countless discoveries in the study of Spanish literature, the great polymath Marcelino Menéndez y Pelayo is to be credited with having pointed the way toward appreciating the connections between Cervantes and Apuleius. His insistence on a deep moral difference between the authors perhaps reflects the nationalist concerns of a bygone era, but modern readers interested in the history of the novel form ignore him at their peril.

2. Monetary manipulation has always had an element of the surreal to it. In 1605, Juan de Mariana marveled sarcastically at the "alchemy" of princes who changed the values of metals on a whim. A modern example is Frank Silver and Irving Cohn's haunting novelty song, "Yes! We Have No Bananas," the original written in 1923 during the hyperinflation of the Weimar Republic. Spike Jones added to the list of things that can be had in lieu of bananas: "And kippers with zippers / and pounds of devaluated pounds." It's a double reference to inflation: (1) an obvious slap at the British pound; (2) an allusion to one of early modern Europe's major inflationary messes, the Kipper und Wipper crisis of 1619–22. How does one go about having no bananas? Why, devalue the currency, of course, and merchants will recoil from selling lots of things.

3. The earliest known reference to the proverb "curiosity killed the cat" is found in the British playwright Ben Jonson's play, *Every Man in His Humour* (1598), which was first performed by Shakespeare. As a novelist, and like Poe, Twain has a far more Cervantine take on cats.

Appendix

"On the Coinage" by Juan de Mariana

Translated from the Latin by Hazzard Bagg

[*De moneta*, Book III, Chapter VIII, pp. 268–78 of
De rege et regis institutione (Mainz, 1605)]

Figure 20.   Title Page of Juan de Mariana's *De rege et regis institutione* and First Page of *De moneta*, Mainz, 1605 *Source*: Google Books

In order to fill a gap in the budget, which is never not a problem, especially in a sprawling empire, certain smart and clever men propose that it would be helpful in many difficult situations if something were to be pulled out of the weight of the coinage or from its quality, by debasing the metal while still retaining its original value. The prince gets to keep whatever is deducted from the quality or the weight of the currency. And what is more amazing, in the absence of harm or complaint on the part of the provincials. This wonderful technique is not a secret but, rather, a useful method by which an incredible amount of gold and silver is redirected into the public treasury without the imposition of any new burden.

I have always typically thought of those men who promise to transform metals by some magical method—to make silver out of bronze and gold out of silver—as being the most untrustworthy sort, like itinerant snake oil salesmen. Now I see that metals are rendered more valuable without any effort; that they are doubled in value without any smelting, controlled merely by the edict of the prince, as if multiplied by some sacred touch or higher power; that the subjects are getting back from the economy what they had before at full value; that there is public utility in the fact that what is left over is handed over to the prince for his use. Who is so unreasonable, or, if you prefer, so insightful, that he would begrudge this happy state of affairs—especially when no innovations are being introduced?

Rather, we tread upon a road trampled by the feet of many, standing upon which great princes from every era have gotten through difficult times. Who will be able to deny that the Romans, under the pressure of the Punic War, reduced their copper coins, which were previously generous, first [p. 269] to two ounces of bronze, then to one ounce, and again to half an ounce . . . and that the government was freed from debt by this technique? That Drusus, as Tribune of the People, mixed bronze into the *denarii* that appeared to be made of pure silver? Plautus's comparison of a new bawdy form of comedy to the new coinage is as wise as it is old.[1] Need I bring up the Jewish people, that superstitious race, who shun everyone else? I note that among them the temple *shekel* is worth twice as much as the common *shekel* for no other reason than that after a while it became clear to the people that half the value had been subtracted from the correct and original weight of the coinage, either all at once in a single stroke or gradually by means of all too frequent acts of deceit (which I suspect is the more likely explanation). There is no need to go on about other countries since it is common knowledge to anyone explaining the past that money has often been made worse by great kings through frequent devaluation.

Or do you suppose you suppose that it is for some other reason that *solidi*, which were first made of gold and then of silver, ultimately ended up as bronze for the most part, unless this was due to an assumed right to contaminate metals by adding some extraneous alloy? What should I say about our own *maravedí*, once gold, not so long-ago silver, and now completely copper? Indeed, who is so confident that he dare criticize a practice employed by all nations at every point in time? Do we seek a higher form of praise in finding fault with institutions? Are we grasping at the empty favor of the masses?[2] Indeed, I shall not deny (for how could I?) that the coinage has often been debased by our forebears and that the type of crisis can sometimes happen in which it is necessary to have recourse to this remedy. I will be the first to say that not everything that our forebears did was without fault[3] [p. 270]. I would also maintain that deceit lies hidden behind the appearance of exceptional and accessible usefulness, that pure fakery exists, that considerable difficulties have arisen from this practice, both for governments and for individuals, and that one must not stoop to this point if we want a healthy situation.

First off, I assert that neither the portable possessions nor the land of subjects is under the legal control of the prince to the degree that he can take these things for himself at his own discretion or hand them over to someone else on a whim. Those who argue otherwise are blowhards and yes-men of the sort that are numerous in the halls of the powerful. Because of this, it is the case that he cannot order new taxes upon his nation without the consent of the people. For he should get his subjects to pay by asking openly, not by cheating them,[4] nor should he capriciously take a cut on a daily basis whereby they are reduced from a state of abundance and prosperity to a state of need. For that would be to behave like a tyrant who measures everything by his own desires, who takes possession of everything for himself, not a king who restrains the power that he has received from willing people with law and reason, and who does not extend his power all over the place. But I do not want to pursue any further a matter that is clearly understood and that has been discussed at greater length elsewhere.[5] I shall only add that of the two it is the case that a king cannot debase the coinage arbitrarily and without the consent of the people. It, too, is a kind of tax by which an amount is extracted from the possessions of subjects. Who would agree to exchange gold for an equal weight of silver, or silver for an equal weight of iron? Generally speaking, why would anyone agree to accept a silver coin for a gold one or a copper coin for a silver one? This happens every time the money is debased. Indeed, it will only be permitted for the king to change the appearance of the coinage, since coinage is listed among the things that are held by royal right under imperial law, provided that the value remains inviolate in accordance with the quality of the money and pre-existing law.

The value of coinage is twofold. First, there is its natural value based upon the quality and quantity of the metal used, which can be called its "intrinsic" value [p. 271]. The second value is its legal and "extrinsic" one, which the prince sets by law, as he does the prices of other goods so that they are not sold for more than what the law without question has ordained. He is a fool who so separates these two values such that the subsequent legal value does not stick to its natural value. Unfair is he who commands that something that is commonly valued at five be generally sold for ten. No one should try to make this happen through effort or strictness.[6] For people are influenced by a common valuation, which is based upon the quality of things and supply and demand; a prince would struggle in vain to tear up these foundations of commerce (which stand better unmoved), to deviate from the common opinion, and to bring a kind of force against their minds. What happens in the case of other commodities should also be extended to money. When assessing value by law, a prince ought to consider the actual price and weight of the metal and should not try to go beyond the small amount that can be added to the value of the metal to cover the cost of minting. For we are also not of the opinion which has hold of great scholars and famous legal experts that a prince must mint the coinage at his own expense, and that he consequently should not add anything to the true value of the metal.

As a general rule, however, if we do not want to fall into error and overturn the laws of nature, the legal value should not be discordant with the natural and intrinsic value. What a sleazy deal it would be if a prince were to keep the extra for himself—and all the more disgusting if anything is subtracted from the quality of the metal or the weight of the money! Or should he be allowed to break into the granaries of his citizens, take a portion for himself, and compensate citizens for their loss by granting the option to sell what is left for the value of the whole pile before his portion had been taken away? Who would not proclaim open robbery, the worst sort of embezzlement? The same scenario could be played out in the case of businesses, farming operations, and any [p. 272] moveable property, but you get the point.

In ancient times they used to exchange things without using money: a goat for a sheep, a cow for some grain. Then they figured out that it would be easier if merchandise and grain were exchanged for metals: gold, silver, and copper. Ultimately, so that it would not forever be necessary to weigh metals out for their dealings and transactions with one another (which is quite a pain), they decided that the various metals should be divided into units by public authority and that these units should be stamped according to the weight of each. This is the proper and natural way to use money that Aristotle tells us about in the first book of the *Politics*;[7] those other ways of turning a trick to cheat the people were developed and discovered by men who could not care less about transparency and fairness. But even if the prince is not taxing the other commodities and is not laying claim to them, he often takes a cut of the currency; this does not mean that there is any less blame in doing this, nor is it any less of a subversion of, and stain upon, the laws of nature. But these mysterious, dolled-up schemes deceive most people with the result that the disease is felt less acutely.

"What harm is there," they say, "if the prince takes a half or a quarter for himself, and if what is left over for individuals is spent at a value that is no less than the original one? Indeed, you buy clothing and food just like before. Where is the loss? For their money is used only to buy necessities." So easily are the people tricked that they put up with the debasing of the coinage! Thus, the prince has more power over the coinage than he does over other commodities. The mints, mint officials, their operations, and the bureaucrats are completely in his power and control. Because of this, he is able to blend metals without anyone stopping him, he can introduce a new coinage in place of the old one [p. 273] stamped with a new mark, with no more honesty than if he were directing the other possessions of his citizens to himself with blatant force.

You might ask, what should be done when a confident enemy challenges in war? Add to that one who is aggressive because of a fresh victory and strong in troops and supplies, and when there is no money available with which a soldier might be recruited or a salary paid. Or will you suppose that he ought to surrender and that every type of misfortune should be endured so that the coinage can remain intact? I would think that every possible remedy should be tried before it should come to the extreme measure of debasing the currency. But if a major crisis is pressing and the safety of the people is in jeopardy and the affected citizens cannot be forced to enter into an agreement whereby the prince can commandeer the other possessions of his subjects to come to the aid of the country in its moment of need, only then will he be able to blend metals or snip off a portion of the weight, but with the proviso that the permission to debase should come to an end along with the war and that the blemish not be permanent, and then that the bad money that necessity forced upon them be straightaway turned in and retired, and that the proper old coinage be restored in place of that bad one for those who were holding it in good faith.

Frederick Augustus, the second of that name, was laying siege to Faenza in Flaminia during a very harsh winter. There was no money for soldiers' pay, everywhere soldiers were slipping away, and units were being abandoned continuously. Lifting the siege was a disgraceful and serious thing, but continuing it was a difficult one. He marked money made of rawhide with the value of a gold coin, and with this conceit he got out of the tight spot. Once he had taken the city as victor, he exchanged the rawhide coins for as many gold ones as he had promised. The source is Collenutius in Book Four of his *History of*

Naples. This example has been followed in similar crises, certainly long ago but also in recent times, and coinage quite often made of hide but sometimes even out of paper [p. 274] has been marked without harm or rebuke. However, if a prince thinks that it is within his purview to debase the currency outside of one of these crises just to fill a deficit in his treasury, something that is more or less always a problem, I proclaim certain destruction—nor will the respite be long-lasting—as the following terrible afflictions demonstrate.

The first consequence will be the high cost of all commodities and food—doubtless not less than the amount that will have been subtracted from the quality of the currency. For people do not value a currency any more than the quality and amount of metal allows—not even if there are strict laws against doing this. Indeed, at that point the people will bemoan the fact that they have been tricked by an illusion, and they will sense that the new currency that has been substituted for the old one is not worth as much as the former currency when they need much greater resources than they used to in order to feed their families. Or are we serving up delusions rather than things that are plain to see from the accuracy of our chronicles? King Alfonso of Castile, known as "The Wise," as soon as he gained control of the crown and possessions of the realm, substituted a bad currency, called the *burgalesa*, for the *pepión*, which was the coinage in use at the time. In order to relieve the high cost of things that immediately followed, he set the value of merchandise with a new law. This solution made matters worse since no one was willing to sell at the set price. And so, this scheme to set prices fell apart right from the start. The problem of high prices went on for a while. I conclude that damage to the coinage was the primary reason for the disaffection of the people and for his replacement by Sancho and his son before the end of his life. For since Alfonso was stubborn, in the seventh year of his reign he recalled the *burgalesa* and introduced a coinage that was called "black" because of the poor quality of the metal.[8]

Alfonso XI, in no way chastened by the example of his great grandfather, also minted a coinage made from metal that was not of high quality [p. 275] that they called *novenes* and *coronados*. So that the prices of food and other items not increase, he took the sensible enough precaution that a mark—that is to say two-thirds of a pound—of silver not be worth more *maravedis* than it was worth previously (that is, 125). This ineffectual measure, however, turned out to be a useless precaution: inflation followed, the value of silver skyrocketed. Enrique the second, the son of this Alfonso, upon gaining the throne after the murder of his brother, King Pedro, had recourse to this solution in order to pay the salaries of his foreign provincial soldiers (to whom he owed his life and his throne) because his accounts were in a lot of trouble, since both the public and his personal treasuries had been exhausted. He struck two types of coinage, *reales* and *cruzados*, doubtless valued above the amount of metal in them. We have examined the *reales* of King Pedro and those of his brother Enrique; indeed, Pedro's are of good silver of the kind that is struck in our own day in Castile; Enrique's are blackish, evidently with a lot of copper added in. In order to alleviate the rise in the prices of things that followed (together with the dismay of people in the provinces), after a fresh appraisal, he was compelled to subtract two thirds from the value of both types of coinage. Thus, things that have been dreamed up so ingeniously to save us do frequently fall the other way. Oh, the short-sighted and blind minds of men!

That much the same thing befell Enrique's son, King Juan, is evident from his laws. For, being out of money because of the wars that he waged, first against the Portuguese and then incessantly against the English, he struck a coinage that he called the *blanca* in order to send the money that he owed to the Duke of Lancaster, his rival for the throne, in accordance with the treaty that he had recently entered into with him. Presently the prices of food went up. To alleviate this problem, he soon reduced the value of the new currency by about a half. But the high prices did not let up, as he himself admitted [p. 276] at the Cortes at Burgos the following year in 1388. Why should I bring up the kings who followed? I find that the same collapse has developed from the same corrupt origin.

So much for high prices . . . Another problem flows from the first: commercial activity that for the most part makes up both public and private wealth is slowed down by a debased coinage. The low quality of the currency clearly frightens shopkeepers and their customers; the high prices that follow on from this problem also frighten them. But if the prince were to set prices for things by fiat (as always seems to happen), instead of a cure, the problem will get much worse since there is no one who will agree to sell for that price, which is so clearly unfair and not squared with commonly recognized valuation. Once commercial activity has stopped, there is no category of problem which does not befall such a people.[9] Certainly, the provincials will be of necessity stretched thin in two ways: first, due to the slowdown in buying and selling, the income from which the majority of the population lives will grind to a halt. These people are craftsmen for the most part and people whose hopes for a meal lie in their hands and in working every day—which is most people.[10] Second, the prince will be forced either to completely withdraw the bad currency which is the cause of the problem or to issue a currency that is worse with its previous value reduced. So it happened that in the reign of King Enrique the second of Castile, in spite of this, he subtracted two thirds from the value of his new currency. Whoever found themselves holding that money suddenly discovered that, by the power of a word, what had been three hundred gold pieces had been reduced to no more than one hundred.

We seem to be kidding. Let us set aside the past. From the moment that he left the Church, Henry, the eighth king of England by that name, ran into many problems. Among these problems he debased the currency. For that which had an eleventh part of copper mixed in was gradually reduced to the point that it retained only a sixth part of silver [p. 277]. With a fresh decree he swept up the old money from the provincials and exchanged it for an equal number and weight of the new, debased currency. The people remained silent as long as they feared the savagery of that man, who thought of bleeding his citizens as a game. But after his death, his son Edward brought it about that the value of this coinage was decreased by half. Edward's sister, Elizabeth, also subtracted another half from the remaining value once she gained the throne. So it was the case that those people who used to have four hundred gold pieces in that currency had it reduced to one hundred once three quarters of the value had been subtracted. And the damage did not stop there; that currency was thereupon taken out of circulation with no way to restore the loss, a scandalous mugging. Sanders, a scholar and at one time in the past a friend of mine, confirms this toward the end of Book One of his *On the English Schism*.

With commercial activity suspended and, as a consequence, with the provincials stretched thin, the pitiable disaster of royal taxes will come to the fore. The prince will be punished in proportion to how much he has enjoyed the profit from that currency. For it cannot be a good situation for a king to have a kingdom which is practically struggling physically; nor will the provincials be in a position to be stretched thin by paying taxes. Also, tax collectors will not bring in as much in royal taxes as they had before. I read that when King Alfonso XI of Castile was a child, royal officials were forced to submit to an audit; I have gleaned that all the royal taxes for the year came to 1,600,000 *maravedís*. Those *maravedís* were worth more than ours and each one was worth about as much as seventeen of ours, still an undeniably tiny and laughable amount. The writer of the history of that king describes how one of the two causes of this disastrous situation was the debasing of the coinage carried out [p. 278] by quite a few of the previous kings. Evidently, with commercial activity brought to a standstill, the subjects were reduced to a state of penury and were unable to bring into the treasury what they had typically brought in during normal times.

Who would not see that this is a tremendous handicap? Who would not admit this? Would you then prefer that there be a universal hatred on the part of the people that will inevitably overwhelm the prince? Is it not preferable to be loved than to be feared? In general, all public failures are blamed on the person in charge. Philip the Fair, King of France, confessed right before his death that he faced the hatred of the people for no reason other than that the coinage had been debased, and with his last words he commanded his son Louis "Hutin" to change it. The source is Robert Gaguin. I do not read anywhere about what Louis did, but it seems to be the case that the demonstrations and hatred on the part of the people did not settle down before Enguerrand de Marigny, the author of the foul scheme, was publicly executed, as the majority of the nobles urged during the proceedings and the entire population applauded. There is no need to mention the fact that the precedent set by this disaster did not discourage Hutin's brother, Charles the Fair, nor their mutual cousin and successor, Philip of Valois, from treading on this same path of debasing the currency in France; nor need I mention the magnitude of the public reaction. Instead, let a limit be placed upon the discussion that has been begun here. I would like to give princes one last piece of advice: if you want your state to be a healthy one, do not touch the primary foundations of commerce—units of weight, measurement, and the coinage. A many-layered swindle lies hidden behind the appearance of a quick fix.[11]

NOTES

1. The reference is to Plautus's *Casina*, lines 9–10: *Nam nunc novae quae prodeunt cōmoediae multō sunt nequiōrēs quam nummī novī . . .* "For the new comedies that are coming out now are much more worthless than the new coins . . ."

2. Mariana says that a sound coinage is important to commoners, alluding to the argument that supporting such a policy is somehow populist demagoguery.

3. The author drops irony and affirms that we are allowed to criticize what people did in the past. A call for seriousness and realism in the study of history, it's also a turning point in the essay.

4. The distinction between lawful and unlawful taxation contrasts a formal request for funds with the act of swindling.

5. A reference to the already controversial passages on tyrants and regicide found in Chapters V, VI, VII, and VIII of Book I of the 1598 edition of *De rege et regis institutione.*

6. Elsewhere in this same chapter, Mariana rails against imposing a debased coinage by force, most notably in his discussion of Henry VIII in the penultimate paragraph.

7. See Aristotle's famous discussion of money in *Politics* (1.9.1257a).

8. The relative blackness of a coin indicates its quality by revealing its relative copper content. The more copper a coin contains, the blacker it becomes over time via oxidation.

9. Mariana's genius is his ability to synthesize and extend the ideas of his precursors. Here, he signals the greater, more global threat to commerce posed by monetary manipulation.

10. Inflation affects the poor more than it does the rich! Mariana has already speculated that he might be accused of pandering to the people for criticizing debasing the coinage. Now, he wears populism as a badge of honor.

11. Note how Mariana essentially endorses tyrannicide in response to currency debasement.

Works Cited

Abril, Pedro Simón, ed. and trans. *Los ocho libros de Republica del filosofo Aristoteles*. By Aristotle. Zaragoza: Lorenzo and Diego de Robles, 1584.

Adams, John. "Letter IV. Biscay." *A Defense of the Constitution of the United States*. https://www.constitution.org/jadams/ja1_04.txt

Adams, John Quincy. "Speech to the US House of Representatives on Foreign Policy." 4 July 1821. https://millercenter.org/the-presidency/presidential-speeches /july-4-1821-speech-us-house-representatives-foreign-policy

Aesop. "The Crow and the Pitcher." https://americanliterature.com/author/aesop /short-story/the-crow-and-the-pitcher

Aeschylus. *Persians and Other Plays*. Trans. Christopher Collard. Oxford: Oxford UP. 2009.

Agulló y Cobo, Mercedes. *A vueltas con el autor del Lazarillo: con el testamento y el inventario de bienes de don Diego Hurtado de Mendoza*. Madrid: Calambur, 2010.

Albornoz, Bartolomé. *Arte de los contractos*. Valencia: Pedro de Huete, 1573.

Althusser, Louis. "Ideology and Ideological State Apparatuses." *Lenin and Philosophy and Other Essays*. Trans. Ben Brewster. French, *La Pensée*, 1970. New York: Monthly Review P, 1970. 85–126.

———. *Machiavelli and Us*. Trans. Gregory Eliot. Ed. François Matheron. New York: Verso, 1999.

Alves, André Azevedo and José M. Moreira. *The Salamanca School*. New York: Bloomsbury, 2013.

"Anatomy." *Encyclopedia Britannica*, 2019. https://www.britannica.com/art/anatomy -literature

Anderson, Poul. "Iron." *The Man-Kzin Wars*. Riverdale, NY: Baen, 1991. 27–164.

Anonymous. *Arabian Nights: Tales from a Thousand and One Nights*. Trans. Richard Burton. New York: Classic Books, 2010.

———. *Calila e Dimna*. Eds. J. M. Cacho Blecua and María Jesús Lacarra. Madrid: Castalia, 1984.

———. *Lazarillo de Tormes*. Ed. Francisco Rico. Madrid: Cátedra, 1987. http://www.cervantesvirtual.com/obra-visor/la-vida-de-lazarillo-de-tormes-y-de-sus-for tunas-y-adversidades--0/html/

———. *Poema de Mio Cid*. Ed. Colin Smith. Madrid: Cátedra, 1989.

Apuleius. *The Golden Ass*. Trans. Jack Lindsay. Bloomington: Indiana UP, 1960.

Arias Montano, Benito, ed. *Biblia regia*. 8 vols. Antwerp: Christophorus Platinus, 1569–73.

Ariosto, Ludovico. *Orlando Furioso*. Trans. Guido Waldman. Oxford: Oxford UP,1974.

Aristophanes. *Frogs and Other Plays*. Trans. David Barrett. London: Penguin, 1964.

Aristotle. *Los ocho libros de Republica del filosofo Aristoteles*. Trans. Pedro Simón Abril. Zaragoza: Lorenzo and Diego de Robles, 1584.

———. *Politics*. Trans. Benjamin Jowett. http://classics.mit.edu/Aristotle/politics .1.one.html

Arrabal, Fernando. *Un esclavo llamado Cervantes*. Madrid: Espasa, 1996.

Auerbach, Erich. *Mimesis: The Representation of Reality in Western Literature*. 1946. Trans. Willard R. Trask. Princeton: Princeton UP, 1974.

Avellaneda, Alfonso Fernández de. *El Quijote apócrifo*. Ed. Alfredo Rodríguez López-Vázquez. Madrid: Anaya, 2011.

Avellaneda, Gertrudis Gómez de. *Sab*. Ed. José Severa. Madrid: Cátedra, 1997.

Ayau, Manuel. *Un juego que no suma cero*. Guatemala: Universidad Francisco Marroquín, 2008.

Bakhtin, Mikhail. "Epic and Novel." *The Dialogic Imagination*. Ed. Michael Holquist. Austin: U Texas P, 1981. 3–40.

———. *Rabelais and His World*. Trans. Hélène Iswolsky. Bloomington, IN: Indiana UP, 1984.

Bandera, Cesáreo. "An Open Letter to Ruth El Saffar." *Cervantes* 1.2 (1981): 95–107.

Barrientos García, José. *Francisco de Vitoria y Domingo de Soto. Un siglo de moral económica en Salamanca (1526–1629)*. Vol. 1. Salamanca: Universidad de Salamanca, 1985.

Bass, Laura. "The Treasury of Language: Literary Invention in Philip III's Spain." *El Greco to Velázquez: Art at the Court of Philip III*. Eds. Ronni Baer and Sarah Schroth. Boston: Museum of Fine Arts, 2008. 146–81.

Bastiat, Claude-Frédéric. "Barataria." *Oeuvres Complètes*. Vol. 7. No. 77. Paris: Guillaumin, 1864. 343–51.

———. *The Law*. 1850. Trans. Dean Russell. Irvington-on-Hudson, NY: Foundation for Economic Education, 1998. http://oll.libertyfund.org/titles/bastiat-the-law

Bataillon, Marcel. *Erasmo y España*. 2 vols. Trans. Antonio Altatorre. México DF: Fondo de Cultura Económica, 1950.

Beauvoir, Simone. *The Second Sex (Le Deuxième Sexe)*. 1948. Trans. Constance Borde and Sheila Malovany-Chevallier. New York: Vintage, 2011.

Berlin, Isaiah. "Two Concepts of Liberty." *Four Essays on Liberty*. London: Oxford UP, 1969.

Bernholz, Peter and Peter Kugler. "The Price Revolution in the 16th Century: Empirical Results from a Structural Vectorautoreggression Model." *WWZ Working Paper*. Basel: University of Basel, 2007. 1–17.

The Bible. www.biblegateway.com

Blackstone, William. *Commentaries on the Laws of England*. Vol. 1. Ed. William Carey Jones. San Francisco: Bancroft-Whitney, 1915.

Blancas y Tomás, Jerónimo de. *Comentarios de las cosas de Aragón (Aragonesium rerum comentarii)*. *Biblioteca Virtual de Derecho Aragonés*. 1588. Trans. Manuel Hernández. Zaragoza: Cortes de Aragón, 1878.

Bloom, Harold. *The Anxiety of Influence: A Theory of Poetry*. Oxford: Oxford UP, 1973.

Boccaccio, Giovanni. *The Decameron*. Trans. G. H. McWilliam. London: Penguin, 2003.

Bodin, Jean. *The Six Books of the Commonwealth (Les Six livres de la République)*. Trans. J. H. Franklin. Cambridge: Cambridge UP, 1992.

Böhl de Faber, Cecilia. [Caballero, Fernán.] *Cuentos de encantamiento y otros cuentos populares*. Ed. Carmen Bravo-Villasante. Madrid: EMESA, 1978.

Böhm von Bawerk, Eugene. *Karl Marx and the Close of His System*. 1896. New York: Wolff, 1949.

Borges, Jorge Luis. "Pierre Menard, autor del Quijote." *Ficciones*. Buenos Aires: Emecé, 1956. 47–59.

Boyd, Julian P., ed. *The Papers of Thomas Jefferson, Vol. 12*. Princeton, NJ: Princeton UP, 1955.

Braudel, Fernand. *A History of Civilizations*. Trans. Richard Mayne. New York: Penguin, 1993.

———. *El Mediterráneo y el mundo mediterráneo en la época de Felipe II*. 2 vols. México, DF: Fondo de Cultura Económica, 1997.

Brewer, Brian. "Quixotic Economy: Comedy, Romance, and Early Modern Economics in *Don Quijote*." *Cervantes: Bulletin of the Cervantes Society of America* 39.1 (2019): 117–34.

Brincat, Shannon K. "'Death to Tyrants': The Political Philosophy of Tyrannicide— Part I." *Journal of International Political Theory* 4.2 (2008): 212–40.

Burke, Edmund. *Reflections on the Revolution in France*. New Haven, CT: Yale UP, 2003.

Burns, James Henderson, ed. *The Cambridge History of Political Thought, 1450– 1700*. Cambridge: Cambridge UP, 1991.

Burton, Robert. *The Anatomy of Melancholy*. 1621. New York: NYRB, 2001.

Byrne, Susan. *Law and History in Cervantes' Don Quixote*. Toronto: U of Toronto P, 2012.

Byron, William. *Cervantes: A Biography*. Garden City, NY: Doubleday, 1978.

Calderón de la Barca, Pedro. *El alcalde de Zalamea*. Ed. Ángel Valbuena Briones. Madrid: Cátedra, 1989.

———. *El médico de su honra*. Madrid: Castalia, 1989.

Calzada, Gabriel. "Solo ante la inflación: Juan de Mariana y su lucha contra los desmanes monetarios." *Facetas liberales. Ensayos en honor de Manuel F. Ayau*.

Eds. Alberto Benegas Lynch and Giancarlo Ibárgüen. Guatemala: Universidad Francisco Marroquín, 2011. 79–101.

Canavaggio, Jean. *Cervantes*. Madrid: Espasa Calpe, 1997.

Cañizares-Esguerra, Jorge, ed. *Encounters between Jesuits and Protestants in Asia and the Americas*. Boston: Brill, 2018.

Cantillon, Richard. *An Essay on Economic Theory (Essai sur la Nature du Commerce en Général)*. Trans. Chantal Saucier. Auburn, AL: Ludwig von Mises Institute, 2010. https://mises.org/library/essay-economic-theory-0

Capon, Lester J., ed. *The Adams-Jefferson Letters*. Chapel Hill, NC: U of North Carolina P, 1987.

Carr, Edward Hallett. *What Is History?* 1961. New York: Penguin, 1988.

Cascardi, Anthony J. *Cervantes, Literature, and the Discourse of Politics*. Toronto: U of Toronto P, 2012.

———. "Perspectivism and the Conflict of Values in *Don Quijote*." *Kentucky Romance Quarterly* 34.2 (1987): 165–78.

Case, Thomas E. "Cide Hamete Benengeli y los *Libros plúmbeos*." *Cervantes* 22.2 (2002): 9–24.

Castillo de Bobadilla, Jerónimo. *Política para Corregidores*. 1597. Madrid: Imprenta de la Gazeta, 1775.

Castro, Américo. *Cervantes y los casticismos españoles*. Madrid: Alfagüara. 1974.

———. *El pensamiento de Cervantes y otros estudios cervantinos*. 1925. Ed. José Miranda. Madrid: Trotta, 2002.

Cerezo Galán, Pedro. *El Quijote y la aventura de la libertad*. Madrid: Biblioteca Nueva, 2016.

Cervantes Saavedra, Miguel de. *Don Quijote de la Mancha*. Ed. Francisco Rico. Barcelona: Crítica, 1998.

———. *El casamiento engañoso y El coloquio de los perros*. Ed. Agustín G. de Amezúa y Mayo. Madrid: Real Academia Española, 1912.

———. *El licenciado Vidriera. Novelas ejemplares*. Vol. 2. Ed. Harry Sieber. Madrid: Cátedra, 1982.

———. *La española inglesa. Novelas ejemplares*. Vol. 1. Ed. Harry Sieber. Madrid: Cátedra, 1982.

———. "Representación de Miguel de Cervantes Saavedra, exponiendo sus méritos y servicios hechos en Italia, en la batalla naval de Lepanto, y en otras partes, con motivo de solicitar uno de los oficios vacantes en Indias." 21 May 1590. http://www.cervantesvirtual.com/

———. *Rinconete y Cortadillo. Novelas ejemplares*. Vol. 1. Ed. Harry Sieber. Madrid: Cátedra, 1982.

———. *Los trabajos de Persiles y Sigismunda*. Ed. Juan Bautista Avalle-Arce. Madrid: Clásicos, 1984.

Chafuen, Alejandro A. *Faith and Liberty: The Economic Thought of the Late Scholastics*. New York: Lexington, 2003.

Childers, William. "Recordando el futuro: los moriscos cervantinos y la inmigración magrebí actual." *Estas primicias del ingenio: Jóvenes cervantistas en Chicago*. Eds. Francisco Caudet and Kerry Wilks. Madrid: Castalia, 2003. 73–98.

Cicero, Marcus Tullius. *The Dream of Scipio (Somnium Scipionis)*. With *On Friendship (Laelius de amicitia)*. Trans. J. G. F. Powell. Liverpool: Liverpool UP, 2004.

———. *Tusculan Disputations (Tusculanae disputationes)*. Loeb Classical Library Series. Boston: Havard UP, 1927.

———. *In Defence of the Republic*. Trans. Siobhán McElduff. London: Penguin, 2011.

Conrad, Joseph. *Heart of Darkness*. London: Blackwood, 1899.

Copernicus, Nicholaus. *Treatise on Coining Money. (De monetae cudendae ratione)*. Trans. George Albert Moore. Chevy Chase, MD: Country Dollar P, 1965.

"Cortes de Aragón." *Gran enciclopedia aragonesa*. Enciclopedia-aragonesa, n.d. Web. 26 April 2011.

Cortés López, José Luis. "La esclavitud en España en la época de Carlos I." www.cervantesvirtual.com/bib/historia/CarlosV/6_4_cortes.shtml.

Crowley, Roger. *Empires of the Sea: The Siege of Malta, the Battle of Lepanto, and the Contest for the Center of the World*. New York: Random House, 2008.

Cruz, Anne J. "Cervantes and His Feminist Alliances." *Cervantes and His Postmodern Constituencies*. Eds. Anne J. Cruz and Carroll B. Johnson. New York: Garland, 1999. 134–50.

Curtius, Ernst Robert. *European Literature and the Latin Middle Ages*. Trans. Willard R. Trask. Princeton: Princeton UP, 1990.

Dante Alighieri. *The Divine Comedy*. Trans. Courtney Langdon. Cambridge: Harvard UP, 1921.

Darst, David H. *Diego Hurtado de Mendoza*. Boston: Twayne, 1987.

Dawson, Christopher. *Los dioses de la Revolución*. Trans. Jerónimo Molina Cano. Madrid: Encuentro, 2015.

De Armas, Frederick A. *Don Quixote and the Saracens: A Clash of Civilizations and Literary Genres*. Toronto: U of Toronto P, 2011.

Defoe, Daniel. *Robinson Crusoe*. 1719. London: Penguin, 2001.

De Jean, Joan. *Tender Geographies: Women and the Origins of the Novel in France*. New York: Columbia UP, 1991.

D'Emic, Michael Thomas. *Justice in the Marketplace in Early Modern Spain: Saravia, Villalón, and the Religious Origins of Economic Analysis*. Lanham, MD: Lexington, 2014.

Dempsey, Bernard. *Interest and Usury*. Washington, DC: American Council on Public Affairs, 1943.

Derrida, Jacques. *The Beast and the Sovereign*. Chicago: U of Chicago P, 2009.

———. "Plato's Pharmacy." *Dissemination*. Trans. Barbara Johnson. Chicago: U of Chicago P, 1981: 61–84.

Doody, Margaret. *The True Story of the Novel*. New Brunswick: Rutgers UP, 1996.

Dostoevsky, Fyodor. *Devils*. Trans. Michael R. Katz. Oxford: Oxford UP, 1999.

Douglass, Frederick. *Life and Times of Frederick Douglass*. 1845. Internet Archive: archive.org/stream/lifetimesoffrede1882doug

Dudley, Edward. "Don Quijote As Magus: The Rhetoric of Interpolation." *Bulletin of Hispanic Studies* (1972) 49: 355–68.

Duffield, Alexander James. *Don Quixote, His Critics and Commentators.* 1881. Folcroft, PA: Folcroft, 1980.

Eagleton, Terry. *Literary Theory.* Minneapolis, MN: U of Minnesota P, 2003.

Elias, Norbert. *The Civilizing Process.* 1939. Oxford: Blackwell, 2000.

"El juramento de los Reyes de Aragón." *El Justicia de Aragón.com.* 27 June 2006. Web. 15 Dec. 2012.

El Saffar, Ruth Anthony. *Beyond Fiction: The Recovery of the Feminine in the Novels of Cervantes.* Berkeley: U of California P, 1984.

———. "In Marcela's Case." *Quixotic Desire: Psychoanalytic Perspectives on Cervantes.* Eds. Diana de Armas Wilson and Ruth Anthony El Saffar. Ithaca: Cornell UP, 1993. 157–78.

———. "In Praise of What Is Left Unsaid: Thoughts on Women and Lack in *Don Quijote.*" *MLN* 103.2 (1988): 205–22.

———. "Response to Cesáreo Bandera." *Cervantes* 1.2 (1981): 108–10.

Emerson, Ralph Waldo. "Montaigne; or, the Skeptic." https://emersoncentral.com/texts/representative-men/montaigne-the-skeptic/

Erasmus, Desiderius. "Exorcism, or the Specter." *The Colloquies of Erasmus.* Trans. Craig R. Thompson. Chicago: Chicago UP, 1965. 230–37.

———. *The Manual of the Christian Knight. (Enchirdion).* London: Aeterna P, 2014.

———. *Julius Excluded from Heaven (Julius exclusus e coelis). The Praise of Folly and Other Writings.* Trans. Robert M. Adams. New York: Norton, 1989. 142–73.

———. *The Sileni of Alcibiades (Sileni Alcibiadis)*, with *Utopia* by Thomas More. Trans. David Wootton. Indianapolis, IN: Hackett, 1999.

Euclid. *Elements.* Ed. Oliver Byrne. London: Pickering, 1847. www.math.ubc.ca/~cass/Euclid/byrne.html

———. *Los seis libros primeros de la geometría de Euclides.* Trans. Rodrigo Zamorano. Sevilla: Alfonso de la Barrera, 1576.

———. *The Thirteen Books of Euclid's Elements.* Vol. 1. Ed. Thomas L. Heath. Cambridge: Cambridge UP, 1926.

Fajardo-Acosta, Fidel. "Don Quijote y las máquinas infernales: vanidad del ejercicio de las armas." *Hispanic Journal* 10.2 (1989): 15–25.

Feijoo y Montenegro, Benito Jerónimo. *Defensa de las mujeres.* Ed. Victoria Sau. Barcelona: Icaria, 1997.

Ferguson, Niall. *Civilization: The West and the Rest.* London: Penguin, 2011.

———. *The Great Degeneration: How Institutions Decay and Economies Die.* New York: Penguin, 2012.

Fernández Álvarez, Ángel M. "Juan de Mariana. Transmisión de las ideas de economía política de España hacia Inglaterra en el siglo XVII." *Iberian Journal of the History of Economic Thought* 2.2 (2015): 32–59.

Fernández-Flores Funes, Francisco. *Los tributos, la moneda y el crédito en El Quijote.* Madrid: Marcial Pons, 2016.

Fernández-Morera, Darío. "Cervantes and Economic Theory." *Literature and the Economics of Liberty: Spontaneous Order in Culture.* Eds. Paul A. Cantor and Stephen Cox. Auburn, AL: Ludwig von Mises Institute, 2009. 99–165.

Forcione, Alban K. *Cervantes and the Humanist Vision*. Princeton: Princeton UP, 1982.

Foucault, Michel. *The Order of Things*. New York: Vintage, 1973.

Freud, Sigmund. *Moisés y la religión monoteísta*. 1939. *Obras completas*. Vol. 23. Trans. José L. Etcheverry. Buenos Aires: Amorrortu, 1976.

Friedman, Milton. *Capitalism and Freedom*. Chicago: U of Chicago P, 2002.

Frye, Northrop. *Anatomy of Criticism*. Princeton, NJ: Princeton UP, 1957.

Galdós, Benito Pérez. *El amigo Manso*. Madrid: Cátedra, 2001.

Gates, Henry Louis. *The Signifying Monkey*. Oxford: Oxford UP, 1998.

Gay, Peter. *The Enlightenment: The Rise of Modern Paganism*. New York: Norton, 1977.

Girard, René. *Deceit, Desire, and the Novel: Self and Other in Literary Structure*. Trans. Yvonne Freccero. Baltimore: Johns Hopkins UP, 1976.

———. *Violence and the Sacred*. Trans. Patrick Gregory. Baltimore: Johns Hopkins UP, 1972.

Gómez Rivas, León. "La teoría del valor en la Escuela de Salamanca." *Modernidad de España: apertura europea e integración atlántica*. Madrid: Marcial Pons, 2017. 321–43.

Gómez Rivas, León and Ángel Soto. "Los orígenes escolásticos de la independencia latinoamericana (en el Bicentenario de la Emancipación: 1810–2010)." *Revista de Historia de Chile y América* 4.2 (2005): 115–45.

González de Cellorigo, Martín. *Memorial de la política necesaria y útil restauración de España y estados de ella, y desempeño universal de estos reinos*. 1600. Ed. José Pérez de Ayala. Madrid: Instituto de Estudios Fiscales, 1991.

González de León, Fernando. "The Don Quixote of Edgar Allan Poe: Reader, Narrator, Detective, Critic." *A Novel Without Boundaries: Sensing Don Quixote 400 Years Later*. Eds. Carmen García de la Rasilla and Jorge Abril Sánchez. Newark, DE: Juan de la Cuesta Hispanic Monographs, 2016. 73–89.

Goytisolo, Juan. *Crónicas sarracinas*. Barcelona: Ibérica, 1982.

Grabill, Stephen J., ed. *Sourcebook in Late-Scholastic Monetary Theory: The Contributions of Martín de Azpilcueta, Luis de Molina, S.J., and Juan de Mariana, S.J.* New York: Rowman & Littlefield, 2007.

Gracián, Baltasar. *Arte de ingenio, tratado de la agudeza*. Ed. Emilio Blanco. Madrid: Cátedra, 2010.

Graf, Eric Clifford. "*Don Quijote* and Materialism: Martin and the Ghosts of the Papacy." *Cervantes and Modernity: Four Essays on Don Quijote*. Lewisburg, PA: Bucknell UP, 2007. 131–55.

———. "The Economy of Asses in *Don Quijote de la Mancha*: Metalepsis, Miscegenation, and Commerce in Cervantes's Picaresque." *eHumanista/Cervantes* 4 (2015): 255–88.

———. "El Greco's and Cervantes's Euclidean Theologies." *Goodbye to Eros: Recasting Forms and Norms of Love in the Age of Cervantes*. Eds. Ana Laguna and John Beusterien. Toronto: U of Toronto P, 2020. 83–116.

———. "From Scipio to Nero to the Self: The Exemplary Politics of Stoicism in Garcilaso de la Vega's Elegies." *Publications of the Modern Language Association of America* 116.5 (2001): 1316–33.

———. "Heliodorus, Cervantes, La Fayette: Ekphrasis and the Feminist Origins of the Modern Novel." *Ekphrasis in the Age of Cervantes*. Ed. Frederick A. de Armas. Lewisburg, PA: Bucknell UP, 2005. 175–201.

———. "Juan de Mariana, *Don Quijote* y la política monetaria estadounidense moderna: Salamanca, Cervantes, Jefferson y la Escuela Austriaca." *De reyes a lobos: Seis ensayos sobre Cervantes*. Newark: Juan de la Cuesta Hispanic Monographs, 2019. 50–80.

———. "La antropología subversiva de Freud y *La novela y coloquio de los perros.*" *De reyes a lobos: Seis ensayos sobre Cervantes*. Newark: Juan de la Cuesta Hispanic Monographs, 2018. 112–37.

———. "La política teológica de *La Numancia*." *De reyes a lobos: Seis ensayos sobre Cervantes*. Newark, DE: Juan de la Cuesta Hispanic Monographs, 2018. 11–20.

———. "The Politics of Renouncing Zaragoza in *Don Quijote* 2.59: Cervantine Irony Framed by Plato, Aristotle, Pedro Simón Abril, and Juan de Mariana." *Revista Hispánica Moderna* 66.2 (2013): 121–38.

———. "The Politics of Salvation in El Greco's Escorial Paintings and Cervantes's *Numantia*." *Signs of Power in Habsburg Spain and the New World*. Eds. Jason McCloskey and Ignacio López Almeny. Lewisburg, PA: Bucknell UP, 2013. 177–98.

———. "Sancho Panza's 'por negros que sean, los he de volver blancos o amarillos' (*DQ* 1.29) and Juan de Mariana's *De moneta* of 1605." *Cervantes: Bulletin of the Cervantes Society of America* 31.2 (2011): 23–51.

———. "When an Arab Laughs in Toledo: Cervantes's Interpellation of Early Modern Spanish Orientalism." *Diacritics* 29.2 (1999): 68–85.

Greenblatt, Stephen. *Hamlet in Purgatory*. Princeton: Princeton UP, 2001.

Grice-Hutchinson, Marjorie. *Early Economic Thought in Spain, 1177–1740*. Indianapolis, IN: Liberty Fund, 2015.

———. *The School of Salamanca*. Auburn, AL: Ludwig von Mises Institute, 2009.

Groenewegen, Peter. "Thomas Carlyle, 'The Dismal Science,' and the Contemporary Political Economy of Slavery." *History of Economics Review* 34.1 (2001): 74–94.

Guevara, Antonio de. *Menosprecio de corte y alabanza de aldea*. Biblioteca Virtual Universal. http://www.biblioteca.org.ar/libros/131878.pdf

———. *Libro áureo de Marco Aurelio. Obras completas*. Ed. Emilio Blanco. Vol. 1. Madrid: Turner, 1994. 1–333.

———. *Relox de príncipes. Obras completas*. Ed. Emilio Blanco. Vol. 2. Madrid: Turner, 1994. 1–943.

Gutiérrez, Gustavo. *Las Casas: In Search of the Poor of Jesus Christ*. Trans. Robert R. Barr. Maryknoll, NY: Orbis, 1993.

Haliczer, Stephen. *The Comuneros of Castile: The Forging of a Revolution, 1475–1521*. Madison, WI: U of Wisconsin P, 1981.

Hamilton, Alexander. *Federalist, No. 1. The Federalist Papers*. https://www.congress.gov/resources/display/content/The+Federalist+Papers#TheFederalistPapers-1

Hanson, Victor Davis. *Carnage and Culture: Landmark Battles in the Rise of Western Power*. New York: Random House, 2001.

Hart, David M. "Bastiat's Use of Literature in Defense of Free Markets and His Rhetoric of Economic Liberty." Association for Private Enterprise Education, Cancún, 2016. http://davidmhart.com/liberty/Papers/Bastiat/DMH_BastiatFrenchLiterature.html

Hayek, Friedrich A. *The Fatal Conceit*. Chicago: U of Chicago P, 1988.

———. *Law, Legislation, and Liberty*. London: Routledge, 1998.

———. "The Pretense of Knowledge." Nobel Prize Lecture, Stockholm, 11 December 1974. *NobelPrize.org*. Sun. 14 Apr 2019. https://www.nobelprize.org/prizes/economic-sciences/1974/hayek/lecture/

———. "The Use of Knowledge in Society." *American Economic Review* 35.4 (1945): 519–30.

Hebreo, León. *Diálogos de amor (Dialoghi d'amore)*. Trans. El Inca Garcilaso de la Vega. Madrid: Fundación José Antonio de Castro, 1996.

Hegel, Georg Wilhelm Friedrich. *The Phenomenology of Spirit*. Trans. Terry Pinkard. Cambridge: Cambridge UP, 2018.

Heliodorus. *An Ethiopian Romance*. Trans. by Moses Hadas. Philadelphia: U of Pennsylvania P, 1999.

Hernández-Pecoraro, Rosilie. "The Absence of the Absence of Women: Cervantes's *Don Quixote* and the Explosion of the Pastoral Tradition." *Cervantes* 18.1 (1997): 24–45.

Herrero, Javier. "Sierra Morena as Labyrinth: From Wildness to Christian Knighthood." *Critical Essays on Cervantes*. Ed. Ruth El Saffar. Boston: G. K. Hall, 1986. 67–80.

———. "The Beheading of the Giant: An Obscene Metaphor in *Don Quijote*." *Revista hispánica moderna* 39.4 (1976–77): 141–49.

Hitchens, Christopher. *God Is Not Great: How Religion Poisons Everything*. New York: Hachette, 2007.

Hobbes, Thomas. *Human Nature. Hobbs's Tripos, In Three Discourses*. London: Gilliflower et al., 1684.

———. *Leviathan*. Ed. Richard Tuck. Cambridge: Cambridge UP, 1996.

Hoffer, Eric. *The True Believer*. New York: Harper, 1951.

Homer. *The Iliad*. Trans. Richmond Lattimore. Chicago: U of Chicago P, 2011.

———. *Odyssey*. Trans. Stanley Lombardo. Indianapolis, IN: Hackett, 2000.

Huerta de Soto, Jesús. "Juan de Mariana and the Influence of the Spanish Scholastics." *Fifteen Great Austrian Economists*. Ed. Randell G. Holcombe. Auburn, AL: Ludwig von Mises Institute, 1999. 1–11.

———. "New Light on the Prehistory of the Theory of Banking and the School of Salamanca." *Review of Austrian Economics* 9.2 (1996): 59–81.

Huet, Pierre-Daniel. *Lettre-traité de Pierre Daniel Huet sur l'origine des romans*. Ed. Fabienne Gégou. Paris, Nizet, 2005.

Hume, David. "Of Miracles." *An Enquiry Concerning Human Understanding*. Ed. Tom L. Beauchamp. Oxford: Oxford UP, 1999. 169–86.

―――. "Of the Academical or Skeptical Philosophy." *An Enquiry Concerning Human Understanding. Project Gutenberg*, 2011.

―――. "Of the Standard of Taste." *Four Dissertations*. London: A. Millar, 1757. 203–40.

Iwasaki Cauti, Fernando. "Borges, Unamuno y el *Quijote.*" *Biblioteca Virtual Miguel de Cervantes*, 2005.

Jaca, Francisco José de. *Resolución sobre la libertad de los negros y sus originarios en estado de paganos y después ya cristianos*. 1681. Madrid: CSIC, 2002.

Jaeger, Werner. *Paideia: The Ideals of Greek Culture*. Trans. Gilbert Highet. 3 vols. New York: Oxford UP, 1960.

Jameson, Fredric. *Marxism and Form*. Princeton: Princeton UP, 1974.

―――. "Religion and Ideology: A Political Reading of Paradise Lost." *Literature, Politics and Theory: Papers from the Essex Conference, 1976–1984*. Eds. Francis Barker, et al. London: Methuen, 1986. 35–56.

Jefferson, Thomas. "Draft for a Bill to Establish Religious Freedom in Virginia." 1779. https://cas.umw.edu/clpr/files/2011/09/Jefferson-Statute-2-versions.pdf

Johnson, Carroll. *Cervantes and the Material World*. Chicago: U of Illinois P, 2000.

―――. *Don Quixote: The Quest for Modern Fiction*. Boston: Twayne, 1990.

―――. "*La española inglesa* and the Practice of Literary Production." *Viator* 19 (1988): 377–416.

Johnson, Paul. *A History of Christianity*. New York: Atheneum, 1977.

Jonson, Ben. *Everyman in His Humour*. 1598. http://hollowaypages.com/jonson 1692humour.htm

Juan Manuel, Infante de Castilla. *Libro de los enxiemplos del Conde Lucanor et de Patronio*. Ed. José Manuel Blecua. Madrid: Castalia, 1988.

Kerrigan, William and Gordon Braden. *The Idea of the Renaissance*. Baltimore: Johns Hopkins UP, 1989.

Keynes, John Maynard. *The Economic Consequences of the Peace*. New York: Harcourt, 1920.

Kilmeade, Brian and Don Yaeger. *Thomas Jefferson and the Tripoli Pirates: The Forgotten War that Changed American History*. New York: Penguin, 2015.

Kojève, Alexandre. *Introduction to the Reading of Hegel: Lectures on the Phenomenology of Spirit*. New York: Basic, 1969.

Kozintsev, Grigori, dir. *Don Quixote*. Lenfilm, 1957.

Kristol, Irving. *On the Democratic Idea in America*. New York: Harper, 1972.

La Fayette, Marie de la Vergne, Comtesse de. *The Princess of Clèves*. Trans. John D. Lyons. New York: Norton, 1994.

―――. *Zaïde: Histoire espagnole*. Ed. Janine Anseaume Kreiter. Paris: Nizet, 1982.

Las Casas, Bartolomé de. *Brevísima relación de la destrucción de las Indias* 1552. Alicante: Biblioteca Virtual Miguel de Cervantes, 2006.

―――. *Historia de las Indias*. 3 vols. Ed. Augustín Millares Carlo. México DF: Fondo de Cultura Econónica, 1951.

Latino, Juan [Johannes Latinus]. *La Austriada de Juan Latino*. Trans. José A. Sánchez Marín. Universidad de Granada, 1981.

Laures, John. *The Political Economy of Juan de Mariana*. New York: Fordham UP, 1928.

Lea, Henry Charles. "Spanish Coinage." *A History of the Inquisition of Spain*. Vol. 1. Appx. 3. London: MacMillan, 1906. 560–66.

Levin, Mark. *Unfreedom of the Press*. New York: Threshold, 2019.

Lewis, Bernard. *Cultures in Conflict: Christians, Muslims, and Jews in the Age of Discovery*. Oxford: Oxford UP, 1995.

Lezra, Jacques. "La economía política del alma: El 'Soneto al túmulo de Felipe II.'" *En un lugar de la Mancha: Estudios cervantinos en honor a Manuel Durán*. Eds. Georgina Dopico Black and Roberto González Echevarría. Salamanca: Almar, 1999. 149–78.

Liggio, Leonard P. "The Hispanic Tradition of Liberty: The Road Not Taken in Latin America." The Mont Perlerin Society Regional Meeting, 12 January 1990, Antigua, Guatemala.

Liu, Benjamin. "Ricote, Mariana y el patrón oro." *Cervantes y la economía*. Ed. Miguel-Ángel Galindo Martín. Madrid: Universidad de Castilla-La Mancha, 2007. 55–66.

Lloréns, Vicente. "Don Quijote y la decadencia del hidalgo." *Aspectos sociales de la literatura española*. Madrid: Castalia, 1974. 47–66.

Locke, John. *Two Treatises of Government*. Vol. 5. *The Works of John Locke*. 10 vols. London: Thomas Tegg, et al., 1823.

López-Baralt, Luce. "El cálamo supremo (Al-Qalam Al-'Alà) de Cide Hamete Benengeli." In *Mélanges María Soledad Carrasco Urgoiti*. Ed. Abdeljelil Temimi. Zaghouan, Tunisia: FTERSI, 1999. 343–61.

Lukács, Georg. *The Theory of the Novel: A Historico-Philosophical Essay on the Forms of Great Epic Literature*. 1920. Trans. Anna Bostock. Cambridge: MIT P, 1971.

Luna, Álvaro de. *Libro de las claras e virtuosas mugeres*. Ed. Manuel Castillo. Valladolid: Maxtor, 2002.

Luther, Martin. *Ninety-five Theses. Works of Martin Luther*. Vol. 1. Eds. and Trans. Adolph Spaeth, L. D. Reed, Henry Eyster Jacobs, et al. Philadelphia: A. J. Holman, 1915. 29–38. *Project Gutenberg*: http://www.gutenberg.org/ebooks/274

Lyly, John. *Euphues: The Anatomy of Wit*. 1578. Ed. Leah Scragg. Manchester: Manchester UP, 2002.

Machiavelli, Niccolò. *El príncipe*. Trans. Alberto Lista. Madrid: EDAF, 2009.

Macleod, Henry Dunning. *The Elements of Economics*. Vol. 2. New York: D. Appleton, 1886.

Madison, James. *Federalist, No. 51. The Federalist Papers*. https://www.congress.gov/resources/display/content/The+Federalist+Papers#TheFederalistPapers-51

———. *First Amendment to the US Constitution*. National Archives: https://www.archives.gov/founding-docs/bill-of-rights-transcript

Maravall, José Antonio. *El mundo social de La Celestina*. Madrid: Gredos, 1964.

———. *La oposición política bajo los Austrias*. Barcelona: Ariel, 1972.

———. *Las Comunidades de Castilla. Una primera revolución moderna*. Madrid: Occidente, 1963.

————. *Utopía y contrautopía en El Quijote.* Santiago de Compostela: Pico Sacro, 1976.

Mariana, Juan de. *De ponderibus et mensuris.* Toledo: Tomás Guzmán, 1598.

————. *Historia general de España (Historia de rebus Hispaniae).* 1592/1605. Trans. Juan de Mariana. Ed. Francisco Pi y Margall. *Biblioteca de autores españoles.* Vol. 30. Madrid: M. Rivadeneyra, 1854.

————. *La dignidad real y la educación del rey (De rege et regis institutione).* 1598/1605. Trans. Luis Sánchez Agesta. Madrid: Centro de estudios constitucionales, 1981.

————. *Tratado y discurso sobre la moneda de vellón (De monetae mutatione).* 1609. Trans. Juan de Mariana. Ed. Francisco Pi y Margall. *Biblioteca de autores españoles.* Vol. 31. Madrid: Atlas, 1951. 577–93.

Mariscal, George. "*La gran sultana* and the Issue of Cervantes's Modernity." *Revista de Estudios Hispánicos* 28 (1994): 185–211.

Márquez Villanueva, Francisco. "El morisco Ricote, o la hispana razón de estado." *Personajes y temas del Quijote.* Madrid: Taurus, 1975. 229–85.

————. "La cabra *manchada.*" *Personajes y temas del Quijote.* Madrid: Taurus, 1975. 77–92.

Marx, Karl and Friedrich Engels. *The Marx-Engels Reader.* Edited by Robert C. Tucker. New York: Norton, 1978.

Mauss, Marcel. *The Gift.* 1925. Trans. Ian Cunnison. London: Cohen & West, 1966. Internet Archive: https://archive.org/details/giftformsfunctio00maus

McCloskey, Deirdre N. *The Bourgeois Virtues: Ethics for an Age of Commerce.* Chicago: U of Chicago P, 2007.

Medina, Juan de. *Codex de Restitutione et Contractibus.* Madrid: Juan Brocar, 1546. https://repositorio.uam.es/handle/10486/2257?show=full

Mendoza, Diego Hurtado de. *Guerra de Granada.* Ed. Bernardo Blanco-González. Madrid: Castalia, 1996.

Menéndez y Pelayo, Marcelino. "La novela entre los latinos." *Doctoral Thesis. Universidad de Madrid.* Santander: Telesforo Martínez, 1875. *Orígenes de la novela.* Vol. 3. Appx. 2. Madrid: CSIC, 1962. 451–512.

Meneses, Felipe de. *Luz del alma christiano.* Seville: Martín Montesdoca, 1555. Internet Archive: https://archive.org/details/ARes7651402

Menger, Carl. "History of Theories of the Origin of Money." *Principles of Economics.* 1871. Appx. J. Glencoe, IL: The Free P, 1950. 315–20.

————. *Principles of Economics.* 1871. Glencoe, IL: The Free P, 1950.

Menocal, María Rosa. *The Ornament of the World.* Boston: Back Bay, 2002.

Mercado, Tomás de. *Suma de tratos y contratos.* 1571. 2 vols. Ed. N. Sánchez-Albornoz. Madrid: Instituto de Estudios Fiscales, 1977.

Merquior, José Guilherme. "Classical Liberalism, 1780–1860." *Liberalism, Old and New.* Boston: Twayne, 1991. 37–67.

Mill, John Stuart. *The Subjugation of Women.* London: Longmans, et al., 1869.

Miller, Nancy K. "Men's Reading, Women's Writing: Gender and the Rise of the Novel." *Yale French Studies* 75 (1988): 40–55.

————. "Emphasis Added: Plots and Plausibilities in Women's Fiction." *An Inimitable Example: The Case for the Princesse de Clèves*. Ed. Patrick Henry. Washington, DC: Catholic U of America P, 1992. 15–38.

Mises, Ludwig von. *The Anti-Capitalistic Mentality*. Auburn, AL: Ludwig von Mises Institute, 2008.

Molina, Luis de. *La teoría del justo precio*. Trans. Francisco Gómez Camacho. Madrid: Editora Nacional, 1981.

Mondino de' Luizzi. *Anatomia*. 1541 [c.1316]. History of Science Collections. University of Oklahoma Libraries. https://hos.ou.edu/galleries//03Medieval/Mon dinoDeiLuzzi/1541/

Montemayor, Jorge de. *La Diana*. Ed. Asunción Rallo. Madrid: Cátedra, 1991.

Monterde Real, Cristofor Joan. *Breve discurso del doctor Christoval Monterde . . . sobre el assiento que se puede tomar para el desempeño de los estados del Duque de Gandía . . . Dirigido a la Magestad . . . del rey Don Felipe II de Aragón y III de Castilla*. Madrid: Alfonso Martín de Balboa, 1613.

Montesquieu [de Secondat, Charles]. "Letter 78." *Persian Letters*. 1721. https://en.wikisource.org/wiki/Persian_Letters/Letter_78

————. *The Spirit of the Laws*. 1748. London: J. Duncan and Son, et al., 1793.

Murillo, Luis Andrés. "El Ur-Quijote: Nueva hipótesis." *Cervantes* 1.1–2 (1981): 43–50.

Nader, Helen. *Liberty in Absolutist Spain: The Habsburg Sale of Towns, 1516–1700*. Baltimore: Johns Hopkins UP, 1990.

Newman, William L. *The Politics of Aristotle*. 1887. New York: Amo P, 1973.

Nirenberg, David. *Communities of Violence*. Princeton: Princeton UP, 1998.

Oppenheimer, Franz. *The State*. New York: Vanguard P, 1928.

Oresme, Nicholas. *Tractatus de Origine, Natura, Jure, et Mutacionibus Monetarum. A Treatise on the Origin, Nature, Law, and Alterations of Money. The 'De Moneta' of Nicholas Oresme and English Mint Documents*. Trans. Charles Johnson. New York: Thomas Nelson and Sons, 1956. 1–48.

Ortega y Gasset, José. *Meditaciones del Quijote*. 1914. *Obras completas*. Vol. 1. Madrid: Taurus, 2004. 747–825.

Orwell, George. *Animal Farm*. New York: Alfred Knopf, 1993.

————. "Inside the Whale." *Inside the Whale and Other Essays*. London: Penguin, 1957. 9–50.

————. "Orwell's Preface to the Ukrainian Edition of Animal Farm." *Animal Farm*. Appx. II. New York: Alfred Knopf, 1993. 108–13.

————. "The Prevention of Literature." *Inside the Whale and Other Essays*. London: Penguin, 1957. 159–74.

Palma, Ricardo. *Tradiciones peruanas*. Lima: Peisa, 1973.

Palmer, Michael. "Mastering Slaves or Mastering Science? An Aristotelian Reprise." *Masters and Slaves: Revisioned Essays in Political Philosophy*. Lanham, MD: Lexington Books, 2001. 1–11.

Petrarch, Francesco. *Sonnets and Songs (Canzonieri)*. Trans. Anna Maria Armi. New York: Grosset & Dunlap, 1968.

Pérez, Joseph. *Los comuneros*. Madrid: Esfera, 2001.

Pérez de Antón, Francisco. "Superstición tenaz, enfermedad incurable." *Tópicos de Actualidad del Centro de Estudios Económico-Sociales* 44.911 (2003): 3–11.

Pérez Lasheras, Antonio. *Sin poner los pies en Zaragoza (algo más sobre el Quijote y Aragón)*. Zaragoza: Rolde, 2009.

Pérez-Reverte, Arturo, ed. *Don Quijote de la Mancha*. By Miguel de Cervantes. Madrid: Alfaguara, 2015.

Phillips, Christopher. *Socrates Café*. New York: Norton, 2002.

Piñero Ramírez, Pedro M. and Rogelio Reyes Cano. *La imagen de Sevilla en la obra de Cervantes. Espacio y paisaje humano*. Seville: Universidad de Sevilla, 2014.

Pinker, Steven. *The Better Angels of Our Nature: Why Violence Has Declined*. New York: Viking, 2011.

Pizan, Christine de. *The Book of the City of Ladies (La Cité des dames)*. Trans. Rosalind Brown-Grant. London: Penguin, 1999.

Plato. *The Laws*. Trans. Tom Griffith. Ed. Malcolm Schofield. Cambridge: Cambridge UP, 2016.

———. *The Republic*. Trans. Allan Bloom. New York: Basic Books, 1991.

———. *Symposium*. Trans. Seth Benardete. Chicago: U of Chicago P, 2001.

Plautus, T. Maccias. *Asinaria*. Perseus Digital Archive: http://www.perseus.tufts.edu

———. *Casina*. Perseus Digital Archive: http://www.perseus.tufts.edu

Poe, Edgar Allan. *Complete Tales and Poems*. Ed. Edward H. O'Neill. New York: Barnes and Noble, 1992.

Polybius. *Histories*. Trans. Evelyn S. Shuckburgh. New York: Macmillan, 1889. *Perseus Digital Library*: http://www.perseus.tufts.edu/hopper/text?doc=Perseus :text:1999.01.0234

Popper, Karl. *The Open Society and Its Enemies*. Princeton, NJ: Princeton UP, 2013.

Postrel, Virginia. *The Fabric of Civilization*. New York: Basic Books, forthcoming.

Quevedo y Villegas, Francisco Gómez de. "Miré los muros de la patria mía." *Renaissance and Baroque Poetry of Spain*. Ed. Elias L. Rivers. Prospect Heights, IL: Waveland P, 1966. 264–65.

———. "Poderoso caballero es don Dinero." *Renaissance and Baroque Poetry of Spain*. Ed. Elias L. Rivers. Prospect Heights, IL: Waveland P, 1966. 292–94.

———. *Política de Dios*. c.1635. Biblioteca Virtual Universal, 2019. http://www .biblioteca.org.ar/libros/131978.pdf

Quint, David. *Cervantes's Novel of Modern Times: A New Reading of Don Quijote*. Princeton: Princeton UP, 2003.

Rabin, Lisa. "The Reluctant Companion of Empire: Petrarch and Dulcinea in *Don Quijote de la Mancha*." *Cervantes* 14 (1994): 81–91.

Rand, Ayn. *Atlas Shrugged*. New York: Random House, 1957.

———. *The Fountainhead*. New York: Bobbs Merrill, 1943.

Randall, Dale B. J. and Jackson C. Boswell. *Cervantes in Seventeenth-Century England*. Oxford: Oxford UP, 2009.

Read, Malcolm K. "Language Adrift: A Re-appraisal of the Theme of Linguistic Perspectivism in *Don Quijote*." *Forum for Modern Language Studies* 17 (1981): 271–87.

————. *Language, Text, Subject: A Critique of Hispanism*. West Lafayette, IN: Purdue UP, 1992.

Redondo, Augustín. *Otra manera de leer el Quijote*. Madrid: Castalia, 1997.

Ricardo, David. "An Essay on Profits." *The Works and Correspondence of David Ricardo*. Vol. 4. Ed. Piero Sraffa. Indianapolis: Liberty Fund, 2004. 6–26. http://oll.libertyfund.org/titles/205

————. *Works of David Ricardo. Vol. V. Speeches and Evidence*. Ed. P. Sraffa. Cambridge: Cambridge UP, 1952.

Rico, Francisco. *Anales cervantinos: Notas al margen de un centenario*. Barcelona: Arpa, 2017.

Ridley, Matt. "Friedrich Hayek and the Collective Brain." https://capx.co/friedrich-hayek-and-the-collective-brain/

————. "When Ideas Have Sex." Oxford: *TEDGlobal*, 2010. www.youtube.com/watch?v=OLHh9E5ilZ4

Rodríguez, Juan Carlos. *Theory and History of Ideological Production: The First Bourgeois Literatures (the 16th Century)*. Trans. Malcolm K. Read. Newark: U of Delaware P, 2002.

Rodríguez de Montalvo, Garci. *Amadís de Gaula*. 2 vols. Ed. Juan Manuel Cacho Blecua. Madrid: Cátedra, 1987–88.

Rojas, Fernando de. *La Celestina*. Ed. Patricia S. Finch. Newark: Juan de la Cuesta, 2003.

Román, Luis Miguel. "Los molinos encantados del *Quijote*." *Alcázar de San Juan Lugar de Don Quijote*. Alcázar de San Juan, Spain: Sociedad Cervantina de Alcázar de San Juan, 2015. 1–19.

Romero-Díaz, Nieves. *Nueva nobleza, nueva novela: Reescribiendo la cultura urbana del barroco*. Newark, DE: Juan de la Cuesta, 2002.

Roover, Raymond de. "Scholastic Economics: Survival and Lasting Influence from the Seventeenth Century to Adam Smith." *Quarterly Journal of Economics* 69 (1955): 161–90.

Rorty, Richard. "Feminism, Ideology, and Deconstruction: A Pragmatist View." *Mapping Ideology*. Ed. Slavoj Žižek. New York: Verso, 1994. 227–34.

————. *Philosophy and Social Hope*. New York: Penguin, 1999.

Rosales, Luis. *Cervantes y la libertad*. 2 vols. Madrid: Cultura Hispánica, 1985.

Rossi, Rosa. *Escuchar a Cervantes*. Valladolid: Ámbito, 1988.

Rothbard, Murray N. *Anatomy of the State*. Auburn, AL: Ludwig von Mises Institute, 2009. https://mises.org/library/anatomy-state

————. *Economic Thought before Adam Smith*. Vol. 1. Auburn, AL: Ludwig von Mises Institute, 2006.

————. *The Ethics of Liberty*. 1982. New York: New York UP, 1998.

Ruiz, Juan. *Libro de buen amor*. Ed. Alberto Blecua. Barcelona: Austral, 2001.

Russell, Peter E. "*Don Quixote* as a Funny Book." *Modern Language Review* 64 (1969): 312–26.

Salinas, Pedro. "La vuelta al esposo: Ensayo sobre estructura y sensibilidad en el 'Cantar de Mío Cid.'" *Bulletin of Hispanic Studies* 24 (1947): 79–88.

Sánchez-Blanco, Rafael Benítez. "Continuidad de la presencia morisca en España después de las expulsiones." *Actas XII Simposio Internacional de Mudejarismo*. Teruel, Sept. 14–16, 2011. 473–90.

Sánchez Martínez de Pinillos, Hernán. "Cervantes y Poe en contrapunto." *eHumanista* 24 (2013): 571–606.

San Pedro, Diego de. *Cárcel de amor*. Madrid: Cátedra, 1982.

Saravia de la Calle, Luis. *La instrución de mercaderes muy provechosa*. 1544. Ed. Elena Carpi. Pisa, Italy: Edizioni ETS, 2007.

Schmitt, Carl. *Political Theology*. Trans. George Schwab. Cambridge: MIT P, 1985.

Schumpeter, Joseph A. *Capitalism, Socialism, and Democracy*. 1942. London: Routledge, 1994.

———. *History of Economic Analysis*. New York: Oxford UP, 1954.

Schwartz Girón, Pedro. *En busca de Montesquieu: Democracia y mundialización*. Madrid: Real Academia de Ciencias Morales y Políticas, 2005.

Scott, James Brown. *The Spanish Origins of International Law: Francisco de Vitoria and His Law of Nature*. New York: Oxford UP, 1934.

Scudéry, Madeleine de. *Clélie: histoire romaine*. 4 vols. Paris: Champion, 2001.

Sears, Theresa Ann. *A Marriage of Convenience: Ideal and Ideology in the Novelas ejemplares*. New York: Peter Lang, 1993.

Sedgwick, Eve. *Between Men: English Literature and Male Homosocial Desire*. New York: Columbia UP, 1985.

Selig, Karl-Ludwig. "*Don Quixote*, I/8–9 y la granada." *De los romances-villancico a la poesía de Claudio Rodríguez: 22 ensayos sobre las literaturas española e hispanoamericana en homenaje a Gustav Siebenmann*. Madrid: José Esteban, 1984. 401–05.

Shakespeare, William. *Hamlet. The Riverside Shakespeare: The Complete Works*. Eds. Herschel Baker et al. Boston: Houghton Mifflin, 1997. 1183–1245.

———. *The Merchant of Venice. The Riverside Shakespeare: The Complete Works*. Eds. Herschel Baker et al. Boston: Houghton Mifflin, 1997. 284–319.

Shell, Marc. *Art and Money*. Chicago: U of Chicago P, 1995.

Skinner, Quentin. *The Foundations of Modern Political Thought*. London: Manchester UP, 2000.

———. "Political Philosophy." *The Cambridge History of Renaissance Philosophy*. Eds. Charles B. Schmitt and Quentin Skinner. Cambridge: Cambridge UP, 1988. 389–452.

Smith, Adam. *An Inquiry into the Nature and Causes of the Wealth of Nations*. 1776. 2 vols. Ed. Edwin Cannan. London: Methuen, 1904. http://oll.libertyfund.org /titles/237

Sowell, Thomas. *Basic Economics*. New York: Basic, 2011.

Spitzer, Leo. "Linguistic Perspectivism in *Don Quijote*." *Linguistics and Literary History: Essays in Stylistics*. Princeton: Princeton UP, 1948. 41–85.

Stirling-Maxwell, William. *Don John of Austria*. 2 vols. London: Longmans, et al., 1883. Internet Archive: https://ia800200.us.archive.org/14/items/cu3192 4088475946/cu31924088475946.pdf

Stowe, Harriet Beecher. *Uncle Tom's Cabin*. 1852. London: Wordsworth, 1995.

Strauss, Leo. *Essays and Lectures by Leo Strauss. The Rebirth of Classical Political Rationalism: An Introduction to the Thought of Leo Strauss.* Ed. Thomas L. Pangle. Chicago: U of Chicago P, 1989.

Sullivan, Henry W. *Grotesque Purgatory: A Study of Cervantes's Don Quixote, Part II.* University Park: Pennsylvania State UP, 1996.

Taddeo, Sara A. "*De voz extremada*: Cervantes's Women Characters Speak for Themselves." *Women in the Discourse of Early Modern Spain.* Ed. Joan F. Cammarata. Gainesville: UP of Florida, 2003. 183–98.

Tanner, Marie. *The Last Descendant of Aeneas: The Hapsburgs and the Mythic Image of the Emperor.* New Haven: Yale UP, 1993.

Tellechea Idígoras, J. Ignacio. "Españoles en Lovaina en 1551–58." *Revista española de teología* 23 (1963): 21–45.

Thucydides. *The Peloponnesian War.* Trans. Thomas Hobbes. 1629. https://oll.liberty fund.org/titles/thucydides-the-english-works-vol-viii-the-peloponnesian-war-part-i

Torre, Felipe de la. *Institución de un príncipe christiano.* Antwerp: Martín Nucio, 1556.

Tucker, Jeffrey. "Hayek: The Knowledge Problem." https://fee.org/articles/hayek-the -knowledge-problem/

Twain, Mark. *Adventures of Huckleberry Finn.* London: Chatto & Windus, 1884.

———. *The Adventures of Tom Sawyer.* 1876. New York: Penguin, 2018.

———. "Corn-Pone Opinions." 1901. http://grammar.about.com/od/classicessays/a /cornponetwain.htm

Unamuno, Miguel de. *Vida de Don Quijote y Sancho.* 1905. Madrid: Alianza, 2015.

———. *Niebla.* 1914. Madrid: Cátedra, 1982.

Valdés y Salas, Fernando. *Índice de libros prohibidos (Index librorum prohibitorum). Les index des livres interdits du XVIe siecle, t. V: Les index espagnols de 1551 et 1559* by Jesús Martínez Bujanda. Sherbrooke, Canada: Centre d'études de la Renaissance de l'Université de Sherbrooke, 1984. 90–120.

Vargas Llosa, Mario. "Una novela para el siglo XXI." *Don Quijote de la Mancha* by Miguel de Cervantes. Ed. Francisco Rico. Madrid: Alfaguara, 2005. xiii–xxvii.

Vasconcillos, Felipe de la Cruz. *Tratado único de intereses sobre si puede llevar dinero por pretallo.* Madrid: Francisco Martínez, 1637.

Vega y Carpio, Lope Félix de. *El arte nuevo de hacer comedias en este tiempo. Preceptiva dramática española.* Eds. A. Porqueras-Mayo and F. Sánchez Escribano. Madrid: Gredos, 1971. 154–65.

———. *La dama boba.* Ed. Diego Marín. Madrid: Cátedra, 1989.

Velde, François R. "Lessons from the History of Money." *Economic Perspectives (Research Department of the Federal Reserve Bank of Chicago)* 22.1 (1998): 2–16.

Velde, François R. and Warren E. Weber. "Fiat Money Inflation in 17th Century Castile." *Research Department of the Federal Reserve Bank of Chicago.* Manuscript (1997). 1–24. http://frenchcoins.net/links/vellon.pdf

Vesalius, Andreas. *The Fabric of the Human Body (De humani corporis fabrica). An Annotated Translation of the 1543 and 1555 Editions.* Eds. D. H. Garrison and M. H. Hast. Basel: Karger, 2003. Digitized: https://www.e-rara.ch/bau_1/content /titleinfo/6299027

Vilanova, Antonio. *Erasmo y Cervantes*. Barcelona: Lumen, 1989.

Vilches, Elvira. *New World Gold: Cultural Anxiety and Monetary Disorder in Early Modern Spain*. Chicago: U of Chicago P, 2010.

Villalón, Cristóbal de. *Provechoso tratado de cambios y contrataciones de mercaderes y reprovación de usura*. Valladolid: Francisco Fernández de Córdoba, 1542.

Virgil. *The Aeneid*. Trans. John Dryden. New York: P. F. Collier and Son, 1909.

Vitoria, Francisco de. *Political Writings*. Trans. Jeremy Lawrance. Eds. Jeremy Lawrance and Anthony Pagden. Cambridge: Cambridge UP, 1991.

Voltaire, François-Marie Arouet de. *Candide and Other Stories*. Trans. Roger Pearson. Oxford: Oxford UP, 1990.

———. *An Essay on Epick Poetry*. Ed. Florence Donnell White. Albany: Brandow, 1915.

Wilson, Diana de Armas. "Homage to Apuleius: Cervantes's Avenging Psyche." *The Search for the Ancient Novel*. Ed. James Tatum. Baltimore: Johns Hopkins UP, 1994. 88–100.

———. "'Passing the Love of Women': The Intertextuality of *El curioso impertinente*." *Cervantes* 7.2 (1987): 9–28.

Wilson, Diana de Armas and Ruth Anthony El Saffar, eds. *Quixotic Desire: Psychoanalytic Perspectives on Cervantes*. Ithaca: Cornell UP, 1993.

Wollstonecraft, Mary. *A Vindication of the Rights of Woman*. Boston: Peter Edes, 1792.

Yerushalmi, Yosef Hayim. *Assimilation and Racial Anti-Semitism: The Iberian and the German Models*. New York: Leo Baeck, 1982.

Zayas y Sotomayor, María de. *El prevenido engañado. Novelas amorosas y ejemplares.* 1637. Ed. Julián Olivares. Madrid: Cátedra, 2014. 295–342.

———. *Estragos que causa el vicio. Desengaños amorosos.* 1647. Ed. Alicia Yllera. Madrid: Cátedra, 1998. 469–511.

Index

About the Author

Eric Clifford Graf was born in Dallas, Texas, and he earned his PhD in Spanish Literature from the University of Virginia in 1997. He has taught literature, cultural studies, and analytical writing at Smith College, University of Chicago, University of Illinois at Urbana-Champaign, College of William & Mary, Wesleyan University, Universidad Francisco Marroquín, and Universidad del Valle de Guatemala. He has published numerous articles and essays at news sites and in journals worldwide, such as *Cultura Económica, Publications of the Modern Language Association of America, Quarterly Journal of Austrian Economics, Modern Language Notes, Bulletin of the Cervantes Society of America, Journal of Spanish Cultural Studies, Hispanic Review, Bulletin of Hispanic Studies, PanAm Post, elCato, eHumanista,* and *Procesos de mercado.* He is author of two other books: *Cervantes and Modernity: Four Essays on Don Quijote* (Bucknell University Press, 2007) and *De Reyes a Lobos: Seis Ensayos Sobre Cervantes* (Juan de la Cuesta Hispanic Monographs, 2019). He is currently working on a comparative study of pre-Hispanic epic entitled *Popol Vuh and Poema de mio Cid: Sacred Violence at the Foundations of Spain and Guatemala.* All of his work can be found at: https://independentscholar.academia.edu/ERICCLIFFORDGRAF.